Managing Archives
and Archival Institutions

Edited by *James Gregory Bradsher*

With a Foreword by *Frank B. Evans*

The University of Chicago Press

First published in Great Britain by Mansell Publishing Limited,
A Cassell Imprint

The University of Chicago Press, Chicago 60637
Mansell Publishing Limited, London
© 1988 by Mansell Publishing Limited and the Contributors
All rights reserved. Published 1988
University of Chicago Press edition 1989
Paperback edition 1991
Printed in the United States of America

98 97 96 95 94   543

Library of Congress Cataloging-in-Publication Data

Managing archives and archival institutions / edited by James
    Gregory Bradsher; with a foreword by Frank B. Evans.
    p.   cm.
    Bibliography: p.
    Includes index.

    ISBN 0-226-07055-7 (paperback)
    I. Archives—Administration.   I. Bradsher, James Gregory.
CD950.M36   1988
025.17'14—dc19   88-15893
                                                CIP

∞ The paper used in this publication meets the minimum
requirements of the American National Standard for Information
Sciences—Permanence of Paper for Printed Library Materials,
ANSI Z39.48-1984

TO JAMES E. O'NEILL

There is nothing more useful for instructing and teaching men, nothing more necessary for clearing up and illustrating obscure matters, nothing more necessary for conserving patrimonies and thrones, all things public and private, than a well constituted store of volumes and documents and records—as much better than navy yards, as much more efficacious than munition factories, as it is finer to win by reason rather than by violence, by right than by wrong.

BALDASSARE BONIFACIO
Des Archivis, 1632

Would it be possible to conceive organized government without records of its acts, its laws, its compacts, its intercourse with other governments and with its own citizens . . . A government without archives would be something like a warrior without weapons, a physician without medicines, a farmer without seed, an artisan without tools. Public records are the solid ground on which the statesman can tread with security in the incessant toil of conducting the affairs of a nation. They are the silent, impartial, reliable and eternal witness that bears testimony to the toils, the misfortunes, the growth and the glories of peoples.

RICHARDO J. ALFARO
Former President of Panama
(at a Society of American
Archivists meeting, 1937)

We think of amnesia in an individual as a dreadful affair, but fortunately one that is usually temporary. Compare it with the kind of permanent amnesia that would set in on a government with the factual records of its past, as represented in its archives, obliterated: The hundreds of thousands of documents that give cohesion and consistency to the organization and conduct of our national Government; the wealth of hard-won experience and knowledge, in all its immense and intricate detail; the documents that by the tens of hundreds of thousands record our rights and duties and status as citizens, and link us as individuals into the great chain of past and future.

WAYNE C. GROVER
Archivist of the United States
(at a Society of American
Archivists meeting, 1950)

Contents

Foreword

The keeping of archives is as old as civilization, but the concept of archives has necessarily undergone evolution in response to changing political,social and economic ideologies and institutions. Nevertheless, from the earliest civilizations until the end of the eighteenth century the basic concept remained virtually unchanged. The clay tablet gradually gave way to papyrus, in turn to be replaced by parchment and then by paper, but the kinds of records preserved and the basic reason for their preservation—to establish and protect the rights and interests of the sovereign—remained fairly constant. Thus, the archives of eighteenth century European monarchs have much in common with those of ancient Babylonian kings and high priests.

During the past two centuries, however, the evolutionary process has accelerated to the extent that changes in the political, economic and social structure have become truly revolutionary. Despite these changes the core concept of archives remains; institutions, both public and private, still preserve certain of their non-current records to establish and protect their rights and interests. However, the range of documentary materials that are now selected—and collected—by archival repositories; the additional purposes these materials are intended to serve; the problems of access, preservation and duplication posed by new media; and the impact of rapidly changing information-handling technologies have all resulted in several differing concepts of archives and of the role of the archivist in the modern world.

Today, most Western European archivists are trained as research scholars in the auxiliary sciences of history and are oriented toward traditional historical scholarship. They are readily distinguishable from Eastern European archivists and those of socialist countries in other parts of the world, who also maintain they serve history but who conceive of history less as an academic discipline than as a tool that enables records and archives to be used actively in development of the socialist society and state. A third conception of archives is now emerging as part of the decolonization movement that followed World War II. In the newly independent countries, archives are highly regarded as essential to national identity which is to be achieved in part through a written national history. But in many countries in Asia, Africa, and Oceania that history must incorporate—in the absence of written records—oral tradition, and requires access to or copies of records of both the former colonial governments and of private institutions, such as businesses and religious organizations, that were active during the colonial period. Problems of economic, social and political instability are also threatening to force an ideological orientation upon many of these new archival agencies.

The most dynamic and fundamental changes in the traditional concept of archives, however, have occurred in the United States and in Canada, with the latter exhibiting a remarkable faculty for selecting—and frequently improving upon—American innovations. The records legacy of the United States is essentially that of Great Britain. French, Spanish, Dutch, and Swedish administrative and recordkeeping practices introduced during the colonial period have had only local and no long-term national significance. Much more significant was the early establishment of numerous and autonomous private and public historical societies and libraries, which collected personal papers and other historical manuscripts, including, occasionally, public records. The first state archival agency was not established until 1901 and a National Archives was not created until 1934. By that time a remarkable variety of policies and practices had emerged for the management of manuscript collections, most of them based upon principles and techniques of library classification and cataloging or upon a strict chronological arrangement of individual documents for each public institution, department or agency. The latter system was defended and explained in a 1913 publication of the Manuscript Division of the Library of Congress, John C. Fitzpatrick's *Notes on the care, cataloging, calendaring, and arranging of manuscripts*. This widely influential work went through three editions by 1928, and actually served as an early manual on archival theory and practice.

With the creation of the National Archives in 1934 and the establishment of the Society of American Archivists (SAA) in 1936, separate archival development began in earnest in the United States. Individual historians familiar with European archives and European archival experience, led by Waldo Gifford Leland, had early introduced the principles of provenance and original order, but very few of these historians held archival positions, and it remained for the National Archives to adapt these principles to the records of a rapidly expanding modern government with a relatively fluid administrative structure and decentralized recordkeeping systems. An initial experiment with classification and cataloging proved ineffective, and by 1941 the National Archives had begun the development of the theory and practice of records appraisal and disposition (to which were soon added scheduling and the range of activities that came to be called records management) and of collective arrangement and description. The National Archives also developed related policies and procedures for accessioning, preservation (including applications of micrographics), reference service, exhibits, and publications (including those on microform), which, when taken together, defined the overall archival program for the records of the national government.

Central to that program was the concept of archives as a very small percentage of the total accumulation of modern government records; their preservation as evidence to establish and protect the rights and interests of both the government and the governed; their availability for use by government in current administration when needed; and their use by scholars and students, genealogists, and others in studying public administration and specific government programs and activities, or for reference or research on a wide variety of subjects because of the unique and valuable information the records contained.

From the outset this concept of archives embraced cartographic, architectural and audio-visual records, but gave relatively little attention to the special problems of appraisal and selection, preservation and utilization which they posed. It also viewed the reference function as an essentially passive one of making records and limited information from records available upon request. Permanent and temporary exhibits and general and specialized information leaflets were regarded as adequate to meet the needs of the public who chose to visit the repository. A range of other publications, including annual reports, occasional pamphlets, journal articles on archival theory and practice, general and specialized guides, inventories, lists and indexes, supplemented by selected and historically edited documents, were aimed primarily at the professional archival community and the preferred research clientele—academic historians and their graduate students.

This was, in general, the concept of archives that emerged between about 1940 and 1965. It is documented in publications of the National Archives and in the pages of the *American Archivist*; it was taught to new staff members of the National Archives, to the hundreds of archivists from state and private archival repositories and to scores of archivists from abroad who enrolled in National Archives institutes; and it influenced archives training courses developed in history departments and library schools in other parts of the country. The fullest expression of this concept is contained in Theodore R. Schellenberg's *Modern archives: principles and techniques* (1956), a work that earned for its author an international reputation and was translated into a number of foreign languages.

A second study by Schellenberg, *The management of archives* (1965), published in the series of *Columbia University Studies in Library Science*, attempted to reconcile modern archival and traditional library methodology by applying archival principles and techniques to cartographic and audio-visual records. This work, however, never attracted the attention or support of

Schellenberg's initial study, and his *Modern archives* still remains the most widely-known and influential American contribution to archival theory and practice.

Yet even while Schellenberg's model was attracting widespread attention, the archival scene in the United States was in increasingly rapid transition. The principles and practices advanced by Schellenberg had been the result of an effort to adapt traditional European experience to the reality of modern America, and the effort was, at best, only partially successful, even when limited to public records. Furthermore, the deep-rooted manuscript tradition had continued and, indeed, experienced a resurgence as the number of archival repositories and practitioners grew rapidly in the next two decades. Most of this growth was in the private rather than in the public sector, particularly in colleges, universities and special collections. The Library of Congress *Notes* were replaced first with Lucile M. Kane's *A guide to the care and administration of manuscripts* (1960, 2nd edition, 1966), and then by Kenneth W. Duckett's *Modern manuscripts: a practical manual for their management, care and use* (1975). Neither work mentions records management, scheduling, or archival (as distinct from monetary) appraisal, but both moved closer to the ideas of collective methods of arrangement and description, and Duckett extends the concept of reference beyond the scholarly user to public services. The next step was the launching by the SAA in 1977 of a series of manuals on specific functions and activities that would help bridge the gap between the fields of "Archives and manuscripts", which was adopted as the general series title.

During the past decade the SAA published fourteen manuals in this series, covering such traditional functions and specialized areas as appraisal and accessioning, arrangement and description, reference and access, exhibits, maps and architectural drawings, reprography, administration of photographic collections, and conservation. These were accompanied by manuals on such relatively new concerns as security, surveys, automated access, public programs, machine-readable records, and law. During this same period the SAA also published and updated a user's manual, a data element dictionary, and a reference guide on MARC (Machine Readable Catalog) for archives and manuscripts.

Paralleling this increasing convergence between the traditional fields of manuscripts and archives has been the further evolution of the concept of archives in the public sector. The Schellenberg model never fully reflected the functions and activities of even the institution on which it was based, and during the three decades since the publication of *Modern archives* these functions and activities have increased in both number and variety. The changes are perhaps most graphically revealed by a comparison of the table of contents of *Modern archives* with that of the present work. Both include the core functions of records management, appraisal, preservation, arrangement, description, and reference. But the present work, reflecting the current broader concept of archives to include manuscripts, and revealing the impact of rapidly-changing media and technology, also includes chapters on personal papers; cartographic, architectural, audio-visual, and machine-readable archives; archival automation; oral history; archival ethics; security; public programs; exhibits; and archival management.

It has been observed that history must be rewritten by each generation to be relevant to its needs and aspirations. The scope and role of archives require similiar reinterpretation and updating if archives are to continue to serve present and future needs in a society undergoing increasingly rapid change. This handbook, reflecting the current state-of-the-art of archives administration, is intended as a contribution to this continuing process.

FRANK B. EVANS
Deputy Assistant Archivist
for Records Administration,
National Archives
and Records Administration,
Washington, D.C.

Preface

American historian J. Franklin Jameson, lobbying for an American national archives, wrote President William H. Taft on November 26, 1912, that "the care which a nation devotes to the preservation of the monuments of its past may serve as a true measure of the degree of civilization to which it has attained". Echoing similar thoughts a dozen years later, Canadian Dominion Archivist Sir Arthur Doughty wrote that "of all national assets archives are the most precious. They are the gift of one generation to another, and the extent of our care of them marks the extent of our civilization".[1]

Because archives are important to society, and to civilization itself, archivists have an important societal role. They fulfil this role by managing their archives and archival institutions effectively and efficiently, and by ensuring that those who create, maintain, and use records of archival value do so in a manner that protects their quality and integrity. These are difficult tasks, given the bulk and complexity of modern records. To meet the challenge of modern records and archives, to ensure that archives will serve the present and the future, archivists must acquire and continue to update a thorough knowledge of archives administration. They must understand the theories and principles that should guide their work, and they must become familiar with and implement practices based upon them.

The knowledge and skills of archives administration can be acquired by various means. Archivists can read appropriate literature, attend lectures and courses, observe other archival practitioners at work, participate in on-the-job training, and receive academic instruction. Although a growing body of periodical literature on archival topics is available to those who desire to acquire knowledge through reading, only a few books covering the whole scope of archival administration have been published.

In 1964, Oliver Wendell Holmes, then executive director of America's National Historical Publications Commission, observed that there were only four works available in English worthy of the archivist's attention. They were the Dutch *Manual for the arrangement and description of archives* (by S. Muller, J. A. Feith, and R. Fruin) written in 1898 (translated into English in 1940), Sir Hilary Jenkinson's *A manual of archive administration* (1937), Theodore Schellenberg's *Modern archives* (1956), and Ernst Posner's *American state archives* (1964). Two equally significant works appeared a year later: Schellenberg's *The management of archives* and a revision of Jenkinson's work.

Although he recommended the four works, Holmes observed that "there is no textbook, indeed there is no one general book in English, or even in other languages, that can be recommended as surveying the subject of archival theory and practice systematically and including good bibliographic references for further reading".[2] Holmes believed that there was neither an adequate number of archivists to create a demand for such a work nor a sufficiently universal experience among archivists upon which it could be based.

Times have changed since Holmes assessed the archival profession. During the past two decades, there has been a staggering growth of archival institutions and archival materials, accompanied by a demand for more and better-educated archivists. The universal experience, considered by Holmes to be essential to the production of a compendium of archival theory and practice, may still be lacking; but sufficient agreement exists as to the general knowledge and skills of archives administration which archivists must possess to warrant an attempt at the compilation of a handbook.

During the past quarter of a century few archival handbooks have been published. They were generally limited in scope and did not adequately incorporate the profileration of periodical literature, nor describe sufficiently sophisticated methodology.[3] The lack of a book-length work providing the most up-to-date information relating to all aspects of archives administration and providing bibliographic citations to the most recent professional literature prompted me to consider producing such a work. Recognizing, as has British archivist Michael Cook, that because of the development of new specialities and the broadening scope of archival work "it is no longer possible for one person to write a complete survey of professional practice in the administration of archives", I turned to seventeen colleagues to assist me in the preparation of this book.[4]

My goal was to produce a book that would provide archivists and archives administrators with the information they need to meet the challenges presented by modern records and archives. I wanted a book broad enough to apply to all types of archival institutions and custodians of archival materials. I also wanted a book general enough to be useful to records and information managers, historians, librarians, and anyone else with an interest in archival materials.

Contributors to this volume have attempted to fill my large order by sharing their varied and informed views. They did so with the realization that the very nature of recorded information necessitates different ways of dealing with archival materials, and that American procedures and practices are not necessarily better than those of other countries; they are merely different. Because of the variety of archival institutions and laws and regulations governing archives, the contributors also realized that it is impossible to apply their general guidance in all situations and circumstances.

Thus, if readers disagree with some of the contributors' views, that is to be expected; indeed, constructive discussion of differences of opinion promotes progress. We have been reminded by a former president of the Society of American Archivists that "Archival practice is not only not an 'exact science'; it needs competing solutions and a diversity of approaches to fundamental problems".[5]

This book, although covering most topics in archives administration, does not cover them all. For instance, the areas of printed archives, reprography, and buildings and supplies are not directly addressed because of space considerations. Also not discussed are the special areas of expertise (paleography, diplomatics, chronology, toponymics, and sphragistics or sigillography) needed by custodians of pre-nineteenth-century documents to read, interpret, understand, date, and authenticate old documents and seals. These were excluded in keeping with the book's emphasis on modern archives.

Space limitations forced the contributors to focus on major theories, principles, practices, issues, problems, and challenges. They have attempted to cover their topics in general terms while providing specific guidance where appropriate. Each has provided a bibliography for further reading.

If this book informs discussion of the theories, principles, and practices of archives administration; if it helps define the dimensions of the current and future archival challenges; if it kindles respect or even enthusiasm for the profession; if it leads some to read more about the subjects addressed; then its purpose will have been fulfilled.

I am in debt to Bruce Ambacher, Bob Brookhart, Frank G. Burke, Frank B. Evans, Michael J. Kurtz, Michele F. Pacifico, Mary Lynn Ritzenthaler, and Sharon G. Thibodeau for a thorough review of the introductory chapter and for so many excellent suggestions. It is much improved as a consequence. They should not be held to account, however, for my views, which often differ from theirs. I would also like to thank Frank Evans for providing me with copies of his lecture notes and several of his articles as well as for writing the foreword.

Numerous people have reviewed various drafts of chapters of this book and I appreciate their time and interest. They include Nancy Allyn, Stacey Bredhoff, James Corsaro, Bruce Dearstyne, Judith Felsten, Kenneth E. Harris, William J. Heyen, Betty Hill, Brenda Beasley Kepley, Nancy Malan, William T. Murphy, Julie Nash, Claudia Nicholson, Kitty Nicholson, David Paynter, Trudy Huskamp Peterson, Judy Pratt, Virginia Purdy, Rodney A. Ross, Nancy Sahli, John Vernon, and James D. Zeender. I would also like to express my appreciation to Adrienne C. Thomas, for being such a thoughtful and understanding supervisor. Finally, I wish to express my appreciation to all the authors for their contributions, which reflect their own views and not necessarily those of their respective institutions. They have been good-natured and cooperative and I wish to acknowledge what a pleasure it has been to collaborate with them.

This book is dedicated to James E. O'Neill who, had he lived, would have contributed a chapter. Unfortunately and tragically, he was taken away from us, his agency, his profession, and his wife and family on March 6, 1987. During his two decades with the National Archives and Records Administration, as the Director of the Franklin D. Roosevelt Library, Assistant Archivist for Presidential Libraries, Director of the Federal Bureau of Investigation Records Appraisal Task Force, Deputy Archivist and Acting Archivist of the United States, Dr O'Neill exemplified what an archivist and archival administrator should be and do.

Notes and references

1. Elizabeth Donnan and Leo F. Stock, eds. *An historian's world: selections from the correspondence of John Franklin Jameson*. Philadelphia, The American Philosophical Society, 1956. p. 153; Arthur G. Doughty. *The Canadian archives and its activities*. Ottawa, F.A. Acland, 1924. p. 5.
2. Oliver W. Holmes. History and theory of archival practices. *In*: Rolland E. Stevens, ed., *University archives; papers presented at an Institute by the University of Illinois Graduate School of Library Science, November 8, 1964*. Champaign, The Illinois Union Bookstore, 1964. p. 19.
3. An exception to the general observation is *Keeping archives*, which was published by the Australian Society of Archivists in 1987.
4. Michael Cook. *Archives administration: a manual for intermediate and smaller organizations and for local government*. Folkestone, Kent, England, Wm.Dawson & Sons Ltd., 1977, p. viii.
5. Maynard J. Brichford. Seven sinful thoughts. *American Archivist*, vol. 43, no. 1, Winter 1980. p. 13.

1

An Introduction to Archives

James Gregory Bradsher

When I was about to leave graduate school to become an archivist, my friends asked me what it was I was going to be doing. My response was somewhat vague. Having looked at a dictionary, I was able to respond that as an archivist I was going to be a "keeper of archives". This, of course, prompted the question, what are archives? My response, also dictionary-based, was that "archives are public records or documents preserved as evidence of facts; as, national or family archives". These explanations elicited the response that archival work sounded dull, uncreative, of limited intellectual scope, and dirty—dealing with old and dusty files, not something important or relevant; certainly not something that a "scholar" would want to do.

Such misconceptions about archivists and their archives are not new. In 1935, shortly after the National Archives of the United States was established, a Washington, D.C., newspaper columnist attempting to define "archivist" for his readers came up with the concept that an archivist was a "dead file clerk". By printing these words without any punctuation it was not clear as to who was dead, the file clerk or the files. In a book about words and expressions first published in 1975, the author observed that the "euphemism" archivist actually means museum or library clerk.[1] As will be seen in this chapter and throughout the book, archives are not dead files and archivists are not museum, library, or file clerks.

This introductory chapter explains what archives are and where they are maintained, and discusses the general principles governing their management. Additionally, by way of introducing the various functions and activities of archivists addressed by the authors, this chapter outlines the knowledge and skills that archivists must possess and exercise in order to manage effectively

1

their archives and institutions. Finally, it contains a discussion of the education, training, and professional development of archivists.

Records, personal papers, and historical manuscripts

What are archives? Before answering that question, it is necessary to understand the nature of records, personal papers, and historical manuscripts, all of which are documentary sources acquired by various types archival institutions. Records are generally defined as recorded information (regardless of form or medium), created, received and maintained by an agency, institution, organization or individual in pursuance of its legal obligations or in the transaction of business. Most records are of a prosaic nature, being fundamentally the record of business or administrative transactions, created to facilitate public and private business. They are used to justify official actions; to record proceedings; to explain and record policy decisions; and to establish and maintain rights under the law for citizens, corporations, and governments.[2]

Recorded information accumulated in the course of official governmental activity constitutes public records. If records are accumulated by non-governmental institutions or organizations, they are private records. Records are generally created and maintained as "series", that is, as groups of records maintained as a unit because they are filed in accordance with a particular filing system and relate to a particular function or subject, result from the same activity, or have a particular form, or because of some other relationship arising out of the circumstances of their creation or use. Records include a wide variety of documentary forms and classes, such as correspondence, reports, maps, photographs, sound recordings, and motion pictures, and they are recorded on a variety of media, such as paper, microforms, audio and video disks, videotape, and reels of computer tape. Records are referred to as current, semi-current, or non-current, indicating their value to users for the conduct of current business. Records also are viewed as having a "life cycle". That is, they are born or adopted (created or received), live actively (used), retire (become semi-current), and, when they become non-current, die (are destroyed) or are "reborn" (become archives).

Information recorded or received by private individuals and employees of a governmental entity or private organization or institution, and not created or received during the course of conducting official business, is generally contained in what are termed personal papers.[3] While archives grow out of some regular functional activity, personal papers are accumulated by individuals or families in the conduct of their personal, professional, and private concerns. The line between organizational records and personal papers is sometimes difficult to define. The distinction is especially important when legal problems of what is and what is not a record are considered. While personal papers belong to and are subject to the disposition of an individual, records are generally subject to laws and regulations or corporate policies and procedures that authorize their dispostion at a specified time and in a specific manner.

In addition to personal papers, which accumulate naturally and thus have an organic character, there are historical manuscripts, which are collected artificially, frequently without regard to source.[4] Both types were once termed historical manuscripts (to distinguish them from literary manuscripts) or historical records. The term historical manuscripts is now generally used to designate artificial or miscellaneous collections. These collections are generally regarded as unorganized groups or individual documents of a private nature, ordinarily created as the product of spontaneous expression of thought or feeling, such as personal letters or diaries. They are collected by an individual or private repository from a variety of sources, because of their special historical significance or literary value, or their importance to research.

Archives

Institutional records and personal papers maintained by an archival repository are frequently termed archives. Such holdings are often mistakenly viewed as a collection of historical records or manuscripts. But archives are not simply unorganized groups of historical documents. They are a body of functionally and/or organizationally related material that has grown organically out of some activity. They are basically the business (legal, administrative, policy, fiscal) records of an individual or public or private entity, that are preserved because of their value, either as evidence of transactions, and/or because of the information they contain about people, places, and things.

Just as no single definition of "history" has ever been accepted by all historians at any period of time, no one definition of archives will satisfy all archivists or serve all archival institutions. It may be said, however, that archives are the official or organized records of governments, public and private institutions and organizations, groups of people and individuals, whatever their date, form and material appearance, which are no longer needed to conduct current business, but are preserved, either as evidence of origins, structures, functions, and activities or because of the value of the information they contain, whether or not they have been transferred to an archival institution. Information in archives is of fundamental and continuing value for administrative, fiscal, legal, evidential, or informational (historical) purposes. The French archival law of 1979 states that certain records are preserved as archives "in the interest of the public, as well as for the needs of administration and proof of rights of individual persons or corporate bodies, either public or private, and for the historical documentation of research".[5]

According to the 1979 French definition of archives, records become archival as soon as they are created or received. American federal records are considered archival when they are formally offered by a federal agency and the National Archives signs a document accepting legal responsibility for them. Yet, when records are first appraised as having enduring value or when they cease to be in current use and are set aside for preservation, they begin to take on the character of archives.

So, while archives are records, not all records are archives. Archives are the small core of records with enduring value; no more than five percent of the volume of all public records. It is this enduring value that distinguishes archives proper from records in general. All records have some value to somebody. However, generally only those of sufficient value, as determined by archivists, are retained as archives, and then only as long as their value is of an enduring nature. Archives are thus retained or preserved indefinitely, but not necessarily permanently; the information contained in them is subject to re-evaluation to determine if they warrant continued retention.

Etymologically, the word archives comes from the Greek "archeion" and the Latin "archivum", both meaning a government office and the papers kept therein. First applied only to bodies of official governmental documents, the term was subsequently used to designate the accumulated files of an institution or a family. From the Latin, the French developed the word "l'archive" and later the collective "les archives". The word "archives", although long in usage on the European continent, was, for the most part, not adopted by the English-speaking countries until the nineteenth century. The words "records" or "historical records" were preferred because the term "records" was used in early English law to indicate something deliberately preserved, and often deliberately created, for future legal or administrative use.

Early in the nineteenth century, in the midst of the Romantic movement, the term "archives" was adopted by many English-speaking scholars to refer to old records. In its American sense the plural was carried over from the French "les archives", to mean not only the body of such records but also the place where they were kept, and the institution or agency responsible for administering them. The last half of the century saw increased use of the term, primarily as a result of historians having trained in German universities where it was well-established. Before the 1930s the term "archives" was usually applied to public records of archival value while the terms "personal papers", "historical records", or "historical manuscripts" were used for non-public records of archival value. Thereafter, the term "archives" generally included non-public records and often personal papers of individuals and families, if they were organically created, consciously preserved, and organized in some logical arrangement, thereby having the characteristics of archival materials.

Archival institutions

Archival materials are found throughout the world in hundreds of thousands of publicly- and privately-funded and operated archival institutions. These institutions, whose function is the preservation and administration of archives, are known either as "archives" or as "manuscript repositories" depending on the type of material they contain and how it is acquired. "Manuscripts repositories" are responsible mainly for personal papers and artificial miscellaneous collections (historical manuscripts) acquired by purchase or donation primarily for cultural and educational purposes. "Archives" are responsible for the archival records of the organization or institution of which they are a part. Most archives hold some personal papers and many manuscript repositories also serve as the archives of their own or some other institution. In common usage the terms "archives", "archival institutions", or "archival repositories", are generally used to denote entities maintaining archives and manuscript collections.

Most national governments and many other official bodies maintain archives. Institutions of higher learning have archives, as do business, religious, labor, ethnic, patriotic, charitable, political, educational, fraternal, and social organizations. Archives, personal papers, and historical manuscripts are also found in large quantities in libraries and historical societies. Archives are maintained in hospitals, museums, and wherever it is important to retain indefinitely those non-current records of the greatest historical value and of the greatest potential use to their creators and other researchers in documenting and understanding the past, dealing with the present, and preparing for the future.

Archival repositories range from large, relatively well-funded institutions providing a full range of archival services to more limited operations, often run by a single archivist or volunteer. The average archival institution in the United States contains about two thousand cubic feet of archives and is staffed by four employees. By way of contrast, America's National Archives contains more than 1.5 million cubic feet of archives that are administered by nearly six hundred employees. Substantial variations exist, not only in the size, nature, and scope of archival holdings, but also in their internal structure and their location within the organizational structure of their parent institution. Often archives are part of a library system, and the institution to which they belong contains the words "library and archives" in its title. Some archives are part of a historical agency, such as a Bureau or Department of History and Archives. Often the term "library" is used to designate a primarily archival institution, such as the Bentley Historical Library or the John F. Kennedy Library. And the term "record" is often used in the title of an archival repository, such as the British Public Record Office.

Archivists

The individuals who are responsible for managing public or private archival materials are generally termed "archivists". They maintain the archives of the parent entity, be it a government, organization, or institution, primarily for their administrative usefulness to the creators or their successors. Because of their connection with the creating entities, some archivists have responsibilities for records before they become archives. In this role they serve as records managers, assisting the creators of records in achieving economy and efficiency in the creation, maintenance, use, and disposition of records; thereby reducing their quantity and increasing their quality. Following archival principles and their institution's policies and procedures, archivists identify records for retention and disposal; accession records that have archival value; and arrange, describe, preserve, promote the use of, and make available their archives or the information contained in them.

"Manuscript custodians" administer personal papers and artificial collections. Although they identify and acquire valuable documentation, maintain and administer their collections in much the same manner as archivists, and are generally bound by the same professional standards and ethics, there are important distinctions between the two professions. Archivists in the public sector are generally restricted legally in what they can do to and with their archives. Curators of manuscript collections are restricted in their methodology only by such private contracts as may have been agreed upon between their institution and the previous owners of the materials. In common usage, most manuscript custodians are today termed either archivists or librarians, depending on the nature of their institution and its holdings.

Archival characteristics and principles

Archival materials, whether public or private, were created in the normal conduct of business, by a particular entity, and maintained in a definite arrangement usually related to the actions that resulted in their accumulation. The most basic characteristics of archives and all archival principles derive from these facts.

The first characteristic of archives is the relationship they have to a creating entity, whether it is an organization, governmental agency, or individual. The archives of a particular entity are accumulated as a direct result of its functional activities, and are intended to reflect the policies, functions, and transactions of that entity alone. From this fact is derived the first major principle of "respect des fonds" or "provenance", that is, maintaining the archives of one entity separate from those of others, thereby respecting the natural body of documentation left by the creating entity and reflecting its work.

Based on this principle, records are grouped on the basis of their organizational origins. For archival management purposes, these groups of records are variously termed "archive groups" or "record groups".[6] They are the largest physical units established in archival institutions and generally comprise the records accumulated by an entity that has separate or distinct functional responsibilities, and for that reason, can be dealt with separately. An "archival subgroup" comprises the records accumulated by subdivision of the larger organizational unit. Within a subgroup, records are maintained in "series", which are archival units established on the basis of their functional origins.

A second characteristic of archives is their organic character. As a transaction progresses, records relating to it grow naturally. Each document in a file is related to, or is a consequence of, some preceding document or documents, and the former is explained and elaborated by the latter. Taken out of sequence, or arranged in a manner different from that in which they were created, archives tell an incomplete or inaccurate story. To retain their quality of reflecting accurately what has gone before, why and how, the original order of records is maintained or restored. This sanctity of the original order is a very important and basic archival principle.

A third characteristic is the official character of archives. Archives are the by-product of the transactions of an organization or institution with individuals or corporate entities, often having legal effects. From this characteristic flows the archival principle that archives must remain in the custody of their creator or its legitimate successor in order to ensure that no tampering has taken place by unauthorized individuals. This assures that archives will be acceptable in a court of law as valid evidence of a transaction.

Another characteristic of archives is their uniqueness. Unlike books, which are mass-produced for cultural and educational purposes, archives are essentially single file units created or accumulated in connection with a specific business or administrative transaction. If a copy of a book is destroyed, another copy almost always exists somewhere. If, on the other hand, archival file units are destroyed, other copies of the documents in them might exist, but it is unlikely they would be maintained in the same sequence or context.

Maintaining archives according to these basic principles provides evidence about the nature of their creator; preserves the values arising from their organic character; provides evidence as to how and why they were created and used; protects their integrity; and allows for them to be arranged, described, and administered efficiently and effectively. Archivists during the last century learned the hard lesson that to rearrange their archives according to subject, rather than retaining their original arrangement, was impossible because of the size of their holdings as well as the complexity and diversity of the information which they contained.

The difference between archives and other reference materials is that the latter do not have the characteristics just discussed. Books in a library or items in a historical manuscript repository are "collections" of isolated pieces that have been put in some sort of logical order. Archives, on the other hand, are "accumulations" and their arrangement is determined as they grow, not afterwards. Other reference materials do not have the official character or relationship with a creating agency that is essential to archives, nor are they unique, at least in the sense archives are. Books are created for general use; archives, in the course of one specific transaction.

Differences and similarities between archives and libraries

Reviewing the differences between archives and libraries illustrates the essential nature of archives and archives administration. Although libraries often maintain archival materials and manuscript collections, their primary function is to house and make available collections of books and other printed materials. Archives, on the other hand, often contain books and other printed matter (generally reference materials), but their primary function is to maintain accumulations of the records or papers of organic entities and individuals, including printed archival materials, such as manuals produced by an agency, organization, or institution. Archives and libraries both exist in order to help preserve valuable information. They share the common objective of making their holdings available as effectively and economically as possible. But they are essentially quite different, not only in the physical and substantive attributes of their holdings, but also in the way these holdings are created, acquired, maintained, and administered.

Archivists are concerned with records, papers, and manuscripts; mostly unique, non-printed material. Librarians are concerned with multiple copies of books and publications. The quality that distinguishes an archives from a library is the uniqueness of its holdings. Although libraries may sometimes contain unique items, for example, rare books, for the most part they contain collections of printed works produced for general use, whereas archives contain accumulations of unique documents, created in the course of specific transactions.

This quality of uniqueness reflects a fundamental difference between archives and libraries. The difference lies in the fact that archival materials are normally created as a result of some regular functional activity of a government agency or other entity. Their significance depends on their organic relation to this body and to other archival materials in the same files, series, or record group. Any cultural values they may have are incidental to their creation. Library materials, on the other hand, are produced primarily for cultural or educational purposes. They usually consist of discrete items, whose significance is independent of their relationship to other items.

Archival institutions are established to preserve the archival materials produced by the body or bodies they serve; they are receiving insitutions. Libraries on the other hand, are collecting bodies, deriving their materials not from particular entities, but from anywhere or anyone.

Archival appraisal, deciding what material should be retained, is usually carried out in relation to organization or function rather than subject. It is accomplished by assessing the value of particular series of records (aggregates, not items) in relation to the entire documentation of an organization or institution. While archivists appraise aggregates, librarians select or collect discrete items, on the basis of either their subject matter or the collecting interests of their library.

Other differences between archival and library principles and methodologies exist. Librarians, in organizing discrete units, use one of the proven, pre-determined, and logical schemes of classification for the arrangement and subject control of their materials. Archivists, in organizing collective organic units, maintain them in their original arrangement, thereby providing evidence of what has gone before. Libraries describe or catalog discrete items while archivists describe aggregates of items, such as record groups or series. Archives provide information on series of records, while libraries do it for individual items.

Despite their differences, librarians and archivists have much in common. They share some common preservation problems, some common views on professional training and development, and a common desire to facilitate the use of their holdings. Developments in information technology mean that, increasingly, they find themselves handling documents in the same physical formats as books, on the one hand, and paper-based records, on the other, are replaced by electronic and optical media. Nevertheless, the ways in which such materials are treated and used in libraries and archives will continue to differ, regardless of their physical form.

The importance of archives and archivists

Regardless of what definition one chooses or where archival materials are kept, archives are important, not only for studying the past but also for the impact which a knowledge of the past has on the present and the future. The preservation and improvement of governments, other institutions and organizations, societies, and even civilization itself depends to some degree on the preservation and efficient utilization of archives.

Nearly everyone benefits from archives, even those who never use them directly. They are the institutional memory of corporate entities which, just like individuals, cannot function without a memory. Archives permit continuity and consistency in administration. In a democracy, they document government responsibility and accountability to the people. They provide citizens with a sense of national identity and are of great value to them in establishing and protecting individual and property rights and privileges. They provide documentation for corporations. They educate, entertain, and enrich our lives by providing appealing and tangible manifestations of our history, as well as useful information. In short, they provide the basis for understanding where we have been, they help orient us to our present, and they provide guidance for our progress into the future.

Because archives are important, archivists, who preserve and manage archival materials, have an important role in society. By preserving and making available the archives in their care, archivists provide an important service to the entities that created them; to citizens establishing their rights and privileges; and to those who evolve new ideas, extend the boundaries of knowledge, or disseminate information and ideas.

Often archivists are viewed as preoccupied with the past. In fact, they are equally concerned with the present and the future. In some respects, particularly in deciding what records are to be preserved, they are professionally concerned with a more distant future than that of any profession except possibly theology and astronomy. They have an important function in society, acting as the trustees and custodians of the past and present for the benefit of the future.

Much to do—much to learn

Preserving the evidence of the activities of individuals and public and private entities so that others may know and understand them is the ultimate goal of archivists. To achieve this goal, archivists have two objectives. Their most fundamental objective is to establish and maintain control, both physical and intellectual, over the records transferred to them. In doing this archivists have a responsibility to preserve the physical and intellectual integrity of their archives, keeping them in order such that they can be produced when required. The archivist's secondary objective is to make their archives, or the information in them, available to researchers in a proper and effective manner. This second objective is impossible if the first is not accomplished, and the first objective is meaningless without the second.

Everything archivists do should be concentrated on this dual objective. If they do not accomplish their objectives in an effective and timely manner, their archives will not afford the legal protection they should guarantee, the pleasure they can provide, or the information and potential knowledge which are available in them. Archivists thus have an immense and important responsibility to society.

To fulfill their responsibility of saving the past for the future, and of serving the present, archivists must possess certain attitudes and knowledge and employ a wide range of skills. They must continually improve these skills, and be aware of all aspects of their profession as well as of related fields that bear on their work. In some large and complex archival institutions there is a growing need for specialization. Despite this, all archivists should have a working knowledge of all aspects of their profession, including technical specialities, not only to develop their own competence, but also to faciliate dealing with experts in other areas, when they need to call upon them. Each chapter in this book addresses a different aspect of archival administration. To provide an integrated overview of these aspects, the remaining pages of this chapter are devoted to explaining (in the same order as the succeeding chapters) what archivists must know and do in order to fulfill their function.

Archivists have an obligation to know what their profession is all about. They must believe in what they are doing. If they cannot justify their existence to themselves, they cannot justify it to others. If archivists are to be respected by other professions and by the public they serve, they must understand and be convinced of the importance of their mission and be able to convince others. Therefore, they must take the time to reflect on the importance of what they are doing, to remind themselves that their roots go back five thousand years, and to remember that archives serve myraid purposes.

Most archivists cannot afford to concentrate only on their archives, letting present (and future) records take care of themselves. Someday, some current records will become archives. Many, if not most, of the problems of the archivist of the future will have their origin in what is done to and with the records that are being created today. If archivists are content to accept and deal only with those records that survive administrative handling and neglect, they will unquestionably find, in the future, that their archives are greatly impaired in intellectual and physical quality. Because of the volume and complexity of the records now being created, and the risk of losing completely information stored in electronic data bases, archivists must be aware of all aspects of the life cycle of records and knowledgeable about records management techniques. They must assume a records management role to ensure that full and adequate documentation is created and maintained until such time as it is accessioned by an archival institution. They also must play a role in ensuring that records are managed effectively to facilitate their disposition and to ease the archivist's future tasks of arrangement, description, preservation, and reference service.

Because the first objective of archivists is to establish and maintain control over records of enduring value, identifying and selecting such records is the first step in the archival process. Making appraisal judgments (deciding what records can be destroyed without legal repercussions or serious historical or administrative loss) is perhaps the most difficult and important archival task. In deciding what records are to be retained, archivists determine what sources will be available in the future. Thus, they need to know how to appraise records so as to be able to identify those that are truly archival. In meeting this challenge, archivists must know what their institution wants and needs to preserve, and help to formulate clear, coherent, and comprehensive retention programs to achieve this.

Archivists must know how to arrange and describe their archives at all levels—namely, those of the repository, record group, subgroup, series, filing unit, and individual item—so that the physical and intellectual integrity of the archives can be maintained and protected, and so that they can be easily used. Because most archives begin their life cycle as records, archivists need to know something of the organization, mission, functions, policies, procedures, and activities of the entity that created them, and how and why they were created, filed, and used. This knowledge is critically important if archives are to take on more meaning in the context in which they are created and used.

Many archival institutions contain personal papers. These share certain characteristics with more formal archives and many of the same principles of management apply. However, since strict archival methods are not always applicable to the arrangement and description of personal papers, it is as important for curators of personal papers to know something of archival methods as it is for archivists to appreciate the character of the personal papers in their charge.

Often, when people envision archives, they picture individual documents, folders of documents in an archival container, or bound volumes. But archives take many shapes and forms, including maps, charts, photographs, motion-picture films, video and audio tapes, and reels of computer tape. These media require special storage, care, and handling, both before and after they become archives. Thus, archivists must be aware of the preservation, storage, and access requirements of such media. They must also possess special skills if they are to appraise, accession, arrange, describe, and administer these materials effectively.

Various technologies are changing the way information is created, recorded, stored, accessed, and disseminated. Increasingly, documentation is originally produced on, or is being transferred to, new media, such as computer tape and optical and video disk. This affects archival procedures for processing and accessing the information, requiring archivists to learn skills that were not dreamed of a generation ago. Increasingly, archivists are being required to become acquainted with the uses, advantages, and limitations of the computer and other electronic techniques as tools in the management of archives and archival information.

Archives also take the form of oral histories (tape-recorded interviews) that are used to supplement the written word, or to fill gaps in source materials. Although the oral tradition has been used to advantage by historians since Herodotus and Thucydides in the fifth century B.C., it was not until the 1940s that "oral history" became a systematic archival form. For an oral history program to be successful, archivists must be aware of its benefits and short-comings, and the financial and legal considerations, and be able to develop sound collection strategies and processing techniques.

Whatever the media, archives must be physically preserved if they are to serve any purpose. The vast amount of paper records and the newer recording and storage media present archivists with enormous preservation challenges and costs. Archivists must have the knowledge, skills, and resources to establish and maintain satisfactory environmental controls and proper storage conditions; to educate other archivists and the general public in preservation fundamentals and handling procedures; to preserve materials by conservation treatment where their retention in the original format is important; to repair damaged or deteriorated documents; and to preserve the information contained in deteriorated materials by reprographic means.

Archives have many enemies. Thus, archivists need to be aware of potential threats and dangers, and understand how to protect their archives from them. Archives must be protected from humans, who would steal them because of their intrinsic or monetary value, and from fire, flood, and other disasters. Archivists must appreciate the importance of archival security and safety, and know how to protect archives from human and non-human foes.

Because archives serve no purpose until they are used, archivists must provide a variety of reference services to facilitate the use of their holdings. Providing these services is no easy task, particularly now, when there is an increasing demand for information contained in archives. The difficulties are due to the growing volume of records and their complexity, and to the lack of resources to adequately arrange and describe them. Nevertheless, archivists must know their holdings and their relationship to the interests of researchers as well as the laws and regulations governing access. They must be diplomatic when dealing with the public, exercising good judgment, common sense, and tact.

Frequently in their careers, archivists will be faced with situations that will test their integrity. These usually arise in connection with collecting policies; with their relations with researchers and other archivists and institutions; and with their own use of their archives for personal research and publication. To deal intelligently and honorably with these situations, archivists must understand the ethics of their profession and deport themselves with a scrupulous regard for what is considered right by the various archival codes of conduct, such as the Society of American Archivists' 1980 Code.

Greater use and appreciation of archives by the public not only contributes to its general education, but usually ensures increased public support for archival endeavors. Thus, archivists must be able to impart to society the importance of the past, the significance and value of archives, and the need for archival institutions to be supported. They must be able to publicize the availability of their archives, to encourage their use, and to interpret archival work to the public and to parent organizations. To accomplish these tasks, archivists must participate in education, exhibition, publication, and other outreach programs, and take advantage of every opportunity to broaden the use of their holdings and enlist support for their programs.

All archivists, especially those in management positions, need to understand and apply the principles of sound management to their work, to provide for the smooth and efficient administration of the archival establishment. They must know how to set goals and establish priorities; how to use both human and non-human resources wisely and efficiently; how to recruit, motivate, train and supervise their staff; and how to develop resources and build support for their programs, both within the parent organization and among society at large. Archival managers, if they desire to have an efficient, effective, and productive institution and staff, need to manage (that is, control) events; to plan for the future; to evaluate their policies, procedures and practices, and measure their performance; and to provide an invigorating, challenging, and creative atmosphere.

Archival education, training, and professional development

What constitutes the best background education for archivists is a matter of debate. Because librarians and archivists share a common concern with the collection, storage, and preservation of information in a wide variety of formats and also share the common goal of providing information through similar services, some have concluded that archivists should have a substantial background in library and information science. They maintain that modern technology makes it difficult to distinguish between published and unpublished documents. This, they maintain, blurs older distinctions between archives and libraries.

Because many archival tasks require judgment based upon a wide knowledge of history, and experience in historical methods, many archivists believe that a substantial knowledge of history and training in historical research should be the main prerequisite to becoming an archivist. Such a background, it is maintained, instills in archivists an appreciation of the value of archives as basic resources for research, and teaches them the research methodologies that are often used in appraising records in the light of their relation to history, in describing them in their historical context, and in providing a reference service based upon them so that their historical significance can intelligently serve researchers.

Those of the historian-trained school often argue that the methodological training given by librarians, which focuses attention on individual items, might lead to a mistaken application of the principles of librarianship to archival materials, or might lead archivists, trained by librarians, to be so engrossed with method as to lose sight of the scholarly aspects of archival work. Those of the librarian-trained school believe that archivists trained in history may not give adequate attention to the technological and methodological changes taking place in the information sciences, which can assist in gaining access to the information contained in archival materials.

Much can be said for both historical and library training. Perhaps a history background, supplemented by formal training in archives administration and librarianship, would produce the best prepared candidate for an archival career. But whatever the background education, it simply provides a foundation for becoming an archivist. Archivists, to be worthy of the name, need a firm understanding of the theories, principles, and practices of archives administration. Such understanding comes from informal and formal training; from participation in professional activities; from reading archives, records, and information management literature; and through learning from related disciplines.

Many archival tasks in appraisal, arrangement, description, and reference require a minimum of theoretical study and a maximum of practical consideration and exercise. On-the-job training is how most archivists learn their craft. But archivists should not rely only on such training. Before entering their job or soon thereafter, and certainly periodically, they should receive formal training in order to acquire a good working knowledge of the basic theoretical concepts and principles underlying the methodology of archives administration. Formal training will provide an appreciation of the archivist's role and functions, and reinforce the correct order of priorities among their duties.

The professional development of archivists should not end with formal and informal training. Rather, such training should be the foundation for professional development where archival skills and knowledge are strengthened by other experience. This professional development is acquired from a variety of sources. Archivists should join and participate in local, regional, national, and international archival organizations. Attending professional meetings and conferences is both an excellent means to become more knowledgeable about a particular subject and an opportunity to learn about new and different opinions and ideas. Archival and records management literature, if read regularly, provides the same opportunity. Keeping abreast of the literature and taking part in professional activities, while meeting daily commitments, is difficult. But such mental stimulation is needed, if archivists are to remain enthusiastic about their profession.

Taking the time to learn from other professions, particularly in the fields of economics, geography, sociology, and political science, not only allows archivists to become more knowledgeable about things that will help them in their work, but also allows them to better appreciate the aims, methods, and needs of related professions. Informed archivists are in a better position to call on specialists in other fields to help in appraisal and similar activities. In exchange, other professions come to know of archival roles and responsibilities, as well as the existence of archival sources that may be of interest to them.

If their second objective is to serve the needs of researchers, then archivists will be more successful if they are familiar with the problems faced by researchers. Possessing historical skills and some reputation for scholarship allows archivists to deal with researchers, including historians, not only as archivists, but also as fellow researchers, thereby reducing the credibility gap that can develop between scholars and archivists. This is particularly true with respect to appraisal, where archival judgments are frequently questioned by historians and others who, if left to their own devices, would prefer to retain almost every record ever created.

Just as contacts with academic disciplines are important, so too are those with the library and information sciences. Archivists can learn from the librarians's information retrieval systems, and from library network development and public outreach programs. By learning from and cooperating with librarians on the management and control of documentation, not only will archivists benefit, but their perspective may indeed enhance library practices as well. Archivists and librarians must work together if they are both to serve scholarship.

Conclusion

Today, just as five thousand years ago when archivists administered clay tablets, their effectiveness depends on their ability to identify, acquire, organize, preserve, and administer records and information of enduring value. This is no easy task, for a variety of reasons, including the bulk and complexity of contemporary records and information.

To meet their ultimate goal of preserving and making available archives and the information they contain, archivists must first remember and understand their ultimate goal and keep in clear perspective the functions and purposes of their institutions. By keeping their eyes on their goal and objectives, they focus their energy on their mission and what needs to be done. Archivists must possess the knowledge and skills to manage their archives and repositories, develop strategies to cope with both the opportunities and problems created by the information revolution, and adapt to changes in the way information is created, stored, accessed, and used. Survival and continued service in the decades ahead will require commitment, efficiency, and imagination by archivists, and require them to make the most of their opportunities, industry, curiosity, common sense, and intelligence. Anything less will mean depriving themselves, their archives, and the public they serve.

Having read this introductory chapter, readers should be aware of the complexities involved in archives administration, and the knowledge and skills which archivists must possess in order to fulfil their ultimate goal of preserving archives and making them available. Readers also should be aware by now that archives are *not* dead files and that archivists are *not* dead file clerks. Furthermore, they should be able to answer the question of if anyone, including a "scholar", would want to be an archivist with a resounding affirmative.

Novice archivists or readers about to undertake an archival career should consider this chapter, as well as this book, as only part of the process of an archival education. Archivists, in order to fulfil their ultimate goal in an effective and efficient manner, must improve their knowledge and skills continually. The professional development of an archivist never ends; neither do the work and rewards.

Notes and references

1. Harry Shaw. *Dictionary of problem words and expressions*. New York, Washington Square Press, 1985. p. xxxv.
2. The communication process has traditionally relied upon the use of the "document", from the Latin "docers", to teach or show. A document is an instrument (piece of paper, book, map, etc.) for the communication of information, usually intended for immediate use for a contemporary purpose. Documents, in larger or smaller aggregates, make up "files", "records", "papers", "manuscripts", and "archives". The term "record", derived from the Latin "recordari" (to be mindful of, or to remember), is almost synonymous with "document", but has in addition the connotation of deliberate creation and deliberate preservation.
3. As a result of the United States Presidential Records Act of 1980, there is yet another term to cope with, "personal records". This term is used in describing strictly personal or political papers of the President of the United States.
4. "Manuscript" comes from the Latin "manu-scriptus", that which is written by

hand. The term has been used to distinguish writing by hand from printed matter. The term is now used to include typed manuscript (typescript) but not machine-duplicated (processed) material.

5. Cited in Michel Duchein. Archives in France: the new legislation of 1979. *Archivaria*, vol. 11, Winter 1980–81. p. 128.

6. It is interesting to note that in England, where the archival institution is called a record office, the record units are termed "archives groups", while in the United States, where the archival institution is called an archives, the record units are termed "record groups".

2

History of Archives Administration

James Gregory Bradsher
and *Michele F. Pacifico*

Early man did not read or write. The only surviving tangible records of his existence consist of fragments of tools and etchings on cave walls. Yet the earliest bands of people were conscious of their history and took measures to ensure that it survived. Many early cultures left the responsibility of preserving the accumulated social memory to some functionary. A "Nar" in third millennium B.C. Sumeria, a "groit" as described in Alex Haley's *Roots*, a tribal elder, a priest, or a bard was responsible for remembering and communicating a group's past experiences. Using speech, song, chant, and dance, early men and women told and retold their people's history, myths, lores and legends. Before writing, the oral tradition kept the cultures of the past alive.

Then came the written word. With writing, mankind was able to further ensure that its experiences were remembered. While the oral tradition did not disappear, records made possible a more precise account of the past. The written word enabled societies to establish and communicate all types of knowledge that could be used in all aspects of life.

Throughout the more than five thousand years that man has been recording experiences and transactions, records have served a multitude of purposes. Through the centuries, historical records have provided information on contemporary problems and issues. Records have lent administrative continuity to governments, institutions, and organizations, and have provided the legal documentation necessary to protect people's rights and interests. Archival records have been used for historical and genealogical research, to educate, and to enrich lives. They have been used as political weapons by warring, conquering, and totalitarian states. They have been used to arouse nationalistic feelings and patriotic sentiments. Archival systems and services continue to serve these purposes and today most countries can boast of a national archives and regional repositories. Municipal, institutional, and business archives continue to grow in numbers and importance. An overview of the historical development of archival organizations and records maintenance provides a context for archivists to discuss and comprehend present-day archival functions and management. Understanding the development of archival administration enables archivists to better plan for their future.

Ancient archives

The desire to keep track of their busy economic and commercial life led the Sumerians to develop writing and to keep records. These earliest records, developed in the middle of the fourth millennium B.C., were clay tablets impressed with cuneiform, or wedge-shaped, characters. As writing spread through the Near East in the following millennia, Mesopotamian and other societies made provisions for keeping records in their temples and in the courts of local rulers. Priests and kings created and maintained records on property, offerings, taxes, and exchanges. Temple priests kept records on the decisions of the gods, merchants retained financial accountings of their businesses, and individuals kept family records, frequently for genealogical purposes.

As governments became more complex and empires expanded, records became important administrative tools. Information recorded on leather, wooden tablets, and papyrus after its introduction in the fifth century B.C., allowed ancient Egyptian bureaucrats to better administer the Pharaoh's empire. Reflecting their centralized administration, the Egyptians developed an extensive archival system in the second and third millennia. Central archival repositories were established to house the records of many government agencies, like the Department of Granary, and archival records were maintained in the House of Royal Writings (the chancery) and the House of Writings (or state archives). Local Egyptian records were maintained in over forty regional repositories.

The Persian Empire, founded by Cyrus the Great in 539 B.C., maintained archives in Babylon, Ecbatana, Susa, and Persepolis. Records made of clay, leather (termed "royal skins"), and papyrus included copies of royal decrees and register rolls. The rolls, called daybooks by the Greeks, were created to record the daily actions of the royal house and were later used by Alexander the Great and his successors to rule the Persian Empire. One such register is mentioned in the Bible's *Book of Ezra* as proof that Cyrus the Great had authorized the Jews to rebuild their temple in Jerusalem.

The Egyptians, the Persians, and other early civilizations also used their archives to develop military plans and to help conquer neighboring lands. The archives of the captured governments were used by the conquerors to administer the newly-acquired territories and to obtain crucial information about their predecessors' relations with neighboring governments.

Alexander the Great initiated the use of daily journals to record all court and empire events. These journals, maintained by chancery scribes, facilitated better administrative practices and could be used to establish and retrace precedents. Preservation of all records, including those of the courts, was deemed crucial to the successful rule of Alexander's empire. Complete historical accounts were so important to Alexander that when records were burned in the tent of his chief of chancery (about 330 B.C.), he ordered his staff to reconstruct them by obtaining copies from his provincial governors and military commanders. Babylon was eventually established as the capital of Alexander's realm and the headquarters for its archives. Just as Alexander had used Cyrus' records to gain control of his land, successors used Alexander's archives to facilitate rule of the non-Grecian parts of the Empire.

In classical Greece, records consisting of information recorded on wooden writing boards were used to document property ownership and protect the rights of citizens. The city–state records of Athens were considered important enough to be housed in the Metroon, the temple of the Mother of the gods. Original records were stored for posterity under the protective eyes of the gods, while copies were displayed for public consultation. Functioning as early as 410 B.C., the Metroon contained General Assembly and Council laws and decrees, minutes of meetings, diplomatic records, budget and financial accounts, public trial records, contracts of the state with private individuals, and copies of the great dramas.

Republican Rome was slower to develop public archival institutions. The Aerarium, Rome's first public archives founded about 509 B.C., contained primarily financial records and copies of laws. A room in the temple of Saturn, Rome's first special facility for public records, was open to all citizens who wished to consult the laws. When the wooden building containing the Aerarium was destroyed by fire in 83 B.C., it was replaced by a large stone building, the Tabularium, to protect against future fires. In the Tabularium, wax tablets (*tabula*) were carefully preserved in wooden boxes. Not all public records, however, were placed in the Tabularium. Magistrates often took their office records into their private *tablina*, and some public records, including lists of magistrates, treaties, statutes, senatorial decrees, and popular ordinances, were housed in other temples. At the same time, private Roman archives abounded and were maintained in "house archives", or *tablina*.

When power shifted from the Senate to the emperors, the Tabularium lost its position as the central archives of the Roman body politic. It did, however, continue to serve as a senatorial archives to the middle of the third century. The emperor's secret archives (*secretarium*) were maintained separate from the Tabularium, by Tabularius, the archivists of the emperors. Outside Rome, large volumes of records were created by the complex government of the Roman Empire. Archives were established by provincial governors, military commanders, and municipal officers to efficiently administer their own territories and to make the mandatory reports to the emperors. The emperor Justinian considered his empire's archives to be so valuable that he ordered magistrates to set aside a public building in each province to store records and to entrust their care to a responsible citizen so that the records would "remain uncorrupted and may be found quickly by those requiring them". In the 530s Justinian was able to use the carefully preserved archives of his empire to compile the "Body of Civil Laws", better known as the Justinian Code.

Egypt, under Greek and Roman rule, adopted the record-keeping practices of its rulers yet also continued the archival traditions inherited from ancient Egypt and the Persian Empire. The centralized government established under the Pharaohs was not only preserved but intensified in this period and transactions of every kind were recorded. Great attention was given to preserving records and providing access to them. A central archives was established in Alexandria, the capital, and regional state archives were set up to ensure that the wealth of Egypt was properly administered. Provincial repositories in Egypt were responsible for sending copies of the governor's diaries to the central archives.

In China, archival records can be traced to the Hsia Dynasty, the first dynasty established after the fall of primitive communes over four thousand years ago. China's earliest records were made of bones and tortoise shells and were used to record events and prayers. By 700 B.C. China's archival material changed to bamboo slips, silk, and stone tablets, and many of the warring states had special buildings to protect their records. After 200 B.C. plant fibre paper was invented in China and safety precautions were taken to protect fragile documents made of this material. One ancient archives in this period was built on a canal in order to get water quickly in case of fire. As China developed, respect for history prompted the continued preservation of historical documents and each succeeding dynasty established its own archives building. By A.D. 50 the Han Dynasty had established the Bureau of Historiography to conserve the records of the dynasty and to write the history of the preceding one. This strong archival tradition continued throughout ancient China, although like most ancient civilizations, the majority of the records did not survive the ravages of time and politics.

The early Mesopotamian societies, the Persians, the Egyptians, the Greeks, the Romans, and the Chinese, all realized the need for records. To efficiently administer and protect their vast holdings and to monitor their citizens, these early civilizations developed institutions to care for their records. From 3500 B.C. to the fifth century A.D., governments and individuals systematically established archives. Consisting of current, non-current, and historical records, books, and artefacts, these ancient archives existed to guide governments and record history for future civilizations. Although no ancient archival repository has survived intact and relatively few ancient records exist today, hundreds of thousands of clay tablets fortunately have survived.

The Dark and Middle Ages

Archival development in Europe was almost non-existent from A.D. 600 to A.D. 1000. During the Dark Ages few records were created because most people did not know how to read or write. Business transactions in and between the self-sufficient feudal communities were usually exchanges made in kind, that is exchanges of goods and services. Government procedures were conducted orally and rituals and ceremonies served as substitutes for written records. Laws and edicts were published by proclamation, and trials (often by "ordeal") and punishments were public so all could witness the delivery of justice. For the most part the elaborate and sophisticated administrative organizations that characterized the Roman Empire disappeared during the Dark Ages. The new German kingdoms of the west, Goth, Lombard, and Frank, maintained records, but most other kingdoms and secular entities did not.

Even if there had been a greater desire or ability to record information in the Dark Ages, parchment was scarce and expensive. Older documents were sometimes erased so new ones could be created. Paper, introduced in the Near East by the ninth century, was not adopted in Europe until the twelfth century and not used in England until the early fourteenth century. Those records that were created were usually maintained by the churches since most monarchs and princes did not have fixed residences.

The few existing archives in the Dark Ages were used for the traditional administrative reasons as well as for religious, legal, and historical purposes. Churches kept records of births and deaths. Charlemagne used older records to develop his codes of law late in the eighth century. In England, the Venerable Bede (673–735), the noted historian, relied heavily on archival materials to write England's church history.

The Middle Ages in Western Europe experienced a growth in ecclesiastical and secular archives as more records were created and preserved. Oral ceremonies and oral transactions gave way to written documentation. Written laws, which had almost disappeared since Roman times, again prevailed. Laws were codified, decisions were recorded, and by the end of the thirteenth century, evidence unsupported by written documents was increasingly found unacceptable by the courts. Churches and abbeys continued to keep records, housing them in "muniment rooms" built with thick walls, small windows, and heavy doors.

Until the twelfth century, kings and princes without permanent residences turned their records over to the church for safekeeping or carried them from campaign to campaign, from castle to castle. As late as 1310, Henry VII of the Holy Roman Empire took his records with him to Italy for his coronation. Unfortunately he died there and his archives remained in Italy. But as the residences of monarchs became fixed and the scope of their administration expanded, secular archives grew. Financial and legal records predominated, although most monarchs were also careful to preserve their correspondence with the Church and each other. France's archives were ambulatory until 1194, when Philip II lost his belongings in battle to Richard I of England. Consequently, Philip created the Trésor des Chartes in Paris to protect the country's charters (documents containing grants of rights and privileges). England finally caught up in the thirteenth century and began to house its Exchequer rolls in the Tower of London. In 1305 the King of England sent a collection of papal privileges to the Tower for safekeeping; in the 1320s records of the Treasury, the Exchequer, and the Wardrobe also were sent to the Tower. By the fifteenth century the Tower of London housed all of Britain's Chancery records.

The late eleventh and early twelfth centuries witnessed the growth of European municipal governments and an increase in trade and commerce. As the monarchies solidified, towns developed, and commerce increased, administrative records again were needed and created. Princes and feudal lords also perceived the economic and organizational benefits of retaining and preserving their records. Cities and towns began registering births, deaths, marriages, and taxes, while business and banking transactions were scrupulously recorded.

By the end of the Middle Ages, the fact that monarchs had fixed and permanent residences resulted in an increased consolidation of official archives. Churches and states took special care of their records, often to prove their title to property, which has resulted in some of them surviving today. On the eve of the Renaissance, archival records began to be viewed as state property, not as the possession of an individual ruler. This brought greater assurance that a king's archival records would be passed on to his successors.

From the Renaissance to the French Revolution

As the Middle Ages ended in Europe (ca. 1460–1520), a renaissance of learning took place. Originating in the twelfth century, this surge of learning was accelerated during the sixteenth century by the invention of the printing press. The spread of learning during the sixteenth and seventeenth centuries stimulated a renewed interest in the past and the preservation of materials for studying the past. The Renaissance was a period of eclectic acquisitiveness, resulting in the creation of libraries, manuscript collections, and archival repositories.

Until the early 1500s archives were used primarily by governments and churches for financial and legal purposes. In the Renaissance period, however, particularly in Europe, archives became increasingly viewed as a source of history. The growing opposition between the all-embracing claims of the Church and the new demands of a more secular age provided the impetus for a renewed interest in civil history. Additionally, exploration during the Renaissance period created a demand for more exact information, historical as well as geographical.

With the invention of the printing press and the growth of administrative governments came a growth in records creation. Monarchs in Western Europe could no longer personally maintain their records in castles or churches and looked to creating royal repositories. European monarchs began to regard their archives as symbols of their prestige and power and consequently planned special treatment, including special buildings, for them. In 1524, Charles I of Spain ordered that the Royal Archives of Castile be transferred to the castle of Simancas to appropriately preserve the country's royal materials and any records necessary for the daily operation of his government. With the start of operations in 1543, the Simancas repository became the first well-defined, distinct European archives facility. In 1560, Francis II of France followed suit by appointing a trusted aide to organize the royal archives. The Swedish Chancery Archives was established in 1618 with records housed in the Riksarkiv. The Danish Royal Archives was established in 1665, although it did not move into its own facility until 1720. In sixteenth-century China, records were still handwritten yet were voluminous and important enough for the Chinese Emperor to plan an archival repository. The Huang Shi Chen, or Imperial Records Repository, was built in 1534–35 by Ming Emperor Jiajing, expressly to store dynastic records. Unfortunately, efforts to establish other national archives, including Francis Bacon's attempt in 1593 to create an English national archives, were unsuccessful.

The Reformation and Counter-Reformation provided a stimulus to churches to collect and maintain documents, primarily to demonstrate the historical validity of their positions. Monastic orders collected medieval records into the eighteenth century to document what they perceived as the civilizing role of the Catholic Church. The Vatican Secret Archives was formally established in 1612 with an appointed archivist and a special facility to house the records of the Pontiff and his Curia.

Spurring historical enquiry during the sixteenth and seventeenth centuries were the problems associated with legal authority and systems of law. In England, both Parliamentarians and Royalists used historical records to justify their political claims. On the continent, legal scholars began consulting ancient legal archives to trace and develop their laws. Archives were used to legitimize governments and provide the continuity needed to govern new territories. Peace treaties began to provide for the transfer of all records belonging to the ceded or conquered territory. Captured archives were used to claim title to property.

With the emergence of the modern state in eighteenth-century Western Europe, governments established ever-expanding administrative machinery, and accumulated large volumes of records as a byproduct of their work. Nations began to centralize and consolidate their records and erect special buildings as proof of their country's importance and commitment to history. In 1713 an archival facility was begun in the Electorate Hanover to store the records of this newly unified country. The Royal Archives of the Kingdom of Sardinia in Turin (1731) and the French Foreign Ministry Archives in Versailles (1761) were housed in architecturally-distinguished premises. Public archives facilities were built in Florence in 1778 and in Milan in 1781. The Scottish General Register House was completed in 1784. One year later, Spain established the Archives of the Indies in Seville, thereby concentrating the country's colonial records in one location.

Other governments either started anew or improved the provisions for their country's archives. The Swedes, who had established their national archives in 1618, archivally influenced the Swedish-ruled Baltic provinces of Estonia, Latvia, and Lithuania. Peter I, also influenced by the Swedes, issued a comprehensive law in 1720 emphasizing the need for the systematic and centralized preservation of historical documents in Russia.

Along with this archival growth came the first guidelines for archival administration. In 1618, Axel Oxenstierna, chancellor of Sweden, prepared a set of rules and regulations for the Swedish Archives. Baldassare Bonifacio's *De Archives* (1632) discussed the history and importance of archives and provided guidelines on how to care for them. His fellow-countryman Albertino Barisoni had written *De archives commentarius* in 1620, although it was not published until 1737.

Despite the increasing consolidation of archives, decentralized archives continued to be more characteristic of the situation in Europe and the Far East. Archival records were scattered in various repositories. Monarchs continued to keep their own records as well as those of appointed government entities. In the decade before the French Revolution there were over twelve hundred archival repositories in France, including over four hundred in Paris. Archives were still poorly organized and rules of archives administration were not developed. Without a centralized archival system and with poor travel conditions, scholars found it very difficult to use historical records to their best advantage. Furthermore, access to archival materials was restricted. The records still belonged to the monarch and access was often difficult if not impossible to obtain.

The French Revolution and the nineteenth century

The French Revolution marked a new age in archival administration. With the triumph of French republicanism came a commitment to establish a nationwide public archives. France and other European states recognized their responsibilities to preserve and care for their citizens' records. Public access to government records was initiated and for the first time archives were legally open to all citizens. The French Revolution brought with it the acknowledgement that public archives were essential to preserve and administer a nation's heritage.

In 1789 the French National Assembly provided for an archival institution to house their parliamentary records, which one year later was named the Archives Nationales. A decree of June 25, 1794, established the Archives Nationales as the country's national repository and reaffirmed the new French government's belief that the records of the past regimes and present government were public property. Access was guaranteed in the newly established public archives. The 1794 decree granted the Archives Nationales jurisdiction over the records of government agencies, provinces, communes, churches, hospitals, and universities. In 1796, it obtained control of the records formerly held in the districts, creating the first centrally-directed state-wide archives system. With the Revolution, the self-conscious new government gave birth to the first modern national archival system. Other countries soon copied France's commitment to preserve its documentary heritage.

The originators of the first modern central archives, however, attempted to go too far with this idea. Napoleon, in his search for an Empire, tried in 1810 to centralize all the archives of Europe in Paris. His armies were ordered to take custody of official and historical records when they seized territories. Napoleon not only hoped to cripple a country's psyche by depriving it of its past, but he also knew that he needed the information to control the new lands. Fortunately his plan for a central European archives collapsed with his fall in 1814 and each European country was left to develop its national archives in its own fashion.

As a result of the impact of the ideals of the French Revolution, nationalism flourished. Romantic nationalism prompted an increase in historical scholarship in nineteenth-century Europe. The search for history and a national identity in turn influenced archival developments. Specialized public archives, modeled after France's central depository, were either created anew with revolutions or grew out of existing archival traditions. After Finland was separated from Sweden in 1809 and Norway was separated from Denmark in 1814, each established national archives. Under Denmark's newly established constitutional monarchy (1848) a separate archives for governmental records was created. The Dutch Allegemeen Rijksarchief in The Hague and the Belgian Archives Générales du Royaume were established in this period. The Italian kingdoms of Naples (1818) and Sicily (1843) set up central repositories for their administrative records.

In England, Sweden, Prussia, and Denmark, central archives evolved from existing chancery or ministerial archives. By an Act of Parliament of 1838 the Public Record Office was established in England as the national archival institution, where all state papers of the central government would be preserved. Six Parliamentary committees from 1800 to 1837, collectively known as the Record Commission, had voiced concern that the country's official records were not being properly preserved. A fire in 1834, which destroyed most of the House of Commons papers housed in the palace at Westminster, served to intensify the concern for England's records. The cornerstone of the Public Record Office was laid in 1851; five years later the records of the monarchy began to arrive. In Sweden, the new central archives evolved from the chancery, the oldest central agency of the country. The Riksarkiv, established in 1618 to house chancery records, gradually absorbed the archives of other governmental agencies by the middle of the nineteenth century. Other nations followed suit and formed or improved their national archives in the latter half of the century. Finland and Norway, both of which established archives in the early part of the century, increased the responsibility of these entities by making them government agencies in 1869 and 1890 respectively. "National archives" were established by the British in India in 1891 and by the Dutch in Indonesia in 1892. And in Italy, Pope Leo XIII (1878–1903) elevated the archivist of the Vatican Archives to a cardinal and in 1880 opened the doors to outside researchers.

In the United States growing patriotism and self-identity in the wake of nationhood resulted in an increased interest in preserving historical records. In the six decades following the establishment of the Massachusetts Historical Society in 1791, more than two hundred state, local, and regional historical societies were established. While there were still no official national or state archives, many of these societies assumed responsibility for their region's records. In South America a national archives was established in Argentina in 1821. In North America the Provincial Archives of Nova Scotia was founded in 1857 and the Public Archives of Canada in 1872.

Regional archival establishments grew in Western Europe during this period as the central establishments realized that the growing quantity of material was too great for one repository to administer efficiently. In the first years after the Revolution, France had seriously considered centralizing all records in one national archives. French archivists rethought the idea and instead developed sectional and local depositories, "Archives Departementales", which were subordinate to the central administration. In 1851 Norway established a provincial archives in the northern part of the country. In the 1890s Sweden and Denmark also began to set up provincial archives for their governmental records.

In conjunction with establishing archives administration as a specialized branch of public service, the French Revolution prompted countries to make archives accessible for public examination. While there are examples of scholars who had previously been privy to their country's records, it had always been by favor. With the new feelings of nationalism, historical writing was encouraged and in some cases sponsored by the heads of states. Publishing documentary sources was also encouraged. European states competed in assembling and publishing archival materials. In England the "Roll Series" and "Calendars of State Papers" and in the United States the "American State Papers" were published. With the emergence of the school of scientific history, historical writing began to emphasize the study and use of primary sources and a reverence for written evidence. This stimulus for archival consciousness led to the establishment of a Historical Manuscripts Commission in England in 1869. In the United States the American Historical Association established the Historical Manuscripts Commission in 1895 and the Public Archives Commission in 1899. Their mission was to locate and publish historically valuable documents. A division devoted to the preservation of prominent manuscripts was also initiated in the Library of Congress in 1897.

With the increased use of archival materials came important changes in archival administration. Until the late nineteenth century, archives were managed by historians and archivists who had frequently been trained in librarianship. Modern records were neglected as emphasis was placed on older records. The needs of scholars resulted in artificial systems, often by subject, for arranging and cataloging records. Records were forced into such special areas as "biographica, topographica, militaria, and ecclesiastica", regardless of their original connections. Finally, in 1840, the French again took the lead in the development of modern archives systems. The principle of "respect des fonds" required that groups of documents created by one office be treated as a unique unit and be preserved accordingly. However, the French continued their attempts to satisfy researcher demands by dividing the files within each office into subject classifications. It was not until 1890 that the principle was extended by the Prussian doctrine of "provenance". Records were not only to be maintained according to their origin, but also would be arranged in the original order used by the respective office. The Dutch gave both principles their sanction in 1898 in the first modern published archives manual, the *Manual for the arrangement and description of archives*, by S. Muller, J. A. Feith, and R. Fruin.

The growth of national and regional archival institutions in Europe and the development of archival theory led to the first organized training schools for archivists. In 1821 the École des Chartes was founded in Paris, for the purpose of providing training in the handling of historical sources. Modeled after it was the Institute for Austrian Historical Research, established in Vienna in 1854. In 1877 Russia began training archivists at the St Petersburg Archaelogical Institute.

The effects of the French Revolution were in fact revolutionary for archives administration and marked the beginning of a new era. Previously decentralized archival institutions in Europe were transformed into central public archives. Nineteenth-century states acknowledged their responsibilities for preserving their documentary heritage and making it accessible to their citizens. The ideas that germinated with the French Revolution profoundly influenced the development of archival administration in the nineteenth and twentieth centuries.

Modern archives

The twentieth century has witnessed the establishment of national archives in the Soviet Union, the United States, the People's Republic of China, and many developing countries in Asia and Africa. Other countries have developed and expanded existing archival operations. Archivists around the world have begun to communicate with each other about their holdings, procedures, and problems. National and international professional organizations have been established to promote cooperation and professionalism among archivists.

Throughout history, archives have been used to bolster new governments and their political ideologies. In this century, the formation of modern governments and the proliferation of paper that accompanied them increased and intensified the maintenance and use of archival materials. Revolutions and wars furthered the importance of preserving archival materials. Records, used to monitor every facet of a nation's existence, became vital tools to the invader and the defender. As socialist governments formed, historical records became important political weapons of the new states. The Soviet Union led the movement to control and nationalize its records.

On July 1, 1918, Lenin signed a decree providing for the reorganization of Russia's records under the Bolshevik regime. All documentary records of the new Soviet Union were nationalized under a central administrative agency which held supreme authority over archival policy and procedures. After World War I a decree of January 30, 1922, further strengthened the government's control and empowered the Soviet Union's archival agency to examine the files of all government offices. This gave the Soviet Union the most highly centralized archival system in the world. With this new system, university-level and on-the-job training programs for Russian archivists were initiated. China and other socialist countries in Eastern Europe, Asia, and Africa followed Russia's methods as they defined their governmental operations.

In the first quarter of the twentieth century, national archives were established in Iceland, Panama, and French Indochina. In the United States the first state archives was formed in 1901 but a national archives was not established until 1934. There were a number of unsuccessful attempts to organize a United States national archives in the latter nineteenth century and early twentieth century, and to bring control to scattered government records, but it took a persistent lobbying effort by historians, genealogists, and military veterans to finally obtain the legislation needed for such an institution. Four years after the establishment of the United States National Archives the first presidential library, the Franklin D. Roosevelt Library, was established, ensuring that United States presidential records, both personal and official, are preserved and made accessible.

Since World War II there has been unprecedented growth in archival development throughout the world. English-speaking countries such as Canada, Australia, and New Zealand sought to catch up with Western Europe and its strong archival traditions. Developing countries, which achieved independence as part of the decolonization process, quickly sought to establish archival institutions as symbols of their new identities. Israel's state archives was established in 1949, one year after the formation of the country. In the 1950s and 1960s national archives were formed in Uganda, Sudan, Malaysia, Thailand, and the Republic of Vietnam. Over one hundred countries have been created since World War II and most have national archival repositories.

While some countries were just beginning their archives, others with established archival systems expanded their local, regional, and provincial programs. In England, although county records had been kept for centuries, the first county records office was not set up until 1924. By the late 1960s, there was at least one archival repository in each British county. The Central African Archives, formed in Southern Rhodesia in 1935, was extended as a joint service for Northern Rhodesia and Nyasaland in 1946. In the late 1950s, New Zealand set up a state archives system. In 1968 the United States National Archives established regional archives branches across the country to house federal records with primarily regional content and interest. By this time almost all fifty states of the United States had developed state archival systems and numerous local archives were active.

Today all Canadian provinces have archival institutions. Most Scandinavian countries have at least seven provincial archives. Most Swiss federal records are maintained in one of the twenty-five government repositories of the individual cantons, not in the national archives building in Bern. Likewise, Italy has an extensive regional system with some ninety-five provincial archives. In France, between 1956 and 1985, sixty-four buildings were erected or adapted for national or "departmental" archives. And in China today, there are 2,600 archives and over 200,000 archivists. Unfortunately not much has been done with regional, state, municipal, or local records in many of the developing countries. Furthermore, many countries lack institutions to house the records of private entities or the personal papers of significant citizens. While throughout the world there has been a significant growth in public archives in the past twenty years, only the United States has had any noticeable development in private archives.

As the archival movement grew and developed, professional archivists organized to communicate with each other about policies, procedures, training, and ethics. In 1910 the International Congress of Librarians and Archivists met in Brussels to discuss common concerns. The archivists in attendance, most of whom were from Western Europe, endorsed the principle of "respect des fonds" as the basis for archival endeavors. Unfortunately World War I temporarily ended any further international professional action.

Following World War I, archivists participating in the newly formed International Institute for Intellectual Cooperation compiled and published the first volume of a projected multi-volume international guide to archives in 1934 and began preparations for an international glossary. However, when Germany withdrew from the League of Nations, the group ceased its work. Once the United Nations Educational, Scientific, and Cultural Organization (UNESCO) was organized in 1946, there was again a vehicle of communication for archivists. In 1950 the International Council on Archives (ICA) was established to promote the scholarly use of archival records and their effective administration. Until 1966, when the United States National Archives hosted an ICA Congress in Washington, D.C., the ICA was largely a Western European organization. Subsequently, the United States and developing countries participated in its activities. Today more than 120 national archives institutions are members.

Although the ICA's primary orientation is public archives, it attempts to represent the interests of all archivists. To improve its own communications and provide for better professional exchanges, the ICA has created nine international regional branches for those countries that became independent after World War II and those now designated as "developing" countries. In 1979 the ICA and UNESCO initiated a comprehensive long-term Records and

Archives Management Program (RAMP) to promote, primarily through publications, the more effective management and use of archives, particularly in developing countries.

Meanwhile, the past fifty years has witnessed the mobilization of archivists at local, regional, and national levels and by special interest. Most nations have national professional archival associations, such as the Society of American Archivists, the Australian Society of Archivists, the Association of Canadian Archivists, and the Society of Archivists (in England). These associations provide their members with various avenues of improving their professional knowledge and skills, including newsletters, journals, conferences, and educational workshops. Most national associations also have within their structure special interest groups, such as labor archivists, religious archivists, and college and university archivists, which enhance communications between archivists with unique interests and problems. Many nations also have regional and local archival organizations for these same reasons.

Conclusion

Archival institutions and the profession continue to grow and mature as governments, businesses, organizations, and individuals continue to record their activities and preserve information of historical value. "Provenance" and "original order" are still the guiding principles of the archival profession, although archivists around the world differ in how they perceive and practice archival administration.

Western Europe's long-established traditions of scholarship and history have dictated how archives are managed. European archivists are educated and trained as historical scholars and for the most part governments control entry into the profession. The United States, on the other hand, has departed from the traditions of Europe and has introduced a new concept to the profession. The "life cycle of records" extends archival administration to include records from their creation to their disposition, thereby increasing efficiency and further ensuring that archival records are not lost before reaching their final destination, the archives. Archivists in North America tend to be versed in records management as well as traditional archival principles, although their training is much less defined than that of their European counterparts. Yet on both continents, in Europe and North America, the right to access that evolved from the French Revolution is still predominant.

In socialist countries, public access to records is not a guaranteed right of the citizen and scholarly research is often prohibited by political obstacles. The archivists in socialist countries are "political functionaries" and the archives exist primarily to serve the interests of the government.

Archives today constitute an informational and cultural resource and a storehouse of knowledge, and are a key element in perpetuating and improving governments, businesses, organizations, and institutions, as well as national heritages, cultures, and societies. Archives throughout the world face many of the same problems. On the eve of the twenty-first century, storage space remains a continuing concern for archivists, and new technologies for storing and accessing information are being addressed. But no matter what the current and future problems are, archives continue to be the primary source for historical information. Archives are used daily for a wide variety of immediate and practical purposes and needs, with tangible benefits to the individuals and societies they serve.

Archives from their very beginnings have been important administrative tools for governments, businesses, organizations, and institutions. No matter what the political orientation of the government is, or whether the archives are public or private, the records document the development, organization, policies, programs, and activities of these entities. Archival records are crucial for analyzing program developments, planning future programs, and evaluating past performances. They assure the clarity and continuity of administrations.

Archives continue to be of great legal and historical value. Daily they are used to document agreements, obligations, personal and property rights, patents, and trademarks. They substantiate claims, provide evidence of citizenship, and define a government's responsibilities. Meanwhile, historians, genealogists, and other researchers use the information in archival repositories to support and develop their studies. A nation's archives contributes greatly to the creation of the national identity, the national consciousness, and the national heritage. That same sense of identity is enhanced by a business archives, a college archives, or a church archives.

In addition to these traditional values, archives today serve many other purposes. Archival materials are used increasingly to educate, entertain, protect, and enrich lives. Copies of archival documents are used in classrooms to provide students with first-hand evidence of past events. Historical photographs, sound recordings, and motion pictures provide pictorial and aural representations of the past. Publications, exhibits, documentary films, and advertising campaigns all use archival materials. Medical researchers use historical records to trace genetic and contagious diseases. Maps, permits, photographs, and reports allow scientists to predict earthquakes, locate toxic wastes, trace climatological changes, and determine nuclear waste disposal sites. Architects, engineers, surveyors, and preservationists consult archival records to plan, maintain, and restore cities, buildings, bridges, highways, and other structures. Writers use archives to give historical flavor to stories, journalists for background to current news, and collectors to date and understand memorabilia.

For more than five millennia, mankind has relied heavily on archives as a basis for understanding its past, to help orient it in the present, and to provide guidance for progress into the future. This has been especially true for the past two hundred years, when archival materials have been centralized and made more accessible. Now, with the information revolution, archives take on an even more important role. Increasingly people are acknowledging that the most reliable way to anticipate and to shape the future is to understand the past. So long as memory is a necessary part of the conduct of current and future affairs, archives and archives administration will be crucial elements of our societies. The Qianlong Emperor of the Qing Dynasty gave sage advice when he encouraged all to "ponder the sacred documents diligently" and to use them "as mirrors to examine ourselves."

3

Archivists and Records Management

Karen Dawley Paul

When he observed that "all of the archivist's problems in arranging, describing, appraising, and servicing public records arise out of the way in which such records are handled in government offices", Theodore R. Schellenberg, a leading archival theorist, put forward a major reason for archival interest in records management.[1] In fact, appraisal, arrangement, and description practices have evolved largely in response to conditions in which records were created and maintained. Basic administrative principles of provenance and original order reflect this fundamental link between archival methods and office management practices.[2] Furthermore, the creation and maintenance of a record, be it governmental or of some other corporate type, largely defines its authenticity, preservation and use. The ability of records to provide authentic and adequate documentation is related to the way in which they are administered, whether they are kept in their entirety without unauthorized alteration or destruction, or whether they are transferred to an archives according to established disposition procedures. Finally, the ease or difficulty of accessing information in an archives is conditioned by initial filing and indexing decisions.

Despite the existence of such fundamental relationships among current records maintenance, disposition and archival practices, interest in records management as a technique to administer records from creation to final disposition developed only as recently as World War II, mainly in response to the proliferation of war-related agencies and a resulting need to administer vast quantities of records in an efficient manner. In 1941, the National Archives of the United States established a records administration program which was designed to promote standard practices in the segregation, filing, and retention of records in order to facilitate their disposition. Records management would be used to improve records administration throughout the record life cycle, enhance the archivist's comprehension of provenance and filing methods, help prevent uninformed destruction of records, and assist with the preservation of adequate documentation of agency policies and programs. Archivists also perceived that records management could improve the quality and reduce the quantity of records, and ultimately facilitate access to information for reference and research.

Responding to the need for expertise in the management of records of increasing volume and complexity, records management subsequently grew into a separate profession with specialized training, independent professional associations, and a separate certification process. Most public and private institutions and businesses today have a need to maintain both records management and archival operations, although they may not be labeled as such. In large, complex entities, such as national, state, provincial, and municipal governments, the two services tend to be more specialized and autonomous, and the normal problems of communicating within a large bureaucracy can exist. In such instances, archivists must conscientiously establish and maintain close working ties with records management professionals. In smaller organizations, the structure and hierarchy vary. An archives may function as part of a records management program or vice versa, or the services may operate independently.

While the two professions generally require different training and skills, they are in fact mutually dependent upon each other for complete success, and share a common concern for the identification and preservation of records essential to the ongoing operations of their institutions. Morris Radoff recognized this in 1955 when the Association of Records Executives and Administrators and the American Records Management Association were organized. In his annual address as president of the Society of American Archivists, he asserted that the two professions did not share common interests, but had only one interest: namely the guardianship of records. He called upon archivists and records managers to recognize their shared goal and urged archivists, in particular, to become masters of the whole field of records, including creation and maintenance. At the same annual meeting, Robert A. Shiff, president of the National Records Management Council, noted that the functions of archivists and records managers were closely related and, to a growing extent, were interchangeable. He pointed out that most businesses were unable to maintain two separate programs and concluded that the business archivist or records manager must serve both functions simultaneously.

Regardless of the particular relationship of archives to records management within a given organization, all archivists should possess a good grasp of records management fundamentals and be actively involved in records management concerns. Whether it is to establish and maintain close working ties with records professionals in an existing program, to engage in records management activities directly, or to instruct specialists in certain duties, archivists must be familiar with those records management functions which will help guarantee the acquisition of quality archives. Effective records management is the best way to avoid the pitfalls of waiting passively for records to be offered.

Records management provides archivists with the means to rationalize and economize archival and information services within a larger institutional structure. This chapter covers records management functions which are vital to a successful archival program. By discussing specific techniques and benefits of records management, it urges archivists who are unfamiliar with the discipline to seek closer, more productive working relationships with their fellow professionals and, where appropriate, to incorporate the techniques into their own archival programs, becoming their own records managers when necessary.

Definition of records management

To support or implement good records management, archivists should have a clear understanding of its scope and methods. Stated simply, its goals are to ensure that unnecessary records are not created, that necessary records are maintained and used effectively, and that records which have served their purpose are disposed of properly. To achieve these goals, records managers survey an organization's holdings, analyze the data with an eye to systems improvements and economies, schedule the records for disposition so that they will remain in active storage space only as long as absolutely necessary, and carry out specific disposition actions.

Of necessity, records management activities are both analytical and promotional. Those involved in records management must provide inspiration as well as expertise in order to initiate and perpetuate a successful program. Such a program includes the identification and collection of adequate documentation; preservation of records vital to the ongoing operations of the organization; facilitating the use of such information in complete form; providing for efficient use of personnel, space, and equipment; and ensuring compliance with administrative, fiscal, and statutory record-keeping requirements. To accomplish these goals, a records management program must collect accurate and complete information on an organization's policies and programs and ensure that recorded information is created and maintained in such a way that it may be identified, segregated, and assigned appropriate disposition.

The *Dictionary of archival terminology* defines records management as "that area of general administrative management concerned with achieving economy and efficiency in the creation, maintenance, use, and disposal of records; i.e. during their entire life cycle".[3] Goals of economy and efficiency, however, must be carefully balanced with the aim of achieving adequate and proper documentation of an organization's policies and transactions. Only by acquiring such information in the first place will records managers or archivists be able to furnish it when needed. Hence, a comprehensive program is designed to ensure that records containing adequate and proper documentation of the structure, functions, policies, decisions, procedures, and essential transactions of the organization are created and preserved, as well as conscientiously disposed.

Adequate and proper documentation for the records manager includes those records which protect the legal, financial, and other interests of the organization and the individuals affected by it. Such records assist the organization's officials and their successors to make informed policy and program judgments, and provide information required by authorized agencies and other oversight bodies on the manner in which any public business has been discharged. Documentation for archival purposes includes records management objectives together with a consideration of historical or research value. Archival documentation goals, for example, encompass broad topical areas, social movements, or categories of scientific endeavor, in addition to documentation needed by a specific corporate body. A discussion of archival appraisal appears in the following chapter.

Records management's role is evolving with the information age and its proliferation of equipment and processes that are resulting in the creation of ever more records and information. Records managers charged with planning and otherwise controlling the creation, utilization, protection, and final disposition of electronic records have been among the first to appreciate the fact that if information systems are to provide maximum benefits and efficiency, they must be scrutinized and managed to at least the same degree as traditional forms of record-keeping.

The new information managers, as they are sometimes called, have broad responsibilities for the selection or coordination of all information management functions within an organization. These include reprographics, word processing, data processing, electronic mail, optical character recognition, telecommunications, micrographics, records and archives management, and special library services; departments that were once independent but which are now undergoing increasing functional integration. Effective management at this level plays an important role in establishing the entire information structure of organizations and in setting policies and standards for the use of such data. Its decisions will affect what information is preserved and the extent to which it is accessible for further research.

Information management is acquiring a higher organizational profile at the policy-making level due to a growing realization that information, whether it is on a piece of paper, a microform, or a magnetic disk, is expensive to create and maintain, that it is a valuable corporate asset, and that it must be managed if it is to be of use. Archivists and records managers should take maximum advantage of this trend. Together, both groups should play a leading role in the development of comprehensive information management initiatives within their institutions, even if it entails crossing departmental boundaries. A failure to become involved will inevitably result in the loss of information that should be preserved, in vital information becoming less accessible, and in a potential breakdown of the systems encompassing records and archival administration.

Archivists and records managers are natural members of an information management team as both are important members of the larger information profession. As such they identify and accession material of interest, either to a records center or an archives, and share the goal of systematic acquisition of useful information. They both perform the tasks of arrangement and description, and provide storage. Records centers, like archives, must establish "intellectual control" over their holdings by maintaining accession inventories and producing finding aids to support collections administration and reference activity. Both services also are "user-oriented", sharing the ultimate goal of any information profession, namely providing quality information.

The archivist's role in records management

The life cycle concept provides archivists and records managers with a framework for conceptualizing records management goals and tasks. Simply stated, records are created, used, stored or maintained for future·reference, and either are disposed of or transferred to an archives for permanent retention. Records management focuses on the creation, maintenance, and disposition phases of the life cycle, while archival administration emphasizes the identification and preservation of, and the provision of access to, records of enduring value—functions which occur at the end of the life cycle. In instances where prior records management controls are lacking, archivists will need to become more deeply involved in records creation and maintenance concerns if they wish to manage the flow of records to the archives and influence collection development.

A sustained interest in records creation and maintenance leads to the development of better archives by facilitating the diversion of valueless material from the archives and ensuring the preservation of valuable information. At a minimum, therefore, archivists should promote the adoption of the essential records management processes of inventorying, scheduling, and disposition. To further refine these basic techniques, archivists can initiate or themselves implement systems analysis, micrographics, files management, inactive records storage, and other specific records management tools as the occasion warrants. Active participation in the establishment and maintenance of record-keeping and data systems ultimately provides the best means for shaping the way information is produced and stored.

Archivists should not passively wait for records to become non-current before identifying those categories having potential historical value. By designating such records as they are generated, or soon after, archivists can encourage appropriate filing and indexing, better maintenance, and timely and accurate disposition. Archival identification of valuable records while still current is especially relevant for records having prolonged administrative use, that are retained in government departments and businesses for a long time because of their sensitivity, or are in high-level political offices that experience rapid or sudden staff turnover and, therefore, retain little continuity of knowledgeable records management personnel.

In a large, complex organization the major work of controlling production and maintaining agency records will probably be performed by records managers and assistants in individual offices rather than by archivists. The records staff will be in charge of adapting good records management principles to particular situations, determine what types of files series to establish and where, and participate in the development of storage and retrieval systems. They will advise on microfilming and compile record disposition schedules which specify when non-current material will be transferred to a records center. They will also do most of the surveying required to compile schedules and disposal lists that incorporate up-to-date statutory, legal, and fiscal retention requirements. In smaller organizations or in situations where a records management program does not exist, archivists should themselves implement and encourage the adoption of these techniques.

Regardless of an operation's size and degree of sophistication in records management matters, archivists have an important and visible role to play in records administration. First, they can serve as catalysts for rationalizing the management and disposition of records by promoting archival and records management goals to agency administrators. During records creation, they can provide the archival perspective in matters ranging from the theoretical to the practical, from providing a comprehensive working definition of records, to selecting appropriate storage media for valuable records, analyzing and selecting information systems, and assisting with index design. Archivists can point out the historical value of records to agency officials to encourage better care and preservation. Through seminars, exhibits, publications, and even receptions, archivists can communicate and cultivate an interest and pride in maintaining archival materials even though they may reside, for the time being, in a working office.

Secondly, archivists should work with records managers to develop and support standards and guidelines in filing techniques, forms design, correspondence management, word processing, source-data automation, reprographics and access and disposition requirements. By encouraging standardization in record-keeping, archivists will be able to make more accurate and efficient appraisal and disposition decisions and will be in a stronger position to identify duplication and waste. Support of standards and guidelines in electronic record-keeping and reprographics will facilitate the archivist's ability to preserve such information. By establishing guidelines for disposition and access, archivists strengthen their own ability to make informed and consistent disposition decisions and better provide uniform access to information of value and use.

Standards and guidelines can range from the promulgation of statutory provisions and rule making to the dissemination of procedural handbooks and manuals and the development of training seminars. In addition, archivists can establish resource centers or clearinghouses that collect and disseminate information on technical and other record-keeping matters. They can set up model office pilot projects and conduct office inspections aimed at evaluating compliance. They may provide record center storage, if not already available, and centralized micrographic services to help preserve voluminous record series. They should be prepared to advise on procedures for compiling record schedules, if they are unable to participate directly.

Thirdly, archivists should regularly remind officials of their responsibility to create and maintain adequate documentation in such a way that it can be identified, selected, and preserved. Finally, in instances where programs are non-existent, archivists should not hesitate to point out the benefits of comprehensive records management and promote its implementation.

All of these activities take place prior to formal accessioning of records into an archival institution. They are projects that archivists can and should seriously pursue. Successful implementation can mean the difference between acquiring quality archives with high informational value, or archives of negligible use.

Many archivists feel that their role in records management should expand in proportion to the use of information systems in organizations. Hugh Taylor, a former president of the Society of American Archivists, concedes that there must always be scholar archivists to meet the demands of preserving historical records for writing history, but goes on to assert that when dealing with automated records, "we must be prepared to abandon the concept of archives as bodies of historical records over against so-called active records which are put to sleep during their dormant years prior to salvation or extinction".[4] Taylor maintains that archivists should be present at the creation of documents and should play a creative and supportive role close to the administration. It is only by playing a more active role that archivists can shape electronic documentation so that it serves administrative ends together with those of administrative or historical research.

To play this role effectively, archivists will need to acquire some knowledge of automation, communication theory, records management, and the use of records in administration, together with academic history. They must establish good working relationships with the administration (including financial, legal, general, and special departments), the special library service, historical offices, and above all the records management program. Archivists acquiring this broad-based expertise and building the necessary professional networks will be in the forefront of records administration in the next decade.

Records management techniques

The following paragraphs provide an overview of records management methods and processes at different stages of the record life cycle. Archivists should be familiar with these various program elements because successful and timely application has a major impact on the quality and completeness of material received by the archives. Where records management programs do not exist, archivists should implement selected techniques on an "as needed" basis. In-depth coverage of management processes can be found in the records manage-ment textbooks cited in the list of sources for further reading. Every archivist's library should include, at minimum, one or two of these standard volumes.

To establish a new program or improve an existing one, records managers utilize the technique of systems analysis. A typical study focuses on simplification of work processes, improvement of filing, or design of an infor-mation storage and retrieval system. Analysis might include identifying rou-tine, repetitive or outdated information in reports, directives, letters, and forms. The purpose is to standardize content and style, and institute procedures to control the distribution and filing of records by matching how records are used to what is being done. When developing series for filing, records managers consider the functions to be performed, the separation of substantive from facilitative records, the degree of detail needed for subject headings, and the level of indexing.

Substantive or program records are those records created or received and maintained by an agency as it performs the substantive functions for which it is responsible. In contrast, facilitative or housekeeping records relate to budget, fiscal, personnel, supply, or similar administrative matters common to all offices and agencies. They facilitate achievement of a functional goal, and generally lose their value as soon as their primary purpose has been accom-plished. Examples of facilitative records include requests for equipment and supplies, work schedules, and general announcements. By creating separate series for substantive and facilitative records, records managers can develop a disposition schedule that complements the filing system, thus facilitating disposition.

Standardization and controls are implemented through a variety of methods. Forms control entails studying the content, format, design, incidence, distribu-tion, and final disposition of forms with an eye to improving the quality and timeliness of information contained therein. Paperwork management includes designating record sets of information, determining the distribution of copies, and setting up files that separate substantive from facilitative information. Directives management concentrates on determining the appropriateness of methods and steps employed for communicating policy and procedure, and mail management seeks to improve an organization's handling of mail, by tracking its receipt, distribution, and filing. This includes form letter design, improving the language of official letters, and designing appropriate filing systems. Other records management duties include devising information secu-rity procedures, implementing a vital records program, and ensuring compli-ance with legal retention requirements.

Management of electronic information systems is an increasingly important aspect of records administration. This work involves assessing the effectiveness and productivity of new systems and working with computer specialists to design data bases of maximum usefulness. Records managers weigh the relative advantages of electronic filing and assess retrieval capabilities. They evaluate organizational formats and indexing, devise operating procedures, and provide for system security, as well as proper records disposition.

When records become inactive and are ready for disposition, records managers oversee their removal from expensive office space to less costly space. Records centers, whether in-house or off-site, are established to store records more economically and efficiently than would be the case if they remained in the office. They are essentially intermediate depositories for records which still have value for the originating agency. They serve as passageways between the beginning and end of the record life cycle. Indeed, they sometimes are referred to as purgatories, places where records wait out their time before going either to the heavenly archives or to the flames (most probably recycling). Centers typically receive, store, service, process, provide security and oversee the final disposition of records.

A well-managed records center attempts to attract maximum numbers of series to its holdings based on the archivist's plan or records schedule, which is a list of records series together with their assigned disposition. Center staff are responsible for applying the disposition instructions contained in such schedules to the corresponding series forwarded from the agency. Archivists rely on center personnel to assist with records acquisition and further their goals of acquiring quality documentation. They should promote the use of such intermediate storage especially to assist with the dispostion of records which must be retained for a long period of time, but which will not be forwarded to the archives. After stored records cease to have further administrative or legal use, they are either destroyed or transferred to the archives according to instructions on the disposition schedule.

Records management activities consist of conducting a thorough survey of all records maintained by the organization, obtaining official appraisal and, finally, compiling and implementing a disposition schedule. Because archivists are ultimately responsible for the appraisal decision, they should if they are not themselves conducting the inventory, work particularly closely with records managers and assistants during the "disposition" stage of the record life cycle or risk not obtaining the information needed to determine the records' archival value.

Records disposition

Records disposition is that portion of a total records management program which deals with semi-current and non-current records. Disposition actions include transfer, either to a records center for temporary storage or to an archives, donation to an eligible repository, reproduction on microfilm, or destruction. A records dispostion program has two main objectives: first, the designation of permanent records, and secondly, the timely and systematic removal of records deemed temporary by the creating office, the organization and authorizing officials. It serves as an important bridge linking those involved in creation and maintenance with those who specialize in disposition and preservation.

Records managers and archivists are partners in the disposition process. Archivists, in particular, have a substantial interest in an effective disposition program which helps to rationalize the complexity of modern record-keeping and provides for the preservation of information maintained in machine-readable formats. The archival role in disposition is a formal one consisting of appraising records to determine their informational and evidential value and designating temporary records and permanent ones. The appraisal decision is incorporated into the disposition schedule.

In the United States, for example, federal archivists have statutory authority to review all United States government agency records proposed for destruction or transfer to the National Archives. Likewise in Great Britain, the Public Record Office staff determines research value as well as value for overall documentation. As in other stages of the life cycle, archivists can also provide technical and professional guidance in establishing a disposition program, and it is certainly to their benefit to lend support to an existing one.

Where comprehensive records management programs exist, records managers serve as liaison between records creators and users within the ogranization, on the one hand, and archivists, on the other. They determine proper retention periods for the creating agency and decide whether non-current records should be stored in the office, in a holding area, or in a records center while they await disposition. Archivists should collaborate with records managers to ascertain the primary value (administrative, legal, or fiscal) for the creating agency. They also depend on records staff to document the location of the most complete and usable set of evidential records. Archivists working without the benefits of an established records management tradition will need to collect information relating to primary value and retention periods directly from agency staff. Agency legal, fiscal, and personnel officers should be consulted together with departmental heads and others identified during the course of completing an inventory. Statutory requirements must also be researched and incorporated into disposition instructions.

If records disposition has a fundamental rule, it is that series should not remain without an appraisal status. Records should not enter a storage system without a specific disposition instruction; moreover, they should neither be destroyed nor transferred to an archives without formal appraisal. Records managers and agency officers generally supply retention instructions for temporary records while archivists determine which records have permanent value.

Disposition instructions fall into five basic categories. A "permanent" instruction should indicate the date of transfer to the archives. "Undetermined" can be used to allow more time for an appraisal decision, but should specify when the appraisal review should occur. "Review" indicates that individual file units need further appraisal and that the entire series cannot be appraised as a whole. "Temporary" indicates that the material has been appraised as non-archival and should include the notation "retain for 'x' numbers of years, then destroy". "Destroy" is used to authorize destruction, but should specify the date. Instructions for microphotography can be included with disposition statements. Above all, disposition instructions should specify when a disposition takes place, such as "from the date of the latest entry", "from the date the file is closed," or " 'x' number of years following the settlement of a case or claim".

A comprehensive records control schedule provides the vehicle for implementing a records disposition program and is the blueprint which outlines the fate of an organization's information resources. Specifically, it describes all records of an institution; specifies those having archival value; and authorizes, on a continuing basis, the disposition of recurring records series. In addition, the schedule provides instructions for the disposition of materials produced by an agency and specifies retention periods for each series of records. The authority granted by a schedule provides for the continuing removal of unneeded records. This, of course, is a great help to archivists who are thus spared from repetitious appraisal. Understandably, the quality of this document is of fundamental concern to archivists because on it hinges the potential value of documentation held in the archives.

General records schedules are useful for identifying and scheduling series of records, often called housekeeping records, common to all organizations. Such records include personnel, payroll, procurement, budget, travel, printing, and other types of administrative records maintained by most offices. Archivists promote the use of these schedules to eliminate future records accumulations and to authorize the disposal of non-permanent records. For records series which are no longer being created, archivists grant a one-time authorization to designate disposition approval.

Besides records disposition, records managers and archivists find other advantages in compiling and implementing a comprehensive records schedule. Primary among them is to use the schedule and the survey process which generates it to focus attention on records management and to improve administrative efficiency. A comprehensive schedule also aids in providing better reference services. Records managers utilize a schedule to designate information resources of value to the organization while archivists use it to locate and identify material outside their immediate custody.

Finally, schedules are useful as educational tools. Within the agency, they can be used to publicize a records management or archival program and to inform staff of the value of particular records, thereby promoting preservation. Schedules can also be used to delegate tasks to record-keeping assistants responsible for implementing the disposition instructions. Most importantly for archivists, the schedule approval process can communicate historical value to records managers and agency officials. The schedule forms a basis of understanding between the organization and the archives staff. Also, because it is signed by required officials, the schedule demonstrates that policies and laws affecting records disposition have been observed. It is, therefore, the single most important mechanism for routing valuable records to the archives and for diverting valueless materials. Further discussion of design and formats for schedules, together with examples of standard forms useful for the administrative aspects of scheduling records and authorizing disposition, may be found in the standard records management textbooks, handbooks and manuals included in the list of sources for further reading.

Record surveys

Records schedules are based on data obtained through a records survey. A survey is a systematic procedure designed to gather information about records not in the immediate custody of the records manager and to allow the manager to achieve intellectual control over the organization's information resources. Indeed, the determination to conduct a survey is usually the result of a basic administrative decision to institute a records management program. In instances where such a program does not exist, archivists should require that a survey be conducted, or themselves conduct one, in order to gather information necessary for appraisal and to facilitate the selection of valuable documentation from the whole body of material. Surveys may also be conducted to discover valuable material or to acquaint potential donors with an archival program.

A survey should be carefully designed and conscientiously executed. If a schedule is the key to a records disposition program, the survey is the heart of the schedule. A thorough survey gathers information on the levels of administration and their respective functions, the relationship of records to office functions, and the relationship of records at various administrative levels. Ideally, the survey should cover all records in all formats and media and involve the entire institution or administrative unit.

A completed survey lists each type of record or series together with a description. The unit of description is the record series which is defined as a group of documents, volumes, folders or other records having the same physical form. These records are either arranged under a single filing system, are related to a particular subject, document a particular kind of transaction, or are produced by the same activity. Records normally are disposed and retained by series and thus should be surveyed by series.

The ideal survey team includes both an archivist and a records manager, each bringing to the task a different perspective. At a minimum, two individuals, one a records manager or archivist, will cause the work to progress more efficiently and will execute a survey capable of supporting a comprehensive disposition program.

A standard survey form should be used. It should be formatted to capture the following information: the name of the administrative unit; the series title, including the commonly used title and a descriptive title supplied by the records manager or archivist; the name of the creating office, if other than the present custodian; the location of the series; the inclusive dates of the records, including the month and day if required for disposition; a description of the files such as a summary of contents, purpose, and relation to specific programs or functions; length of time needed for current use; series volume and rate of accumulation; arrangement or filing scheme; type of series, such as case files, correspondence, subject, or chronological; special record types such as maps, photographs, microimages, duplication in other records; frequency of use; statutes governing retention or disposition; finding aids; restrictions; and suggestions for retention or transfer.

The survey should be conducted in as short a time as possible, in order to obtain data on an organization's holdings at a particular point in time. A separate worksheet should be used to describe each series. When completed, the worksheets can be sorted by function and analyzed by type of series and frequency of use. In addition, by comparing worksheets, decisions can be made as to which series are duplicative or redundant, and which are complementary. The sheets should then be retained for control purposes.

Analysis of the survey is presented in a management report which identifies series for removal from expensive office space and also makes recommendations on regular file closings or "cutoffs". The report should provide recommended retention periods for each series. A detailed report can serve as an outline for the records schedule, and should be discussed at staff meetings which include instructions for implementation. Publication of the report together with the corresponding records retention and disposition schedule is recommended for wider publicity and distribution.

Disposition of electronic records

Computers, office automation, and electronic records pose new challenges for records managers and archivists because of the ease with which electronic information can be transmitted, updated, and deleted. There are four major documentation areas affected by automation. First, electronic data processing creates data files and data bases which are constantly updated. Hence, records managers and archivists face the problem of determining the point at which a record copy should be preserved. Second, word processing systems, especially when configured as networks, raise the possibility of loss of important documentation which was formerly retained in substantive paper drafts and major manuscript revisions. In addition, micrographics, including computer output microfilm and computer-assisted retrieval, are now important components of information systems and must be managed as such. Finally, telecommunications supporting document facsimile transmission and teleconferencing require especially careful planning for information retention.

Changes in information technology are resulting in increased decentralization of computer applications, which in turn makes it more difficult for records managers and archivists to gather necessary information about such systems and establish management controls. Archivists and records managers must grapple with problems of incompatibility among records storage formats together with those of hardware and software obsolescence while they seek the development of information interchange standards.

Technology developments and their corresponding challenges have reinforced records and information management as an activity central to management planning. To establish effective controls, records managers and archivists should be involved during the system design phase. Records should be evaluated as they are created, and designated for short-term, long-term, or potential archival retention. Assistance with document naming, filing, and indexing conventions should be provided. Archivists and records managers must cease to focus exclusively on *what* is being created, but should instead assess *how* it is created and stored. Planning for system use and disposition of information at an early point in its life cycle is the best way to ensure the preservation of valuable information.

Above all, archivists and records managers should ensure that information in electronic form is properly documented, filed, and retained in usable condition. For data files, documentation should include a record layout and codebook. The layout describes the contents, size, and position of the fields together with all data elements in each logical record. For microcomputer formats, written documentation should include the brand and model of the microcomputer and disk drive; the name, version, and release of the operating system; a list of contents, a narrative description of the contents of each file, and the dates the files were created.

In addition to appraising records for long-term value, archivists should decide what is necessary for adequate retrieval of information stored on automated sytems. Ideally, systems should be able to retrieve, sort and store documents according to any of these categories: name of the sender (with provision for authentication of authorization, when appropriate), name of recipient, dates of transmission, office of origin, filing code, unique document identification, security/access classification, links to previous documents, and subject keywords.

Other systems design considerations include the need to ensure that systems automatically retain preliminary drafts of certain categories of documents, record the date of any alterations, and prevent the deletion of certain categories of documents. It is particularly important that hardware, software, format, and network standards be configured in such a way as to guarantee that electronic data can be converted when systems are upgraded. Finally, when such files are ready for transfer to an archives, they should be readily covertible to an archival storage medium. Archivists should help determine which medium is most appropriate. The choice of medium will, to a certain extent, reflect the archivist's appraisal decision which takes into account future use and the format which best supports it.

Archivists and records managers need to emphasize that electronic records require special maintenance and storage throughout their life cycle, and should work closely with data processing professionals and systems operators to ensure that preservation requirements are met. Successful management of electronic records depends on cooperative efforts among archivists, records managers, program directors, and technical personnel. Records managers and archivists should also stay well informed about new technological advances, such as the development of universal software formats, document interchange formats, and optical disk technology, which will dramatically increase and improve information storage and retrieval options.

By implementing programs to identify, survey, describe, and schedule electronic records, archivists can avoid situations where electronic media remain in inactive storage for months or years before being brought to their attention, thereby making preservation difficult if not impossible. The basic steps of inventorying and scheduling, modified to account for the special characteristics of electronic records, should be rigorously applied to automated records. Surveys, for example, are best conducted on a "system" basis, a system being the organized collection, processing, transmission, and dissemination of information according to defined procedures, including inputs and outputs. The following information must be collected in order to appraise and schedule an information system: system title, description of the program it supports, program authority, purpose, source of the data, contents, system outputs, and major users of the information. This data may need to be supplemented with additional information such as restrictions on access, documentation, and technical information, depending on the particular system. Further discussion can be found in the chapter on machine-readable records.

Before beginning a survey, it is wise to obtain an overview of an organization's systems. Information may be found in a variety of sources. Internal reports, newsletters compiled by central computer centers or by computer user-groups, budget and equipment requests, and special guides to information systems frequently describe major systems and applications. It is advisable to review as much information as possible from these sources before interviewing individuals. Unlike a survey of textual records, visual inspection is not sufficient to determine the scope, contents, and volume of electronic records files. Regardless of the method used, office visits, telephone interviews, or mail questionnaires, a survey of electronic files will rely heavily on information obtained from individuals familiar with the system and its contents. A direct interview will also allow the opportunity for clarification of information provided. As with textual records, a standard data collection form should be used to ensure collection of complete data.

Records disposition schedules should be compiled for all automated systems within an organization, including master data files and data bases, office automation systems, systems existing in networked configuration, and electronic mail. Systems can be scheduled individually, or a comprehensive schedule that includes disposition instructions for paper source documents and printed output together with instructions for conversion to microfilm or another archival storage medium can be drafted. A comprehensive schedule has the advantage of allowing records managers and archivists to identify all available versions and formats of information associated with the system. System documentation should always be scheduled for transfer with the corresponding electronic records. The disposition schedule should contain information similar to a textual records schedule, but archivists and records managers should expect to work more closely with data processing staff and office automation systems administrators to ensure implementation. Detailed instructions for inventorying and scheduling can be found in volumes cited in the list of sources for further reading, especially *Archives and manuscripts: machine-readable records* by Margaret L. Hedstrom and recent issues of the *Records Management Quarterly*.

To better understand automation's effects on records management and archival records, the National Archives of Canada conducted a well-documented study involving the Department of Communications. Of special interest to records managers and archivists was the development of document and task management, a logging and tracking function, and an archiving function whereby completed documents were automatically sent to the originator for subsequent transfer to the archives. In addition, keywords provided a basis for content analysis, and retention periods were included in the document index.

The study revealed that records managers have an important role to play in designing and maintaining office automation systems because the most challenging problems are managerial rather than technical. Managers can contribute to effective system planning because they possess a full understanding of the agency's mission, current records management practices, and information products. The study also showed that functions designed to ensure archival control will work best if they provide the user with a real service.

Because archivists appraise records for historical value and their ability to do so is tied to system design and use, they should also be ready to participate in system planning and, in fact, should insist on it. Both archivists and records managers should be active participants in formulating policy and program initiatives such as design and documentation standards. They should be active participants on project teams and work to establish control over automated systems by documenting and scheduling them, and by helping to develop a corporate perspective that takes into account the information management needs of the entire organization. Electronic records disposition is an instance where archival involvement best occurs at the beginning rather than the end of the record life cycle.

Micrographics

Micrographics is a favored records management tool consisting of the photographic reproduction of documents, on either continuous roll film or individual mounts, to control voluminous series of records by reducing the size of the permanent collection, facilitating handling and reproduction, and creating a bound order for better document control and security. When integrated with sophisticated computer-assisted storage and retrieval systems, micrographics provides a relatively stable and universal storage medium that can be produced to meet archival requirements for storage and preservation. When properly administered and maintained, micrographics also meets criteria for evidential documentation.

Microimage storage and retrieval generally is applied to records having a high level of reference activity where users need immediate access to an entire records collection. Managers weigh the capacity of the existing paper or electronic systems to meet user requirements as effectively as a microform-based system.

Archivists who deal with voluminous contemporary records should promote the full integration of micrographics within a comprehensive disposition program. Judicious use of the technique provides advantages similar to those derived by records managers; namely, space savings, preservation of original order, preservation of a complete record, and enhancement of reference service. In addition, archivists utilize micrographics as a conservation measure when they film frequently used or valuable records and retire the originals from everyday use. Archivists also find that micrographics can be used to build or round out their holdings by allowing them to acquire complementary material in microform copy.

In order to derive maximum benefits from microfilming and to be able to accession a microform copy in place of an original, archivists must ensure that established standards for filming, processing, and intermediate storage are met. They should insist that adherence to such standards is incorporated into the disposition program and they should require certification to that effect. Specific standards can be found in records management texts noted in the list of sources for further reading. Generally, micrographics standards for producing a master copy include creating a silver halide emulsion of a certain purity and resolution; checking chemical composition after processing; preparing diazo copies for reference use; and storing the film in a fireproof area, with relatively constant temperature and humidity (18–20 degrees centigrade, 30 percent relative humidity).

Besides insistence on filming and storage standards, archivists can promote a number of procedures which enhance the usability of filmed material and encourage records managers to elevate them to standard practices. The following filming techniques are helpful—place any indexes at the beginning, followed by the records themselves; include information about the reduction ratio on an introductory guide card; film a density card; prepare and film a title card containing the series title, inclusive dates, roll numbers, and any other explanatory information about the documents filmed; include information on the date and place of filming; prepare and film guide cards, as necessary, to further identify records groupings; film records with frame numbers on each frame, using an automatic counter; label reel boxes, cassettes and cartridges; and for microimage publications, prepare necessary textual material.

While archivists realize that they can derive many benefits from micro-photography, they should not regard it as a panacea for all records management ills. They must understand its specific applications and benefits and recognize that it cannot, by itself, replace the implementation of a comprehensive records and information management program. Archivists therefore should promote the use of micrographics within a wider program which has improved documentation and systematic disposition as its ultimate goal.

Records management literature and assistance

A number of associations and organizations are devoted to education, professional development, and furthering communications and knowledge in the records management field. They include the Association of Records Managers and Administrators (US), the General Services Administration (US), the Institute of Certified Records Managers (US), the National Archives and Records Administration (US), the National Archives of Canada, the Public Record Office (UK), the National Association of Government Archives and Records Administrators (US), the Society of American Archivists (US), the Society of Archivists (UK), and Unesco. These organizations, together with others of more specialized purpose, serve the profession through publications programs, conferences, workshops, and institutes.

Indispensable for keeping abreast of current developments in a rapidly evolving field are the scholarly journals and newsletters published by these organizations. Other publications include basic manuals and handbooks in the areas of filing, record center operations, scheduling and disposition, vital records, information systems planning and evaluation, micrographics, and paperwork management. The handbooks and manuals, especially when combined with records schedules produced by private and public institutions, can provide useful models in developing or improving a records management program.

Conclusion

Archives have two fundamental purposes: they are essential administrative parts of the governments, institutions, or organizations they serve, and they are cultural resources established to preserve and provide materials for research. To fulfill their administrative role, archival programs must be committed to objectives shared by records management, namely the control of records and information throughout their life cycle and the establishment of records disposition systems that provide for appropriate disposition.

Accomplishment of the second goal hinges on the first. To conserve knowledge for the future, archivists must serve the present in an efficient manner. Records management is their indispensable tool. Today, the need to work closely with records managers and to implement solid records management techniques is even more pronounced as increasing proportions of historical records are created and stored on fragile and reusable media. New technologies deny archivists the luxury of making appraisal judgments months or years following a record's creation.

The actual extent of archival involvement in records management will depend on the scope of existing records programs, the nature and extent of an organization's information management problems, and the character of the existing archives program, whether or not it has a records administration component. For institutions having no distinct records program, archivists themselves should provide guidance on proper creation and maintenance. Where a solid program exists, archivists will focus more exclusively on disposition activities related to inventorying, scheduling, and appraisal. In either case, however, archivists have a major responsibility to act first, to provide leadership in promoting good records management, to serve as catalysts in getting programs started, and to lend their continued support.

Notes and references

1. Theodore R. Schellenberg. *Modern archives*. Midway Reprint. Chicago, University of Chicago Press, 1975. pp. 26–27.
2. Provenance is the principle that archives of a given records creator must not be intermingled with those of other records creators. It is frequently referred to by the French expression, *respect des fonds*. A corollary, usually designated as a separate principle, is the registry principle, or the principle of the sanctity of the original order (*respect pour l'ordre primitif*). This principle maintains that archives should be retained in their original organizational pattern or structure and in their original filing arrangement in order to preserve all relationships among individual series, thus enhancing their evidential value. Evidential value refers to the value of records for providing authentic and adequate documentation of an agency's organization and functioning.
3. Frank B. Evans, Francois-J. Himly, Peter Walne. *Dictionary of archival terminology*. International Council on Archives: ICA Handbook Series. Munich, etc., K. G. Saur, 1984. p. 139.
4. Hugh Taylor. Information ecology and the archives of the 1980s. *Archivaria*, vol. 18, Summer 1984. 30–31.

4

Records Appraisal and Disposition

Maygene F. Daniels

Archival appraisal is the process of determining which records should be accessioned to an archival repository. Although archivists of earlier generations could be relatively little concerned with this process, it has become an essential part of archives administration in the twentieth century due to the very abundance of modern documentation. Archival resources are not now sufficient—and never will be—to care for all modern records without limit. In fact, even if archives could store and care for all of the voluminous and complex files, reports, memoranda, photographs, charts, computer records and other documents of a modern organization or institution, the very extent of the materials would make them effectively unusable. Researchers inevitably would be overwhelmed by a mass of undigested materials. Archivists therefore must either actively choose which records to care for or randomly accept files until shelves are full. Most archivists believe that the active choice of the most valuable materials is their most important archival responsibility.

Appraisal is often difficult. Every piece of paper, photograph, map, or computer tape has some potential use for some researcher or administrator of the future. In fact, one could construct an argument for keeping virtually everything. Judgment, therefore, is at the heart of archival appraisal. Various values in the records must be balanced against the costs of maintaining them, current and future uses must be considered, the views of one person or group must be weighed against the needs of others. Furthermore, appraisal decisions must be reached before the materials are inadvertently lost or unnecessary resources are expended to keep them in costly office space.

Although much has been written about archival appraisal, no formula has yet been found—or is likely to be discovered—that will provide a simple way to infallibly evaluate records for archival retention. Thus records appraisal is a constantly demanding job. Techniques are available, however, to ensure that appraisers' time and energy are used effectively, that repetitive appraisals are avoided, and that institutional resources are expended wisely. Standards also are available to provide guidance in weighing values in records and determining which are most likely to have sufficient long-term importance to justify archival retention. These appraisal techniques and factors will be the subject of this chapter.

Many appraisal concepts and processes were originally developed for institutional archives. The techniques described in this chapter will therefore be presented within this context. Twentieth-century archival developments have given some appraisal concepts wider applicability, however. Once clear distinctions between the characteristics of documents created within an institution and of those produced by a family or individual have become blurred. Now, both personal papers and organizational records may be either well-organized or in chaos, voluminous or filled with gaps, and, with the advent of modern technologies, on paper, on film, or produced by computers. Similarly, although many archives may be primarily responsible either for their own organization's records or for acquisitions of personal papers from other sources, virtually every institution holds both records and personal papers. Thus many appraisal concepts and techniques are appropriate for evaluating not only institutional records but also personal papers.

The process of appraisal

Archival appraisal can be understood best in its relationship to the life cycle of records: the predictable pattern of creation, maintenance and use, and disposition of records within an institution.

As natural byproducts of organized human activity, records are created in the first phase of their life cycle to communicate, facilitate transactions, or document events, activities, or situations. The physical form, content and other characteristics of the records are established during this first phase. During the second phase, that of maintenance and active use, the records may be referred to, revised, refiled, and reorganized. Eventually, however, most records have served the function for which they were created and are no longer needed for the conduct of current business. At this point they enter the final phase of their life cycle in which their ultimate disposition is determined. Immediate destruction, transfer to a records center for temporary storage and ultimate destruction, or transfer to an archival repository for long-term retention are among possible disposition actions.

Appraisals can take place at any stage in the life cycle. Early appraisal has the important advantage of ensuring that valuable records are carefully identified and protected until they are accessioned to an archival institution. These records can be housed in archivally approved conditions in order to minimize future preservation costs. Such precautions are particularly important for fragile computer records and audio-visual materials. Temporary records identified for destruction early in the life cycle may be disposed of promptly whenever they are no longer needed for current business.

On the other hand, many appraisal decisions may be difficult to make when records are still active. In these instances, archivists may choose to defer appraisal until a certain date in the expectation that new information or a clearer perspective will be available to facilitate the process at that time. Appraisal decisions must be as well-founded and broadly based as is humanly possible. Speed in itself is not a meaningful appraisal goal.

Although entire series of records are not always retained or disposed as units, appraisal itself is almost always conducted at the series level. A series of records has been arranged by its creators in a unified filing scheme or has been maintained as a group because of some other unifying factor. Although documents in a series may be created or received at different times, they are maintained and used together and are related to one another by subject or circumstance. Much archival theory is based on the important recognition that individual documents have their greatest meaning and importance within the natural context of the series. Out of this context, they may be subject to misunderstanding or may even be meaningless.

Appraisal at the series level is both efficient and effective. It avoids the time-consuming need to describe and evaluate individual documents and ensures that all documents are considered and evaluated within their natural context so that their full meaning and research potential can be considered.

Appraisers first must learn as much as possible about the nature and characteristics of the records they are evaluating. They must determine the extent, arrangement, and physical condition of the records, the physical types of materials included and the subjects they concern. The date span of the materials and periods of special concentration should be determined. Principal correspondents, particularly noteworthy types of materials, and subjects of special import should be identified. Extraneous or unusual materials found within the records also should be noted.

Effective appraisals depend on a thorough understanding of the character of the functions and activities for which the records were produced. Appraisers must carefully identify the organizational origin of the records they evaluate and the function or purpose for which they were created. They must be students of administrative structures and organizational histories and must conduct specific research about each organization whose records they evaluate. Box or file lists and other written finding aids provide an appraiser with important information concerning the scope and arrangement of the materials. Interviews with individuals who created or worked with the records also may provide substantial assistance.

Appraisers almost always must conduct a personal on-site survey of the records to gain essential information. In most instances, appraisers can make a straightforward survey of the materials, providing that sufficient time is taken to accurately establish their character. Careful notes must be taken to avoid repetitive examinations and to create a comprehensive record of the appraisal. A statistical or representative sample may be taken and recorded to provide more quantifiable and accurate information should the importance, complexity or extent of the materials require such an approach. Appraisers must also learn as much as possible about related series of records. Records surveys and schedules permit the appraiser to evaluate records within the broader context of the available universe of documentation and thus to make better informed decisions.

In records surveys, archivists summarize information about the physical characteristics and informational content of the records of an organization, or a unit within it, as comprehensively as possible. Surveys may include records in active office files as well as materials that have been retired from active use. By gathering comprehensive information about all documentary resources of an organization or institution, a survey provides full information about choices and options for records disposition. An appraiser's judgment thus can be based on the fullest possible information.

Records disposition schedules provide written instructions for retention and appropriate disposition of continuing series of records. Typically, schedules cover records of a single administrative unit or office and are based on a survey of its record-keeping systems and an analysis of its information needs. Records schedules are subject to amendment should the unit's functions, organization, or record-keeping practices change. Because schedules incorporate appraisal decisions, they must be based on the same procedures, research and review as other appraisals. Disposition schedules also can describe records commonly found in a number of offices. These "general records schedules" provide guidelines concerning institutional policy for maintenance or disposition of such documents wherever they may be encountered. Routine housekeeping records and documents such as desk calendars, extra copies of correspondence, and working papers all might be included in such "general records schedules".

Records disposition schedules permit an organization to ensure that appraisal decisions are consistently applied to continuing series of records and that reappraisals of the same groups of materials are avoided as far as possible. Schedules thus permit an organization routinely to dispose of most of its records at the appropriate time. They also permit the organization to identify continuing series with permanent value early in their life cycle. Most significantly, the use of schedules for recurring records permits appraisers' energies to be reserved for the initial appraisal of continuing series, for the evaluation of unique groups of records, and for the most difficult appraisal issues.

Acquisitions policies

Every appraisal judgment is made within the context of the goals, resources, and policies of a particular archival repository. Clear definitions of institutional acquisitions goals are, therefore, essential for effective appraisal.

An archival acquisition policy defines the types of records that the repository seeks to add to its holdings. Policies of institutional archives usually attempt to ensure adequate and complete documentation of the institution, its functions, and its activities. The policy therefore identifies priority subjects for acquisition and the types of materials most likely to provide important information about the institution. Acquisitions policies also may specify the administrative units that are most likely to create essential documentation. An archival acquisitions policy also identifies categories of personal or family papers and other non-institutional collections that should be sought and accepted from outside sources. All appraisals and acquisitions of documentary materials must take place within the guidelines and policies that an institutional acquisitions policy establishes.

Acquisitions policies also may define acquisitions in relationship to the holdings of other archival institutions. Many such institutions are concerned with documentation of similar subjects and serve the needs of the same researchers. Because duplicate or redundant documentation is of little value to these scholars and absorbs valuable archival resources, acquisitions policies may specify that the holdings of other institutions should be considered when records are evaluated for accessioning. Similarly, institutions may cooperatively choose areas of specialization or may agree that records or papers should be placed in institutions already holding relevant related documentation.

Institutional resources

All appraisals must also be conducted with cognizance of the scope and limitations of an institution's ability to care for the records. Appraisers therefore must consider in their evaluations the cost of maintaining records.

A number of separate factors affect the cost of retaining records in an archives. Among these are the volume of the records, the time needed to process them, their physical condition, and their form. More staff time is needed to move, box, and handle a voluminous series and more shelf space is required to house it than is required for a smaller series. As a result, voluminous series cost more for an institution to maintain than do smaller groups of records. Poorly organized or unarranged records require more time to process than do carefully arranged and registered materials. Similarly, records in poor physical condition may require expensive conservation treatment or reproduction that would not be required for records in good condition. Finally, documents in certain physical forms, including parchments, glass plate negatives, and computer tapes may require specialized storage environments and careful physical or technical monitoring that is costly for an institution to provide.

Although cost alone can never be the primary criterion in an appraisal decision, it must be weighed in appraisal judgments. An extremely valuable series of records may well be worth retaining despite high costs. On the other hand, a series of doubtful value might not warrant retention in the face of the substantial cost its accessioning would entail. Appraisers must consider the best use of limited resources among the many complex factors in each appraisal.

The appraiser

Because the appraisal process depends on analysis and judgment, the qualifications of appraisers and the circumstances in which they work are exceptionally important.

Archival appraisers should be experienced archivists with a thorough understanding of the principles and practice of archives administration. They should also be familiar with the research uses of records and research trends. Many appraisers have academic training in history, political science, or other disciplines that depend on research in primary resources. Personal experience in conducting research in archives is also an important means of obtaining the sophistication and understanding of the many considerations that contribute to any appraisal decision.

Because archives serve many users, no individual can be trained or have personal experience in all relevant disciplines. Yet appraisers must be sensitive to the needs and concerns of all. Effective appraisers therefore are open to learning as much as possible about the goals, techniques, and problems of all information-based activities. Wide reading, attendance at professional meetings of the various disciplines, and discussions with users of archives provide invaluable knowledge that an appraiser requires for effective evaluation of records.

Successful appraisers must be able to assess records and their values accurately, creatively determine potential uses, and realistically judge their importance. An alert, open and curious intellect is thus the appraiser's most essential tool.

Appraisers may perform their work either individually or in teams depending on the scope of the project and the nature of its problems. Typical appraisals are likely to be handled by a single appraiser working independently. Exceptionally large or complex projects may be managed more efficiently by teams of several appraisers with different subject-matter expertise or varied types of experience.

Appraisal depends on analysis of the characteristics and values of records and judgment of their importance within a specific institutional context. Because records and institutional requirements differ, every appraisal is unique. Uniformity in appraisal, therefore, is impossible. On the other hand, appraisers within each institution should always ask the same questions and apply similar criteria in their evaluations.

In every instance, written documentation of an appraisal, including both a thorough description of the characteristics and content of the records and an analysis of factors considered in the appraisal decision, should be complete and adequate in order to permit review both at the time of appraisal and in the future.

Although appraisers often work alone, they should never work in isolation. Every appraisal should be subject to review and discussion by colleagues within the archival repository. Often discussion will reveal previously unexplored possibilities or new considerations that will affect an appraisal. Experiences of other archivists also may provide useful insight into ways of handling new problems.

Appraisers also should consult with knowledgeable individuals outside the archival profession to ensure that the best possible information is available for their appraisals. Creators of the records or persons performing related functions can provide important information concerning why the records were created, why they were given their particular form or organization and what continuing importance they might have. Creators also can bring to appraisers' attention important information about the strengths, weaknesses or potential uses of the records. In many instances, individuals who created or used the records also instinctively provide thoughtful and accurate analyses of their long-term value.

Archivists should also consult with potential users of the records. This can be done informally in conversations with researchers using similar records in the repository. Informal consultations can also be supplemented by discussions with scholars and users of archival resources at professional meetings and other gatherings and through study of contemporary publications based on archival sources.

Archivists may also formally ask scholars or other subject experts for advice. Formal consultation has both benefits and pitfalls. Whether voluntary or paid, it is a means of receiving specialized information relevant to appraisal of the records. Particularly when an archivist is considering records in a specialized or technical field such as the sciences, medicine, or law, the professional insight of consultants may be an important source of information and can save the appraiser many hours of work. In such instances, the expertise of an outside consultant may be invaluable. Consultants should not be expected to make archival judgments, however. Lacking the experience and viewpoint of the archivist balanced by the practical realities of archival administration, consultants may easily become advocates for retaining virtually all records in their area of interest irrespective of other considerations and competing interests. Archivists therefore must ensure that outside specialists are consulted for their subject expertise alone. They should not be used as a substitute for the appraiser.

Archival appraisers must consistently meet the highest standards of professional conduct. Their statements form the basis for decisions concerning whether records should be retained or destroyed. The work of appraisers therefore must be uniformly accurate and complete. Appraisers must respect the conditions of privileged access that they are given and keep in confidence information that is not available to others and that they receive as part of their work. While respecting necessary confidentiality, appraisers must also be open and honest about their deliberations and decisions. They must not hide unrestricted information that would be of use to others in or outside the archival profession.

Evaluation of records

Effective appraisal depends on determining whether records have sufficient value to warrant long-term retention in an archival repository. To do so, appraisers must understand the different values that records may possess and be able to identify such values in the records they appraise.

As natural byproducts of human activity, all records are created for a purpose and, for at least some period, have value for that purpose. This is known as their primary value. Primary values may be administrative, legal or fiscal. That is, records may have value for the transaction of business, for protection of legal rights or interests, or for financial administration. Most (though not all) primary values diminish with time as administrative transactions are completed, fiscal books are closed and the passage of time reduces the need for legal concern about routine matters.

Records also have secondary values for purposes other than those for which they were created. Generally, secondary values relate to research uses. Unlike primary values, these secondary values do not necessarily diminish with time. They are the principal concern of archivists.

Secondary values of records fall in two categories, evidential values and informational values. Evidential values are the values of the records for documentation of the operations and activities of the records-creating institution. The evidential value of records is used to determine the organizational structure of an institution, document its procedures, policies and activities, and evaluate its effectiveness. Evidential values are particularly important to ensure public accountability of government organizations and for studies of administrative history.

Informational values are the values that the records have for the information they contain on persons, places, subjects, and things other than the operations of the organization that created them. Informational values in records are used for studies concerning historical events, social developments, or any subject other than the organization itself.

Most records have both evidential and informational values to a greater or lesser degree. Consideration of certain records of the United States Census Bureau may help clarify the distinctions between these values. Among other functions, the Census Bureau is responsible for gathering information on every person in the United States every ten years. Records of the decennial census eventually are transferred to the National Archives of the United States and are made available for research use there after the passage of sufficient time to ensure appropriate confidentiality. Scholars and others who examine the records for information about the Census Bureau and its work are interested in evidential values of the records. That is, they are examining the records for what they reveal about the Bureau's organization, structure, functions and activities. Researchers seeking specific biographical or genealogical information about individuals listed in the census use its informational values. They are not concerned with the Census Bureau itself but rather with information on other matters found in census records.

Appraisers identify and analyze both primary and secondary values during the appraisal process. Most records with significant primary values—that is, records still important for the purposes for which they were created—generally are needed for the conduct of current business. Immediate transfer to an archival repository therefore would be unwise and appraisal or accessioning might be deferred (other considerations in the timing of appraisal and transfer decisions are discussed more fully below). Those few records with continuing primary values that will not diminish over time—for example, an organization's constitution and by-laws—would also be identified by the appraiser. Such records could appropriately be transferred to an archival repository for long-term retention whenever they are no longer needed frequently for current use.

Secondary values in records must also be considered. These are the values of records for continuing research use and thus are a principal concern of appraisers. A number of factors including source, informational content, uniqueness and usability affect the secondary value of a group of records. Although these factors can be independently identified, they must be weighed together to establish the long-term value of the records for archival retention.

Levels of activity

Records are created in the course of various types of organizational activity ranging from top-level policy formulation through program management to routine program support and housekeeping functions. High-level offices with the broadest overview of institutional activities are the most likely to make and receive records containing substantive information about important subjects and transactions and providing the best overview of the organization's functions and activities. Thus high-level records of policy development are most likely to be rich sources of significant documentation. Program management records may provide important information concerning significant issues providing that the program is important or relates to significant people, places, or subjects or events. Housekeeping records are least likely to have continuing importance because the matters that they document are of relatively little import. Thus the level of activity at which records were created offers the appraiser important insights into their long-term value.

Significance of function

The significance of the function for which records were created must also be considered in appraisals. Even the most important policy documentation of a trivial function has relatively little long-term value. On the other hand, relatively slight documentation of a very important function with far-reaching implications may have substantial importance, particularly if no better source of information is available. Appraisers therefore must identify not only the level at which records were created but also the significance of the function or activity that they document.

Uniqueness of information

To have importance for archival retention, records should contain information that is not available elsewhere in a similar or more easily used form. If a group of records contains only information that is readily available in published form, they are probably relatively unimportant. A researcher would be able to retrieve needed data more quickly and economically from the published source than from the records. Similarly, a series of records that contains the same information as another, more accessible, group probably has little, if any, additional value irrespective of the importance of the subject concerned.

Usability of information

The appraiser must also evaluate the extent to which information in records is usable and accessible. In general, the more important the information that records contain, the more effort researchers might be willing to expend to extract it. Thus usability must be balanced against importance in every appraisal.

Various factors affect the ease or difficulty of using records. If the volume of records is particularly large relative to the information they contain, identification and use of the information becomes tedious and impractical. Legibility also is an important factor. The arrangement of records also may either aid or impede access to information. The presence or absence of detailed indexes and other finding aids may affect the availability of information as well. Access conditions too have an important impact on the usability of records. Records that will never be available to researchers or will be available only under very restrictive conditions are obviously of limited use.

Relationship to other records

The relationship of a records series to other records may also affect its value and should be considered in every appraisal. Records may supplement or enhance a related group of records on an important subject and thus have particular archival importance. On the other hand, if important related documentation is missing, the materials may be little more than a relatively meaningless fragment. Appraisers must see each group of materials as part of a larger universe of documentation and must evaluate its importance accordingly.

Appraisal recommendations

To permit efficient evaluation and to ensure that the records are understood within their most appropriate context, appraisal almost always is conducted at the series level. Similarly, most appraisals recommend retention or destruction of a series as a whole in order to protect the integrity and full informational content of the records. Certain alternatives, such as weeding, sampling or selection may be appropriate under some circumstances, however.

Weeding consists of removing individual extraneous documents from an archival series to reduce its volume and make it easier to use. An appraiser may recommend that a series of records be accepted for long-term retention but that certain specific types of documents be weeded—removed and destroyed— during processing. Extra copies, routine transmittals, specific types of transactional documents or unrelated ephemera are typical of materials appropriate for weeding.

Weeding is an effective way to reduce the volume of a series that includes valuable information but is large in volume relative to the importance of the information. It may also make a voluminous series easier to use by removing useless materials that interfere with the accessibility of more important documents.

Weeding must be employed with caution. Appraisers must ensure that it is limited to purely extraneous materials that are irrelevant to the significance of the series or the meaning of the remaining documents. Materials appropriate for weeding must be easily identified and unmistakable. Otherwise, in the process of weeding, valuable materials may be accidentally destroyed. Weeding instructions must be clear and easily followed. Unclear or confusing instructions may lead to a tedious process that is far more costly than retaining the series as a whole. Weeding therefore should be employed only when the benefits to be gained outweigh the dangers and costs. Archivists responsible for processing should ensure that careful records are maintained of the policies and procedures that are followed and the documents to which they are applied.

Sampling and selection are also methods of reducing the volume of records through appraisal within a series. These processes are normally considered for large series of case files that apparently have some value for research but are too voluminous to warrant retention as a whole. Sampling consists of the application of statistical or other systematic procedures to obtain a sample intended to be typical or representative of the series as a whole. Random number tables may be used, for example, to obtain a mathematically accurate random sample. Systematic or statistical samples are intended to permit researchers to draw statistically correct conclusions concerning the character of the larger body of records from which the sample has been drawn.

Selection or qualitative sampling consists of identifying for archival retention certain categories of files or individual examples with particular importance. Unlike statistical sampling, selection or qualitative sampling is intended to obtain a non-representative group of files. Precedent-setting case files, documents concerned with issues of particular significance, or other categories of materials might be specified for selection.

Both sampling and selection depend on the assumption that each case or file is essentially independent of the others with which it is associated. Unlike most records, the meaning of such files should not necessarily be enhanced by association with the other files in the series. Because both sampling and selection are used to identify records for narrowly-defined purposes, both processes also assume that the appraiser is able to identify with reasonable certainty ways in which the records will be used by future researchers.

In practice, both assumptions often prove faulty. In most instances, even case files relate to one another in important ways. Examination of one file may lead to further investigation in others. Furthermore, future important uses for records are often unforeseen. A selection intended to serve one research goal probably will be inappropriate in the context of another. Both procedures thus are extremely limited. They should be applied only when no other alternative is available. In many cases, upon closer examination a recommended sampling or selection procedure could be replaced by deferred destruction of the series as a whole.

Accessioning

Accessioning is the process of transferring records to the physical custody and legal control of an archival institution. It is the culmination of the appraisal process. Records accessioned by an archival institution become its property and responsibility. They must be cared for and made available to researchers in accordance with the institution's policies and regulations. The timing and circumstances of accessioning are therefore important appraisal concerns.

Records ordinarily should be accessioned to an archival institution only when they are no longer needed frequently for the conduct of current business. If records are transferred to an archival repository too early, the archives is forced to serve the functions of a file room in order to respond to the daily administrative demands of the creating organization. On the other hand, accessioning should not be delayed excessively. Records no longer needed for current business usually are of no further interest to office staff. They may be subject to careless handling, haphazard storage and damaging physical conditions. Even records needed occasionally for on-going business may be mishandled. Files may be removed and never returned and boxes may be opened, reviewed carelessly, and abandoned. Ordinarily, therefore, records appraised for archival retention should be transferred to archival care as soon as they are retired from active use.

Research demands and access limitations should also be considered in the timing of accessioning. Records that will not be available for research use for a significant period need not be transferred to a repository immediately, particularly if their physical protection is assured in the interim. In contrast, records that will receive immediate and intense research interest might be transferred to the archival repository as soon as possible to serve this research need, even if some administrative demand for the records continues. Archival administrators particularly must note that records requiring extensive processing must be transferred to archival custody sufficiently in advance of anticipated research need to permit this processing to take place.

The most appropriate physical form for records must also occasionally be considered during accessioning. Some records must be retained in their original physical form because of some quality or characteristic that gives them intrinsic value. Files directly associated with famous events or people, documents that may be appropriate for exhibit, or questioned documents that must be kept in the original to provide physical evidence for future investigators, are examples of records with intrinsic value. Documents that cannot be adequately reproduced by usable copy must also be accessioned and maintained in their original form. Other documents, however, may be accessioned to an archival repository in any form that adequately retains their full informational character. Although existing forms of reproduction all have significant disadvantages that discourage extensive use, new forms of information storage may offer archival repositories practical and economical alternatives.

Written documentation of the transfer of records is also an important part of the accessioning process. At this point, an archival institution should ensure that a dossier on each appraisal is complete, including information on the offer of records, the appraiser's analysis and recommendations, administrative review of the appraiser's conclusions, and conditions concerning transfer of the records. Legal documentation of archival ownership—whether forms documenting transfer of responsibility within an institution or a deed of gift transferring ownership from outside—is critical. A receipt recording physical transfer of the records should also be included in the dossier. Comprehensive documentation of the appraisal and accessioning provides essential legal documentation of archival ownership as well as an important information base for processing the records and providing data about them to future users.

Reappraisal

The appraisal and acceptance of records for long-term retention in an archival repository should not be viewed as a promise that they will be permanently retained. Instead it should be seen as an important institutional commitment based on available information and opinion at a particular time. Appraisal depends on a complex interplay of factors and on judgment that weighs values inherent in a group of records against an institution's resources and goals. It is also based on human judgment, which is never uniform or infallible. Archival institutions therefore should anticipate that judgments will be made that later, in the light of future considerations or new information, may appear incorrect. Reappraisal offers a systematic means of reviewing an archives' holdings on a regular basis to identify records that may have been appraised erroneously or brought into the archives without an appropriate appraisal.

Reappraisal is most effective if performed systematically at established intervals. It may begin with a simple survey of archival holdings and a preliminary assessment of whether a question exists concerning the value of any series of accessioned records. Accessioned records identified for reappraisal should be evaluated essentially as if they were being considered for accessioning for the first time. They must be described and analyzed in terms of their values, the costs of maintaining them, and institutional acquisition policies.

All records need not be reappraised at the same intervals. Some should be permitted to remain in an archival repository for an extended period of time before reappraisal, particularly if they are restricted or if use is expected to increase in the future. Others, particularly those that can be immediately opened for research use and that concern issues of contemporary research interest, might be considered for reappraisal more quickly. Reappraisal permits the archival repository an opportunity to reconsider its holdings and to ensure that its limited resources are devoted to the care of those records found to be most valuable in the light of the best possible information at all times.

Conclusion

Records preserved and maintained in archival institutions will provide the basis for future study and evaluation of contemporary life and activities. The selection of this documentation is the most critical archival function. In many ways, the success or failure of an archival program depends on its effectiveness in determining which records should be accepted for long-term retention. The greatest challenges for the appraiser, however, lie not in identifying the most valuable records whose importance is obvious nor in marking for destruction those records that are unarguably limited in their value. Rather, the difficult decisions are those in which values, costs, and institutional goals must all be balanced to reach a decision that may result in maintaining records despite their limitations or destroying them despite some values that they may have.

Appraisal must always be conducted with care, intelligence and thoughtful judgment, yet it will never result in uniform conclusions. Furthermore, no objective criteria exist to measure an appraisal's correctness. In fact, only investigators of the future can determine whether an institution's appraisals have been wise or unwise and its program a success or failure. Appraisal can thus be seen as the archivist's most important, challenging, rewarding and unmeasurable task.

5

Archival Arrangement and Description

Sharon Gibbs Thibodeau

If the chief purpose of establishing an archives is to extend the useful life of valuable records, then a crucial component of a successful archival program must be the implementation of professional arrangement and description practices. Records that are merely accumulated, and never arranged or described, are as unavailable to future users as records that have been destroyed. Because the importance of good arrangement and description has long been recognized by archivists, there has been much discussion of its distinguishing characteristics. These many discussions, including this chapter, can themselves be described as variations on certain fundamental themes.

The fundamental themes of archival arrangement and description, first articulated in Europe over a century ago, and still important today, can be couched in modern terms as follows:

1. Maintain the identity of a body of records and preserve as much information as possible about its origins and custodial history. (This is the fundamental principle of *respect des fonds* or provenance. It acknowledges the importance of maintaining the link between records and their creator.)
2. Whenever possible, take advantage of the intellectual control established by the creator or the previous custodian of a body of records. (This is the fundamental principle of *respect pour l'ordre primitif*, first established by French archivists and later refined by their Dutch colleagues. It argues for the maintenance of the original order of a body of archival material.)
3. Let the arrangement and description of a body of records reflect a knowledge of its custodial history as well as an understanding of any previously established methods of intellectual control.

Provenance

The archival principle of *respect des fonds* or provenance requires that archivists judiciously preserve both the integrity of a body of records received from a given source and the identity of the source. In implementing the principle of provenance, archivists link each distinct body of archival records to a creating organization and avoid at all costs intermingling records from various organizations. The importance of implementation of this principle derives from the fact that documents achieve their status as *records* through linkage with the entity which created or maintained them as records. When the link with its creator or official recipient is broken or obscured, a document's role as a record is destroyed and its usefulness as a source of factual information is greatly lessened. From a practical perspective, maintenance of the link between records and records creator is essential to an understanding of the activities of the creator. Conversely, much can be learned about records from a knowledge of the context in which they were created.

In preserving the integrity of a body of archival materials, archivists engage in the process of recognition of archival *series*. The crucial nature of this recognition process has prompted various attempts at its definition. All these attempts emphasize the recognition of shared characteristics as essential to series identification. Archival series have a common creator or collector (e.g. the Widget Development Division of the Large Corporation or the Widget Testing Branch of the Widget Development Division), and they generally have a common format (all ledgers, all notebooks, all photographs). Typical series of file units originating in the nineteenth century include the "central files" of organizations, sometimes divided into separate series of "letters sent" and "letters received". Twentieth-century organizations also created central files, but in more recent years these have tended to be replaced by files maintained by individual offices.

When archivists take custody of more than one series from a given source, they are responsible not only for maintaining the identity of each individual series, but also for recognizing the important relationships which may exist between these series. For example, a series of letters received by a nineteenth-century organization is almost certainly related to a series of letters sent by the same organization, and both of these series may have been abstracted or indexed by yet another series of records. The archival principle of provenance prescribes that the group identity of these related series be preserved as well as the identity of each series comprising the group.

Straightforward as the principle of provenance may seem, it can sometimes prove difficult to apply. As traditionally implemented, the principle links each series, or group of functionally related series, to a single source. In an era of joint projects and shared functions, however, it may be necessary to relate a given series to multiple sources. For example, a series of automated records that results from a data-gathering activity that was commissioned by one agency but actually carried out by another is evidence of the activity of two distinct agencies. Lest researchers be deprived of valuable clues, it is this dual heritage that must be preserved.

Original order

Archival records (as distinguished from personal papers) most often originate in an institutional setting. To have been accessible during their active life to more than one member of the institution's staff, the records had to have been organized acording to an easily interpreted plan. The principle of the sanctity of original order merely advocates the preservation of this pattern even after the records become inactive and are placed in an archival environment. Applied in its strictest sense, the principle means that archivists need only understand and perhaps perfect arrangement patterns imposed by others. In his classic development of this fundamental theme, Oliver W. Holmes identified several distinct levels at which the ability of archivists to recognize arrangement patterns may be tested.

In general, archivists must first be able to recognize the arrangement of documents within a file unit. For older, nineteenth-century documents, the file unit may be a bound volume; in the twentieth century the most common forms of file unit are the file folder and the "acco-fastened" case file. Whether bound or acco-fastened, documents in a file unit are generally found to be chronologically arranged.

Secondly, archivists must be able to recognize the arrangement that identifies a body of file units as an archival series whose identity must be preserved. The ability to recognize the arrangement patterns of series is essential to their use both as evidence and as sources of factual information. The arrangement patterns or file plans of series of records originating in the nineteenth century are many and various. Those originating in the twentieth century tend to reflect a desire to organize the filed documents according to the subjects to which they relate.

At first glance, the archival principle of the sanctity of original order seems quite straightforward and relatively easy to implement under normal circumstances. Problems may arise, however, if through some discontinuity in its custodial history, the order imposed on a series at the time of its last active use is obscured. Archivists must, in that case, impose a workable arrangement pattern, keeping in mind the most likely requirements for user access.

Modern records in automated form pose a special challenge for archivists familiar with the principle of the sanctity original order. The ease of manipulation which is characteristic of automated records renders irrelevant any concept of original order. Because it provides the same crucial key to the informational content of automated records as a file plan provides for textual records, the documentation prepared in connection with an automated file or system deserves the *respect* normally reserved for the *l'ordre primitif* in textual records.

Description

The archival principles of provenance and original order are rooted in a desire to ensure that archival records will be accessible to researchers. Thus it is not surprising that the principal means of encouraging access, i.e. archival description, must reflect an understanding of these principles. Descriptive compositions involving variations on these classical archival themes may proceed along either traditional or modern lines depending on the orientation or experience of the composer. The goal is harmonious description; that is, description that is appropriate, efficient and effective.

Specific descriptive activities undertaken by archivists may be considered appropriate if these activities represent the best investment of available archival resources. Records should be accorded the descriptive attention they deserve. The goal of descriptive activity is to assist researchers in locating pertinent documents. To achieve this goal, archivists must analyze the records prior to description and attempt to anticipate their research potential. Uniquely interesting items, such as individual motion picture films, maps, photos, or letters exchanged by luminaries, may warrant individual descriptive attention; but for the most part, archival descriptive activity is appropriately focused on the record series. In general, archival description comprises clear, accurate and objective reporting of the common characteristics of documents which were maintained as a group by their creator.

Over time, the effective reporting by archivists of the common characteristics of records grouped into series has evolved into a relatively widely-adopted format. The format incorporates—at a minimum—five categories of information: a title phrase; a reference to dates associated with the series; an indication of the quantity of records in the series; a description of the physical arrangement of records in the series; and a summary of the informational content of the series. The conventions adopted for reporting in each descriptive category may vary slightly from institution to institution, but the categories are universally utilized and, as such, warrant further discussion.

Categories of information

Because it is often the only category of information associated with a series of records, the title must be bestowed with particular care. It should be both specific and distinctive. For the most part, specificity is achieved by reference to the type of records constituting the series—correspondence, reports, cases files, photographs. Distinction is accomplished by qualifying the reference to record type with an indication of the subject-matter to which the records relate, their creator, their function, or their frequency. Examples that employ these techniques include:

Correspondence Relating to Widget Design
(type + subject)

Annual Reports of the Widget Development Division
(frequency + type + creator)

Widget Price Determination Case Files
(function + type)

Of the dates that could be reported in describing a series of records, the most important from an archival perspective are those of creation or accumulation of the records in the series. These dates place the records in the context of the history of an organization, and thus establish the records' status as archives. The preferences of the archival repository may dictate whether the dates reported always refer only to the accumulation period of the bulk of the records in the series (i.e. bulk dates) or whether they stretch beyond the bulk of the records when necessary to include chronological outliers (i.e. inclusive dates). Either approach is acceptable, as long as it is implemented consistently and explained carefully to researchers.

In determining the dates of accumulation of a series, archivists generally must rely on clues provided by the records. Assuming records are filed soon after they have been created or received, it follows that the dates of existence of the series may be inferred from the dates recorded on the documents in the series.

Archivists report the quantity of records in a series in order to enable researchers to estimate the density of the information contained therein. (A series 200 feet long covering a period of ten years may be assumed to contain much fuller evidence than a series only two feet long covering the same period.) Once again, reporting conventions may vary depending on repository preference; but, in general, the quantity of textual records is reported in linear (rather than cubic) units. Measurement preferences for non-textual media are media-specific; however, all involve counts of items, whether motion pictures, photographic images, or machine-readable data files.

If carefully phrased, a description of the arrangement pattern characteristic of a series of records can so sufficiently supplement information contained in the title, dates, and quantity as to eliminate the need for further clues to the research potential of the series. Carefully-phrased arrangement statements are both precise and complete. Though it may be the case that the complexity of some arrangement schemes—particularly those prevalent in nineteenth-century American bureaucracies—defy precise description, most are relatively straight-forward chronological, alphabetical or numerical patterns. It is helpful to explain that a chronological arrangement organizes records by the date of their receipt or by the date of their issuance. The reporting of alphabetical or numerical patterns must always be modified to indicate what was alphabetized or numbered. Typical statements are:

Arranged chronologically by date of receipt.

Arranged alphabetically by name of correspondent.

Arranged according to a numerical classification scheme designed to ensure that records relating to the same subject are filed together.

Arranged by project number.

For more complex patterns, the various levels of arrangement should be specified:

Arranged in annual segments and thereunder alphabetically by name of correspondent.

Significant gaps in the pattern should be reported, as in:

Arranged alphabetically by name of state and thereunder alphabetically by name of city. There are no records for California and Colorado.

These examples by no means exhaust the possibilites for arrangement patterns. They omit, for example, an interesting pattern described by Ernst Posner in his *Archives of the ancient world*. Posner notes the existence of a collection of ancient papyri excavated from the bellies of mummified royal crocodiles found at Egyptian Tebtunis. Current custodians have preserved the "crocodilian" arrangement of these papyri, because they believe that this arrangement provides important clues to the papyri's administrative origins.

The fifth category of descriptive information—the summary of the informational content of the series—has traditionally taken the form of a narrative paragraph that conveys pertinent details. Generally these details focus on the typical series component, but they may occasionally alert the researcher to an unexpected item. The kind of detail eligible for inclusion in the content summary of a series description includes, for example, amplification or clarification of the record type mentioned in the series title ("the letters contain sketches"). Additional detail appropriate for inclusion would be specification of persons, places, events, or topics substantively documented in the records ("the letters contains sketches of proposed designs for widgets, whatnots, and thingumbobs" or "the reports include eyewitness accounts of the explosion at the Peculiar Widget Factory on September 15, 1946"). Lest this latter category of descriptive data mislead the researcher, it is best to impose some order and some limits. Often subjects are listed in order of decreasing frequency of mention in the series. When the list of pertinent references threatens to become unwieldy, it may be easier to suggest what is missing ("the reports describe diplomatic relations with all Latin American nations, except Guatemala").

In addition to record types and topics, the content summary may elaborate on the activity that led to the creation of the records in the series ("the notebooks record the results of tests of the ability of widgets to withstand exposure to high temperatures"). By relating these notebooks to a testing function, the archivist conjures a very useful image of their informational content—i.e.

columns of recorded measurements. A similarly informative image is called to mind by the functionally oriented phrase "investigative reports".

While the content summary should concentrate on the common denominators of a series, it can also bring uncommon or unexpected informational content to light ("most correspondents are official weather observers, but there are a few letters from amateurs, including a report from Edgar Allan Poe concerning a particularly violent coastal storm"). It is also useful to describe in the content summary any changes in the nature of the records which may have occurred over time ("beginning in 1950, the reports include a section devoted to discussion of the quality of performance of the laboratory staff in addition to the previously included sections on the condition of instruments and the progress of current research").

Finally, it is important to keep in mind in summarizing the informational content of series, that researchers particularly welcome mention of the availability of any detailed finding aids (i.e. indexes, folder lists, or file plans). Also helpful are indications of the existence of related series with references to their location.

Automating the descriptive process

As more archivists begin to recognize the possibilities for automating the process of retrieving information about archival series, the sometimes lengthy narrative descriptions which have traditionally supplemented series titles and arrangement statements are dissolving into data elements or data fields. With such names as "subject reference", "geographic reference", "finding aids", and "notable items", these data fields are merely convenient new containers for familiar distilled descriptive information. A comparison of traditional and automated approaches to the same series description reveals their close relationship.

1. THE TRADITIONAL APPROACH
   Subject File of the Widget Section
   1910-1961   8 feet
   Arranged alphabetically by subject and thereunder chronologically. A copy of the file plan is available.
   This file contains letters, memoranda, reports and published materials. Filed together are records relating to the following subjects: general widget research; standardization of widgets; manufacture of widgets; and uses of widgets, particularly as doorstops. Of particular note are the eyewitness accounts and sketches of an explosion at the Peculiar Widget Factory on September 15, 1946, filed under the subject "Disasters".

2. AN AUTOMATED APPROACH
   Title: Subject File of the Widget Section.
   Start Bulk Date: 1910   *End Bulk Date:* 1961
   Quantity: 8 feet.
   Arrangement: alphabetical by subject and thereunder chronological

Specific types of materials: letters, memoranda, reports, publications
Subject references: widgets, research, standards, doorstops, industrial accidents
Corporate reference: Peculiar Widget Factory
Notable items: (Disasters File) eyewitness accounts with sketches of explosion at Peculiar Widget Factory on September 15, 1946
Finding aids: a copy of the file plan is available.

The automated approach fragments the more traditional format for the purpose of facilitating the Boolean searches so readily conducted with the assistance of computers: "find all series where materials equals reports, and subject equals widgets, and date equals 1946". The success of computer-assisted retrieval such as this clearly demands both careful definition of data elements and general agreements as to their use. For some data elements, like subject reference, agreement on use may extend to the development of a controlled vocabulary of authorized terms. Unless a controlled vocabulary has been imposed, a search for all series relating to floods will overlook those series which have been described as relating to inundations.

Over the last several years, working groups established in Australia, in Canada, in the United Kingdom and in the United States have each undertaken the task of analyzing the archival descriptive process with a view to developing standards essential to the effective automated exchange of descriptive information. Full realization of the potential for this approach to providing access to archival records depends on the accumulation of a critical mass of data of consistent quality. For further discussion of the automation process, see Chapter Ten.

Archival family trees

If archival series were as intellectually independent as books in a library, it is quite likely that archival description would more closely resemble library cataloging. As it is, few series of records stand alone in archival repositories. Most form families of series, related because they have a common provenance or because they result from related activities or were maintained according to related record-keeping practices. The descriptive programs of archival repositories have tended to emphasize these family relationships, with a view toward achieving thereby desired economies of language and more efficient characterization of the informational content of very large quantities of records. Since its introduction by the National Archives of the United States in 1941, the published "inventory" has served as a widely-adopted model for conveying descriptive information about families of archival series.

An archival inventory describes an extended archival family tree (called a "record group" in the National Archives). In the context of the federal government, this tree generally represents a department, a bureau, or an agency. The branches of the tree described in an inventory may be either bureaucratic or functional subdivisions of the family mission (called "subgroups"), and the leaf-bearing twigs attached to the branches are the series. Descriptive information presented in the inventory proceeds from the general to the specific. It begins with a general introduction to the record group and continues with "chapters" devoted to each subgroup with its component series. By devoting each section of an inventory to a specific level of information, and clearly indicating the relationship between these levels of information, tedious repetition is avoided. Each level of description can be briefer for the reason that it need only supplement previously supplied information. When all levels of information combine in a well-planned inventory, the researcher's access to a body of records is significantly expanded.

For all of its value in introducing efficiency into the descriptive process, the analogy of the archival family tree, on which the inventory is based, is somewhat deficient. The analogy conjures up an image of a stable relationship between component parts. In fact, at least in a modern bureaucracy, instability may be the norm. Any given "branch" of a bureaucracy may enjoy independent growth for a while, then be absorbed by another stronger branch, then grow independently again, and then, perhaps, be cut off from the original tree and grafted on to another. If the record-keeping activities of the branch remain the same, then each series maintains its identity despite its bureaucratic odyssey. Lest researchers be misled, this odyssey must be explained. The efficiency which should be a characteristic of the inventory disappears as more and more descriptions have to be qualified with explanations.

There is hope, however, for archivists weary of explaining the apparent vagaries of bureaucratic entities. Through the use of computers equipped with relational data base management systems, it is possible to simulate the organic nature of a bureaucracy by describing the various configurations of a branch and at the same time preserving the link between that branch and any series created by it. As more archivists realize the potential of automation for mitigating the descriptive deficiencies of the printed inventory, it is increasingly likely that the "inventory" of the future will be a machine-readable data base.

Guides and lists

At the risk of belaboring the arboreal analogy, it is possible to liken large archival repositories to groves of family trees. The descriptions in inventories published by the repositories focus on the individual trees, leaving researchers to prepare their own subject "field guides" to the grove. Conducting subject searches in an archives—where for the sake of efficiency, the emphasis has been placed on the "where from" rather than the "what about" of records—is no easy task. It is not surprising, then, that researchers encourage archival repositories to include comprehensive subject guides as part of their descriptive programs.

The production of a subject guide can absorb considerable repository resources. It is thus a project to be undertaken only if it is likely to greatly facilitate reference activity or effectively "showcase" the repository's strength in an area important to a crucial constituency. In developing guide entries, archivists survey any existing inventories and *ad hoc* series descriptions to identify likely sources of pertinent information. Then they examine the potentially pertinent series so identified in order to provide specific citations to relevant records. Confirmed citations are then organized in a manner that promotes both efficient presentation and effective use of the information. To this end, most guide entries at the National Archives are organized so as to preserve record group and subgroup identities. As with other aspects of archival description, the production of subject guides will undoubtedly be faciliated by the implementation of automated descriptive techniques, particularly if this involves the adoption of controlled vocabularies.

Not all guides prepared by archival repositories are designed to appeal to researchers with specific and well-defined interests. In fact, the type of guide most frequently prepared by repositories is one which provides an overview of their entire holdings. Such general guides are most useful when they contain enough information to encourage those researchers who should be using the facility and to discourage those researchers who shouldn't. This delicate balance can be achieved by carefully outlining the repository's collecting policy in an introduction and by including in the body of the guide, to the extent that it is reasonable to do so, the title and dates of each series in the respository's custody.

The "big picture" presented by inventories and guides can be sharpened by the inclusion of indexes. Indexes are essential when the picture to which they relate is large and complex. Even indexed guides and inventories, however, fail to assist researchers who have progressed beyond the initial stages of a project or who have very specific information requirements. Description in an inventory or guide only suggests the potential relevance of a series. For its relevance to a particular query to be confirmed, the series itself must be examined.

Series examination is always facilitated by the availability of detailed descriptive information about the components (file units or documents) of the series. This can take the form of a file plan, a folder list, a list of documents, or a name or subject index to the filed documents. Helpful as this level of descriptive detail can be, it can be very costly to produce. It must be available to researchers, however, if it is essential to utilization of the information in a series. Ideally, any descriptive detail that is truly essential has already been prepared by the creator of the series and need only be accessioned with it. Essential detail that is not available from the creator must be provided by the archivist. The provision of detailed information need not be limited to instances where it is essential. It can be justified whenever it facilitates access to a heavily-used series.

Goals and priorities

In recent years, the archival community has placed particular emphasis on the identification of goals and the establishment of priorities. This exercise of "taking stock" can be conducted broadly, as reflected in the work of the Goals and Priorities Task Force of the Society of American Archivists, or it can focus on a circumscribed area of archival activity such as arrangement and description. If, in summarizing this chapter, the narrower focus is attempted, it can produce the following results:

The goals of successful archival arrangement and description are:

1. Arrangement that preserves both the integrity and the identity of a body of records acquired from a given source, and
2. Description that facilitates access to bodies of records whose integrity and identity have been preserved.

Priorities for action to be taken to meet these goals within an archival repository should include:

1. Establishment and maintenance of a minimum level of intellectual control over the archival holdings of the repository. (Because it both reflects an appreciation of archival principles and represents the best investment of archival resources, the series level seems an appropriate minimum.)
2. Development of a comprehensive descriptive program that accommodates enhancement of the minimum level of intellectual control. (The program may include the production of inventories of groups of records, as well as general or subject-specific guides to the holdings. It should involve description of individual items whenever their unique character or importance warrants it. The provision of access to motion picture film and machine-readable data sets regularly requires enhancement of detail available at the series level.)
3. Exploration of the potential for applying automated techniques to descriptive activity, with a view to facilitating both the preparation and the retrieval of descriptive information.
4. Cooperation with other repositories in the exchange of descriptive information.

When the identification of goals and the establishment of priorities lead to the implementation of practices that increase the availability of archival material, the whole archival profession benefits. Archival records which are made accessible through professional arrangement and description are recognized as valuable resources by the user public. Recognition of the value of information resources, in turn, leads to recognition of the value of the institutions, the programs and the people that preserve these resources. A strong, professional arrangement and description program is an investment in the archival future in more ways than one.

6

Personal Papers

Megan Floyd Desnoyers

Archival institutions may hold two different yet similar types of material: archives, on the one hand, and personal papers, also called manuscripts, on the other. Archives are the non-current records of an organization or institution which are preserved because of their continuing value. Personal papers are natural accumulations of documents created or accumulated by individuals or families, belonging to them and subject to their disposition. Archival repositories hold mainly archival records with, perhaps, complementary collections of personal papers. The holdings of manuscript repositories, by contrast, are largely comprised of historical manuscripts. These are documents of historical value which were written by hand, typewriter or the equivalent in single or multiple form. There are three categories of manuscripts:

1. bodies or groups of personal papers with organic unity—the "archives" of a person, family, or organization;
2. artificial collections of manuscripts acquired by private collectors from various sources, usually gathered according to a plan but without regard for their origin; and
3. individual manuscripts acquired by an institution because of their special importance to research.

Modern manuscript collections are usually personal or family papers, literary papers, organizational records or collections organized around a past event. Although archives and personal papers have many common characteristics, there are subtle differences between the two that necessitate variations in their administration.

    The first difference between archives and personal papers is the language their custodians use to describe them. Materials produced by or relating to individuals are generally called papers, and they are grouped in collections and described in registers and catalogs. Materials produced by or relating to organizations are called records, and they are grouped in record groups and described in inventories. The difference in terminology, however, is often greater than the actual differences between the two media. Both personal papers and archives are materials which were created or accumulated by individuals or groups while pursuing their interests and responsibilities. Both consist of a number of loose items which have to be grouped together and described in order for them to be used by, first, their creators and, later, custodians and researchers.

Institutions collect and save archival records and personal papers for different reasons. Archives are kept primarily to meet the needs of the creating organization. Personal papers are collected to foster the study of the subjects with which the repository is mainly concerned. However, the line between institutional archives and personal papers is frequently not clear-cut, and the place where they are housed is often merely an accident of custody. Often historical manuscripts are really archival records which happen to reside in a manuscript repository. In many offices, personal papers and official records are not maintained separately, as they should be, but are interfiled. When office holders leave their positions, they take complete files with them. Such stray official papers often include some of the more historically important and interesting items. In addition, not all organizations and institutions maintain archival facilities, so private repositories fill the gap by collecting and preserving orphaned files. Often, that is the only chance the materials have to survive. Regardless of what materials are called and where they are housed, scholars and students need both archives and manuscripts to provide as complete a documentary record as possible.

Archival and manuscript repositories also differ in size of holdings, staffing and type of work done. Archives tend to have huge quantities of material which receive only minimal levels of processing, so they have smaller staffs in proportion to their holdings. Manuscript repositories collect groups of items and single disparate items and devote greater attention to arrangement, preservation, screening, and description to make them as accessible as the record groups of archival material found in archives. Therefore, manuscript repositories tend to have more staff in relation to the size of their holdings.

Acquisitions

Archival record groups generally come to archival repositories as part of well-defined administrative procedures. Records creators and archivists agree that certain records are no longer needed in offices for current use and should be transferred to the archives, and that is done. Manuscript repositories must define the focus of their institutions; solicit personal papers collections; and, since donors control the disposition of personal papers, negotiate the donation of the papers and the terms of access to them. Unlike archival repositories, manuscript repositories gather their holdings from a multiplicity of outside sources. Rarely do their holdings come from a single source.

Collecting policy

Manuscript repositories exist to serve scholars and students. Their primary responsibility is to create a focused body of research material that informs researchers on a specific subject. They do this by defining a collecting policy after taking into consideration the available institutional resources, the existence of other collections of research materials on the same subject elsewhere in their geographical area, and the public they serve now and want to attract in the future. When assessing institutional resources, archivists look at available supporting materials, such as secondary sources; economic consequences; staff needs; and the physical facilities required.

The collection focus should be well thought-out and provide carefully defined objectives for a rational collecting program. The collection development policy is usually limited by geography, chronology or some other common denominator. The aim or theme should give meaning to the institution, avoid duplication of effort, allow for expansion and contribute positively to scholarly research. It should be one that will be of continuing interest and relevance to scholars as a research and teaching tool. Institutions want to attract a clientele broad enough to be supportive and interested now and in the future. Competing with neighboring institutions for the same kinds of material will merely reduce the number of appropriate collections each institution may acquire and divide the interested public who would use the materials and support the institution. There are more collections of personal papers in private hands than all the repositories in the world can house. It is not necessary to compete with neighbors.

Solicitation

To implement collecting programs, institutions should prepare very clear, one-page statements of purpose. Then they should publicize their collecting efforts in every possible way, such as through local-interest interviews in newspapers and magazines, speaking to groups, and sending solicitation letters.

A well-organized solicitation of potential donors enables repositories to acquire collections whose contents support their collecting focus. Once institutions have determined what the focus of their collections will be, they identify the types of papers needed to document that focus and try to discover who has such papers. They conduct surveys of papers within their geographical location or in a particular subject-area and prepare lists of potential owners of suitable materials. In doing so, institutions should consider both famous and not so famous owners and originators of papers, to avoid the mistake of collecting only those papers which document the role of the élite in the events with which they are concerned.

Once located, each collection is appraised on an individual basis and secured as a result of selective appeals. Collections are evaluated for evidential or informational value and their relevance to the institution's collecting focus and existing holdings. With people becoming successful at relatively early ages and living longer lives, it is not unusual for individuals to have several different careers or avocations. Their papers will be equally diverse. One institution may be interested in only one aspect of the person's career and may not want to house papers dealing with other aspects. While this would seem to be logical in terms of closely following the institution's collection focus, it may give rise to ethical problems for the archivists involved. First, this may be the only chance these papers have of being transferred to a repository. Secondly, personal papers, by their nature, document the whole career of the person. Generally, someone's papers should be kept intact in one institution regardless of differences in subject. The institution should then make a point of informing researchers of the existence of material on a subject other than its main collection focus. If an institution feels that it cannot take all, or even part, of a personal papers collection, but that the papers are worth preserving, its archivists should suggest to the donors the names of other institutions which might be interested in the papers, and inform these institutions that the papers exist and that the donors have been referred to them. Sometimes, donors, because of their divided loyalties, will insist that a collection be split between two institutions. If they cannot be dissuaded and neither institution is willing to give up the papers, the collection may be reproduced (by photocopying or microfilming) or divided along natural lines (by function or time) for deposit in both institutions.

The next stage in solicitation is field work. Institutional field representatives identify, locate, negotiate for, and secure personal papers collections for their institutions. In small institutions, one staff member may have responsibility for field work and everything else. Field representatives follow all leads to gather data about prospective donors and the types of documents and subjects in their collections.

Field representatives need to keep very careful records. They should maintain files of leads on log sheets or cards with some form of reminder of the next steps required in the solicitation process. They should also examine the solicitation program periodically to determine if the institution's approach is adequate and successful.

Negotiation for personal or family papers can be quite prolonged and often must be very personalized. The first contact may be by letter or telephone call. Records should be kept of each contact. After the preliminary contact, field representatives should follow up as often as necessary, whilst at the same time being very tactful toward and sensitive of donor's feelings. Timing may be especially important. Sometimes field representatives must respond immediately when a home or office is being moved or closed, or a person has died.

Donors may want to sell their papers to institutions, or benefit from tax deductions allowed with respect to gifts of such materials, so archivists and field representatives should be familiar with the market for papers and with tax laws. In either case, staff members should *not* provide financial appraisals for collections which are being deposited in the institutions where they work. This would create a conflict of interest. Instead, institutions should prepare lists of reputable, independent appraisers and make them available to donors, who usually pay for appraisals since they are getting the tax deductions. If an institution is thinking of purchasing a collection, it will want to have an appraisal done on its own behalf.

When visiting donors, archivists evaluate their collections in terms of their content and relevance to the collecting focus and other holdings of the archival institution which is considering their acquisition. If the institution decides to accept a collection, the archivists should arrange for the papers to be transferred to the repository with minimum disturbance to their original order, no physical damage, and as little cost as possible. Donors may occasionally underwrite the cost of transfer and, very rarely, the cost of processing. Local transfer may be easily carried out by staff members by car, van or truck. Whenever possible, it is helpful for staff members to be present when papers are boxed for transfer so they may discuss the origin, arrangement and use of the papers with donors and make any minor adjustments in arrangement and notes about preservation and screening. When the papers have arrived safely, the archivists should write or call the donors to advise them of this fact and to thank them for donating the papers. It would also be thoughtful to have a notable person affiliated with the institution write and thank donors.

Initial control

The institution should have a well-equipped receiving area or room where papers may be brought and where initial control can be achieved. This consists of identifying critical preservation needs, boxing papers in uniform storage containers labeled with accession number and collection title, and achieving immediate intellectual control. This is achieved when four tasks are accomplished: accessioning; preparing an initial inventory and processing proposal; making a case file; and negotiating a deed of gift. Any major preservation problems, such as insect infestation, should be identified and rectified before the papers are moved to the same storage area as the existing holdings.

Accessioning is a record-keeping procedure under which materials are recorded as having been taken into physical custody by the institution. An accessions log is maintained in either card or book format. A number is assigned to the collection and the title, dates of receipt and acknowledgment, donor's name and address, approximate size, general subject-matter, comments on restrictions, notes on transfers, and shelf location are recorded. If the collection was purchased, the name of the seller and purchase price are also included.

An initial inventory is a list of all the identifiable units (folders, volumes, etc.) which were found in each box when the papers were received. After an inventory has been prepared, archivists should evaluate the qualities of the papers in order to establish appropriate processing requirements for each series or collection, and record these in the processing proposal.

Processing consists of the four activities which facilitate the use of personal papers: arrangement, preservation, screening, and description. The range of processing that is possible for each body of material is very broad, ranging from doing nothing to the other extreme of treating each item on an individual basis. Some collections require very little processing, some, a great deal, but most fall somewhere in the middle. The processing proposal states what needs to be done to each series and how long the work will take. When preparing the proposal, archivists should also consider restrictions on the use of the collection and suggest when it should be processed in relation to other unprocessed collections. For example, if a collection is to be closed for ten years, only immediate preservation work would be done upon arrival; all remaining processing would be done just before the restrictions were about to expire.

A collection file, case file or processing file is a folder titled with the name of the collection. It contains the initial inventory, all correspondence relating to the collection and its acquisition, copies of legal agreements, publicity photographs of donors, and articles about the papers or their donors.

Personal papers are owned by the donor. The donor may choose to give or sell them to an institution. In legal terms, title to the property passes from the giver or seller to the recipient, from the donor to the repository. Such a gift requires a clear offer, acceptance of the offer, and delivery of the material. Before accepting the gift, archivists should ask tactful questions to ensure that the donor is the sole owner of the papers and is legally competent to dispose of them.

All archival materials, including personal papers, have both a physical and an intellectual component. The transfer document should record both in an unambiguous fashion. The transfer document may be an exchange of letters, a written will, a deed of gift, or a bill of sale. Occasionally, donors may say they will give something to an institution and then deliver it. If the intent is very clear, the oral statement and physical delivery may be adequate if there are no further complicating factors which need clarification.

A deed of gift is a written instrument which effects some legal disposition and is sealed and delivered by the disposing party. It is prepared after consultation between donor and recipient, and is signed by both to indicate both the offer and its acceptance. A typical deed of gift includes the names of all donors and recipients, the date of transfer of title, a description of the material, clear definition of who holds the copyright, any restrictions on use and who can impose and lift those restrictions, a statement of their scope and coverage, a determination of who has disposal authority, and a provision for subsequent gifts. A well-designed deed of gift will cover as many of these factors as are appropriate to the nature of the papers and the circumstances of the donation. The deed is a contract between the two parties in which the donor promises to give the materials and the repository promises to respect any conditions stipulated by the donor.

When negotiating with donors, archivists are responsible for providing complete and accurate information about copyright, literary rights, appraisal value and privacy issues. Copyright and literary rights may be governed by local, state, and federal laws. Archivists should understand the relevant laws and their application. Personal privacy issues could be of great concern to donors, especially when dealing with recent family or personal papers. Donors may want to avoid future embarrassment from disclosure of the papers and may consider withholding some of the more sensitive items. In such cases, the institution's agents should suggest that the collection be donated intact, but that appropriate restrictions be imposed on its use. This will preserve the integrity of the collection while honoring the donor's concerns.

Providing unlimited access to information in contemporary personal papers creates a risk of damaging living people and exposing to public view communications and revelations which were made in complete confidence. Donor-imposed restrictions may solve this problem for donors, but can create other problems for researchers and archivists. The kinds of restrictions which donors may specify include the removal from a collection of certain types of information or kinds of material, the requirement that researchers obtain the permission of the donor to use the collection or to cite or quote from it, closing the material for a specified period of time, or closing it to certain types of users.

If donors require archivists to identify and remove certain types of information or kinds of materials, archivists have to screen the papers on an item-level basis to locate and remove such items. This is very labor-intensive and time-consuming and considerably raises the cost of processing the papers. A privacy restriction that is fairly commonly applied to personal papers is that the institution will identify and remove all financial and personal records of living people and any material which could personally injure living persons. When any item is identified and removed, it should be replaced by a withdrawal sheet which identifies withdrawn items as specifically as possible without revealing the information which donors want to be protected. Withdrawal sheets usually include information on the date of the item, the number of pages, author, recipient, subject and general reason for closing, such as "financial information".

Donors who want researchers to get their permission to use and cite or quote from the papers, must be prepared to be regularly bothered by researchers seeking such permission. Archivists need to be certain that donors will grant access on a rational, equitable basis, because they, the archivists, will have to invest time and effort in processing the papers to get them ready for research use and will also have to deal with researchers and their reactions to donors' responses to their requests for permission.

Should a donor decide to completely close a collection for a specified period of time, the archivist should seriously consider whether the length of closure is compatible with the repository's needs and eventual research use of the material. The institution will have to house the papers during the period they are closed but researchers will not be able to use them. If the period of closure is quite long, it might not be worth while for the institution to invest time and effort in storing the papers; research interest in them might have disappeared by the time they are opened.

If a donor tries to require that a collection be closed to certain types of researchers, the archivist will face serious problems in enforcing the restriction. In the first place, such a restriction is discriminatory and archivists should treat all researchers as equally as possible. Secondly, the restriction is almost impossible to enforce. If a donor should say, for example, that the papers are to be closed to journalists, how do archivists determine who is a journalist and who is not? How do they differentiate between the person who is writing an article for a newspaper (a "journalist") and the same person who, on leave of absence, is writing a book on some current political event (a "writer")?

Donors sometimes deposit personal papers in repositories under agreements which merely deposit the material and state that they intend to transfer title to the materials to the institution at a future date. Archivists should seriously consider the deposit status of a collection when scheduling processing. If a collection is only on deposit, it may not be wise to process it. If it must be processed, archivists should first attempt to negotiate a written understanding between the institution and the donor that once the papers are processed, they may be made available for research use. This is especially important with relatively young donors who may go on to other, different careers. If creators or donors deposit papers from earlier careers only under deposit agreements, they may, when they embark on new careers, decide to transfer all their papers to a repository associated with their new careers. If the papers are not legally donated to the first institution under a deed of gift, donors have the right to do this. If the institution has not yet processed the papers, it will not lose much if they are transferred, but if it has already invested time and materials in processing the papers, it will lose a great deal.

The other thing that can happen is that another institution may decide to name a facility after a famous donor and the donor may, very logically, wish to transfer his papers to the second institution. This is especially likely to occur when donors with long and successful careers retire.

Processing

Processing facilitates the use of personal papers and manuscript collections. It comprises the archival processes of arrangement, preservation and description, plus the activity of screening, which is unique to personal papers. Because of their quantity, nature, and use, archival records are maintained by their custodians as close to the original order as possible, with a minimum of arrangement and description. Personal papers, on the other hand, are generally processed more extensively by their custodians.

In the past, the major difference between archival records and personal papers was their quantity. Archival records were massive, while personal papers tended to be smaller in quantity and more likely to be comprised of disparate items. Little needed to be done to the large quantities of archival records because, since they were institutional, they were in better order and easily used by their clientele. Personal papers consisted of small numbers of personal diaries, letterpress books or holograph letters and often came with major preservation and arrangement problems. Twentieth-century technology has changed all that. With the development of mechanical means of production and duplication, manuscript curators are now faced with massive collections of personal papers which only occasionally include individual items as meaningful and valuable as those of earlier periods. Most of the items in twentieth-century personal papers collections are individually of relatively little value.

Traditionally, manuscript repositories processed all personal papers to a standard level of processing which the institution considered professionally responsible. That system worked well as long as there were adequate resources to deal with incoming collections.

Unfortunately, larger collections began arriving at the same time as staff resources either declined or had to be spread over more activities. Severe processing backlogs developed. Researchers were frustrated that collections were not available because they had not been processed and began pressuring archivists to get them processed and open for use. In the worst cases, donors became upset because institutions were not living up to the terms of deeds of gift by processing papers in a timely manner.

With no increase in resources, archivists had to look at the way they processed collections to see if it could be done more productively. They came to the conclusion that all series and all collections did not need to be processed to the same level. Like custodians of archival records, they tried to use whatever they could from the way the papers were when they were received. This approach is called adaptive processing. For each of the four processing activities, archivists have a range of choices from which to select for each collection or series. After considering the found state of the papers, the requirements and interests of donors and users, and the qualities within the papers themselves, archivists decide what level of arrangement, preservation, screening, and description is needed for each series and whether the work is to be done sequentially or concurrently. Archivists then know how long it will take to process the papers and what will be done to them. This is recorded in the processing proposal at the time of initial control.

Archivists responsible for processing papers will want to keep records of what collections an institution has that need processing and schedule such processing only after considering the relative merits and costs of dealing with each collection. Such records should, at least, be kept in one place, perhaps in chart form. If available, a computerized data base facilitates such record-keeping and is easy to update.

Arrangement

Arrangement is the scheme by which items, groupings and collections are ordered to reveal their contents and significance. The objects of arrangement are:

1. to restore and present to researchers, as far as possible, the original order of the papers as evidence of how they were used by their creators and why they were created; and
2. to provide a basically rational order in which individual documents or facts can be found with a modest amount of search and analysis.

Keepers of archives, as distinct from personal papers, are fortunate in terms of arrangement of their materials because the records were created in and maintained by an office in an organized way for its documentation and use. Personal papers may or may not reflect the activities of their creators or be arranged in a usable manner. Often, if they are, it is because of an unusually well-organized creator or efficient secretary. Because of the nature of their holdings, archivists strive to preserve the original order, while curators of personal papers are prepared to impose an order based on a combination of archival principles, manuscript techniques and researcher needs if a collection is disarranged.

The archival principles of *respect des fonds*, provenance, and sanctity of the original order are applicable to personal papers as well as archival records. But these principles of arrangement presume that the initial order was rational and bore a direct relationship to the work of the creating office, organization, or person and this is less likely to be true for personal papers. There are two problems in applying the principles to collections of personal papers:

1. not all original order is rational, nor are all people who create or collect papers orderly; and
2. original order is for the filer's convenience.

In considering the arrangement of personal papers, archivists should use these two facts with the three principles of arrangement as reference points, not as immutable rules.

There are five levels of arrangement. Each level may have an arrangement which is coordinated with, but different from, the others. The first is the *repository* level. Arrangement at this level is governed by convenience in retrieval and guided by a desire to avoid shifting the location of holdings any more than necessary. Most manuscript repositories find it easiest to shelve their holdings in accession order.

The second level, that of the *collection*, is the level on which *respect des fonds* applies. The collection level for personal papers is the same as the record group level for archival records. Collections and record groups are equivalent units of bodies of material related by organization, activity or creator.

The *series* level is the third level of arrangement, and the one that most completely expresses the character of the materials in the collection. A series is a grouping of like materials. Collections usually arrive with some series, but the series are often not titled. Some series are the result of organic activity, created by their creators for their own purposes, such as correspondence, speeches, clippings, subjects. Others are created by archivists to produce logical order, such as by merging smaller units into larger series. Personal papers tend to be more disordered and require more arrangement at the series level than do archival records. This is also the point at which archivists of personal papers leave archivists of records behind. Personal papers archivists continue with processing below the series level as far as is necessary. Archivists of records generally stop arrangement and description at the series level and are much less concerned with preservation and screening because of the nature of their holdings.

If a personal papers collection arrives in total disorder, archivists may have to create series from scratch with few clues as to the original order to aid them. It is very labor-intensive to sort materials into series. Further, it is possible that a file unit could be filed in more than one place.

Once series have been established, they are ordered either from the most specific series to the most general, or vice versa. When series are arranged by type of material, correspondence, diaries, or minutes are usually filed first because they describe most completely the work of their creators. If two series seem to warrant being placed first, the series containing the older material or that containing the most material is filed first. After the most important series, it is helpful to order other series parallel with the career of their creator, so that they end up largely in chronological order. Subseries may be used as another level if necessary.

The *file unit* is the fourth level of physical arrangement, and may, be represented by folders, minute books, ledgers, notebooks, and so on. File units are usually arranged within their series chronologically, alphabetically, or by type of material.

The fifth and final level of arrangement is the *document* level. Documents within file units are usually arranged chronologically, alphabetically, or by a combination of both. If items arrive in no order and not in file units, archivists generally arrange them chronologically or sort them by name of correspondent.

There is no one way to arrange a collection. Archivists try to achieve what they perceive as the arrangement that will best show respect for the origin and integrity of the papers while considering the needs of the users. Usually the simpler the arrangement, the greater its usefulness. A simple arrangement is easier for researchers to use and for archivists to implement. On all levels, materials may be divided up by:

1. type of material—generic groupings such as minutes;
2. chronologically by period in the creator's life or career;
3. alphabetically;
4. or a mixture of any of these.

The selection of the appropriate method will suggest itself on the basis of the apparent order as received, the most useful order for search and retrieval of information, or the simplest means of acquiring control over the papers. Archivists are responsible for deciding which arrangement is most appropriate at each level and making sure that arrangement makes sense in relation to the other levels and parts and to the whole.

Preservation

Like custodians of archival materials, manuscript curators are concerned with the preservation of their holdings. They house them in secure facilities with constant temperature and humidity controls. They evaluate all collections to determine the need to protect them from their containers, from self-harm or destruction (such as from deteriorating chemicals or metal in, on or near the documents), and from damage or destruction from theft or careless handling. As necessary, they re-folder materials in acid-neutral folders filed in acid-neutral archives boxes rather than the larger records center cartons generally used for archival records. As appropriate, they fumigate, clean, flatten, repair, encapsulate and restore individual items. To protect intrinsically valuable items from damage and theft, they replace them with photocopies and maintain the originals in secure locations. The greatest preservation problem in contemporary personal papers collections is the vast quantity of material on poor-quality paper which is yellowing and disintegrating quickly. Given the relatively low value of individual items in many contemporary collections, the most useful solution has been to photocopy these deteriorating items and replace them with copies. If the originals have intrinsic value, they are segregated and saved with other valuable items.

Screening

Screening is the process of examining the papers to determine the presence of restricted items or information and removing them from the file. Screening is done to meet the needs of donors as specified in deeds of gift. Screening is probably the least flexible and most sensitive and immediate of the four processing activities. If donors impose restrictions on the use of personal papers, the papers must be screened prior to opening. Screening also has the greatest impact on the labor-intensiveness of processing the collection, the length of time needed, and the resulting expense. Archivists review donor's deeds of gift to determine what restrictions have been imposed on the papers. Once the pertinent restrictions are identified, series titles are examined to determine which series might require screening. Within such series, archivists review folder titles for those whose contents have to be examined. Finally, they review each item in the identified file units. Items removed from the file are identified on, and replaced by withdrawal sheets following such a review.

Items which have been closed under donor restrictions need not remain closed forever. Often, with the passage of time, the reason for closing an item will no longer be valid. Institutions should develop procedures under which closed items are periodically reviewed for possible opening, or researchers may appeal closures and archivists will examine the closed items and decide whether or not they may be opened.

Description

Description is the process of establishing intellectual control over holdings through the preparation of finding aids. Intellectual control is necessary because archivists need to know what they have, what it contains, and where it is. Personal papers are collected and maintained to document the collecting focus of an institution. It is important to make information about the holdings known to researchers so that they may come and use them. Researchers need to know that the institution exists, what its collection policy is, what collections it has, what materials it has on specific topics, and what is in each collection.

The first level needing description is the repository level. Repository-wide description may include listing the institution in any national data base of manuscript repositories, publishing a guide to holdings, and creating accession lists, shelf lists, card catalogs, indexes or specialized brochures. A guide to holdings may be a very simple list or a detailed booklet, but it should list all the holdings of the institution, describe them briefly, and state the availability of each collection. All collections held by the institution should be listed, regardless of their availability. They may then be identified as "open", "permission required", "closed under donor restrictions", or "closed pending processing". When researchers write or call to ask about the institution's holdings, archivists may send them copies of the guide. Card catalogs of holdings are more likely to be found in manuscript repositories than in archival institutions. When a collection is processed, cards are prepared for the title of the collection and for notable subjects and names which appear in the collection. This record may be computerized if resources are available.

The next level needing description is the collection level. Collection-level description for personal papers may include a listing of the collection in any national union catalog of manuscript materials, a container list (as discussed under initial control, above) or a register. A manuscript register is somewhat like an archival inventory. If it is to be published, the register will include a preface which states the institution's policy on the production of finding aids. The introduction gives an overview of the contents, origins, and research strengths of the collection, briefly summarizes its nature and content and gives its title, size, dates, provenance, restrictions, and the status of copyright. It should provide any information which would be of immediate interest to the researcher. A biographical sketch should give the significant mileposts in the life of the creator, while a scope and content note should describe the extent and depth of the collection, and its strengths and weaknesses, putting the papers in the perspective of the individual's career. Such a note gives processors the opportunity to pass on to researchers their unique knowledge of the papers. It should also relate the collection to the institution's holdings and tell researchers of other personal papers of the creator which are held in other facilities.

The series description gives the title, dates, size, type of material, arrangement and subject of each series. The folder title list is just that. Very rarely, archivists will decide that each item in the collection is historically important enough to warrant an item listing or index. But the value of such an index or list should always be weighed against the cost of preparing it. The American tradition has been to use the register as the primary form of description for personal papers. The British tradition has been to item index all correspondence. This has produced a large cataloging backlog but has been a delight for researchers.

In deciding what form of description is appropriate for each individual collection of personal papers, archivists should consider the nature of the collection, the needs of researchers, and the resources of the institution. For example, if a collection contains literary manuscripts by an extremely important author, the institution might decide to describe the collection down to the item level. But most contemporary personal papers collections are adequately described by a register that goes to the folder level.

Conclusion

While personal papers have much in common with archival records, there are enough differences between the two to warrant different approaches to their administration. Personal papers archivists have borrowed useful techniques from archivists of records and from librarians and have created solutions of their own to meet the needs of their institutions and holdings. First, they undertake aggressive and well-organized acquisitions programs to ensure that the institution has holdings to support research on its collecting focus. Then, they evaluate the collections they receive to determine what processing is needed to facilitate research use of the papers. Finally, they complete the necessary arrangement, preservation, screening and description. Personal papers archivists will find support and ideas in archival literature and from their colleagues in local, regional, national and international associations. Many professional associations have subgroups specifically designed for them, such as the Personal Papers Section of the International Council on Archives.

7

Managing Cartographic and Architectural Archives

John A. Dwyer

Maps, plans, and drawings have been used for centuries to communicate information and knowledge about space on the land, the sea, the heavens and about structures. From pre-historic cave-wall paintings to computer printouts, these records provide information while perfecting the depiction of space through the use of symbols, lines, shading, and coloring. The forms taken by these cartographic and architectural records, or artefacts, range over time from clay tablets and creations utilizing bones, animal skins, ivory, sticks, and shells to the more familiar written and printed words and symbols. The camera and the computer produce other, more current and more modern, forms for these records.

The map, plan and drawing are commonly understood resources for communicating information and knowledge. We may even create our own form of this type of record when, orally and with body gestures, we provide directions to a lost traveler or describe a structure. While the concept is thus quite familiar, the format of these records can be intimidating.

Cartographic and architectural records share a number of common features, all quite different from the more familiar textual (or written) archival records. They are primarily pictorial linear representations employing a mathematical scale and utilizing symbolic devices to convey information. They are often in color and can be artistic depictions of the information they convey. Size, however, is their most common and obvious difference from textual records. Maps, plans, and drawings are normally of such large and varying physical dimensions that using them and managing them requires special handling and care. Regardless of these special characteristics, the basic principles of archival management apply equally to cartographic and architectural records.

While standard archival criteria for appraisal, arrangement, description, conservation and reference activities apply to the management of such records, special skills, techniques, and knowledge also have to be applied. Archivists who are responsible for managing such records have to have a considerable knowledge and understanding of geography, cartography, aerial photography, and architectural history, some mathematical ability, and an understanding of the terminology associated with these fields. Additionally, the fact that, while these records normally comprise series in archival institutional settings, they are almost always used individually, and often independent of the series, to which they belong. This requires the staff responsible for them to possess skills enabling them to work with individual records as well as voluminous series. This chapter addresses the application of basic archival principles and procedures to cartographic and architectural records.

Definitions

Cartographic records consist primarily of maps, charts, and field survey documentation. Maps are scaled representations of the world or parts of its land mass, while charts are scaled representations of the earth's water and air spaces. Field surveys are a means of gathering data used to prepare maps or charts, and the records related to such surveys frequently become part of cartographic files. They are normally written descriptions and mathematical calculations of areas being measured for the development of scaled representations. In recent years, the development and use of aerial photography has supplanted the earlier field notebooks. The interpretation of aerial and satellite photographic imagery, and the plotting of contours from the photographic image, has streamlined the process of creating maps. Current technological developments in the computerization of information in digital or other electronic form are also being used in the creation of cartographic, as well as architectural, records.

Architectural records include scale plans, drawings and models relating to the design and construction of buildings and other structures. They can also be unscaled, freehand, initial representations known as "preliminary sketches" and "presentation drawings" (or renderings), and may include site plans, perspective drawings, landscape drawings, working drawings, "as built" drawings and structural, mechanical, electrical, shop and standard drawings. "Engineering drawing" is a term applied to scaled representations of moveable structures such as ships, aircraft, vehicles, mechanical devices, and other non-building structures. "Model" is the term normally applied to a scaled representation of a building or structure in three-dimensional format.

Both cartographic and architectural records share physical formats such as paper, mylar, blueprints, tracings, linen and diazo prints. Globes, atlases, wood engravings, copper plate engravings, panoramic views and aerial photographs are more commonly found in cartographic holdings, while Van Dyke prints are commonly the reserve of the architectural record. Models are usually associated with architecture but cartographic records may include three-dimensional relief maps.

Appraisal

The same principles, procedures, and techniques used to appraise textual records apply to cartographic and architectural records. They have legal, evidential, administrative, informational, and intrinsic value the same as textual records. The purpose for which the records were created, and the information they portray, can provide evidence of the organization, functions, decisions, and operations of the entity creating or using them. Explorations and surveys, as well as plans for transportation systems or construction developments (whether accomplished or not) provide visible evidence of the policies, purposes, and activities of a government, business, or institution.

Cartographic and architectural records depict sites and locations of structures, changes in the land (shoreline and boundary changes, for example) and its structures and, with the aerial photographic record, provide precise visual evidence of what an area looked like and what it contained in the past. Whether changes occur as the result of natural, evolutionary environmental forces, by acts of wars, by human policies involving urbanization, transportation or similar activities, cartographic and architectural records provide visible evidence of the nature of the land, the landscape, and the planned or built structures in a given area over a certain period of time. They may provide information and evidence, for example, by depicting the site of Indian burial mounds; showing the former course of a river, trail, or road; showing changes in the land caused by natural evolutionary erosion; identifying boundaries of nations and land-owners; and showing the location and plans of structures of the past. They are useful resources when planning to make changes in the land. Records showing site locations of previous civilizations and the historical use and composition of the land can assist planners to make decisions on proposed changes. Documents containing such information form an important part of the official, historical record of a government, business, or institution.

The intrinsic and aesthetic value of cartographic and architectural records, as with other records, is in the "eye of the beholder", but there are many instances where the differences are clear to the informed observer. Over time, maps and drawings have been created by individual mapmakers, architects and draftsmen employing the best art and craft known to them. Their skills are reflected in their precise use of symbols, line widths, coloring, shading and printing techniques. The hand tools used for these purposes in the eighteenth, nineteenth and earlier twentieth centuries are now giving way to modern machines and electronic manipulation. Maps and architectural drawings that exemplify the stages in the technological development of graphic construction and reproduction can certainly be regarded as intrinsically valuable and should be retained as artefacts in their original forms.

Maps and drawings of the past frequently exhibit beautiful workmanship. Consider the frequent cartouches and border embellishments that, in addition to the beauty of their design, often show historical and geographical information not obtainable elsewhere. In addition to representing the "state of the art", many of these documents are truly "works of art".

On the other hand, multiple copies of routine maps and drawings of the types frequently found among modern archives (blueprints, brownline prints, and Van Dyke prints) have less and less value with each duplication, and it is normally necessary to keep only one or two well-preserved reproductions from a stack of identical duplicates. Photocopies that duplicate the original linen tracings from which they were made are considered disposable when the original linen is already being preserved. Blueprints and similar photocopies that bear manuscript annotations are a different story, each is a unique document that must be considered on the merits of the annotations.

Archivists need to be aware of the varying qualities of the cartographic and architectural records they are appraising as well as the sources of such records. Likely sources of these records in municipal, county, state, and national governments are the offices responsible for planning, zoning, transportation, defense, and natural resources. The use of such words as "construction", "design", "engineering", "graphics", "real property", and "survey", as well as "map", "plan", and "architect" in the title of an office or institution may point to its being a possible source of such records.

Arrangement

Ideally, accessioned records are kept in the order in which they are received, reflecting their use by the creating organization. Unfortunately, many cartographic and architectural records arrive in archival institutions in disarranged bundles or rolls. Without guidelines, there is a temptation to re-arrange such bundles according to simple logical schemes. Cartographic and architectural records can fit naturally into arrangement schemes based on geographical location, type of structure or name of building. However, provenance concerns dictate that the first level of arrangement must be by the agency or office that created the records, and thereunder, if there is an arrangement scheme hidden among the bundles, by that system. If the arrangement scheme is something other than geographical or by structure, retrieving individual records depends on good finding aids. Such finding aids often exist because these records had to be accessible during their use in the originating office from which they were accessioned. Only after giving up the attempt to salvage a workable original arrangement scheme or in cases where no finding aids accompany the records should the archivist create an artifical arrangement system. The simplest and most effective systems for cartographic and architectural records are by geographical area and architectural structure.

Although there may be any number of intellectual arrangement schemes, the oversize nature of maps and drawings suggests that arrangement by size is a logical and practical way to physically store these records while gaining efficient use of space. An entire collection can be arranged according to several categories by size and format provided that each record or folder is identified individually so that its original filing order and source is not lost, and provided that the archival staff maintains a perfect accounting of the various file locations in the form of shelf lists. Institutions with a small volume of cartographic and architectural records may be able to keep track of their provenance from both an intellectual and a practical perspective if the records are arranged according to size. This saves space and contributes to the preservation of individual records. Such policies and decisions are best made according to the individual institution's needs, requirements, and abilities.

Another issue involving the arrangement of cartographic and architectural records concerns the question of whether those that began life as enclosures to textual records (reports or correspondence) should be housed independently or remain attached to the original record. When large maps and drawings are part of a report or similar document, they are usually folded. With use over time, the unfolding and refolding of these records will likely result in a variety of folds and they will eventually crack or tear. Such handling can also distort the scale inherent in the record.

In an ideal world, all large maps and drawings would be stored flat in map cases or in specially constructed, oversize archival boxes stored on wide shelves. Removing original maps and drawings from textual records for flat storage in special containers, like arranging them by size, requires a perfect system of cross-referencing so there is never any question where the enclosure is located when it is required for research use. Identification of the record by record group, series, and item number should be noted in pencil on the reverse side as it is removed from its boxed home. Withdrawal notices on archival bond paper can be placed with the textual record from which it was removed, and a system of cross-references can be developed as a finding aid. Again the issue of provenance versus practical preservation is raised and each institution must determine its own policy. If carefully done, the separation of cartographic and architectural records from textual records will not interfere with the archival integrity of the record.

Aside from these issues, arrangement procedures for cartographic and architectural records are similar to those for textual records. A basic difference, however, is that most cartographic and architectural records require that attention be paid to each individual item. The arrangement process begins with the initial unrolling, unfolding and flattening of these records upon their arrival at the archival institution. Archivists need to be alert to potential problems inherent in the physical composition of the records and should consult conservators when these initial processes may result in damage. During this initial process, the records can be screened for identical duplicates and non-record material. Identical duplicates should be removed and, if legally possible, offered to institutions with an interest in such documents. Non-record material (kraft folders and other separating devices) should be removed and discarded. To make the records easier to work with, they should be flattened at this time by placing them face down between clean acid-free blotters or folders on a flat surface large enough to accommodate them. A large, flat object can be placed over the protected records and weights added atop it. Such a process may require a few days or a few weeks to flatten the records sufficiently to allow the arrangement process to begin.

During the arrangement process, identification of the record group, series and the individual item number should be written in pencil on the back of each record to preclude future misfiling. If the composition of the record is such that pencil will not work, or if the record is of extremely high intrinsic value, it should be placed in an acid-free folder with the identification on the folder. Identification labels can be added later when some of these records are encapsulated. This is also a good time to use individual slips of paper or cards to note the title of the record, its file number and other information which can be useful during the description process. These completed cards can be used during the arrangement process by organizing them to attain a proper arrangement. The records then can be put in the order created by the card arrangement. This reduces the amount of handling of the record. Once the cards have fulfilled this use they can then be used as a guide or index to the series of records.

This initial processing provides an excellent opportunity to identify records requiring preservation work. Those needing preservation immediately should be identified with their file designation, removed, and given conservation treatment. Those requiring conservation treatment in the future can also be identified and noted.

As the maps and drawings are arranged, they should be placed in acid-free folders, and filed in map case drawers. In instances where records are small enough to fit in archival boxes, they should be boxed and stored flat on shelving. Records that arrive rolled, for example, railroad right-of-way maps or plans of ships and aircraft, should be unrolled, examined, and identified with pencil notations on the reverse. Such records often may be from five to twenty feet long when unrolled and too large to flatten and store in map cases. Extra long items should be stored rolled and can be placed in map case drawers or filed in archival quality "pigeon hole" cases. When records must be stored rolled, ideally they should be rolled around interior supports (such as acid-free tubes) to prevent damage. Additionally, they can be further protected by encasing the roll in acid-free paper, plastic sheets, or similar coverings.

The arrangement of aerial photographic records, in printed or film format, employs similar procedures. Arrangement of prints follows the same procedures indicated for flat filing of cartographic and architectural records. If in film negative format, the individual images are normally on rolls, 9½ inches wide by 200 feet long, in the sequence in which they were photographed. Each image usually has a unique alphabetical or numerical code which identifies the project or area of coverage. These records are normally arranged by film container or roll number. It is essential that such records be accompanied by indexes, to enable the user to gain access to individual images. The indexes can be arranged geographically by name of area or by a "degree-square" system representing latitude and longitude.

Description

If note cards were used during the arrangement process, they can serve as a brief descriptive card index to the records. Some institutions may develop card systems which can provide specific information about the records. The title of each item, the dates, "author", scale, dimensions, physical format, record group, series and file unit designation should be placed on the card. Some card systems may even be designed with a map of the region so that the cataloger can plot the coverage of specific cartographic records. Other systems may include pre-printed cards containing basic descriptive information plus any other thematic, political, topical, cartographic, and architectural terms required to provide information about, and access to, the record. Duplicates of these cards can be used to provide access by geographical area, date, building, "author", or similar characteristic, regardless of record group and series. Users of cartographic and architectural records generally request records by the name of a specific area, subject, building, mapmaker, or architect. A basic descriptive system using cards can provide numerous access points without altering the physical arrangement of provenance of the records.

Institutions with large holdings of cartographic and architectural records and a small staff to manage them will probably consider the preceding suggestions as ideal, but impractical. While such a system may be time-consuming in the beginning, it can be extremely efficient in the long run in helping the staff to answer requests for records, especially when they are responding to repeat requests for the same or similar information. Researchers visiting the institution may also use the card system to guide them to the information they seek.

Institutions with large holdings of cartographic and architectural records and a small staff that precludes the item cataloging of each individual record can provide general series descriptions using the archival techniques employed for the description of textual records. The title of the series, inclusive dates, the number of items, and a narrative statement about the contents can aid the retrieval of the records. Whenever possible, the title of the series should be that used by the creator. If a title is created by the archives, it should always describe the type of records (topographic maps, site plans, design drawings) in the series and the information depicted on a geographical area, activity, or subject. The dates should include the earliest and latest dates of the records in the series. The narrative should be brief but include as much pertinent information as possible. Depending on the volume of the series, this can take the form of simply listing the records it contains, providing a brief statement about each individual map or plan, or writing a general summary of the whole series. The arrangement of the series, the existence of finding aids, the relation of these records to textual records, if any, and any restrictions on the use or copying of the records should also be explained.

Preservation

Decisions regarding the preservation of cartographic and architectural records can be made during the initial arrangement process or during later use. Determining which records require immediate attention and which can wait may be simple or complex. Managers of such records need to know their composition and physical properties. The records may be on a variety of papers, films, linen, cloth, silk, plaster, and photographically processed support materials. These supports may bear a variety of media, including crayon, charcoal, pastels, watercolor washes, pencil, and pre-printed paper or plastic words and symbols glued to the records (commonly known as "stick-ups"). Decisions regarding the treatments required to preserve these records should be based on an understanding of their composition and physical and chemical properties, as well as their archival value, and should be made jointly by archivists and conservators.

To prevent any damage from handling, records determined to be of great historical significance or importance or of extremely high intrinsic value should initially be filmed and stored in a separate, secure area. A print can be made from the film copy for reference use and the negative used for future reproductions. An additional film negative copy may be used as a security copy.

Series of frequently used records are prime candidates for preservation filming to prevent damage by frequent handling. Some institutions find that filming cartographic and architectural records in a traditional 35 mm format does not provide adequate detail, but that the 105 mm format is excellent for this purpose. This is the size of a microfiche. When jacketed in an archival quality polyester sleeve, the 105 mm image can be stored in a small filing cabinet for use by staff and researchers. This procedure precludes the use of the original record for research and allows the negative to be used to reproduce the record.

The large, oversized nature of cartographic and architectural records requires that special attention be paid when moving or using them. They should be moved in their folders on carts large enough to accommodate them. They should be used flat and not draped over a table or bent for easier reading. At all times, staff managing these records must ensure they are handled carefully and be alert to the preservation needs of records which are frequently handled and used. If flaking media or other deteriorations are found, the record should be removed from further handling and use by placing it in an acid-free folder with proper identification and sending it to the conservators for preservation treatment. Aside from removing loose dirt and dust and flattening records in relatively good condition, archivists should rely on conservators to clean, deacidify, encapsulate, mend tears and creases, and otherwise physically support and preserve these records.

A minimal preservation procedure for those records most actively used is encapsulation. This process uses material similar to the polyester sleeve placed on many film negatives. For cartographic and architectural records, because of their large size, a 3 to 4 mil thickness of archival quality polyester transparent film is used to enclose the record. A seal created by ultrasound, heat, or double-sided archival quality tape around all four sides protects the record from fraying and tearing as well as from abrasion, dust, dirt, and the oil on human hands. Records should be stable and deacidified, if appropriate, prior to encapsulation. Encapsulation is not a permanent treatment altering the integrity of the record. The record can be removed without harm simply by unsealing the polyester film envelope. Cartographic and architectural records containing flaking pigments, charcoal, pastels, and "stick-up" should not be encapsulated because the static electricity in the polyester may lift and transfer these materials from the record to the polyester.

The use and handling of cartographic and architectural records over time requires that attention be continuously and assiduously paid to preservation concerns. Even with the most careful care and handling, the size of these records is such that they can be damaged inadvertently.

Storage

Individual cartographic and architectural records should be stored in flat storage boxes or horizontal storage units (map cases). Small and infrequently used records should be stored flat in acid-free boxes with reinforced corners. The boxes should be about one inch in depth with the remaining dimensions varying according to the size of the records to be placed in them. They should be strong enough to accommodate stacking.

Map cases vary in size and in the size and number of drawers they contain. Their exterior dimensions may vary in height (from 15 to 18 inches), width (from 28 to 50 inches), and depth (from 40 to 80 inches) to accommodate these large-sized records. They can be constructed with four, five or ten drawers with interior drawer depths of one, two or three inches. The cases and drawers should be made of durable steel and free of impurities in the steel, paint, finish or other components that would affect the life of the records they house. Drawers should run on ball-bearings for smooth movement and ease of access, with a rear hood on each drawer to prevent records from sliding out the back. The cases should be constructed so they can be stacked atop each other securely. A stack of three cases high allows the average-sized person to use the top of the stack easily when removing records from the drawers. A stack of two cases high provides an ideal flat workspace for arranging and doing other substantive work with these large records.

The ideal depth of drawers within the map case is one inch. It provides an ideal space for up to five acid-free folders containing 10 to 12 maps or plans each. Such storage offers maximum safety in handling the records and allows for ease of access to, and refiling of, the records. Map cases with deeper drawers should be reserved for rolled records and larger records (such as plaster relief models) which cannot fit into one-inch drawers. The deeper drawers should have a dust cover in each to help prevent dust and dirt from entering. Flat cartographic and architectural records can be stored in these deeper drawers, but they should never fill more than half the depth of the drawer. Filling two- or three-inch deep drawers with flat records can lead to damage of the records during the retrieval and refiling processes.

Storage of bound atlases and portfolios is determined by their size also. Oversized volumes should not be stored upright, as library books, but flat in custom-made archival boxes, or in map case drawers deep enough to accommodate them. Flat storage provides the support which such heavy volumes require. Bound records that are too large to fit in the deepest drawers, or with deteriorated bindings, can be rebound in post-binding format. Post binding is a process designed to reduce the thickness of a bound volume (some of which can be four, eight, or more, inches thick) or replace a deteriorated binding so the records in the volume can be better stored, preserved and serviced. The record is not altered at any time during this process, but large bound volumes can be divided into parts which are more easily handled. Care must be taken during this process to ensure that the correct order of the individual sheets is maintained. In this process, individual sheets (pages, plates) are removed, undergo any necessary conservation treatment, and then encapsulated with an extra-wide reinforced margin into which holes can be punched to accommodate "posts" (a metal screw and receptacle) of varying lengths which are used either to bind the volume together again with a hard cover, or to make the initial single volume into two or more parts. Such a binding will allow the individual record to be used when necessary for reproduction (the binding can be unscrewed) and allows the bound volumes to fit into map case drawers or archival boxes.

Aerial photographic prints can be stored flat in archival boxes, while film negatives can be stored in their original film containers. Before placing the metal film canisters on shelves, they should be examined carefully to ensure they are free from rust and sharp projections. Dents, depressions, and protrusions in the metal canister and the spool containing the film should be repaired to ensure the roll of film is safe and properly sealed in the canister. Canisters should be stored upright to prevent the film from sagging around the spools (reels).

Reference

Providing reference service in cartographic and architectural records often requires the reference staff to assist researchers in reading, understanding, and interpreting the records. Reference staff members will often have to teach researchers how to read a map, drawing, or aerial photograph. Since individual records, rather than entire series, best provide the information which researchers seek, the reference staff must be able to elicit the details of the inquiry in order to provide the specific items relevant to a researcher's request.

To provide records in answer to such requests, the staff member often performs a small research service, becoming a companion to the researcher in the investigation of the subject. Because this often requires substantial time, it is useful to maintain a reference file of responses to inquiries on subjects requiring substantial research or on subjects likely to be requested again. This not only serves as a useful aid to the staff but also as a finding aid for researchers.

One way for reference staff members to become more adept in responding to inquiries is to learn as much as possible about the records. This can be accomplished by their sharing in the appraisal, accessioning, arrangement, and description processes.

A separate public area for reference to cartographic and architectural records should be set aside within the institution. It should be located close to where the records are stored, away from direct or indirect sunlight, and staffed by personnel skilled in the handling and interpretation of these records. The size of the records requires adequate flat table-top space so that the records do not have to be folded or hung over tables to be used. Atlases, gazetteers, and similiar reference materials should be available in the public research area to answer general inquiries regarding locations, place-names, and boundaries. These materials can reduce the need to provide archival records to answer general questions.

Reference archivists must ensure the preservation of archival records when they are used by the public. Records always should be delivered to the research area in sturdy folders or on carts large enough to accommodate oversize items. During their use in the research area these fragile maps and drawings are most susceptible to damage from careless handling. So instructions on the care and handling of these records must be given to researchers before they are allowed to handle them.

Because of the damage that direct and indirect sunlight can do to cartographic and architectural records, lighting in the research area should be filtered to eliminate ultraviolet radiation. Light-sensitive records (such as blueprints) should always remain in their folders or be placed face down when not actively being used in lighted areas. The research rooms must also be kept clean to avoid dirt and dust being transferred to the records when they are being used.

The variable size and format of cartographic and architectural records demand some expertise by the staff in the reproduction of records. Skills are necessary to assist researchers in determining the best type of reproduction required to satisfy their needs and to calculate the best-sized photographic reproduction of an aerial image, map, or drawing to most accurately reproduce the records according to a particular size or scale. It is therefore important to have direct communication and consultation between the archival staff and technical photographic duplication specialists. Like conservators, photographic duplication specialists should be partners with the cartographic and architectural records staff when specific decisions regarding reproduction capabilities for these large, variable-sized, colorful, and detailed records are required.

In addition to the concerns outlined above, the reference staff must know of any restrictions on the accessibility or reproducibility of such records. Such restrictions may have been agreed upon at the time of accessioning or may be inherent in the record itself. Some of these records may also be subject to copyright laws.

Conclusion

The variety of tasks and knowledge required to manage cartographic and architectural records makes the care and handling of them a unique activity within the archival institution and clearly puts them into a "special" category within the archival setting. Their physical size, variable format and often sensitive physical composition require that special care and attention be paid in handling and storing them.

Their compatibility with their more familiar sister record, the written document, is clearly recognized when their purpose to convey information and knowledge of a spatial nature is understood and accepted. Cartographic and architectural records are visible representations which portray physical elements of the history of a nation, state, industry, or institution. The basic principles of archival management for the written record apply to these "special" records. All that is required is an adjustment of one's point of view toward "records" and an ability to physically maintain, preserve, and administer these special documents.

8

Managing Audio-Visual Archives

William H. Leary

It all began in 1839 when the Frenchman Louis J.M. Daguerre announced that he had captured a photographic image on a silver-coated copper plate. In 1877 the remarkable Thomas Alva Edison successfully recorded sound on a rotating tin foil cylinder. A few years later, in 1893, Edison introduced the first commercially successful motion picture device known as a kinetoscope. By the late 1920s, motion pictures featured both sound and color, and commercial television was introduced in Great Britain and the United States in the late 1930s.

Today there are few places left in the world where audio-visual means of communication are not commonplace. Few if any historians or archivists dispute the importance of photographs, sound and video recordings, and motion pictures in documenting the past. The demand for recorded sound and pictures (still and moving) to recreate the life and times of any people will undoubtedly increase as we rely more and more upon aural and visual means of communication.

Most national archives and a growing number of smaller archival institutions have accepted the responsibility to systematically acquire and preserve audio-visual records. The most ubiquitous and accessible audio-visual records are still photographs, and they are the ones most likely to be found in an archival institution. Archives of motion pictures and sound and video recordings are widespread enough to have generated three international organizations: the International Federation of Film Archives (FIAF), the International Federation of Television Archives (FIAT), and the International Association of Sound Archives (IASA).

While most archives now regularly acquire some audio-visual materials, particularly photographs, many archivists remain bewildered, even intimidated, by audio-visual media. They assume, quite incorrectly, that managing materials physically so unlike traditional paper records must require radically different archival principles. Not surprisingly, the most daunting challenge for archivists newly introduced to audio-visual media is the apparently endless variety of sizes and formats, each of which may require different handling.

A selective sample of still photographic processes, for example, would include daguerreotypes, calotypes, platinum prints, cyanotypes, ambrotypes, tintypes, glass lantern slides, albumen prints, stereographs, carbon prints, and autochromes, and would still leave us in the nineteenth century without any mention of different negative types. The variety of motion picture formats reflects different combinations of film type (nitrate, acetate, or polyester), gauge or size (most commonly 8 mm, 16 mm, 35 mm, and 70 mm), color, sound (optical or magnetic sound track), and generation (everything from the camera original to a projection print via several intermediate steps).

Sound has been recorded on cylinders coated with wax and other materials; on discs coated with shellac, cellulose nitrate, cellulose acetate, zinc, and vinyl; magnetically on wire and tape of many different formats; and, most recently, sound has been digitally encoded on tapes and disks. Even the relatively new video recordings have changed format repeatedly since the introduction of videotape in 1956. Videocassettes (¾ inch and ½ inch) have already replaced 2-inch and 1-inch videotape for many applications, and further changes can be expected in this rapidly changing field.

The essential principle underlying the physical variation in audio-visual media is that they all consist of an original or master copy produced by the camera or the sound or video recorder, which in turn can be used to produce a copy for viewing or listening. Motion picture sound productions usually involve added intermediate steps between the camera original and the projection or release print, which combines sound and moving images. These intermediate versions can include an optical sound track and a fine-grain positive or duplicate negative.

Modern negative and positive film materials consist of a support material known as the base, which is coated with an emulsion that is sensitive to light and has a dull appearance. Similarly, contemporary audio and video recordings consist of a base, such as polyester, with a magnetic coating that is sensitive to electronic signals produced by sound or light.

Each audio-visual medium has unique characteristics that archivists must recognize. Nevertheless, most guidelines for the archival management of any one type of audio-visual record will also apply to the others with only slight variations. Also, despite their special physical characteristics, many of the basic principles of archival appraisal, processing, preservation, and reference, should be applied, with occasional modifications, to audio-visual records.

This chapter will survey the management of audio-visual archives under the separate headings of appraisal, arrangement and description, preservation, and reference. While discussing each of these topics separately contributes to clarity, the working archivist soon learns how inextricably these tasks are related to each other. Appraisers of audio-visual records must remember, for example, that whenever new materials are selected, presumably they have committed the archives to a substantial burden of preservation, cataloging, and servicing. Accessioning new materials without the realistic prospect of processing them contributes little to the advancement of knowledge.

Preservation priorities quite properly will reflect a considered judgment about the reference demands on materials as well as their condition and relative value. There is little point in undertaking expensive preservation of an audio-visual collection if the archives does not have the resources to describe and service the materials. On the other hand, it would be irresponsible to make fragile materials available to researchers without first performing proper preservation. Similarly, the quality of description and reference services in an audio-visual archives will certainly affect the institution's ability to preserve materials. In summary, responsible decisions cannot be made about any single aspect of managing audio-visual archives without careful consideration of the inevitable effect upon other archival tasks.

Appraisal

Because of the relatively late archival interest in audio-visual records, the most urgent challenge for audio-visual archivists has been to save as much as possible of a heritage too long neglected. After a generation of serious attention, however, most audio-visual archivists now recognize the need to develop guidelines for the appraisal of visual and aural materials. While the work of salvaging the early audio-visual record must continue, modern audio-visual records pose an equally demanding and more complex challenge for audio-visual appraisal archivists.

The widespread use of low-cost, easy-to-operate equipment has contributed to an exponential growth of audio-visual production that shows no sign of slackening. In the United States alone, for example, about 10 billion photographs are produced annually. Obviously only a small proportion of that output can or should be preserved indefinitely. As the volume of audio-visual records continues to increase, we can assert categorically that appraisal, meaning selection of some and rejection of others, will have to take place. The responsibility of archivists is to make the appraisal process as rational as possible.

The essential prerequisite for systematic appraisal is a well-defined and coordinated acquisition policy for each institution that has a serious program to preserve audio-visual records. Without complementary and circumscribed collecting strategies that are respected by other institutions, the elusive dream of saving all audio-visual materials of historical value will become a certified impossibility. Only by sharing the expensive and escalating burden of preserving the audio-visual record can archives hope to avoid both excessive repetition and the loss of currently unfashionable but important materials.

Proclaiming the need for coordinated acquisition policies is much easier than divining the means to accomplish such a transformation. Who should acquire what is a question that will be answered differently from country to country, depending upon the legal mandate of the national archives and the nature of other institutions seriously engaged in accessioning audio-visual records. Each institution must first determine its official or legal obligations and identify the major themes or characteristics of its current holdings. Information about the current holdings and acquisition policies of audio-visual archives must then be shared widely. FIAF, FIAT, and IASA have sponsored important work in collecting and disseminating such information, especially by encouraging the preparation of national filmographies. Audio-visual appraisers must consult such sources and confine their active collecting to materials that are not already the responsibility of existing archival agencies.

The archival appraiser of audio-visual records needs to follow several general operating principles as well as applying specific appraisal standards. The preparation for appraisal should begin with a thorough analysis of the institution's current audio-visual holdings. No archival institution can hope to build from strength, fill in gaps, or avoid excessive redundancy if the appraiser does not know about the undescribed, infrequently used materials on the top shelves as well as the heavily used collections. Appraisers should also be familiar with current historical literature and the history of each audio-visual medium.

Audio-visual records have archival importance almost exclusively because of their informational value. They rarely provide unique evidence about an organization's operation, although there are occasional exceptions to this rule. Audio-visual materials are worth preserving in an archives, therefore, in direct proportion to the extent that the appraiser can anticipate researcher interest in the information they contain. The best way to measure such informational value is by studying past and present researcher inquiries at the appraiser's institution and elsewhere.

The most important criteria for appraising audio-visual records are age, subject content, uniqueness, quantity, quality, and identification. Old age confers value on audio-visual records, but the determination of what constitutes old age obviously varies according to many circumstances. For example, instantaneous disc recordings of radio broadcasts from the late 1920s and early 1930s are extremely valuable because of their scarcity and fragility, whereas relatively abundant and stable commercial 78 r.p.m. records from the same period would have to be appraised on the basis of other criteria.

A crucial factor in appraising all audio-visual media is determining the point at which technology and other factors accelerated production levels sufficiently to require archivists to make selections from the quantities of material available. That dividing line will differ from country to country and medium to medium. In the history of still photography, two dates are particularly important: 1888, when George Eastman invented amateur photography, and 1932, when the 35 mm camera began to transform the nature of photography.

Audiotape cassettes and videotapes introduced in the 1960s clearly were watershed developments in the history of audio and video recordings. Motion picture film production has resisted the transformation from professional to amateur status. Nevertheless, film productions escalated in most parts of the world after World War II and must, therefore, be judged more skeptically than earlier films.

Subject-matter is the most difficult appraisal criterion to define and apply. Who can say with certainty what subjects will interest future researchers? It is essential, however, to ask the question. If the appraiser cannot anticipate continuing interest in the informational content—the subject-matter—of audiovisual records, then questions of age, quality, and quantity are largely irrelevant. Fascinating subject content, on the other hand, will compensate for deficiencies in other respects.

When evaluating subject content, appraisers should recall that a special virtue of audio-visual records is their ability to document the mundane, the trivial, the everyday texture of life so often ignored by more traditional records. Clearly, it is not only impossible but undesirable to compile a list of non-archival subjects for appraisers. Nevertheless, each institution should attempt to identify the subjects that will receive the highest priority as well as the lowest. The National Archives of the United States, for example, has given advance authorization for the disposal of photos of routine ceremonial activities and film footage and video recordings of routine surveillance and routine scientific, medical, or engineering activities. Local historical societies, in contrast, may attach greater significance to photos of routine ceremonial occasions that help to document a community's social history. The Imperial War Museum's Sound Records Department has suggested another approach by developing a rather detailed list of subject priorities for future collecting based on a careful analysis of their current holdings.

Because all audio-visual records are meant to be reproduced, it is especially important to apply the archival appraisal standard of uniqueness. Emphasizing the acquisition of camera originals or magnetic masters will help avoid the unknowing accessioning of materials that are duplicated at other institutions. It is also appropriate to consider carefully the extent to which information is duplicated in another medium. The audio recording of a prepared speech, for example, diminishes in value significantly if a printed version is also preserved, and its value may be totally supplanted if a film or video recording is also available. Indeed, the archival value of spoken word recordings in general will be tested severely by the inevitable spread of inexpensive video recordings. Similarly, appraisers should consider carefully the relative merits of still and moving pictures of the same subject. If the motion and sound do not add significantly to the information conveyed, a photograph or even a file of photos—can be preserved more inexpensively than a film. If a motion picture has been or will be accessioned, however, it may not be necessary to acquire similar photographs.

Some institutions give insufficient weight to the standard of uniqueness because of the mistaken notion that an archives can always afford to accept a few more audio-visual records. But, even though the volume of audio-visual records is smaller than paper records, their numbers are growing dramatically and their handling costs per unit are substantial. Therefore, volume is a pertinent concern for audio-visual appraisers. The cost of preserving a 30-minute nitrate film, for example, may be a hundred times the cost of conserving a cubic foot of paper records. Weeding and sampling, the traditional archival remedies for excessive volume, can be applied usefully to audio-visual records in special circumstances.

Time-consuming weeding of voluminous files to eliminate ephemeral subject-matter, unneeded duplicates, and poor-quality materials can be undertaken most efficiently in conjunction with other archival processing work. Whenever possible, therefore, archives should seek the right to weed materials after accessioning according to standards negotiated during the appraisal process. Such weeding is particularly warranted for motion pictures because of the great expense of processing a single item. Sampling has been used most effectively in making selections from the massive amounts of material generated by radio and television broadcasters, especially the more ephemeral materials such as soap operas and other entertainment series, sports broadcasts, and daily news bulletins.

Because audio-visual materials are studied for details and are meant to be reproduced, appraisers must emphasize the importance of satisfactory technical quality, which includes proper exposure, clear focus, good composition, and audible sound. Even when actual or potential preservation problems can be alleviated — as with deteriorating nitrate, diacetate, or color film— appraisers must realistically balance the potential research value against the likely costs and institutional capabilities. If an archives cannot afford to copy a collection of deteriorating nitrate films, for example, they may not remain available for research for very long. Appraisers should take care to identify potential problems so that threatened collections can be treated or copied before it is too late.

The importance of uniqueness and quality requires that an archives make every effort to acquire the original camera negative or master recording, as well as a reference copy. For film records, particularly motion pictures, the archives should also try to accession any master positives or duplicate negatives, which are crucial for long-term preservation. On the other hand, cost considerations may dictate that the archives should not accession every production element and all unused footage for each motion picture appraised as archival.

Finally, appraisers should remember that without some identification of the who, what, where, and when for audio-visual materials, their value as historical evidence is severely limited. It is true that photographs and complete audio-visual productions (unlike most unedited film footage or incomplete productions) contain internal evidence that compensates for inadequate identification. Nevertheless, one of the appraiser's most important tasks is to locate and ensure the accessioning of all related documentation that will explain the provenance and enhance the usefulness of any audio-visual collection.

Several categories of documentation should be accessioned if they can be located. Production files that document the origin and development of materials could include scripts for motion pictures or video productions, transcripts of oral history interviews, and any other information about who made the pictures or recorded the sounds, how, and why. This information is particularly crucial for unedited film footage, incomplete productions, or poorly captioned photographs.

Also important are any finding aids used by the creator such as still photo caption lists, shot lists that describe motion picture film, and indexes and catalogs for any medium. Any information about how materials were used or publicized, such as publication data, movie stills, and materials related to the publicity surrounding a finished production will enhance their research value. Finally, it is essential to gather all available information about any copyrights or other restrictions that the archives must enforce.

The key to systematic appraisal and planned development of an audio-visual archives is an active records management program. The audio-visual archivist as records manager can and should encourage the use of archival materials and processes to create archival records, promote filing schemes that separate significant materials from the trivial, encourage necessary weeding of sprawling files, and encourage proper preservation practices—all of which will lessen the burden of archival management.

The basic archival objective of records management is to identify and schedule the transfer of historically valuable records as soon as possible in their life cycle. This is especially important for audio-visual records because they are usually less stable than paper records, and their creators are often reluctant to part with them. The scheduling process should identify precisely all the elements of an audio-visual record that are archival—negative, print, etc.— their location at the time of scheduling, and any related documentation.

The unfortunate reality is that the boxes of audio-visual records shipped to archives frequently show few signs of informed records management prior to their arrival. Not uncommonly, the new treasures will be disorganized, incomplete, dirty, inadequately identified and, in some cases, clearly damaged. Establishing physical and intellectual control over new materials must begin by recording some basic information at the time of accessioning. Keeping the accession register simple will help to ensure minimum descriptive control for all new acquisitions as soon as they arrive. This register will provide the only intellectual control over materials until more extensive cataloging can be completed.

The basic categories of information required for all media are: a unique accession number, date received, source, title, and storage location. For still photos, also record the number and type of containers and a brief description of the collection's contents. For film and sound or video recordings, indicate the number of reels, tapes, or cassettes and their gauge or size—35-mm or 16-mm for most film; for tape, 2-inch, 1-inch, ¾-inch, ½-inch, or ¼-inch.

Arrangement and description

Planning ahead as carefully as possible is the essential first step in processing audio-visual records. Plans must balance institutional objectives, an evaluation of current holdings, researcher interests, and staff and funding limitations. Sophisticated cataloging systems, for example, are unnecessary for only a few hundred items and not feasible without sufficient well-trained staff. Because there will never be enough time to catalog and preserve every item ideally, priorities must be established. A user profile provides valuable information in making the difficult choices. Institutional resources should be concentrated on processing the collections likely to be used most heavily.

As a general rule, arrangement and descriptive cataloging should precede systematic laboratory preservation. This will permit weeding of unnecessary duplicates and irredeemably poor-quality materials and more careful identification of the items that warrant expensive preservation treatment. The traditional archival principle of provenance applies to the processing of all audio-visual media. Documenting their organizational and functional origins helps to explain the crucial question of why materials were created, preserves the interrelationships among materials created in a series, and maintains the connecting links between visual images or recorded sound and related documentation.

The closely-related principle of the "sanctity of the original order" is normally pertinent only for still photographs, thus distinguishing them from other audio-visual media. Since motion pictures and sound and video recordings can only be examined by using a machine—since researchers cannot browse through them—the archivist's traditional concern to discern and perfect an arrangement pattern is largely irrelevant. The arrangement of these materials is important only to the extent that some order (usually numerical) is needed to enable staff to retrieve them efficiently from storage. Therefore, item-level cataloging of these materials is normally required to provide minimal researcher access.

The still photo archivist, in contrast, must normally cope with a much greater volume of material than the archivist who deals with moving images or sound recordings. A master catalog of all images or reorganizing all photos according to a single filing scheme is not only prohibitively expensive in most cases but unnecessary. By maintaining the separate integrity of series that have some internal coherence and by preserving the original order of photos whenever possible—that is, by exploiting fully the principles of provenance and original order—the still photo archivist can rely upon description at the series or group level to provide satisfactory access to most photographs. General description of a collection of photos combined with information about their arrangement pattern enables researchers to browse through pertinent parts of a collection in search of the right image.

The first step in arranging and describing photographs is to determine the unifying characteristics of a collection—why they were created or kept together— which probably will include one or more of the following: they are the work of a single photographer or firm; they relate to the activities of a particular office; they depict the same subject, place, person, or event; or they comprise a similar format, such as a collection of daguerreotypes or 35-mm negatives. Totally unrelated items that are not part of any identifiable collection can be placed in a general picture file, in which photos are normally arranged alphabetically by assigned subject headings.

The assigned subject headings may be derived from published lists or an authority list developed by the institution. As in so many other aspects of archival processing, effectiveness depends upon simplicity and a thorough assessment of the institution's holdings and researcher needs. Keep the main headings as general and limited in number as possible, relying upon subheadings to provide more detailed access as needed, but *only* as needed. One good way to cross-reference pictures that require more than one subject entry is to file electrostatic copies under the appropriate multiple headings.

The arrangement patterns of discrete series or collections of photographic prints may not be readily apparent but archivists should analyze the system and improve it as needed, or impose an internal order where none exists. The most common arrangement schemes for prints are chronological, numerical, or alphabetical by subject, place, or surname. Occasionally, these patterns may be combined to arrange prints, for example, alphabetically by subject or surname and thereunder chronologically or numerically. Simple numerical arrangement provides no intellectual access to prints. Negatives, in contrast, which should never be used for reference, are normally arranged in numerical order to facilitate the retrieval of specific items for reproduction.

While refining the arrangement of photographs, archivists should gather the information needed to describe each series or collection. The essential categories of information are the following: collection title, based either on content or origin; inclusive dates of coverage; description of the contents that explains the who, what, why, and where with particular attention to any noteworthy or unexpected images; description of the arrangement of both prints and corresponding negatives; number of items and storage containers, such as boxes or filing drawers; format; including the type of prints and negatives and their size, accession number; numbering scheme for each item; storage location; access restrictions, if any; and identification of any finding aids.

Adequate physical control requires a unique identification number for each photograph; it can also be used to determine the precise location of each print and negative. For example, in the number 210-G-12H-118, 210-G identifies the series; 12H refers to the box and folder where the print is filed, alphabetically by subject; and 118 is the unique image number identifying both the print and its corresponding negative.

More detailed intellectual access to photographs can be provided by various finding aids, some of which may have been produced by the creator. One of the simplest finding aids to produce is a box-contents listing of folder titles, which is particularly helpful if prints are organized by subject. Some institutions attempt to identify all credited photographers and index the collections in which they are represented.

The most practicable way to provide general subject access to photographs is to describe each collection with a limited number of subject-index terms derived from the same subject authority list used to organize a general file. In that way researchers are directed to all collections that contain photos on a given subject. Indexes to individual photographs are so time-consuming to create that they can rarely be justified, even if the archives has access to a computer.

The description of motion pictures and sound or video recordings, for reasons explained previously, normally involves cataloging each unique item. In a sense, each film and video or sound recording constitutes a collection of organized pictures and sounds. A one-hour film, for example, contains 86,400 individual frames or pictures. The degree of detail required to describe the thousands of individual images or sounds must be determined by realistically balancing researcher needs and institutional resources.

Fully detailed cataloging of each unique reel of film, sound, or video usually produces a steadily growing backlog of totally uncataloged materials. Researchers are better served by a policy that emphasizes minimal but timely cataloging of all materials and more extensive description only in limited, carefully prescribed circumstances.

The cataloging of film and video involves gathering information from the record itself and from secondary written sources. Flatbed viewing machines should be used to examine films. At some major film archives the responsibility for collecting film histories and other secondary sources is assigned to a separate documentation department. The basic descriptive elements are the title, country of origin, producer, director, date, physical description, a brief summary of the contents, unique identification number, identification of supplemental finding aids, and restrictions on reuse.

The preferred title is the original release title; if that cannot be determined, record the title that appears on the film or in related documentation. In some cases, particularly for unedited film, it will be necessary to devise a descriptive title. The title for newsreels and certain other serial productions, especially television programs, will be a series title and the sequence within the series. The producer credit may include a government agency or other sponsor as well as an individual or production company. For edited productions, record the date of release and for unedited material, the date of shooting.

The physical description should indicate whether the item is film or video, its running time in minutes, whether sound or silent or both, color or black-and-white or both, and the film gauge (8 mm, 16 mm, 35 mm, 70 mm) or tape format (cassette or open-reel tape and its width). The unique identification number specifies the collection and unique item within it. More elaborate numbering systems may also incorporate information about the film type, format, and preservation status of individual copies.

The summary should describe the who, what, where, and why of the production as briefly, objectively, and specifically as possible. It should give some attention to the sound aspects of the production and identify the genre or type of film or video, such as feature film, newsreel, documentary, cartoon, etc. For complete edited productions a summary of the main theme or themes is normally adequate. For unedited film or tape that lacks an overall coherence, more detailed description is appropriate. Normally, a brief summary of each unrelated scene is recommended. The precise location of scenes can be indicated by noting the reel number and footage count.

Additional optional information includes other credits (writer, camera, editor, narrator, and leading cast members of feature films) and subject headings for indexing purposes. Subject headings should be based on the summary and should highlight important persons, places, events, activities, and themes. Most major film and video archives attempt to provide some level of subject indexing as well as a separate title index. FIAF also recommends indexes arranged according to director, country of origin, and year of production. The most effective ways to produce several indexes are either to make multiple copies of the basic catalog card—including one for each assigned subject heading—and file them accordingly, or to create an automated data base that can sort information in many ways.

The cataloging of sound recordings follows most of the guidelines for film and video, though normally in less detail. Series-level descriptions will furnish adequate access to closely-related, repetitive recordings, such as recurring official committee meetings or field recordings of bird calls. Even when cataloging at the item level, a descriptive title may provide sufficient intellectual control. Summaries of the subject content are not standard but are reserved for unique and particularly significant collections.

The title line will vary according to the type of recording. The title of a commercial recording, especially music, is usually apparent, but a title must often be devised for non-commercial recordings. Speakers and performers (rather than producer, director, and cast) should always be identified as well as any other pertinent information to establish context, such as the main subjects of an interview.

The physical description of a sound recording should identify the format of the original recording (disk, cylinder, tape, etc.) and its total running time. Information about the date of the recording, restrictions on use and reproduction, unique identification number, and related finding aids is comparable to the cataloging information for other audio-visual media. Indexes—by date, title, speakers or performers, or subject—are the most common type of finding aid for sound recordings.

Film, sound, and video archives, because of their reliance upon item-level cataloging and indexing, understandably have sought to use computers in description work. Despite obvious advantages, the use of computers entails planning and labor costs in addition to the purchase and maintenance of equipment or services. The successful use of computers requires very precise language and format, including adherence to a thesaurus for subject indexing. The cataloging staff must also recognize that alterations to an established computer program are expensive. In summary, computers can improve the cataloging of audio-visual materials but only if there is very careful advance planning.

In addition to describing each collection as fully as possible, all audio-visual archives should prepare a general guide to their holdings. Since the guide will introduce most researchers to the archives, it should be attractively designed and carefully edited. It should describe the purpose of the archives and its reference procedures, and briefly summarize the subject and date coverage of the holdings and their quantity and highlight a few of the most notable collections.

Preservation

Preservation is a particularly important responsibility for audio-visual archivists because audio-visual records are generally more perishable than paper and their preservation costs per unit are so relatively high. This discussion will highlight broad preservation guidelines applicable to all audio-visual materials and briefly review a few special requirements for each medium. The details of laboratory preservation processes are beyond the scope of this chapter and they are covered more extensively in the professional literature than any other aspect of managing audio-visual records.

An archival preservation program for audio-visual materials must reflect the obligation to prolong the life of all accessioned materials, few of which may be exquisite treasures. This obligation leads to a greater emphasis on preventive maintenance for the total holdings than on providing the most elaborate preservation and conservation treatment available for the most valuable items. Effective preventive maintenance requires protecting audio-visual records from the two primary contributors to deterioration, improper storage and improper use, and recognizing the signs of deterioration in time to take corrective action.

Proper storage requirements include adequate environmental controls and satisfactory storage containers. Recommended environmental standards for most black-and-white film and sound and video recordings are temperature and humidity levels that do not exceed 65 to 70 degrees Fahrenheit—and 40 to 50 percent relative humidity. Maintaining consistent levels of temperature and humidity is as important as strict adherence to preferred readings. For nitrate and color film, lower temperature and humidity readings of about 35 degrees Fahrenheit and 30 percent relative humidity are advisable but difficult to maintain. In general, lower temperatures retard deterioration, especially the fading of color dyes. Excessively high humidity promotes the growth of harmful fungus while excessively dry conditions can contribute to brittleness and the shrinkage of film and magnetic tape. Filtration of air pollutants is also recommended, particularly for magnetic recordings, which can be seriously damaged by dust.

Proper use involves careful handling safeguards, observed by archivists and researchers, as well as special attention to protecting the original negative or master recording. The latter requires storing originals separately from other copies and ensuring that they are not used for reference. Duplication is an essential ingredient of an audio-visual preservation program, not only to make reference copies when needed, but to replace or back-up deteriorating or especially valuable originals. Because of the costs of duplication, priorities must be assigned by evaluating the actual and potential use of the record, its physical condition, and its relative value. Conservation treatment should be undertaken cautiously, only by trained professionals, and only on the most valuable items or when necessary for duplication.

All archivists must learn basic preservation skills so that preservation actions can be integrated into all aspects of processing and reference. Cataloging and reference staff should routinely make note of problems since they handle the records more extensively than anyone else. They must also follow the general guidelines for careful handling of audio-visual materials, which include: wearing cotton gloves; keeping the records away from food, drink, or smoke; writing on the back of photographic prints only with a graphite pencil; not using pressure-sensitive labels or tape on records; and removing extraneous objects such as paper clips, rubber bands, staples, or acidic papers (after extracting any useful information they contain). Within this framework of general policy guidelines, each audio-visual medium has specific preservation needs, particularly with regard to storage containers and duplication.

Still photographic negatives should be individually stored in enclosure made of paper with a neutral pH (about 7.0) or inert plastic, such as polyester. Ideally, prints also should be individually sleeved. Since this is sometimes not feasible, concentrate on providing such protection for original, or vintage, prints or those needing extra protection. Other prints can be stored in non-acidic folders. Avoid the use of kraft paper, manila envelopes, or glassine envelopes, all of which are acidic.

The duplication of still photographs is warranted most frequently by the absence of a reference copy and the deterioration of nitrate or unstable safety (diacetate) negatives, which is to say virtually any negative produced prior to the mid-1950s. The deterioration rates of nitrate and unstable safety negatives vary, but they should be inspected regularly. The gaseous byproducts of deteriorating nitrate film can harm other photographic materials in close proximity. Although the inflammability of nitrate still negatives has been exaggerated, they should be stored separately from other materials. The onset of nitrate deterioration can be detected by discoloration, brittleness, stickiness, or an acrid odor. The decomposition of unstable safety negatives results from shrinking that causes the emulsion to separate from the base and produces an acrid odor.

When copying positive or negative originals to create reference (positive) copies, the options to consider are electrostats, photographic prints, microfilm or microfiche, or video disk. The cheapest but poorest quality option is an electrostatic copy. Photographic prints provide the best quality, but they are the most expensive option, especially when producing them requires the creation of a copy negative.

The advantages and disadvantages of microforms and video disks are similar. Their per unit cost is much less than photographic prints, but considerable expertise and preparation are required for satisfactory results and special equipment is needed for viewing. Both microforms and video disks can be reproduced inexpensively for subsequent distribution. Because of the initial start-up costs they are most appropriate for copying very large and widely-used collections.

When making preservation negatives, the options are duplicate or copy negatives (made from film interpositives or prints), microfilm, or direct-duplicate negatives. Copy negatives can be produced in any size from 35-mm to 8 × 10-inch format. The larger the copy negative, the greater the quality and expense. Direct-duplicate negatives are a less expensive option than duplicate negatives made from interpositives because they are only one step removed from the original, but some experts have questioned their long-term stability.

Motion picture film should be stored on cores, not reels, in non-corrosive metal or inert plastic containers stacked horizontally, six to eight high, to prevent warping. Nitrate motion picture film should be maintained in separate storage areas in containers that are unsealed to permit the ventilation of harmful gases.

Unstable and inflammable nitrate film is the most urgent preservation problem confronting film archives. Fires caused by the spontaneous combustion of deteriorating nitrate film have destroyed millions of feet of archival film. Virtually all 35-mm film produced prior to 1951 is nitrate while 16-mm film has been manufactured on a safety base since 1916. Cellulose diacetate film that was widely used from the 1920s to the late 1940s is not flammable, but it tends to shrink with age and become brittle.

The only way to preserve these films is by duplication on to 16-mm or 35-mm polyester film before deterioration becomes too advanced. Video tapes are not satisfactory preservation copies because of their uncertain longevity. Increasingly, however, film archives rely upon video cassettes for reference copies because they cost less than film copies and they are easier for researchers to use.

Duplication must be performed by skilled laboratory technicians using archival quality equipment and supplies. Ideally, for each film the archives should have a master copy (preferably the camera original), an internegative or fine-grain positive used to print additional copies, and a reference copy. For stable materials that are reproduced infrequently, a master and a reference copy will suffice. All copies should be made on the same size film as the originals. Most archives produce a separate picture and sound track for 16-mm film to ensure that optimum quality is preserved for each.

The only practicable way to prolong the life of color dyes is by cold storage, as previously recommended. A more reliable means of preserving color films is by producing a black-and-white separation master for each of the three primary colors, an approach that is prohibitively expensive for all but the most valuable films. Some film archivists believe that future advances in holography will provide more effective means to preserve color films.

Regular inspection is an essential component of a film preservation program. It should begin with an inspection of each new accession to identify the following: number and length of reels, the gauge of film or video tape, the emulsion type (negative, positive, fine-grain), base type (nitrate, acetate, polyester), black-and-white or color, silent or sound, image and sound combined (composite) or separate, the projection speed (which varies for silent films), the general physical condition, and the date of inspection.

The inspection of physical condition should include a check for shrinkage, brittleness, excess hypo and underdeveloped halides, discoloration, tearing, scratches, dirt, and other damage, many of which can be detected visually and corrected or alleviated. This information should be recorded and updated as additional regular inspections or preservation work are performed.

The chief preservation problems of sound archives involve recordings made prior to the era of magnetic tape, with the exception of modern long-playing records made of durable vinyl. The chief villains are dust, careless handling, and poorly-maintained equipment. Many phonodiscs can be stored safely in their original packaging, provided that the cellophane shrink-wrapping is removed to prevent warpage. Polyethylene envelopes are preferable to paper or glassine for most disks. Non-acidic paper envelopes are recommended for instantaneous recordings made on nitrate or acetate disks and for shellac 78s. Records should be stored vertically, snugly supporting each other. Cylinders should be stored vertically with some support in the center. Tape reels should also be shelved vertically, stored in their original boxes and sealed in the polyethylene bags usually provided with new reels.

Cylinders and instantaneous recordings are the most fragile sound recordings. They should never be used for normal reference and, therefore, must be copied on to magnetic tape. Wire recordings, early shellac disks, acetate-base tapes and magnetic tape cassettes are also not suitable for long-term preservation and should be duplicated on to tape reels in priority order, as resources permit. The preferred preservation format is 1.5-mil polyester tape. Thinner tapes have many undesirable qualities.

Tape cassettes are acceptable and convenient as reference copies, but archives should use only good-quality cassettes of the C60 length. By using cassettes with screw fittings, the cassette can be dismantled for repair. Digital compact discs are the latest innovation in sound recording and are still too new to recommend with full confidence. Because of their impressive trouble-free quality, however, they may become the standard audio preservation format in the near future.

The preservation requirements for video tape are comparable to those for audio magnetic tape. The best approach to safeguarding them is to store the archival original properly and use only a copy for reference. Periodic inspection and careful rewinding of the master tapes are also recommended.

Reference

Reference services for audio-visual records differ from traditional archival practices in three significant ways: first, examination of motion pictures, sound recordings, and video recordings requires the use of specialized equipment; secondly, copyright restrictions are not uncommon on audio-visual records; and thirdly, the variety of reproduction formats and the technical quality expected by researchers are greater than for paper records. A realistic assessment of the laboratory's capabilities and a prepared order form that lists all types of reproductions furnished and their costs will reduce the number of repetitive inquiries and subsequent complaints. Audio-visual archives should ensure that laboratory staff are adequately trained and equipped and charge patrons accordingly. Many film and sound archives furnish only full-reel reproductions because of the excessive labor costs involved in copying selected portions as well as possible damage to the film or tape.

Professional-grade playback equipment for film, sound, and video records is not inexpensive but is essential for reliability, durability, and satisfactory quality. It is important to keep the equipment clean and maintained properly. Film archives should provide flat-bed viewers rather than projectors to reduce wear and tear on film copies. The recording mechanism should be disengaged on magnetic tape players and the tabs knocked out of cassettes to prevent accidental erasure. For sound records that have not been dubbed to tape, most archives require staff to play the recording for patrons, who may listen on earphones at a remote listening station. Sound tapes should be played all the way through and not rewound after reference so that the emulsion side of the tape is toward the inside of the reel in what is referred to as the "tails out" position.

Audio-visual archivists frequently encounter copyright questions because many audio-visual records are considered creative works that are entitled to copyright protection. The users of audio-visual archives are also more likely than most researchers to have commercial plans, which increases the need for archival safeguards. Archivists must recognize that all audio-visual records not produced by government employees are subject to copyright and learn as much as possible about the national copyright law.

In most countries, the concept of "fair use" permits archival institutions to make copies for non-commercial purposes. Archivists must furnish researchers with as much information as possible about the copyright status of any material and advise them of their obligation to respect copyright claims. Some potential problems can be avoided by attaching to all archival reproductions a credit line that identifies the creator, any known restrictions on reuse, and the unique archival identification number. Still photo archivists should insist that publishers use the full credit line, including the identification number, which will assist in the retrieval of previously published photographs.

Conclusion

Audio-visual records differ from other archives in important ways. Their complex and diverse physical attributes pose special problems of handling, storage, and preservation; effective management requires specialized knowledge of their distinct characteristics and some special equipment. Satisfactory control and accessibility of audio-visual records require more detailed description than archival institutions normally undertake.

Despite their distinguishing characteristics, however, the basic principles of archival management apply to audio-visual records, with some qualifications. Archives acquire and maintain pictures and sounds for the same reason they preserve written documents: to provide a usable record of the past. Audio-visual archivists must remain ever mindful of their obligation to preserve and make available their entire holdings, not merely the most precious items. The reward for providing the best affordable care to all items is the opportunity to work with materials that not only inform in revealing ways but often delight with aesthetic qualities rarely found in other archival records.

9

Managing Machine-Readable Archives

Bruce I. Ambacher

As citizens and consumers we are well aware of the astounding growth, use, and impact of electronic data processing and computers in every facet of our lives. Computers are used to guide rockets into space and regulate highway traffic; to maintain current inventories and to determine costs and prices; to compute salaries and issue paychecks; to predict weather; to maintain and produce our newspapers, magazines, inter-office mail, manuscripts, and home recipes; to provide administrative record-keeping; and to enhance our leisure and play.

The computer has revolutionized the historical record by altering the ways in which personal, corporate, and governmental records are created, used, maintained, and destroyed or preserved. Over the past few decades, electronic data processing has been introduced first to ease the administrative burden, then to produce and maintain records, and finally to facilitate access to records through automated finding aids and other electronic data bases.

The contemporary integrated office system offers word processing to create, revise, and print text; electronic spreadsheets for statistical information; electronic mail to transmit documents and messages; logging and tracking routines to mark the progress of documents; automated indexing to locate items; and graphic capability to illustrate reports with charts and graphs and permit desktop publishing. Additionally, the automated office environment offers the capability to share this information with virtually any site in the world which is similarly equipped. Increasingly, more advanced computer systems include knowledge systems or expert systems which attempt to replicate human experience and solve problems that previously required human intelligence. These systems are discussed in Chapter Ten. Archivists and records managers are being required to accept and care for the data bases, techniques, and systems adopted by their sponsoring agencies, archival clients, and other records creators.

In a growing number of instances, archivists and records managers are also eagerly adopting this new technology to reduce their own administrative burdens in word processing; records and collections control, description, and access; automated tracking and monitoring systems; and even in preservation efforts.

In the past, most archivists were not part of the computer generation. Computers did not play a significant role in their daily activities and work assignments. This, of course, has changed significantly. Now they must become computer literate. They must understand what machine-readable records and automated techniques are, how they are created, and how they are used. They must be able to communicate with the creators and custodians of machine-readable records, to instruct them in scheduling their data bases, to determine the archival value of their automated creations, and to guide them on the maintenance and use of both machine-readable records and automated techniques.

Understanding the computer system

In order to understand the implications of electronic data processing and machine-readable records, archivists must understand both the technology itself and the environment in which it will function (and create). Failure to do so will separate archivists and records managers further from the current main stream of information management and make them appear to play a less vital part in the information cycle, thus further reducing their influence.

Modern computer systems operate at speeds that are hard to imagine and perform incredibly large volumes of work in a very short period of time. Machine errors, as opposed to human errors, are almost unknown. Their ever-increasing storage capacity offers great advantages, not only to automation users but also to archivists and records managers. Computers also are versatile and can be assigned and complete a multitude of tasks almost instantaneously. This results from the variety of programming instructions which control these operations and from the capacity of the computer to separate programming operations, processing operations, and data representation operations from each other and perform these diverse functions simultaneously.

Computer systems consist of the hardware, including the computer itself and a variety of peripheral equipment, the software, which gives processing instructions to the computer, and the information or data that will be processed. The physical configuration of the computer has undergone immense changes since the first electronic digital computer was developed in 1946. The Electronic Numerical Integrator and Computer (ENIAC) occupied a room sixty feet by twenty-five feet. It contained 18,000 vacuum tubes, 70,000 resistors, and miles of wires. In four decades this thirty-ton computer has been replaced by the modern microcomputer that has thirty times the computing capacity and fits into a briefcase. It is this reduction in size, coupled with the quantum growth in computing power that has moved the computer from its traditional mainframe computer center to the desk-top.

The physical equipment associated with a modern computer, regardless of its size, consists of input devices such as punchcard readers, video display screens and keyboards, tape and disk drives, and scanners to encode the information that is to be processed by the computer; the central processing unit (CPU) which performs the actual computations; and output devices such as keyboards, video display screens, and printers to receive and display the processed information.

The CPU consists of an arithmetic and logic unit (ALU), a control unit, and registers. The ALU is the real "brain" of the computer. It carries out all arithmetic and logic computations and directs the resulting data to the control unit. The control unit regulates the movement of data from input through computation to output. Data is processed within the CPU and control unit at speeds of up to one billion operations per second. Therefore, data resides in the CPU's core storage or integrated circuits for only a fraction of a second.

Electronic data processing operations are controlled by computer programs or instruction packages commonly referred to as software. Through precise steps or actions, taken in an exact sequence in order to produce the desired results, these programs operate or instruct the computer equipment on how to manipulate the data within the CPU and in what form to display or produce the results.

The computer programs which reside permanently within the CPU and control the technical and mechanical aspects of the computer operation are the operating system software. This controls the internal ordering of operations, access to the system, and the storage and retrieval of information.

Applications software consists of commercial programs and custom-designed programs which direct the CPU through a specified series of steps in a specified order to produce the desired results. There is a wide range of commercially-available pre-designed software packages which require a minimum of additional details and instructions in order to perform elaborate manipulations of information. This relieves computer users of the need to learn and use a computer programming language.

Information within a computer system is represented as binary data. The binary digit or *bit* is the smallest or lowest common denominator within the computer. It is the only value which a computer recognizes. It is encoded as the presence or absence of a hole on a punchcard or the presence or absence of an electronic impulse in the CPU or on a magnetic medium such as computer tape. All information must therefore be converted or translated from natural language (letters, numbers, and symbols) into combinations of zeros and ones.

Computer programs contain instructions to combine bits in certain reserved configurations to represent natural language characters and symbols. The process of combining letters to form words, words to form sentences, and sentences to form paragraphs, is the same process utilized within a computer to combine bits into bytes, bytes into fields, fields into records, and records into data files.

Today the two most common codes of reserved configurations used to represent natural language symbols are the Extended Binary Coded Decimal Interchange Code (EBCDIC) and the American Standard Code for Information Interchange (ASCII). In the EBCDIC Code, for example, the reserved combination for a zero is 11110000.

Over the past four decades a variety of storage media has been used to store data for processing electronically. The initial storage media of punchcards and paper tape have virtually disappeared. The most prevalent storage media, in addition to the computer itself, are magnetic tape and magnetic diskettes and disks. Magnetic media consist of a mylar base, a magnetic oxide coating to accept the electronic signal, and a binder or sealer to hold the coating to the mylar surface. The current standard magnetic tape is half an inch wide and 2,400 feet long. Data were first encoded on magnetic tape at 200 bytes or characters per inch (b.p.i. or c.p.i.). Presently, data are encoded at 6,250 b.p.i. At this level of compaction a standard reel of magnetic tape can store up to 180 million characters or the equivalent of 50,000 pages of text. The same amount of information, stored on paper, would occupy up to 135 cubic feet of space.

Benefits of surveying

The process of surveying, inventorying, and scheduling machine-readable records is based on the process for textual records discussed in Chapter Three. Properly implemented, the schedule should significantly reduce both the number of magnetic storage media required and the length of time for which non-permanent information has to be retained. Thus, proper scheduling results in reduced costs and greater efficiency, a significant concern given the cost and the reusability of magnetic tapes, disks, and diskettes. Transferring the records to an archival repository also places the cost burden of reference on that repository and its researchers, not on the program budget of the creator.

Surveying machine-readable records also assists researchers. Surveying promotes the identification, scheduling, and transfer of records to archival facilities where they can be made available to researchers. To date, most machine-readable records remain untapped for secondary analysis. In addition to increasing the amount of records available to researchers, scheduling improves the description of them. By learning about the purposes, themes, and scope of current projects, archivists increase their awareness of current research and gain a better basis for assisting today's researchers, anticipating future research trends, and determining which records to preserve. Surveying permits archivists to provide researchers with information on whether the records they desire exist, where they are, whether they are now, or will in the future, be available for research use, and when.

Surveying does even more to promote the preservation of machine-readable records than it does for the preservation of textual records. Magnetic media are a fragile, non-permanent means of recording information. If they are stored improperly, information encoded as magnetic or electronic impulses can become unreadable through deterioration of the physical surface, interference with the electronic signal, distortion of the data due to improper tension or shrinking or expansion of the tape, or erasure of the information. Additionally, machine-readable records cannot be inspected or interpreted visually. A computer is needed to read such records, and its operation must be based on documentation which describes the content, meaning, and location of specific information and helps to facilitate the translation of the information from machine-readable to eye-readable form. Without this documentation, a computer file may be useless. A survey also promotes preservation by alerting responsible personnel to the existence, volume, and value of the machine-readable records within their area of responsibility.

A machine-readable records survey identifies improper environmental storage conditions and leads either to their improvement or to the relocation of the records to a proper environment. It ensures that documentation adequate for the future use of the records is available and properly scheduled. It also permits the survey archivist to determine how the records will be preserved. In many cases, the same or similar information may be available in more than one physical form. In such cases, it is necessary to decide whether to preserve it either in machine-readable format or in the form of the final printed report or output document, or both. If some cases, it may be desirable to preserve the original information in the form in which it was collected, the machine-readable records derived from it, and the output report.

As with surveys of textual records, the machine-readable records survey furthers an archives' collecting program. Survey archivists know the strengths, weaknesses, and orientation of the repository's collections. A survey can be used as a vehicle to promote acquisitions that will complement or expand current collections.

A machine-readable records survey can also improve the planning of archival programs. Knowledge of the existing volume of records, the portion which is scheduled permanent, and the projected transfer dates permits the archives to better project workload, allocate resources, and train personnel for the most efficient management of machine-readable records.

Finally, a machine-readable records survey, like any other records survey, can be a vehicle for educating and training records managers and archivists. The survey and the accompanying preplanning and research permits records managers and archivists to learn the organization, operations, programs, and missions of the record creator and the principles, regulations, and procedures which are part of working with machine-readable records.

The goal of an inventory or survey is a comprehensive schedule which, combined with general records schedules, covers all records made or received by the records creator. This schedule places all records in the unit of creation regardless of their physical form. Thus, the disposition of all records of an administrative project such as a survey of public school pupils or a study of household food consumption—the study proposal, the questionnaire, the processing tape, the machine-readable master file, and the preliminary and final reports—should be scheduled together. This establishes the relationship of the records and their disposition. It permits the appraisal of textual and non-textual records as an integrated whole. Finally, it can also reduce the volume of records accessioned.

Survey preliminaries

In every case, the actual inventorying, scheduling, and appraisal of machine-readable records is preceded by a detailed study of the creating unit. Survey archivists examine organization charts, mission statements, the annual report, and other publications to understand the creator's mission, programs, and types of records created. The organization charts and the budget provide information on who creates, uses, or processes machine-readable records. The study of existing records disposition schedules and of records which have been previously accessioned from the same institution and its predecessors provides another way to determine the major focus of the agency, the types of data collected, and the probable sources of machine-readable records. The enabling legislation or charter of incorporation and other statutory reporting requirements provide another way to uncover machine-readable records. Finally, preliminary discussions with the records manager help to focus the survey effort and shape the content of the survey instrument.

The survey instrument

The survey instrument should include the name of the agency and the responsible records managers and the names and positions of the program and data processing personnel associated with the records. The series or system title, dates of coverage, and generalized descriptions of the records containing the purpose of the system and types of subjects are also included.

Technical information should indicate the volume of the records, stated in terms of both the physical volume occupied and the number of units of the recording medium used; the arrangement of the records, in terms of both their physical order on the computer reel or disk and the accessing sequence in a disk pack or data base management system; and what user guides or other documentation are available.

The survey form also should indicate whether the records are "software-dependent". If they are arranged in a manner dictated by the pre-programmed computer processing language, the same software will be required for using the records. If this is the case, the difficulty, expense, and technical expertise required to reformat the file into a software-independent format must become an appraisal consideration. The survey should also determine if the records are in a data base management system or if they are instantly accessible because they are maintained in the central processing unit of the computer, that is "on line", at all times. Such records are subject to frequent updating, amendment, and change. This raises the question of which version of the information is the "record" copy. It also raises the question of when the records should be transferred.

The level of detail in the records is another important consideration. The most detailed information possible is the most desirable since it is always possible to create totals, to create a summary record from the detailed responses. The reverse is not possible.

Finally, the survey instrument should deal with the issue of restrictions on access to the information. Access to the records may be restricted because of privacy implications, national security considerations, or because they contain proprietary information. Only a small part of the machine-readable records in any collection will have any kind of restriction on access.

Inventorying and scheduling

The process of inventorying machine-readable records differs from that for textual records only in the extensiveness and diversity of the contacts made outside regular records management channels. These additional contacts may include management personnel responsible for approving the machine-readable project which creates the records, program personnel responsible for creating and using them, data processing center personnel responsible for maintaining and manipulating the records to produce the information and statistics desired, and records managers and archivists responsible for scheduling, appraising, and preserving the data.

A crucial first step in the scheduling process is the creation of a file inventory. It is important to remember that no one list or source will provide all the information required. Data processing center personnel should have a library listing of all machine-readable data files on computer tape or disk pack. This list may or may not contain full titles, dates, creator, and disposition. Combining this list with lists of studies authorized in the budget and studies which produced internal agency reports of some kind and with conversations with various agency personnel should provide a comprehensive inventory of machine-readable records in the agency. Another valuable source may be the agency's public information office's list or directory of files currently available.

Once the inventory process is completed, the scheduling process can begin. Indeed, some series may have been scheduled tentatively already. Disposition decisions should be made in terms of the relationship of the machine-readable records to textual records series, when such a relationship exists. This includes the supporting textual records such as questionnaires, input forms and data collection documents; output reports and lists; and the code definitions, record layouts, and other supporting documentation necessary to process, use, and understand the study.

Disposition decisions should also be made in terms of the detail of information in the records, their manipulability, and whether or not they can be linked with other records to provide a more comprehensive data base. It is relatively easy to make "disclosure-free" versions of the information available while maintaining both appropriate restrictions and individual rights of privacy.

In most cases, only the most complete, most final, most detailed, software-independent version of machine-readable records will be scheduled and retained. Various intermediate stages of the data—processing files, raw input data, print tapes, and previous generation files—are generally disposable. Another consideration when scheduling machine-readable records may be requirements imposed on the creator to maintain such records permanently or to erase them after a specified event or period of time.

Inventorying, scheduling, appraising, and transferring machine-readable records should occur early in their life cycle. Ideally, it should occur during the system-design phase prior to the creation of the records. In almost all cases, it should occur within three years after they have been created. The need for a proper environment, the erasability of the storage medium, and the requirement for complete documentation to access the information requires the earliest possible attention. Those responsible for machine-readable records do not have the luxury of time and events to determine which records have permanent value. They cannot wait for records to be offered. They must be proactive.

A machine-readable records survey is a vital part of any machine-readable records accessioning program. It is both more difficult and more important to the archival program than its textual counterpart. Any repository seeking to accession machine-readable records must be prepared to allocate a more significant portion of its resources to surveying, inventorying, and scheduling them. The end result should be the development of disposition policies and practices that meet all legal concerns, satisfy institutional requirements, and minimize the burden on the creator, the custodian, and the institution as a whole.

Appraisal considerations

The appraisal of the contents of machine-readable records focuses on the archival values developed in Chapter Four. Appraisers ask similar questions in determining whether machine-readable records warrant continuing preservation as permanent records of the creating institution or its archival repository. The traditional archival considerations, however, must be applied with a full knowledge of the special uses and physical characteristics of machine-readable records.

Machine-readable records generally contain demographic information, socio-economic information, information about attitudes and opinions, or some combination of these. The majority of the records currently being preserved were appraised for their informational value; the majority also comprise numeric data preserved for statistical purposes. However, machine-readable records are increasingly appraised and preserved also for their evidential and legal value.

Records with evidential value, whether textual or machine-readable, document the existence, organization, functions, and activities of the creating institution or agency, or contribute to the policies or decisions of that body. Those with evidential value, like textual records, are usually preserved because they also have enduring informational value.

Increasingly, machine-readable records are being appraised and preserved for their legal value, especially when combined with inherent informational value. In a growing number of situations the machine-readable record is the "record" copy, that is, the original form in which the information was collected, used, and maintained. This is especially true in areas such as finance, banking, health, education, social services, trade, commerce, and licensing. While machine-readable records are not accepted as evidence in legal proceedings in all nations, they are in some. Their admissibility and use in this context is dependent upon satisfying concerns that the records in question are as valid and accurate as any others in the system, and that the system itself was not subject to unauthorized or undocumented use and modification.

In spite of the increase in the retention of machine-readable records for evidential and legal purposes, most are retained for their informational value, for their utility in secondary analysis and for research. Several traditional appraisal considerations assume additional significance when considering the informational value of machine-readable records. These include the uniqueness of the information, both in terms of other types of records and of other machine-readable files; the level of aggregation—micro-level data has more research potential than summary data; the ability to link machine-readable records through common internal elements such as address, personal identity number, date of birth, or age; the significance of the information; the institution that collected or created it; and the purpose for which it was used.

The appraisal of machine-readable records is also dependent upon technical considerations which are equal to or may override decisions as to the long-term value of the information which the records contain. These technical factors cannot be overlooked: the readability of the records, the adequacy of the accompanying documentation, the size and internal arrangement of the file, hardware and software considerations, restrictions on access, and preservation requirements.

Appraisal archivists must determine that the physical quality of machine-readable records has not deteriorated since creation or storage. This is accomplished by placing the magnetic tape or disk in a computer and instructing it to read the information. Initial readability problems may be caused by surface dust and blemishes which can be removed by using a tape cleaner. In more persistent cases, data can be recovered by recopying on to a new medium. Both the National Archives of the United States and the National Archives of Canada consider a file to be unreadable if more than 5 percent of the records cannot be used. Such files are not accessioned.

All machine-readable records require textual documentation to help the user to interpret and use them. A record layout and a code book constitute the minimum acceptable level of documentation. Record layouts define the item of information, the length, and the position of each field in the logical record. A code book contains the codes used to represent specific information and establish the acceptable limits for each field or variable. The more complex the records, the more complete the documentation required to use them. It may include the sampling technique and size, instructions to interviewers, the questionnaire, and reports or other analyses of the information. Archivists must review the available documentation from the perspective of an appraiser, a data processor, and a secondary user to determine whether it is sufficient or whether it can be acquired or recreated.

As a part of the initial processing of a machine-readable data file, the size and internal complexity of the file should be determined. If the file is too large for effective use, archivists may determine that a sample should be retained. Any sample must be both statistically valid and preserve the informational value of the whole file.

While the actual physical arrangement of machine-readable records on a computer tape or disk is rarely a problem, any unusual character code, software program, or hardware requirements must be considered when appraising the records. The costs involved in processing the file, whether they are associated with reformatting it or acquiring the necessary software or hardware, must be considered from the perspective of both the repository and the researcher. Due to the costs involved in making machine-readable records both software- and hardware-independent, archival repositories which have accessioned machine-readable records are now re-assessing their policies. Some may begin to accession machine-readable records "as they exist", document their technical requirements, and make them available to researchers in their original format.

Restrictions on machine-readable records arise both from traditional considerations such as privacy and from proprietary considerations such as imbedded software or contractor control over access to the information. Records may be restricted when personal identifiers such as name, address, or personal identity number are included. With textual records, the entire document would have to be restricted for a predetermined time period. With machine-readable records, a disclosure-free version which suppresses the personal identifiers from any copy used by a researcher, or which combines the information of a given subgroup within the records, could be made available, thus providing the information for research use while protecting privacy and honoring restrictions.

Records restricted due to proprietary considerations may include those produced as part of a contact or grant, or those purchased in the course of carrying out normal activities. Gaining clear legal title to machine-readable records produced under contract can be a problem. The contract may have required the delivery of only a final report. The raw data remain the property of the contractor. Indeed, the raw data for this contract may be part of data used for other purposes. Contractor-controlled records may not be available for secondary analysis. Acquiring clear title to the data file resolves this. Contracts should specify that the contractor is to deliver both the raw data and the final report or other specified product.

Information which is accessible only through a proprietary software package has, in essence, a restriction on access. This type of restriction is unique to machine-readable records—only those who have acquired the software have access to the records. Reformatting the information into a software-independent format removes that restriction.

When compared with the considerations and costs involved in a preservation program for textual records, those involved in such a program for machine-readable records become a primary consideration when appraising these records. Since machine-readable records have traditionally been accessioned on reels of magnetic tape, preservation costs are calculated in terms of the cost per reel for accessioning and processing. This includes the creation of a new master copy and a new back-up copy, periodic recopying, and establishing and maintaining a proper environment. Preservation costs also encompass a routine maintenance program with regular physical inspection, annual or biannual cleaning and rewinding under controlled tension, and annual checking of the readability of a small sample of the records.

The appraisal of machine-readable records thus involves a rigorous consideration of both traditional archival values and unique technical considerations. The complete process of identifying, inventorying, scheduling, appraising, accessioning, and initial preservation can cost up to $400 per reel when expressed in terms of both personnel and computer hardware and accessory costs. However, this cost must be assessed against those involved in performing the same steps for the equivalent amount of information in textual format. The enhanced intellectual control and the ease of performing reference on the records also favor machine-readable records rather than textual records.

Accessioning

Accessioning machine-readable records into an archival repository represents a significant action for that repository. Initially, the repository should utilize time-sharing and service contracts with a computer center to provide the computing services necessary to accession, preserve, and provide reference service on machine-readable records. Initial accessioning actions include physical transfer of the records from the creator to the archives. The related documentation and technical specifications required to access and use the records should be transferred at the same time. The machine-readable information should be recopied on to magnetic tape for processing and preservation. Both a master copy and a duplicate or back-up copy should be made.

The quality of the information is confirmed through verification of the data, comparing a sample computer printout or "partial dump" with the documentation. When making this comparison, archivists can confirm the validity, accuracy, and completeness of the record layout and the codes and may uncover errors in the data. the only way to guarantee that a file is error-free is through statistical analysis of the data. When this printout is created, the computer center can provide a record count, that is the exact number of logical records in the file.

Archivists should note any data errors in the documentation package and other descriptions of the file. The contents of the file should not be altered. It is a basic archival principle that all records, regardless of their physical medium, are preserved "as received". To do otherwise could affect the evidential value of the records and the reputation of the repository.

Description

All accessioned records should be included in the repository's basic finding aids, guides, and other descriptive efforts. Most repositories which have accessioned machine-readable records describe the documentation and the records as separate series. The documentation is a basic finding aid, index, or guide to the machine-readable records. In its most usable form it closely resembles a microfilm publication guide and contains a mix of materials created by the records creator and the repository.

Typically, the documentation package includes a title page; an abstract prepared according to an archival information exchange format such as the Machine-Readable Catalog (MARC) Archives and Manuscript Control (AMC) format; a table of contents; an introduction to the records or a project history; a statement on restrictions on access; the code book; source documents such as a survey questionnaire, sample form, or input document; notes by the processing archivist; appendices, if necessary or desirable; and a partial printout of the records.

Reference service

The range of reference services that a repository provides for accessioned machine-readable records will depend on the range of services it provides for other records. It will also depend on the range of computer services it can provide. Repositories with machine-readable records provide access to them by creating copies of the records and the documentation for the user. The user pays the repository for the costs of making such copies. The provision of reference service is developed in Chapter Twelve.

Some repositories with machine-readable records offer more sophisticated services to their users. These include computer searching of the records and the creation of an extract of just the requested information, preparation of a disclosure-free version of the data, statistical analyses of the data, and reformatting the information into a configuration requested by the user, such as a mailing list.

Expanding the archivist's role

All archivists involved with machine-readable records must be proactive. They must focus first on managing information, then on controlling the medium or physical entity which houses it. They can become a recognized, valuable component of the information management team. This requires them to contribute to the design of information systems both to facilitate the creation, maintenance, and use of machine-readable records and to ensure their proper disposition.

Playing a role in the acquisition of computer equipment is a crucial first step. All new equipment must be compatible with existing equipment. If this is not the case, provisions must be made to transfer information from existing to new equipment. Compatibility should be a concern both to archivists and to computer staff. Essential questions in this area relate to the compatibility of computer operating systems and the ability to exchange information between systems through software processing packages such as the Document Interchange Format.

During discussions before a computer system is acquired, especially a system designed to provide an integrated, automated office environment, or during the design phase prior to acquisition, archivists should work with computer staff to ensure that the system provides for both short-term needs and archival management and information control. These include automated indexing of documents to permit both the retrieval of complete documents and full text searching within documents. A second criterion should be the "automatic" assignment of retention or disposition instructions. This is accomplished by incorporating the office filing plan into the applications software to associate index terms with file-plan categories and disposition periods. This feature can be extended into a third criterion, the automatic creation of an archival data base, either by deleting non-permanent information, or by moving permanent information into an archival data base. The latter may require special file-conversion routines. In such cases, archivists should consider incorporating a routine to convert and transfer the file in an archival information exchange format such as MARC AMC or ISO 8211 to facilitate broader access to and use of the file.

Archivists should play a major role in designing a new office automation system. Case studies have demonstrated repeatedly that automation does not overcome poor records management practices. Indeed, it can exacerbate them. Archivists should evaluate each component of the present system and develop an effective records management plan. Linking records management concerns, especially the life cycle of all records, to broader management issues will result in a cost-effective application. It will also enhance the role and perceived value of archivists in managing machine-readable information.

10

New Automation Techniques for Archivists

Thomas E. Weir, Jr

Since people first scratched a permanent record in stone, records keepers have confronted and used changing technology. Records keepers who moved from stone to clay, to papyrus, to parchment, to paper sought, like their modern counterparts, an easier or cheaper way of creating, storing, or retrieving information. Archivists today face analogous changes in information creation, storage, and retrieval. These new record-keeping techniques originate from various methods of automation. Because of the expense and specialized expertise needed to use these techniques, archivists must be exceptionally sagacious in selecting and using them.

Strategic planning and systems analysis

Before examining specific automation techniques, archivists should be familiar with decision-making techniques for automation planning. Two major parts of an automation plan must be the identification of institutional long-range goals and the subsequent study of the needs and possible solutions leading to the implementation of an automated system. These parts of an automation plan are *strategic planning* and *systems analysis*. The strategic plan identifies the goal of the journey into automation. Systems analysis plans and tests the route.

The basic premise of a strategic plan for archival automation is that automation is not a goal; it is a means to a goal. An automated system should not be chosen for an institution simply to have automation; but only as a tool, when appropriate, to meet an institution's archival and management goals. Examples of legitimate goals are to decrease the cost of services, improve the delivery of services, or to provide services that were not practical with a manual system. Selecting these goals and deciding to examine automated techniques to fulfil them is strategic planning. The strategic plan need not be an elaborate document. For a small institution, a one-page memorandum may be enough. No matter how informal the process, identifying long-term institutional goals is a prerequisite to automation planning.

Once goals are identified, an institution must analyze current needs and plan solutions. A premise frequently mentioned in automation studies is: automation cannot succeed unless an effectively operating manual system exists. This admonition should be taken with a grain of salt. An automated mess will still be a mess, only faster and more expensive. If, however, an archives simply automates a manual system and tries only to reproduce its services, the institution may lose opportunities for enhancing its program with capabilities that were impractical with the manual system. More should be sought from automation than an automatic page turner. The rule, therefore, is not: perfect the manual system before automating. The rule is: understand institutional procedures and goals before automating.

Systems analysis consists of several steps. The steps will not be carried out sequentially in practice. Two or more steps will almost always be carried out simultaneously. Furthermore, analysts may "loop" through steps repeatedly until they reach an acceptable solution.

Defining what operations the system will cover is the first part of systems analysis. Will the system generate management statistics as well as provide a means of retrieving information from the holdings? Will it be used only to create a final descriptive product or will it cover all operations from acquisitions through to the final descriptive product? It is important to define the scope of automation in such a way that a workable system can be implemented. The system should not be defined too narrowly, however; it is also important to take full advantage of the capacity of an automated system to produce a variety of outputs and serve a variety of needs. It would be pointless, for example, to create a sophisticated system for producing document descriptions that could not also be used to support equally sophisticated reference services. Defining the scope of the system is therefore crucial to the successful implementation of an economically justifiable system.

Following the definition of system limits, the goals of the specific project should be related to the larger institutional goals laid out in the strategic plan. One cannot complete a journey without knowing one's destination. This step insures that goals, not means, drive the analysis.

After setting goals, systems analysts must make a detailed study of the current manual system and of any operating limitations on the design of an automated system. If competing institutional needs impose an absolute budget limit or a maximum amount of computer access time, this is the time to understand effects of those limits on the chosen goals. In one of many loops made in analysis, the first two steps may have to be re-analysed at this stage because of the limits imposed.

Once the project's scope, limits, and effects are understood, analysts should produce possible solutions. Several possible solutions should be laid out in a draft document for discussion with external users, institutional staff, advisors, funding institutions, or relevant superiors. At this point it is not the choice of hardware and software which is at issue, but the services expected from the system and the automation techniques which will be used to provide them.

When the preferred solution has been identified, the software and hardware required to implement that solution should be determined. At this time it may be necessary to return again to an earlier point in the analysis if the hardware and software chosen so overrun the budget that a simpler system must be designed. A re-analysis of the system goals can be done quickly because the basic information is readily available. This step is crucial because once the computer resources have been selected and purchased, the possibility of change is radically reduced.

The next step is to instal the system, resolve any problems which may arise, and begin operations. As a practical matter, this always takes longer than imagined. The installer will find a variety of problems from minor software errors to unanticipated implications of the chosen solution. If the earlier steps in the analysis have been carefully completed, the risk of unpleasant surprises at this stage should be much reduced.

System maintenance is the final step. Novice automation planners frequently overlook the need to continue investing resources in an automated system after it is installed and working. The need for improvement will become apparent as the system is used. Implementing improvements will require staff time. Also, software and hardware vendors improve their products over time. To decide whether or not the institution should buy such upgraded products will require further analysis. If upgrades are bought, additional staff time or money to hire consultants will be required to introduce them. Eventually, the hardware and software will have to be replaced as they wear out or as newer, improved products become available. Many early systems implemented in archives suffered from inattention to the need for continuing improvements in the system. Systems therefore failed to perform optimally and proved inconvenient to their users. Maintenance and upgrading are as important to successful archival automation as planning and installation.

Because of the cost, the expertise needed, and the potential disruption of institutional programs, careful planning is a prerequisite to successful automation. As a part of the planning process, archivists must be aware of the automation techniques that will affect the archival profession over the next ten years.

The MARC AMC format

One new technique is the MARC AMC format for data exchange between archival systems. MARC stands for Machine Readable Cataloging. AMC stands for Archival and Manuscript Control. By way of analogy, the MARC format has two parts: a standardized box in which to put data and a standardized packing list explaining what may be in the box. The standardized box insures that data packed up by one machine can be unpacked and used by a second machine. The packing list provides a variety of fields intended to capture information in one machine and transfer that information to another. The standardized listing helps the archivist understand the content of a MARC AMC record. Although choosing which fields to use and which fields to index are local decisions, use of the MARC AMC format will lead to more standardized descriptive practices in archives.

The MARC AMC format is an outgrowth of the use of the MARC format in the library field. Libraries began using the MARC format for books in 1968. The chief reason for the format was to exchange cataloging information, first on printed cards and then on magnetic tape, between the United States Library of Congress and other libraries. Later, many libraries used the format to exchange information about cataloged books. The Library of Congress introduced a MARC for manuscripts format in 1973. Archivists did not embrace the format because it primarily supported the cataloging of single items or the manuscripts of published books. The lack of automation experience in the archival profession and the lack of experience in sharing standardized data, whether automated or not, hindered the development of MARC for manuscripts.

In the mid-1970s, the archival profession in the United States became concerned with the potential for duplication of effort between the *Directory of archives and manuscripts*, published by the National Historical Publications and Records Commission, and the *National union catalog of manuscript collections*, published by the Library of Congress. The Society of American Archivists decided to broaden the examination of the issue into an overview of the possibilities for sharing archival information. To this end the National Information Systems Task Force (NISTF) examined several issues. As one outcome, NISTF reworked the MARC for manuscripts format into the MARC AMC format. Major changes supported modern archival collective description of bodies of material rather than the earlier emphasis on item description.

Simultaneously, several major research universities and the Research Libraries Group also considered changes to the MARC manuscripts format. This group reached conclusions similar to NISTF and reinforced the possibility of using the MARC format for the exchange of archival information.

In addition to work in the United States, Canadian archivists have announced their intention to base the development of descriptive standards on the MARC AMC format. With some variations, the MARC for books format is used in many European countries. Although the various European formats do not have the AMC extension to MARC, additions to the national formats could be made to carry archival information. The Swedish National Archives is exploring the possibilities for exchanging data with a specially adapted MARC AMC format. Further developments are likely over the next few years as the work in the United States and Canada becomes more widely known.

Each MARC record in the data base has a leader, a directory, and variable-length fields. The leader and directory are used mainly by the computer itself to process the MARC record. The numbered variable-length fields contain the data with which the practising archivist works. A MARC record may contain information on any level of archival description from a single item to an entire record or archive group. Each record provides a variety of fields divided into eight groups, as follows:

1. Fields 0–99 contain coded or numerical data such as a unique number to identify a specific record or coded geographic or subject data.
2. Fields 100–199 contain the name of the creator of the records, which may be a corporation such as a company, a university, or a government agency. A separately numbered field exists to identify individual creators.
3. Fields 200–299 contain the title of the material being described.
4. Fields 300–399 record the physical attributes of the materials. These may include linear or cubic measurements as well as item counts where appropriate. Information about the arrangement of materials is considered a physical attribute and is described in field 351.
5. There are no fields numbered 400–499 in the MARC AMC format. Fields 500–599 contain a wide variety of descriptive notes. Narrative notes can be lengthy and distinguish the use of the MARC format for archives from its use for books. Field 520 is the primary note and contains the scope note. There are approximately twenty-five other types of notes fields provided for information such as restrictions on access, restrictions on use, the availability of related material, history of the creating agency or biography of the creating person, and actions taken on the material.
6. Fields 600–699 contain the major indexing information such as subject or geographical terms, and the names of persons and corporations that are the subjects of the records. Although locally-defined information may be included in these fields, the data entered generally conform to a shared standard. This is because MARC AMC records are a means of sharing descriptive materials and, therefore, a means of searching the materials must also be shared. In the United States, the Library of Congress name authority list for personal, corporate, and geographical names and the same organization's list of subject headings are the standards most often used. Use of such authorities is not part of the MARC AMC format and not mandatory. In the absence of specific archival standards, however, the use of these standards is widespread in the United States.
7. Fields 700–799 primarily contain added entries. These are generally the names of co-creators of the material being described. Field 773 contains the identification of a superior description in the data base of which the material being described is a part. For example, it can be used to identify the record or archive group of which a series or class is a part. The 773 field thus allows identification of hierarchical relationships between the parts of a collection and the collection as a whole.
8. Fields 800–899 primarily contain the address of the repository holding the material.

MARC does not make the use of any field mandatory. Local system designers make such decisions. Also, MARC AMC contains the 600 type fields which may hold standardized index terms, but the use of standard terms is not mandatory. Indexing can be supported locally by allowing the searching of the text of the note fields or by building an index of the 100 and 700 type fields that allowed searching only for the name of the records creators.

The MARC AMC format is a constantly evolving standard that can increase the availability and utility of descriptive information in archives. Use of the format can increase both the use of archival materials and the value of archives to institutions that support archival repositories as research resources.

Optical disk systems

Optical disks derive their name from an optical technique that creates and reads the message on the disk. This distinguishes optical disks from more customary means of recording information in machine independent forms, such as normal audio records that have a mechanical reading mechanism, namely a needle which physically rides on the disk and "feels" the bumps and grooves to reproduce the message. Magnetic recordings on tape or disk are a more recent machine-readable recording method. In magnetic recording the read head reads magnetic signals stored on the recording medium to reproduce the message.

The three optical media under discussion—video disk, write-once digital optical disks, and CD-ROM—use the same general method to record the message. A high-power laser beam transforms the surface of a metallic disk so that when the disk is read by focusing a weaker beam on the surface, the beam is reflected off the disk in varying degrees of brightness. Areas hit by the "write" laser will have a different reflectivity than other areas. The differences between the reflectivity of affected and unaffected areas constitute the means of storing the message. How the message is encoded, how the disks are produced, and the most appropriate uses vary from one type of disk to another.

Video disks were the first commercially available form of optical disk. Information is recorded on video disks as an analog signal (the other disk types are recorded digitally). "Analog" means that the information is recorded in a manner that resembles a wave form, not the discrete on/off sequences of a digital disk.

Video disks are played back on to a television screen. Because of the inherent limitations of resolution on a television screen (524 lines for the entire screen in the United States), video disks are not suitable for the reproduction of written documents because the finer writing or printing on a document would be unreadable. The video disk is useful for the reproduction of photographic images and motion pictures. (Video disks can, technically, be used to record digital data, but this is not the chosen technique for recording such data and will not be discussed here.)

Video disks have been used successfully for the distribution of still and motion picture images. A video disk can hold about 50,000 still images or seventy-two minutes of audio and sound for a motion picture. It can also hold a combination of still and motion pictures, audio, and large-type text.

Video disks can also be used creatively as a teaching tool to support archival reference. Not only can they carry both still and motion pictures, they can be indexed so that it is possible to jump from one part of the disk to another. Random access allows a microcomputer and a video disk to provide customized instructions based on users' reactions to specific questions put to them through the system. Building a sophisticated system to introduce users to an archives, its finding aids and records is a potential reference use of video disks. No archives currently uses such a system but training based on video disks is widely used in a variety of self-instructional situations in the United States, Europe, and elsewhere.

Optical digital "write once, read many" (WORM) disks are another major form of optical media. Optical digital disks contain information stored in binary form: in ones and zeros, on/off marks, or black and white. Each one or zero represents what in computer jargon is called one bit.

Information is stored on the disk by having the laser burn small holes in the disk or otherwise transform the surface. The holes represent ones and the spaces between them represent zeros. This method of recording can be used to store either images or characters. When the disk stores images, the on/off marks indicate the presence or absence of black or, in more sophisticated systems, gradation of grey or even different colors. The number of dots per inch used in reproducing the image determines its quality. Most systems work at 200, 300, or 400 dots per inch. At 200 dots per inch, a A4 sheet of paper would be represented by 3,740,000 dots. Compression techniques can reduce this by about 90 percent, making it possible to represent an A4 page by some 374,000 dots. This is still a lot of dots, but fortunately these disks hold one gigabyte (a billion dots) on each side.

When a basic system scans a document, the machine must decide whether to record a grey area as black and white. The difference between white and black is decided by a "grey area threshold", which can be adjusted from one document to the next to improve image quality. Because the dots are so fine, mixing black and white dots in a small area will make it appear grey when reproduced. Adjusting the grey threshold can considerably enhance the image; for example, a dark background can be dropped out, allowing the text or image to be much clearer. Image enhancement is one advantage which an optical disk has over more traditional storage technologies such as microfilm.

When the disk stores characters (letters, numbers, or common punctuation or mathematical symbols), it stores information similarly to text created and stored by a word processor. Both image storage and character storage have advantages. Image storage is advantageous because it allows a facsimile reproduction to be stored and enhanced. Character string storage is advantageous because text can be searched or indexed like any text document. Furthermore, much less space is needed to store the text as characters than is needed to store the same document as an image.

To understand the capacity of a digital system to store text, return for a moment to the standard 8½ × 11 inch sheet of paper. Assume 52 single-spaced lines of text. Each line of text has 64 characters (including spaces). Therefore, there are 3,328 characters per page. Eight bits are required to represent each character; a total of 26,624 bits per page plus a small amount for line terminators, top and bottom margins, and similar requirements—say, 26,700 bits per page. This is less that 10 percent of the space needed to store the same document as a compressed image. Text-compression routines may reduce this storage requirement even further.

Optical digital disks can store both facsimile images and characters simultaneously. The United States Patent and Trademark Office (PTO) is currently developing an optical disk system that will have most of the patents issued after 1970 stored as both text and image. The system will also store images of all patents issued before 1971. When the system is complete, the PTO will have thirty terabytes (a terabyte is a trillion bytes) stored on-line with a maximum recall rate of ten seconds for the first page and a maximum of one second for flips to following pages. This permits the text to be searched and also allows the image to be displayed.

The primary application of this technology in archives is to store enormous amounts of information for rapid recall. Documents can be randomly retrieved from disks and displayed, printed on paper, reproduced on a microform, or copied to magnetic tape. The United States National Archives is currently working on a test of a WORM system that will include the scanning of over one million images of the compiled military service records of Tennessee Confederate soldiers during the Civil War. The test will examine the costs of scanning large volumes of handwritten and printed nineteenth-century documents as well as the advantages and costs of document image enhancements. The report on the test will be available by September 1988.

WORM systems have several practical limitations. Because there are no standards for WORM drives, the disks cannot be exchanged between systems. The information from the disk can, of course, be reproduced as mentioned previously but the disks themselves are not transportable.

A second major limit is the start-up cost. WORM systems are expensive. Even if an off-site contractor scans the documents, the simplest single disk playback system costs thousands of dollars. To justify such costs, an archives needs an enormous amount of data that requires rapid recall.

The need to convert data from optical disks to whatever the next storage system will be is an additional limitation. How long will optical disk systems be used? How much will it cost to get to the next storage system? Whatever the life of the disk itself, the system that supports it will probably disappear before the disk does. Conversions in machine-readable media are becoming standard procedures and are therefore not likely to be prohibitively costly in the future. And the advantage of having information in digital and therefore manipulable form will offset cost problems in some cases.

CD-ROM, Compact Disk-Read Only Memory, is a special variant of the optical disk. It is a close cousin of today's CD-Audio disk. Like the CD-Audio disk, most CD-ROM disks are 120 mm, or 4.72 inches, in diameter. Information to be stored on CD-ROMs is scanned by the same method as other optical digital disks: read by a laser and stored digitally as an image or a text string. It is also read back the same way—by a weaker laser running over the disk and noting the variations in the disk surface as either ones or zeros.

There are two major differences between WORM disks and CD–ROM disks: standards and end-user disk creation. Standards for CD–ROMs exist for both the physical medium and the file structure. The standard CD–ROM disk holds 550 megabytes of data or approximately the contents of 2,500 floppy disks of the type used in an IBM PC or compatible microcomputer. The standard may increase to 660 megabytes in the near future. The data are recorded on the disk in a single spiral three miles long with 16,000 tracks per inch. (An IBM PC disk, by comparison, has ninety-six tracks per inch). The existence of standards makes the CD–ROM suitable as an exchange medium because many systems can read the same disks.

Unlike WORM disks, which are written directly on the storage medium, CD–ROM disks are produced by a stamping process. After the document is scanned and the image or text file is stored, a master disk is created. Negative stamper disks are made from the master and distribution copies stamped from the negative stampers. The original mastering costs about $3,000. Disks delivered in quantities of over 1,000 can now be as cheap as a few dollars. As blank disks become more readily available, the price should fall even more.

Another price-reducing factor for CD–ROM systems is their close relation to CD–Audio players and disks. The same machine, with minor modifications, can play both CD–Audio and CD–ROM disks, making it possible for the players to be relatively inexpensive.

Drawbacks do exist, however. Although a CD–ROM can hold document images, few people are using them for image storage systems. Most disk producers are selling information stored as text files. The capacity of a CD–ROM disk is considered too small for image storage. If an image storage system is needed, video disks for in-house use and external distribution, or WORM disks for in-house use only, are the media of choice.

When storing text files, however, shortage of space is not the constraint. The opposite problem occurs. CD–ROMs may be too large for an archives to use. A CD–ROM can store 270,000 pages of single-spaced text. The *Grolier academic American encyclopedia* (without pictures) takes up only about 20 percent of a disk. If the storage of retrieval software and overhead such as indexes are taken into account, usable disk capacity shrinks to about 160,000 pages, still an ample amount. A typical large-size reference book of 1,000 pages can be stored more than a hundred times on a single CD–ROM disk.

The obvious solution to this embarrassment of riches is a shared program. This might result in the distribution of a collection of finding aids related to a region or subject on one disk. For archives of political subdivisions, archival finding aids might be just one type of information available on a "regional information disk". Also on the disks might be a regional government personnel directory, a government organizational manual, local laws, and a bibliographic file of relevant government publications.

A ready market exists for reference disks. Libraries throughout the world are beginning to buy information stored on CD–ROM. Currently the primary users are business and academic libraries but as the price of players and disks falls and as the amount and variety of information distributed on CD–ROM increases, CD–ROM players will also be used in public libraries. CD–ROM is a most promising means for the distribution of archival information to both academic audiences and the general public.

Optical character recognition

Optical character recognition (OCR) converts typed or printed documents into machine-readable files. Services that can convert handwritten material into machine-readable text files are evolving. The primary utility of OCR for archives is the conversion of existing finding aids into machine-readable text files so that they can be stored or distributed on other media.

There are several options for text conversion. Service bureaus will take an archives text and return a machine-readable file with a predetermined accuracy rate. This may be the best approach for many archives, particularly those with many finding aids printed with varying type fonts.

An alternative is the purchase of an OCR machine. Large OCR machines cost tens of thousands of dollar and are out of the question for a one-time conversion program for archives. Small desk-top machines that can read a wide variety of fonts are now available for well under $3,000. (The same machine would have cost $15,000 only two years ago). These machines are designed to read modern typewriter typefaces. In one test using typed documents from older (1930s and 1940s) typewriters, the OCR machine successfully read about 60 percent of the typewritten documents fed to it. Although the machine supports only a limited number of typefaces, that was not the major problem. Most typefaces, even those created on older typewriters, were readable only if the type was clean and the letters aligned.

Small OCR systems or the use of a service bureau will prove to be the answer to the question facing many archivists: "how do I get those finding aids on my shelf into this neat and shiny new electronic filing system on my desk?"

Artificial intelligence

From the first conception of a computer, before a practical working machine was even built, researchers began to ask, "why can't a computer be more like a person?" Computer scientists hoped to endow the computer not only with the ability to carry out complex procedures at blindingly fast speed, but also to give it the ability to reason. The general field of building computers that can reason is known as artificial intelligence. Although the field is broad and in many ways still Utopian, two areas are of special interest to archivists: expert systems and natural language systems. Both of these approaches to artificial intelligence have had some practical success outside of academic settings.

Expert systems attempt to capture both the knowledge of human experts and the rules of thumb they use to reach a conclusion. It has long been noted that human experts do not seem to follow a straightforward progression through a set of rules to reach a conclusion. They make all sorts of leaps of logic during problem analysis, and also seem to be able to derive a conclusion from a brief examination of an issue. Human chess players usually choose the correct move on first guess. They then systematically examine a set of alternatives, but the first guess is usually right. Determining how chess masters select the first guess and how they limit the set of alternatives is an example of the problems met in developing expert systems.

Capturing expert information and recording it in a manner useful to a computer is called "knowledge engineering". To develop an expert system, the expert systems specialist works with the domain expert (for example, with one or more archivists in an archival institution). The systems specialist builds both a knowledge base representing the factual knowledge the expert possesses and a set of rules of thumb representing the analytical tools he uses. There may be from several hundred to several thousand rules. The expert system is usually programmed with either a specialized language such as LISP or Prolog or with an "expert system shell", a specialized program for expert systems development.

In an experiment carried out by a contractor for the National Archives in the United States, the contractor used a small expert systems shell to develop a successful test of the principle of using expert systems in archival reference. The contractor, working with an archivist, developed a knowledge base and a set of rules. The system was designed to answer questions about the trans-Mississippi West in the late nineteenth and early twentieth centuries.

In the test, when the archivist and the expert system answered the same set of questions, the archivist did better than the system. The system did, however, recommend several series that the archivist had overlooked. On review, the archivist agreed that the series recommended by the system met the requirements of the researcher. The expert system also recommended the series in the order that it calculated was most likely to be of use to the researcher.

The expert system experiment was a success. There were clear limitations but most were traceable to the severe limits of the software and hardware or the thesaurus. The errors were, in principle, repairable.

There are at least three uses of expert systems to support an archives program. An expert system could be created to be the "front end" for a standard data base. It would contain rules, not about the information in the data base, but about how to use the data base. It would help new users to learn to use the data base and would analyze the queries of even experienced researchers to find logical gaps, queries likely to return absurdly large number of descriptions, or other problems.

A second method would assist researchers directly by suggesting series or collections to use as the result of a query. With this type of expert system, researchers would conduct research on the content of the finding aid data base directly through the expert system.

A third possible use is to support archival staff in day-to-day work and to train new staff members. Rather than allowing the public to be the primary user of the expert system, the staff might use it to help the public. Because the staff use the system regularly, less emphasis on ease of use would be needed. Furthermore, because a good expert system not only provides answers but can explain how it arrived at them by explaining the rules of thumb that it invoked, it can capture and transfer to new staff the rules of thumb for searching used by experienced staff as well as their factual knowledge.

There are drawbacks. Cost is a major factor. To build a fully useful expert system would, until recently, have required at least a minicomputer or a specially dedicated machine designed from the ground up to support artificial intelligence systems. Furthermore, because the field is new, expert systems programmers or knowledge engineers are few and expensive. Fortunately, the newly released Intel 80386-based microcomputers will support sophisticated expert systems at a reasonable cost. As these systems become more cheaply available and more expert systems are implemented, experienced programmers will become more readily available. Expert systems are an area of archival automation that needs much more research but is likely to provide a path of development for archivists.

Natural language analysis is a second method of artificial intelligence that may support archival reference. Natural language systems attempt to "understand" a natural language such as English the way a human understands it. Natural language systems should be able to remove ambiguities from a text. A natural language system would not interpret the sentence "Time flies like an arrow" to mean that a species of flies, called time flies, have formed an attachment to an arrow shot from a bow but rather would understand the sentence the same way that a human speaker would understand it—time, a measure of temporal existence, passes as swiftly as an arrow passes.

Currently available on-line natural language systems generally translate user queries from an English sentence into commands the computer can understand. In these applications, the natural language system acts as a sophisticated thesaurus, not really interpreting the full meaning of the sentence in the manner of a full-blown natural language system. If the development of natural language systems can be accomplished, queries can be asked of a data base in natural language. Instead of forming a query using specific commands and the exact terms from a controlled vocabulary such as "FIND SUBJECT PHRASE UNITED STATES HISTORY, REVOLUTION", or whatever is appropriate, the machine could be queried in plain English, "What have you got on the Revolution?" The machine might reply, "Which Revolution are you interested in?" The dialog would continue until the machine thought it had a searchable query.

Not only may the query be in natural language, but the text of a finding aid or document may be searched in natural language. A user might search the text of a finding aid directly without resorting to a standardized index terminology. The natural language system would interpret the meaning of the words of the text in the context of the finding aid and reduce the ambiguity common in natural language so that searches would find a high percentage of relevant information. This would reduce the need for the time-consuming and expensive task of establishing controlled vocabulary terms from a thesaurus and might conceivably pay for itself in a large system.

The primary problem with natural language systems is that the researchers have a long way to go to find anything like a generalized solution that can handle text with a wide variety of subjects. Progress is extremely slow, but it is being made. It will probably be several years before sophisticated support will be available.

High-speed text retrieval

Many archivists would like to be able to support the direct searching of document text at high speed with or without a natural language interface. The text searched may be either that of finding aids or that of the records themselves. Current systems generally provide text searching by building an inverted index, a list of words from the text file which are recorded in an index file with pointers to their locations in the original documents. This method has several limitations. A large amount of memory is required to maintain the inverted list. As the list grows, the machine requires increasing time for each update of the index. Finally, the index may grow so large that it slows down searches. Though inverted indexes may be useful in small data bases of a million characters, larger data bases need a different solution.

A newly-available hardware solution now allows faster searching of the text directly without the creation of an inverted index. This new technique is called "associative processing" and uses parallel processing technology. With an associative processor, no inverted index is created. The processor scans text directly. Instead of scanning words one at a time sequentially as in a word processor, many words can be scanned simultaneously. This provides a high-speed text search.

High-speed text searches may be used to search text in a straightforward manner in the same way as an inverted index. The most powerful use would be in the support of a natural language artificial intelligence system. With such a system, text could be gone through rapidly and analyzed by the natural language system. High-speed searches supporting a natural language system might bring startling results to text searches that are now slow and inefficient.

The drawbacks are obvious. Parallel processing is new and expensive. Natural language search techniques are not fully developed. While the hardware part of searching systems will become much more readily and inexpensively available within three years, it will be some time before sophisticated natural language systems become readily available.

Searching the text of documents directly

Perhaps the ultimate finding aid is no finding aid. In the future the techniques discussed above may eventually bring about the conversion of many documents to machine-readable form, allow their storage on a compact medium, and support their searching with minimum indexing and only skeletal finding aids. All the necessary techniques are at least well-defined now, and some are in operation. Within a few years we will see at least some parts of this scenario being carried out.

When can we expect to find our favorite archives in a box under the Christmas tree? Well, not soon. Although there is reason to be optimistic about new automation techniques, there is a long way to go before any are both widely available *and* affordable. There will be an even longer time before some of them will work in the day-to-day real world.

Professional developments

Some of these techniques can and should be developed for use by archivists. No institution, however, can develop them alone. To bring advanced automation techniques to a practical state before archivists can begin to use them, archivists must work together to support and fund research and the development of practical automated systems. Some issues, such as indexing, need a wide variety of points of view. Work by one archives will not apply directly to all others. The development of shared approaches will require the work of many and varied institutions. Some automation issues facing archivists, such as CD–ROM, require cooperation to effectively use the large amounts of storage made available.

Archivists must work together to use automation effectively to meet the continuing basic goals of archival programs: to provide better and more efficient service to more users.

11

Oral History

William W. Moss

Concept and basic principles for archivists

The concept "oral history" is generous, making precise definition difficult; but most oral history fits into the idea of deliberate and systematic recording of oral testimony based on human memory and experience. Its purpose is to enrich the store of historical evidence available for historians and other social scientists. Those who value oral history presume and assert that human memory and testimony of human recollections and reflections or transmission of oral traditions contain evidence that must be taken into account for successful historical analysis.

Oral history includes oral tradition, folk wisdom and folk history that have traditionally been handed down from generation to generation solely by word of mouth, but that more recently are recorded on audiotape, motion picture film, or videotape. It includes deliberate and systematic interviewing of contemporaries, and the recording of those interviews to capture personal recollections and reflections about matters known at first-hand by the present generation, or matters derived from immediate experience with parents' and grandparents' generations.

Two common sorts of oral history are the interviewing of one person by another about his life or his role in historically significant events, and the recording by one person of an example of an oral tradition narrated or recited by another. Combinations of these two modes, and multiple interviewers or multiple respondents are less common, but not without significant examples. The medium of recording is most commonly magnetic audiotape, but videotape is used increasingly, and oral history in sound motion pictures and other media such as disk recordings, wire recordings, or even stenographic notes is not unknown. Oral history archives may include audio recordings, visual recordings, and written transcripts.

Initially scorned by historians accustomed to the immutable, if not altogether more reliable, evidence of written documents, oral history has come to be an accepted addition to the historical evidence which is available for research. It requires appraisal and comparison with other evidence for effective use just as does documentary evidence. Archives are being required to accept and administer increasing volumes of oral history, just as they are also accepting other forms of non-paper documentation that were uncommon in archives of an earlier generation. Archivists accession oral history materials collected by others, but they also collect and record oral traditions and contemporary interviews themselves to broaden the base of documentation. Oral history has become a part of archival experience, and archivists must know and understand it in order to meet their professional obligations.

The first and most critical principle of oral history is that one should never confuse the record produced with the original events, nor even with the underlying memories of those events. The record produced by the oral history collection process is a recording of an interview or a narration. It is not, properly speaking, a record of past events, even if those events may be narrated, recited, recollected, reflected upon, examined, or evaluated in the course of the recording. Historians consult this record to seek and find evidence of what took place in the past, and after suitable weighing of the value of that evidence in the context of all other evidence, may employ it in historical description and analysis. For those who manage oral sources, "the record" is the recording of an interview, narration, or perhaps a conversation among several people that occurred at a time and perhaps in a place well removed from the events narrated.

A second principle is that the original recording as it came from a recording device is the archival item requiring custodial integrity. It, and only it, is the best evidence of what occurred in the interview or recording session. Neither subsequent copies nor transcripts, no matter how carefully prepared and no matter how useful they may be, are equal to original recordings as evidence of what transpired. The best standard for any copy is the original itself. The task of archivists is to preserve it.

The third thing archivists must understand is that when they themselves engage in oral history collection, actually conducting interviews or recording oral tradition, they participate in and to some extent determine the nature and content of the record produced. This is fundamental engagement in record creation with the inherent dangers of bias and self-interest. Sharing in the creation of the record puts archivists in unfamiliar and perhaps invidious positions which may jeopardize their preferred status of neutrality regarding record content. This involvement threatens their integrity as impartial servants of all research interests. In oral history, both interviewer and respondent are joint creators of the record. They share responsibility for its validity and integrity. Archivists cannot, as did the ancient British historian, Bede, disclaim responsibility for errors in what others have recounted for the record. This is uncomfortable ground for those whose traditional responsibility has been limited to ensuring the continued integrity of records delivered into their custody, and has not extended to ensuring the integrity of the records' creation. Supporters of archival involvement argue that it is archivists, with privileged access to sources, who are best able to find genuine *lacunae*, and who thereby can focus effectively and economically on oral sources that truly are fruitful. In certain cultures, particularly those without written archives, collection of a cultural "archive" may require heavy reliance on oral sources and collecting them may be a primary task of archivists.

Beyond these principles, archivists must understand basic differences between oral history and oral tradition, the genesis and development of modern oral history as it is practiced in the latter half of the twentieth century, and the normal procedures of its collection, processing, preservation, and reference use.

Oral history and oral tradition

Oral history and oral tradition share a common oral nature. There are differences between them, but the distinctions are difficult to maintain in practice. There is much similarity in how they are collected, processed, stored, and made available to researchers, and in the equipment required to record and preserve them. Both those who focus on oral history and those who collect oral traditions tend to call themselves oral historians, and they have much in common.

Oral traditions are accounts and other relics from the past, orally transmitted and recounted, that arise naturally within and from the dynamics of a culture. They are shared widely throughout the culture even though they may be entrusted to particular people for safekeeping, transmittal, recitation, and narration. They are organic expressions of the identity, purpose, functions, customs, and continuity of their cultures. They would exist, have existed, and continue to exist without benefit of written notes or sophisticated recording devices. They are not direct experiences of their narrators, and they must be transmitted by word of mouth to qualify as oral traditions.

Oral history, on the other hand, is usually an academic process of inquiry into memories of living people who have direct experience of the recent past. This inquiry and the responses it generates are recorded to supplement written records that have been found wanting in some measure for historical analysis. It is a studied, abstract, analytic practice of historians and other social scientists. It relies heavily on recording devices. Oral history was developed partly to remedy deficiencies in written records. It presumes an existing context of written records, in which research identifies deficiencies that may be remedied somewhat through recording testimony by participants in, and witnesses to, significant events. Oral history's product is subject to textual criticism and content analysis by the same standards of value, integrity, consistency, congruity, and utility that are applied to other forms of historical evidence.

Oral traditions may be collected as an academic exercise and thereby subsumed under oral history; but in their very nature they have an inherent additional social function and value in contributing to the cohesion, dynamic evolution, and durability of the culture they represent. Oral traditions are changed in the very act of recording them from dynamic, developing, and evolving self-consciousness into fixed and static "snapshots" of the culture and its oral tradition at one point in time. By being recorded, they are abstracted from the cultural process that creates and nurtures them. Thus, from the moment of their recording, recorded traditions become anachronous except as historical samples. Recorded recollections and reflections of direct experience are also "snapshots", of someone's changing perspective on the past, conditioned by intervening experience. These recordings must be seen as samplings rather than as being pervasive through time. However, upon close examination, even written documents that arise organically out of the transactions they represent are themselves similarly limited as discrete historical samples, points along a continuum of chronological development.

Oral traditions exist in highly literate societies with impressive written archives as well as in those without them. The written record may often have a parallel oral tradition that serves its social function best when unrecorded. Paradoxically, capturing that oral tradition may be essential to understanding the full history of a literate society. The most important use of oral tradition, however, lies in documenting societies without written records. In many cases it may be the chief way in which the society's past may be reconstructed and recorded for future research, even though archaeological evidence may also survive.

Oral history—genesis and development

Oral historians are fond of seeking and finding the source of their craft in antiquity. In the Zhou Dynasty of China (1122–255 B.C.), officers of the court were appointed to go out among the people to collect their sayings for the information of the emperor and court historians. Somewhat more recently, Herodotus and Thucydides relied on eyewitness accounts for their histories. Certain eighteenth- and nineteenth-century European historians such as Voltaire and Michelet did not limit their sources to written documents of state and official archives. Both relied on recollections and reflections of eyewitnesses. Every generation in every land has probably expressed some regret that more of the lives and experiences of participants in great events were not more often and more extensively committed to written records for the benefit of future generations. We may assume that oral history, or something very much like it, has roots in basic human need as well as in practical utility for historians. It is also evident, from the viewpoint of the latter half of the twentieth century, that the sea change of democratic revolutions throughout the world has encouraged the emergence of a form of popular history intended to redress the historical balance for those neglected by legalistic and bureaucratic histories and archives that favored church and court.

Oral history initially met strong resistance from documentary historians of the schools of Leopold Von Ranke and Charles Seignobos, and it is only in the latter half of the twentieth century that it has come to play a large role in general historiography and archives. Three factors are responsible for this development.

Political and economic evolutions and revolutions throughout the world, particularly in the twentieth century, have produced a growing popularization of government and the participation by broader masses of people in every aspect of modern life, from production and commerce to government and scholarship. In a world of widespread literacy and information sharing, history is no longer the exclusive property of church, state, or even of academic historians, as historical writing by journalists amply demonstrates. Increasing literacy and non-literate mass communications mean that more and more people both receive information and shape its creation, organization, and dissemination.

A second factor in the development of oral history has been a series of products of the technological revolution, particularly since World War II. Technology has, on the one hand, deprived historians of at least some documentation they relied on in the past. At least some matters that might in an earlier age have been committed to writing are now communicated by telephone, radio, television, or even in face-to-face talks through the relative ease and speed of modern transportation. At the same time, modern technology has provided new recording media to capture information that otherwise might have been lost. Television brings us the horrors of war or natural calamity in ways that an earlier generation could not imagine without direct experience. Oral history, at least in its present scale and scope of practice, could not have been possible without the development of light-weight, highly-dependable, high-fidelity devices such as audiotape and videotape recorders.

A third factor in the development of oral history has been the disciplined work and creative imagination of a number of historians, notable among them Allan Nevins of Columbia University, who saw and appreciated the potential of accurately recorded inquiries and memoirs as a means of supplementing written documentation. Paralleling the efforts of Nevins in what has come to be known as "élitist history", were those of anthropologists and "social historians" who sought the oral traditions and testimony of primitive peoples and ordinary common folk for use in better describing conditions of the past, and who, in using tape recordings to do so, found themselves allied with Nevins and the élitists in technological novelty.

Proliferation and popularization have been mixed blessings for oral history. As in all growth industries, unruly development has produced uneven quality, and a need for discipline. Two lines have been taken to bring some order into the field. One is an assumption that oral history is primarily a technique to serve a parent discipline such as history, anthropology, or political science. When in such service, it should be measured by the criteria of the discipline served, not by other criteria, even if "oral history" seems to urge historiographic standards. The second line is efforts by professional oral history societies to set standards by example, to develop a literature of exemplary practice, and to reflect upon and issue guidance for evaluating oral history activity. The 1981 *Oral history evaluation guidelines* published by the American Oral History Association are the clearest, most complete statement of standards developed to date for the craft of oral history.

Oral history collecting

Oral history usually enters archives in one of two ways. It may be accessioned incidentally, along with other documentation, as part of a transfer of records or a donation of papers; or the staff of an archives or an associated office may engage in active interviewing and recording of oral sources to supplement and enrich the documentation already in hand.

Active collection of oral sources is very demanding of archival resources, and stinting of resources produces a poor product. Unless archivists are convinced it is worthwhile, and unless they are willing to accept some share in record creation as an archival responsibility, they should not make the commitment required. They should leave oral source collecting to other agencies, and content themselves with receiving its products.

For those who choose to engage in active collecting, after thoughtful deliberation and weighing the costs and benefits, the list of sources for further reading may prove helpful in making the most of opportunities and resources.

Oral history collecting and oral tradition collecting have some significant differences. While both forms require primary focus on the memory of the person delivering the testimony or narration, the role of the collector or interviewer in each case is different. For oral traditions the collector goes to extraordinary lengths to avoid intruding his own influence into the recorded product. His objective is to record the tradition as close to its pure form as possible. Once the presence of a recording device as an intruding influence is accepted as a tolerable cost for gaining the product, the collector then avoids to the greatest extent possible any initiatives on his part that might influence the course or content of the material being narrated or recited.

In oral history interviewing, however, the collector is at least a catalyst who prompts responses and provides opportunities to draw out as much as possible from the memory of the person being interviewed. This activity may extend to critical challenge so as to account for suppressed evidence, opposed views, or information at variance with the testimony presented. Intrusion of the interviewer, far from being inadvertent, is intentional and essential to a successful product. Those who are best at oral history interviewing try to suppress their own biases, seeking thereby to acquire products useful to the broadest possible range of potential users; but that is different from avoiding intrusion entirely.

Factors affecting quality

Oral history, whether from intrusive interviewing or oral tradition collecting, is most productive as a useful source for history when it is deliberately and thought-fully conducted. It is least useful when it is redundant to common knowledge already recorded elsewhere or cluttered with trivial information lacking histori-cal significance. It shares these characteristics with all other records and docu-mentation. Careful planning and preparation are required to be certain that oral history is the best means for obtaining the information required; that a represen-tative sample of the best available people experienced in the matters to be researched and recorded is chosen; that interviewers and collectors are selected carefully for their knowledge of the pertinent subject areas and for their inter-viewing or collecting skills; and that interviewers and collectors are matched with those to be recorded so as to produce the best opportunities for fruitful results.

Orderliness of procedures and strict accountability of all materials are required to assure the integrity and authenticity of the product. Legal and ethical concerns with respect to the property of the product (the record and its intellec-tual content), the relationships between collectors and respondents, and those between collectors and the sponsoring archives, all must be established to mutual satisfaction so as to avoid future contention over use of the product, and to avoid excessive self-interest in project design and execution.

The historical value of each recording is dependent in great measure on the mastery that an interviewer or collector already has over the subjects to be dis-cussed or gathered in the recording. This mastery, grounded in research in avail-able sources prior to the recording event, must be sufficient to give respondents confidence in the integrity and capability of the person doing the collecting. Early respect for the knowledge and understanding of the collector by respondents is the most effective device for assuring the integrity and usefulness of their own contribution. Quality may depend on the choice of location and the circum-stances of recording. In some cases, options are limited to either accepting a particular situation or losing the opportunity entirely. In others, the recording site may be chosen carefully to encourage maximum cooperation from the respondent and the best possible recording conditions free from irrelevant back-ground noises.

Quality is also dependent on the equipment used to make a recording. Again, options may be limited by circumstances to using poor equipment or making no record at all, but the better the initial recording the more likely it is to survive and be useful in the future across a broad range of possible uses. Collectors should keep in mind possible exhibition and broadcast use of the product, and use the best possible recording equipment and tape that the situation and available resources will allow.

Quality of the record is further dependent upon mastery of listening, record-ing, and interviewing techniques by the collector. Although it is difficult to dem-onstrate the degree to which good technique contributes to the value of a product, it is easier to discover instances in which poor technique has destroyed a good opportunity , and perhaps ruined the chances for others by creating disdain for oral history by respondents.

The final ingredient on which quality depends is the willingness and ability of respondents to deliver testimony that is as rich and useful as expected. Not all respondents live up to their apparent potential, and not all wish to be cooperative, even under the best conditions or under persuasion of the most skilled inquirers.

Records of collecting

Although record content is the primary object of value in oral history, a good record of the collecting process itself is essential to establishing the authenticity and integrity of the product. Collectors must keep careful and accurate records, particularly in identifying the record and the circumstances of its creation.

All communications about seeking and securing the cooperation and participation of respondents should be kept in a basic case file pertinent to the recording of that person. The recording itself should be labeled clearly to identify it completely, including information such as the name and title of the respondent or narrator, the date and location of the recording, the name and title of the collector or interviewer, the project or program under whose auspices the recording was made, and technical information about the recording itself, such as its duration in hours and minutes, recording speed, and the equipment employed. If more than one tape is required, each should carry a label with the same information and each should be numbered sequentially. This information or a copy of the label for each tape recorded should go into the case file. The collector should also note in the file when the process of collecting from that particular source is completed and what remaining *lacunae* there may be, or note if further recording is warranted, perhaps at a later date.

Opinion is divided on the ethics of notes by collectors on the circumstances of the collecting event and on the character or appearance of the narrator or respondent. In collecting oral tradition sources, such notes are extremely valuable in later assessments of the authenticity and integrity of the oral tradition in its social context. The role of the collector is often accepted as one of appraisal as well as collection in the tradition of anthropology, so there is little argument against such notes or against their becoming a part of the case file. In oral history interviewing, such notes may have similar value, but some practitioners balk at making them or putting them into the file on the grounds that surreptitious note taking abridges the terms and conditions under which cooperation of the respondent was secured.

Archival management of the record

Archival management of the oral history record involves appraisal, accessioning (the establishment of custody, legal dominion and control), preservation, arrangement, and description, as for any other documentation brought into an archives. However, oral history requires some minor variations.

Appraisal of an oral source record must be made on the basis of both its provenance and its contents. Standard archival judgment about the integrity of provenance, intrinsic value of the record, primary and secondary values, administrative and historical values, evidential and informational values, enduring values for future use, and so on, all apply to oral source records just as they do to written sources, and in much the same fashion except that the record must be watched or listened to in order to form a good opinion.

Many programs, more so in collecting oral history than oral tradition, offer those who have been recorded an opportunity to review and approve the recording prior to its formal donation and deposit into the archives. Some respondents may insist on review as a condition of participation. It is by no means universal, however, and is rarely practiced in collecting oral traditions. Even for the interview form of oral history there are those who vigorously oppose this practice, arguing that the integrity of the original record may be jeopardized if respondents, upon reflection, choose to modify their original candid spontaneity. Proponents of review argue that it may be the only way to obtain the record and that the well-considered second thoughts and additional contributions that often come from review add to the value of the product.

Ownership, property rights, and participant consent to and control over the use and administration of the record and its content are large issues for archivists, and they vary according to provenance of the material. Participants may have statutory property rights to the intellectual content of the recording, as they do in the United States, or they may have "moral rights" to the shape and content, as in France. Although the proportion may vary widely in each case, participation in creation of the record is generally believed to be inextricably shared and indivisible, requiring therefore the consent of both collector and donor in determining disposition of the record and its property rights. The duty of archivists is to determine what these rights are, how best to handle them within a given legal system, to see they are properly handled, and to record appropriate solutions in a deed or other formal agreement.

In some cases, the voluntary participation of a narrator or respondent may be conditional upon granting him or her a predominant and controling share in the rights and in control of disposition and administration of the record. As with paper and written documents, oral source records may have to be accessioned into archives with restrictions on use imposed by the originators or donors. Care, similar to that for restricted written documents, must be given to oral source records. Clear and precise statements of the terms and conditions of use are essential so that administration may be unequivocal and consistent.

Arrangement of oral source materials in archives usually falls into one of two major patterns. One is arrangement strictly by provenance: oral source records received as items within a larger corpus of documents in various media, integral to that collection or record group. If oral source records within the larger group are many and relatively coherent in provenance or subject, they may form a discrete series within the larger group. However, they may also be few, disparately distributed among and integral to file units within series. Applying the principles of *respect des fonds* and sanctity of the original order, the oral source records are left in their "found" file and series locations, as with written records. Preservation concerns urge the removal of tapes from the file for storage and handling with other audio-visual materials; but some withdrawal notice is kept in the file location from which the item was removed. That location remains the item's "file location of record" for finding aids and description. The withdrawal notice, of course, should have a cross-reference to the tape's actual storage location for retrieval.

The other major pattern is to create a sub-archives of oral history materials into which newly collected material is placed as created. This form is most common to archives that do their own collecting or are the depository for discrete oral source collecting efforts by others. Provenance again plays a role, of course, and oral history records from the same program or project are grouped together in collections or series. Within each project series, oral source records are usually arranged alphabetically by the name of the principal individual or group of people recorded. For each such "file unit" (in some cases perhaps big enough to be a subseries) the records are arranged chronologically by date of recording, perhaps with consecutive serial numbers. Successive tapes from one recording occasion are usually numbered consecutively in the order they were recorded and the arrangement of tapes and transcripts follows that numbering.

Oral source records are often transcribed into written form because users are accustomed to read rather than to listen or watch, because the written page is easier to scan rapidly for what is wanted, and because of the inconvenience of indexing audiotape or videotape contents and retrieving particular segments for close study. Modern technology will undoubtedly make it easier to use audiotapes and videotapes for research, but transcription remains an option chosen by many archives. A benefit of transcription, particularly if done immediately after the recorded event, is that participants in the record are available to identify and resolve ambiguities in the sound recording and thereby avoid possible misinterpretations. It is not uncommon for different people to hear quite different things in a sound recording, and verbal ambiguities such as the similarity in sound of "white shoes" and "why choose" can be misleading, particularly when unfamiliar regional accents or arcane terminology are involved.

There are two major drawbacks to transcription: the transcript is often used wrongly as a sufficient substitute for the original record; and accurate transcription is very expensive. No written transcript, even those employing complicated symbols to indicate pauses of varying lengths or non-verbal interjections, background noises, etc., is ever precisely an accurate representation of the sound or video recording. The original sound recording remains the best and ultimate standard against which any copy tape or any transcript must be measured. No transcript meets that standard, and most fall far short. A transcript is, at best, a very expensive finding aid to what is on the tape. Even when word processing computers are used (and they improve the speed of transcription significantly) the time required to draft, review, and perfect an acceptable finished transcript without significant errors or omissions may be from ten to twenty hours of work per hour of tape.

Preservation for oral source recordings depends on the medium (magnetic tape, paper, phonograph disc, videodisk, wire recording, motion picture film, etc.), and the preservation methods commonly used for each one apply equally to oral source records. As noted above, the better the quality of materials and equipment in the original recording, the better the quality of any copy, and the longer the record will last. The most common medium at present for oral history is magnetic tape. Material composition of the tape is important to preservation, and mylar-based tape is preferred. The wider and thicker the tape and the faster the speed of recording, the better the resulting sound quality of the product. This means that if you need excellent quality, you also need large and cumbersome equipment. Unfortunately, quality of recording must often be sacrificed for convenience, particularly when recording is done in the field. Nevertheless, since the original recording is the standard by which all others must be measured, it should be of the best quality possible under any given circumstances.

Another consideration is that every playing of magnetic tape (or motion picture film or grooved disk) produces wear that diminishes the recording quality over time. For this reason, the original recording should be used only once, to create a "production master" from which subsequent copies may be made without resorting to the original. Storage conditions of the tape are also important. Recent but as yet unpublished studies by the United States National Bureau of Standards have found that magnetic tape preserves best in sub-freezing dry conditions, and the original tape and production master should, whenever possible, be so stored. Low temperature and low humidity tend to prolong tape life, but fluctuations, particularly when temperature is close to freezing (30 to 34 degrees Farenheit or -1 to $+1$ degree Celsius) are as damaging to magnetic tape as they are to film. Constantly stable conditions are essential.

When oral source materials are received as part of larger records accessions, administrative control of the oral records is subordinate to and part of administrative control of the larger body. What follows applies primarily to administrative control and processing of oral source records placed in "sub-archives", the second broad pattern of repository-level arrangement.

The basic unit of oral source recording for archival control is the individual, discrete interview or session record. It may be simple or complex. A simple record is one recording (one reel of tape) of one event (interview, recitation, narration, etc.) in one place at one time, with a clear beginning and end. Complex units involve several tapes covering a long, continuous session or several discontinuous sessions with the same subject (respondent or narrator) over time. For each unit, the identifying data given earlier under "records of collecting" are the basis and source for all control and description, hence it is important that they be accurate and complete. Accessioning in many oral history and oral tradition situations may not occur until after preservation processing, transcription, and execution of a deed of gift or other agreement on terms and conditions of ownership and use. Still, some means of registering each tape or other recording brought into the archives is needed for orderly control. Some archives merely use the common accession register, a practice that requires a later de-accession if the donor refuses to give rights, title, and interest in the property to the archives. Others create a separate register of recordings received for all incoming oral source records. They wait until the legal agreements have been concluded to enter items in the accession register.

"Processing" is to oral history what arrangement and description are to paper archives. Many degrees of processing can be applied, depending on the degree of intellectual and administrative control and preservation sought. At the simplest level of minimum processing, copies are made of the original recording, the original is retired to cold, dry storage, and a brief synopsis of contents is added to the basic identifying data on the label of each unit. The reference tape and accompanying description are then stored for future use. A slightly higher degree of processing improves upon this simple summary description of contents by providing a schedule of contents, which is a sequential list of topics in the order that they appear in the recording. There may be simple and abbreviated notes or complex and extensive descriptions for each new topic or event covered. Each entry may be keyed to a notation of the elapsed time from the beginning of the recording to the start of that topic or event in the recording. Some programs employ a two-track stereo tape system in which one track carries the substance of the recording and the other carries an elapsed time message, signalling the passage of every five or ten seconds. In this way, a written schedule accompanying each tape provides a ready means of locating any given segment.

The ultimate description for any oral source record is a written transcript. It, too, may include a time schedule that keys portions of the transcript to their approximate time locations on the tape.

Beyond the basic elements of description and processing noted above, the most common form of finding aid for oral history and oral tradition collections is a catalog or list for each collection, arranged by the name of the principal participant. Each name entry in the list contains sufficient description and identifying information to help most researchers find most of what they need. This may be in page or card form or accessible on computer. If the descriptive entries are extensive, there may be an index of principal terms from entries keyed to catalog headings in the list. Some programs provide name and subject indices to each recording (based on terms appearing in transcripts or schedules of contents). Some provide indices across whole collections. The degree of sophistication varies with the resources available for such work.

Reflections on the literature of oral history

A number of published works rest entirely or in part on a collected oral sources, and they are often called "oral history" in their titles and advertisements. They are not oral history in the form usually found in archives, but are rather books, films, or broadcast productions, often as much literary or dramatic as historical, that use such stuff of oral interviews as suits the artistic or literary purpose of each author or producer. They produce useful perspectives on the past, just as impressionist painters do, but their work is not oral history in the strict historiographic and archival terms considered in this chapter. Alex Haley, notable for his book, *Roots*, and Studs Terkel, notable for his books, *Hard times*, *Working*, *The good war*, and others, will be familiar to many readers. There are also television and motion picture directors, producers, and playwrights who employ a technique similar to that of oral history. In France, Marcel Ophuls is highly regarded for intensely crafted juxtaposition of personal testimony and the broader scope of historic events. In Great Britain, the British Broadcasting Corporation broadcast a series of recorded personal testimonies and reflections by participants in the Vietnam War, entitled *Vietnam: many reasons why*. Other examples could be cited. All these are as essentially different from archival oral history as written histories and historical novels or dramas are from manuscript collections, for many of the same reasons. Archivists should not be confused at their being called "oral history" in common usage. The chief distinction is that "archival oral history" is raw material, gathered for academic study, and not intended for immediate publication, but rather for inclusion in a chain of evidence supporting historical analysis.

Academic literature on oral history, its methodology and uses, is less exciting than the dramatic works cited above, but more useful to the archivist. It borrows heavily from traditional historiography, anthropology, and journalism, and much of it is given over to manuals of procedure and technique. Several of these are listed in the list of sources for further reading and are worth careful attention by archivists who must deal with oral history materials.

Conclusion

The foregoing should warn archivists not to venture lightly into oral history. It is an expensive form of documentation that may use up resources needed for preservation, arrangement, or description of sources already in hand. On the other hand, it is also often a rich source of information not obtainable otherwise. It can be the means of finding new sources of documentation beyond the oral testimony recorded. Many oral history interviews have led to the discovery of caches of written documents, photographic materials, or artefacts of great value to historians. Oral history is also inescapable. The archivist who seeks to avoid it will sooner or later have to deal with it, and ought to be well-informed when that necessity arises.

12

Reference Service and Access

David R. Kepley

Make a listing of the contributions that archives claim to make to society: they preserve a cultural legacy of a people; they inspire a sense of respect for the past; they enable policy makers and citizens to learn from the past; they permit citizens to ascertain their legal rights; and they allow individuals to discern the truth about formative episodes and personalities that shaped their culture. In Western societies, with their heritage of an informed citizenry making important political decisions, archives take their place as part of the wider network of educational and cultural institutions that seek to educate and to remind societies of their heritage.

The place that reference occupies in this wider view of the role of archives in society is pivotal: those involved in reference service serve as vital links between the treasures of their institutions and those interested in exploiting them. In other words, if archives are to have meaning in society, reference archivists are an important linchpin in the process. This is not, of course, to belittle the obvious importance of conservationists and those who process archival materials, only to emphasize the role of those involved in reference.

Reference service

The principal goal of an archival reference program is to facilitate the use of materials in the custody of an institution. Crucial to its success is a commitment by the institution to the basic concepts that govern other service-oriented institutions. These include stating clearly what is expected of the patron and the archivist, and treating each researcher seriously and fairly. It also means that those in charge of a reference program must be sensitive to the psychological stresses involved in constant daily contact with the public. The best reference archivists are those who combine a knowledge of the materials they administer with an ability to deal with the general public. In spite of the good intentions that must permeate a reference program, factors exist that limit an archives' ability to provide complete access to its materials. These include preservation concerns, the amount of staff time available, records that are not yet processed, the extent to which the institution should do research for the patron, and the sensitivity of the information which some records may contain.

The heart of the reference process lies in understanding the researchers' questions and suggesting the kinds of records that the institution and other related repositories have that may be of use. Because archives are arranged and described according to the principles of provenance and original order, reference archivists become translators between the subject-oriented questions that researchers usually pose and the records they administer. The crucible of the reference experience lies in the reference interview. Here the reference archivist must be a careful listener who attempts to discern the level of the researcher's work and identify clues that will point to specific bodies of archives likely to be of use. For instance, for amateur researchers, the archivist can suggest secondary works or published primary sources that may satisfy the researcher's questions. In all of this it is important to remember that archivists should avoid placing themselves in the position of judging the worth of researchers' topics. No matter how trival some requests may seem, archivists should treat each one with respect.

The most crucial thing that archivists must understand when they perform reference service is that they have entered the world of service industries. The archives' reputation in whatever constituency it serves is dependent on how its researchers perceive the way in which they are treated. A reputation once established, either good or bad, is not easy to change. It will inevitably affect other goals of the institution. One can easily imagine prospective donors, learning of an archives' poor relationship with its researchers, donating their materials to another institution.

Much of the psychology that governs the approach of other service industries to their public, concerns the public's expectations of what constitutes acceptable service. For example, in the restaurant industry, customers expect such things as: to be greeted, shown to a table, told what is available, treated in a courteous manner, and given what they ordered in a reasonable amount of time. These expectations are defined by norms learned from previous experiences with restaurant service, as well as by standards for good service developed by the industry. But suppose one went to a foreign country where the norms were different? Simply being in a strange place puts one on the alert for things that are at variance with the norms of one's own society. In this situation, individuals learn to look for cues that will inform them of the foreign country's norms; they are waiting to be told what is appropriate behaviour for them and for the providers of service.

This is exactly the position many people face when they enter an archives.

Most people do not know what archives are. Upon entering an archives for the first time, they, like the foreign traveler, are looking to be told what is appropriate behaviour, what they must do for themselves, and what they can expect archivists to do for them. People often equate archives with libraries, so the differences may confuse and annoy them: they must sign in; they must sign for records; they may not borrow materials; there may be copying restrictions; and there is no card catalog. It is critical, therefore, for reference archivists to be sensitive to this and to develop ways to advise people of the expectations that archivists have of their patrons and what patrons can expect of the archivists. This educational process may include explaining why certain procedures, such as signing in, are necessary, and why it takes a certain amount of time to provide materials for patrons. When the basic policies and procedures of an institution are explained at the outset, the reference process can go much more smoothly.

Another principle of good service borrowed from other service industries is the doctrine of fairness. In Western democratic countries with their egalitarian traditions, this expectation has become universal. These principles are sometimes expressed in the acronyms: LILO and FIFO, which mean "last in last out" and "first in first out". In other words, archivists should make every effort to answer letters or in-person requests in the order in which they were received. Another dimension of the fairness doctrine is simply to try to treat all researchers with the same amount of courtesy and efficiency.

Archives face ethical problems with regard to the fairness doctrine: who is permitted to use the archives generally and who is permitted to see specific materials. The latter point will be dealt with in the section on access. In the pre-modern era, archives were the private reserve of the powerful who ruled with the dictum that information is power. As archives evolved in the nineteenth and twentieth centuries, from repositories established for the sole benefit of the creators of records to institutions that permitted third-party access, access was often restricted to the highly educated. This was done on the theory that only these individuals were in a position to appreciate and utilize the resources of the institution. Excluded were genealogists, curiosity seekers, journalists, and the general public. These individuals, it was argued, could not understand the materials, posed an additional reference burden on the archives' staff, and could mishandle records. In the case of investigative journalists, for instance, there was the additional fear that they may sensationalize the information they viewed, to the possible embarrassment of a donor.

Such policies are antiquated and élitist. If archives are to achieve the larger goal of becoming an integral part of the cultural and educational network of a nation, then they should encourage use by all comers. Only in this way can they demonstrate their social utility to the constituencies they purport to serve. If this is done effectively, new sources of funding may become available as more individuals come to believe that the archives is not an exclusive club. The concern that the uninitiated may mishandle materials means that efforts need to be made to teach people the proper ways to handle archival materials. Fears that journalists may misuse information are best alleviated by establishing sound general restriction policies, as described in the section on access, so that truly sensitive information is not disclosed. Then a better understanding of the respective roles of archivist and researcher can emerge. Archivists are in the business of administering records, while the task of researchers is to interpret them. Archivists cannot be held responsible for the misinterpretation of the records in their charge.

To this point, the discussion of the reference process has focused on the researcher's expectations and needs, but the other side of this process is no less important—the psychological toll that reference service can exact on reference archivists, sometimes referred to as "burn out". Good reference archivists are trained to listen to researchers and respond to their needs. They are constantly hammered with questions and asked to drop one task to respond to the next inquiry. They must subsume their own egos, opinions, and interests to concentrate on what their patrons think is important. Combine this with the unpredictability of reference workflow, from telephone calls, walk-in patrons, and mail, and reference archives can soon lose a sense of control over their time and themselves. This can be exhausting and demoralizing. The signs of burn out can include irritablility with researchers' questions, a loss of patience, and a decreased desire to respond conscientiously to their questions.

Reference archivists and their supervisors must recognize the stresses inherent in providing reference service and take steps to alleviate them. Possibilities include having someone to take messages on reference telephone calls for a specified period each day so that postal inquiries can be answered. The most frequent questions, ones that can easily become annoyances to reference archivists, should be answered with handouts, signs in the research room, form letters, or tape-slide programs. If possible, archivists should be rotated through the reference desk for specified periods to keep them fresh. All general letters and brochures should stress to researchers that for the archives to give them the best service they should give advance notice of their arrival; this will help to reduce the number of unexpected visits by researchers. For researchers who have large orders, for records, copying, or screening, a mutually agreed schedule can be established for getting the job done, rather than working to exhaustion to meet everyone's requests simultaneously.

While the goal of a reference program is to provide records to researchers, there are practical, ethical, and legal constraints on the reference process. One issue that affects all archivists is the concern over how much research it is appropriate for the institution to perform on behalf of the researcher. Archivists are nearly always on sound ground when they provide information about the records they administer. Typically a researcher may ask if the institution has any information on a specific topic. The archivist responds by citing the series or items that appear to apply, quoting the cost of copying them, perhaps providing a copy of the appropriate finding aid, and inviting the researcher to visit the institution, at the same time giving pertinent facts about the operation of the archives. The research involved in this kind of response is confined to identifying the relevant materials. If researchers have not been sufficiently precise in their queries, then a more general response asking for more information and greater precision may be in order.

Where archivists begin to stray into a grey area is when they interpret the record for the researcher. For instance, if a researcher wants the archives to provide copies of the items of correspondence of a prominent politician that best illustrate his point of view on organized labor, the archivist should beware. The researcher may later publish a piece based on the archivist's recommendations. If a colleague points out that documents from the same institution that were not cited could give a different impression of the politician's perspective, the original researcher will be most distraught. Such a situation could, indeed, involve the archives in legal difficulties. The archivist in this example should notify the researcher of the types of records that are available and invite him to visit the institution and judge for himself what are the "best" records on the subject. An exception to this advice is when the archives, as part of its mission, is playing the role of institutional memory for its own institution.

Another limitation on reference service is an eminently practical one—time. The reference staff is limited in size and each request deserves a fair share of staff time. Researchers who write involved letters with numerous questions, or who have extensive reproduction orders, can be advised of the time constraints and perhaps told that their letter will be answered in part and that a reply to the next section will be forthcoming after all other letters received have been dealt with. In-person researchers pose the same problems. It is entirely appropriate to limit the number of units (boxes, folders, documents, volumes) provided in a day. Otherwise a single researcher, who is able quickly to go through large quantities of materials, will easily dominate the time of one or more staff persons to the detriment of other researchers.

While this author has argued for a policy of opening archives to the widest possible audience, there are times when it is appropriate to deny access to archival materials. If a collection has not been processed, it is not advisable to permit researchers to use the records. Archivists are unable to provide much assistance to researchers in these cases and, more to the point, the institution has not yet learned what is in the collection. The materials may contain documents that the creator had forgotten were sensitive or of high monetary value. Another case where access must be restricted is when a document is so fragile that merely handling it poses a threat to its physical integrity. In both of these cases, restriction on the use of the records should be of a temporary nature. If the collection is unprocessed, then a processing schedule should be established and the researcher advised of it. Institutions that take years to process collections do themselves, the research community, and their donors a disservice. If the documents are in poor condition, definite plans should be made to repair them expeditiously.

Another instance where access to documents should be restricted is when there is another copy of the records available in either microform or letterpress. The most important cause of the degradation of historic documents is use. If another version of the document is available, archivists should require the enquirer to use it. The exceptions to this policy are those cases where the physical document itself is the subject of research, such as watermarks, film technology, or in cases where the authenticity of the original is in question.

Access

The most important and difficult area in which archivists are compelled to deny access to their holdings concerns the specific restrictions that the laws of their country and the donor impose on them. In Western Europe, until the eighteenth century, the access policy for both official records and private papers was relatively simple: the creators of, or the successors to, the records had the right of access and others did not. During the nineteenth century, the rise of democratic governments with their emphasis on the rights of individuals and the concomitant rise of the historical profession, opened the doors of archives to third-party users. These users were generally exploring historical topics in the remote past that were relatively unthreatening to the custodians and creators of the records. The period after World War II changed all that. Many historians shifted their focus to the more immediate past and in many cases were concerned less with great affairs of state than the day-to-day occurrences of ordinary citizens. By the 1960s and 1970s, with the passage of a spate of "freedom of information" laws in most of the countries of Western Europe and North America, the concept of access to government information had evolved from a privilege to a right.

While the various freedom of information laws differ considerably, they generally apply strictly to government records, not personal papers, and they attempt to restrict certain categories of information. There is, for instance, a clear recognition that the government may restrict information that relates to national security and the conduct of foreign affairs. In addition, because governments have played increasingly greater roles in the lives of their citizens, they have collected huge amounts of data on their personal lives. Freedom of information laws have, therefore, recognized that governments have an obligation to protect information, the release of which may invade the privacy of individuals. Governments similarly collect huge amounts of data from businesses. Because release of this information may give rival businesses an advantage in the marketplace, governments are likewise obliged to maintain this information in confidence. Other kinds of information may be unavailable to researchers under other statutes, as in the United States, for example, where federal law prohibits federal employees from disclosing income tax information.[1]

Archivists must thus be completely conversant with the laws in their jurisdiction that regulate access, as well as any donor-imposed restrictions on personal papers. They have an obligation to release as much information to researchers as is consistent with their obligations to protect confidential information and with what the law requires. Archival administrators should establish and publish general rules of access that apply to all classes of records in their custody. The advantage of such a procedure is that it establishes a common standard for all records in an institution that apply equally to all researchers. This will assure equal access to researchers and can be helpful when negotiating with donors, who can be assured that no special restrictions are required because all records will be processed according to the general restrictions of the institution. Such general restrictions should include restrictions on records, the release of which might jeopardize national security, invade the personal privacy of individuals, divulge business and commercial secrets, reveal investigative information, or may be prohibited by law or other government regulation.

In making decisions on whether to release materials, archivists should in each instance weigh the benefits that can accrue to society in releasing information against the harm that may be caused through doing so. Crucial, in making the judgments required by this balancing act, is the understanding that circumstances exist that may permit the release of information even if it comes in one of the restricted categories. The most important of these circumstances is the passage of time. All data, no matter how sensitive, lose their sensitivity over time. This is particularly true of business confidentiality. It is hard to imagine that the release of twenty-and thirty-year-old business information could do much harm to the rapidly changing companies of Western Europe and North America. The same principle is involved in the declassification of national security information. In the area of personal privacy, the death of the person who is the subject of the information removes nearly all of its private character. The only remaining concern is for other living individuals whose privacy may be affected. Finally, once information has been publicly released, it is considered to be public information. [2]

One final note concerns the way in which materials are opened to research. Once records are open, the archives should do everything it can to facilitate research in them. Such practices as opening materials for research and refusing to permit copying or permitting researchers to look at materials and take notes, but then requesting that they submit their notes for review, are counterproductive and pointless.

Ethical concerns

The greatest ethical questions that confront reference archivists involve questions of equal access to materials, discussions of the work of one researcher with another, and the obligations that archivists who are involved in research on their own have toward the researchers they serve. As noted above, the equal access question has two parts to it: excluding certain categories of researchers from the institution, on the one hand, permitting privileged access by some researchers to specific collections or parts of collections that are not available to others. This applies mainly to third-party users, since it is safe to assume that the creators of the records or their legal representatives can have *carte blanche* access to their own materials. Permitting third-party users to obtain access to materials that are unavailable to others must be avoided. This can arise when an authorized biographer is working with a collection and wants to get exclusive access to it before it is released to his competitors. To agree to such terms is unacceptable.

A somewhat thornier problem relates to the degree to which archivists should discuss the work of one researcher with another. Archivists and scholars are supposed to be part of a larger enterprise in which they are both attempting to expand mankind's knowledge about the universal problems illuminated in their holdings. If this were the only concern, they could freely exchange information and the ethical problem would be non-existent. But in the real world, authors do compete on the same subject and much can be at stake—careers, jobs, tenure, and revenue from book royalties. The easy way out would be never to say anything to anybody about any other research done on similar topics. But some researchers want others to know of their work in an area, either to put others on notice or to exchange information.

Probably the best policy in these situations is to ask researchers during the registration process if they mind if the archives advises others of the general nature of their topic. A corollary question might be whether researchers object if the archives provides to others detailed lists of the records they saw and had copied. In this way the archives can shift the onus of disclosure to the researcher. In the absence of such permission, archivists are obliged not to reveal to one researcher the work of another.

The final ethical problem that may confront reference archivists can occur when they themselves are also researchers in the collections they administer. If a researcher arrives and is working on the same or a very similar topic, what are the obligations of the reference archivist? In general, he is supposed to assist the researcher in locating materials that will aid his project. The fact that the reference archivist also has another role, as a researcher in his own right, does not mitigate this central obligation. The first obligation in this case is to the client.

The administration of reference service and access policy

Problems relating to the administration of reference can be handled in a number of different ways, often depending on certain practical considerations. Addressed in the following pages are solutions to problems associated with registration of researchers, research room procedures, copying policies, access for disabled researchers, the administration of access, and the collection of user statistics.

All researchers using the archives should be required to register on a brief form in which they identify themselves and their institutional affiliation and describe the topic of their research, and on which they sign a statement agreeing to abide by the rules of the institution. The researcher should provide a positive form of identification. This might also be a good time to ask researchers if they have any objection to the archives' sharing the nature of their research topic with others. In addition, researchers should sign a log each day they use the research room.

These procedures serve several purposes. Besides knowing with whom they are dealing, it may be helpful to the reference staff if, for instance, the researcher is an author whose works are well-known to them. It is also imperative if the researcher has been involved in document theft. More to the point, the registration documents and daily research room logs can be vital evidence if any documents are later discovered to be missing or damaged. The registration process, particularly signing a statement to the effect that the researcher understands and agrees to abide by the regulations of the institution, reinforces the concept that access to the institution is a privilege that can be revoked if his behavior is improper. Finally, because the researcher was asked to identify his topic, the form serves as a point of departure for the initial reference interview.

A wide variety of issues relating to the administration of the research room need to be decided, written down, distributed, and explained during the registration process. To return to a point made earlier, because archives are unfamiliar terrain for most people, it is important to alert them to appropriate behavior at the outset.

What kind of writing implements will be allowed in the research room? Certainly fountain pens should be prohibited because of the possibility of an accidental spill of ink near documents. While this argument cannot apply to ballpoint pens, there is the possibility that a researcher might make an inadvertent (or otherwise) mark on a document that would be indelible. To be truly safe, researchers could be restricted to using just pencils. If a document became marked it could then more easily be repaired, but the quality of the researcher's notes might suffer, since notes taken in pencil can smudge and at some point might be unreadable.

How many records should researchers be allowed to view at their work station at any one time? Here security and the physical integrity of the records must be weighed against the time of both the staff and the researcher. The maximum security situation consists of researchers being given one document at a time, with the pages being examined and counted before and after use to be certain that researchers return unaltered all that they view. Little chance exists, in this case, that records will become disarranged, stolen, or mutilated. But such a situation grossly impedes research and completely dominates the time of the staff. Minimal requirements might be to deliver all of the records that researchers wanted at the same time. Clearly this reduces the time the staff would have to spend in checking an individual researchers. But with so many boxes, perhaps from different collections, there is a greater possibility that researchers could intermix the contents of one box with those of another and there would be no practical way for the staff to ensure that all that was provided was returned unaltered.

While there is no single answer to this question, permitting researchers to have materials from more than one collection at one time is probably not a good idea. Exactly how many documents, folders, or boxes should be provided at once depends on the institution's resources and the type of collection being requested. In any case, researchers should be required to sign a form that identifies exactly what records they have received. This will be invaluable later if the institution suspects that a researcher altered or removed a document. For a further discussion cf research-room security, see Chapter Fifteen.

What kind of researcher-owned equipment will be permitted in the research room? The answer relates largely to logistical and preservation issues. Researchers have a wide variety of equipment to aid them in their research, including computers (both lap-top and desk-top models), cameras, copiers, tape recorders, and typewriters. So, much of the answer to the question depends on the physical layout of the research room. Are there outlets near the work stations such that people will not trip on electrical cords? Will the power capacity of the room be overtaxed by the equipment? Is there enough room for others if the equipment is permitted? Will the operation of the machine in any way disturb other researchers or staff? The major preservation concerns are the effects that the machines, especially copiers and cameras with high-intensity lights, may have on the documents. For a discussion of the light levels appropriate for documents, see Chapter Fourteen.

Will personal effects be allowed in the researcher room? The principal issue here is security. The more personal effects that are permitted in the vicinity of the records, the more the security of the records is endangered. While it may be simple to require coats to be placed on a coat rack, what about a researcher's notes? What about a woman's pocketbook? In the former case, to deny researchers access to their notes hampers their ability to do research. Some institutions issue paper and note cards free of charge with a hole punched in the corner. This better enables the attendant to check the notes to determine whether materials leaving with researchers belong to them. If the archives insists that more valuable possessions of the researcher, such as a woman's pocketbook, be removed from the vicinity of the records, it must provide a secure environment for these valuables.

There are only a few absolutes in dealing with research-room procedures. Eating, drinking, and smoking should be prohibited around documents, because accidents can happen that pose a permanent threat to their physical integrity. It should be made clear that the alteration, mutilation, or theft of any document may be grounds for legal action. Researchers must be told not to disarrange the records; if they believe that the records are out of order, they should inform the archivist. Researchers should not be permitted to trace, bear down, or write on top of documents.

Since researchers seem to have all but abandoned the practice of taking notes, the copier has become an indispensable part of the research room. The two major issues that the use of copiers pose are those of copyright and of whether the copying should be done by staff or by the researchers themselves. Archivists need to be completely familiar with copyright laws and the extent to which the use of copying equipment may constitute an infringement. A disclaimer statement with reference to the copyright laws posted near the copier may suffice.

Probably the simplest and cheapest copying policy is to permit researchers to copy materials themselves. The only major problem with this approach is that the copying process may damage fragile or bound documents. To minimize the possibility of damage, the archives could instruct researchers to submit any document they wish to copy to the research-room attendant for inspection prior to copying. If the document is judged to be too fragile for copying, every effort should be made to repair it, so that a copy can be made. Another option is to have the staff do all of the copying. This presents less danger to the documents, but ties up staff resources.

An archives should be sensitive to the needs of the disabled, though this does not mean that it need restructure everything. For the blind, an archives could keep on hand a listing of local organizations that provide the services of a reader. To assist those who are restricted to a wheelchair, the distances between tables should not be too narrow and the stairways leading to the archives should be negotiable by elevators or ramps. It may be advisable for one of the reference staff to become skilled in using sign language in order to help the hearing-impaired. The key in this as in all reference service is attitude—the demonstration that the institution is willing to help people.

Once a general institution-wide set of access restrictions has been established and specific collection restrictions clarified, there are a number of procedures that need to be instituted to make the process work. The institution should commit its restriction statements to writing, screen its materials, withdraw restricted documents, establish a parallel file, and institute procedures for returning restricted materials to the publicly-available file when their sensitivity has lapsed.

Because the whole process of restricting access is something that can be an annoyance to researchers, it is important to be very clear about what is being withheld and for what reasons. One hedge against this problem is to have clearly-defined rules on access that are written down and are available for distribution. This will reassure researchers that the institution is not acting arbitrarily. Another institutional obligation is to identify exactly what has been removed from a file and why. This can be accomplished by placing a withdrawal notice in the file at the point at which the original document was removed or by annotating the finding aid if entire series are unavailable. The withdrawal notice should identify what was removed (letter from Smith to Jones, July 5, 1952), for what reason (personal privacy), and when the restriction will expire (on the death of Smith).

Ideally, the screening of records should take place at the time of processing, but it can often be postponed until the records are requested. The problem with the latter approach is that it will make researchers wait until the particular boxes they want are screened. In either case, as each restricted document is removed from its original file, it should be placed in a folder bearing all the information necessary to return it to the original file. All the restricted documents should be placed in different boxes in another part of the archives; this is the parallel file. By maintaining restricted information separately from publicly-available information, the possibility of inadvertently providing restricted information to the researcher is reduced. Clearly noted on the parallel file folders should be the date or event that will cause these documents to become part of the public file. Computer assistance may be desirable when many documents with varying release times are involved. In any case, on a periodic basis, the restricted materials should be reviewed for return to the publicly-available file.[3]

Because archival reference service is similar to other service industries, archival institutions should maintain statistics on the use of the archives to better serve its clientele. An archives should keep track of the number of reference inquiries (at a minimum, the number of letters, people who signed into the research room, and copies produced) and the time taken to complete these services, to enable it to account for its resources and plan for the future. Beyond this, the archives should attempt to note with some precision what kinds of materials, say by collection, are getting the most attention and for what reason. This can have a number of benefits. It can inform and perhaps adjust the collection policy and appraisal process. It can provide the justification for moving a particularly active set of records nearer the research room or perhaps microfilming them. Such statistics can also point to areas that the staff knows are rich, but are just not being used. This should inspire a talk by a member of the reference staff at the next meeting of a client group's professional organization, extolling the value of a particular set of records that has been underutilized.

Conclusion

Archival institutions are an important part of the cultural heritage of a nation and the reference process is crucial in bringing together those who interpret such materials and the materials themselves. In order to facilitate this process, archival reference programs must be imbued with the concepts of good service, which stand at the center of other service industries. These include anticipating researchers' reactions to the special requirements of an archives, treating each request seriously, and being fair in dealing with researchers. It also means encouraging the use of archives by the widest possible audience.

Restraining this impetus toward openness are several important concerns. They include preservation, the extent to which the staff will do research for the researcher, limitations on staff time, whether a collection has been processed, and the existence of restricted information. When restricting access based on the information in the records, archivists must be completely familiar with the laws of their jurisdiction and any restrictions imposed by donors. when they can exercise discretion, archivists must weigh the benefits to society in opening records over the potential damage done to individuals and corporations in releasing information. None of this must obscure the fact that archives are meant to be used for the enrichment of their society.

Notes and references

1. Michael Duchein. *Obstacles to the access, use and transfer of information from archives.* Paris, Unesco, 1983. pp. 10–30.
2. Gary M. Peterson and Trudy Huskamp Peterson. *Archives and manuscripts: law.* Chicago Society of American Archivists, 1985. Chapter 3.
3. Peterson and Peterson, *Law, op cit.* Chapter 4.

13

Archival Ethics

Karen Benedict

Introduction

Imagine that one archives is in conflict with another over the acquisition of a collection of records. The present archival code stipulates that archivists do not compete for collections when the competition would endanger the integrity or the safety of the records or papers.

An archivist from one of the archives in question, who is responsible for acquistions and donor relations, is under pressure from the administration, which in turn is under pressure from the institution's board of trustees to acquire this collection. The collection better fits with the holdings of the competitor. The archivist knows that it would benefit researchers if the collection went to the other institution, which has complementary records, and also has greater financial and staff resources. The other archives will be able to process the collection more quickly, and has better facilities available for research. However, it would enhance the prestige of the archivist's own repository if it acquired the collection. The director, who is the archivist's supervisor, has said that it is likely to lead to an increase in funding for the institution if they manage to secure the collection; and that if they are successful, the archivist will certainly be in line for a substantial raise. The integrity and safety of the materials are not really in jeopardy. The archivist knows that the repository is a good one, although it is currently underfunded and understaffed. This situation provides the archivist with an opportunity to help correct these deficiencies.

On what basis should this archivist make a decision whether or not to aggressively pursue the collection? The code of ethics does not state what is appropriate behavior under these circumstances. Yet, this is clearly a question involving both ethical professional action and personal integrity. What would you do if you were faced with the hypothetical situation described? On what basis would you make your decision?

Ethics is a complex area of philosophy. There is more involved in fostering a sensitivity to ethical concerns in a profession than creating a code of ethics for the group. In addition to establishing general rules of behavior to govern actions when members of a group encounter certain problems or conflicts, ethics also encompasses educating individuals to make reasoned judgments whenever personal values, personal convenience, institutional values, institutional loyalties, principles of morality, or duties and obligations to society come into direct conflict.

Conveying a knowledge of ethics is more complicated than teaching one's personal beliefs of what is good or bad, right or wrong given a certain situation. It is the building of an intellectual, philosophical framework upon which to base decisions, and the provision of training in evaluating decision-making in a wider context than the immediate situation with which one is presented. Do we do a disservice to our colleagues and to our profession by placing so little emphasis upon understanding ethics, with the concomitant inability to judge our actions upon firm ethical principles? I believe that we do. Can we, and should we, provide background and training which will give the individual archivist a basis upon which to make such decisions independent of personal consideration and provide a later defense for such decisions based upon accepted ethical principles of behavior? I believe that we can and should do so.

While a knowledge of ethics would not necessarily make daily decision-making involving questions of principle any easier, it would force upon us a greater awareness of the basis upon which we make such decisions. It would also encourage further evaluation of the implications of those decisions for ourselves and our society.

There are many situations where a code of ethics alone may not enable an individual to make a difficult decision. As described earlier, the decision may require a weighing of values and morals, and a choice of which good to serve—personal, institutional, societal, or the larger good of all mankind. A code of ethics cannot specifically address all of the critical situations which may arise, nor can it adequately provide the basis for ethical decision-making. That is not the purpose of an ethical code. The creation of a code of ethics is a part of the process of providing an ethical framework for a profession. It is a guide to appropriate behavior for the profession and the public when facing certain expected conflicts.

Definition of terms

First, let us define what we mean by the term ethics. It can be: (a) a system of moral principles; (b) the rules of conduct recognized in respect to a particular group, culture, class of human action, etc., e.g. medical ethics, Christian ethics; (c) moral principles as of an individual; or (d) that branch of philosophy dealing with values relating to the rightness or wrongness of certain actions and the goodness and badness of the motives and ends of such actions.

The study of ethics is a branch of philosophy, and involves investigation, on an abstract level, into the fundamental principles and concepts which govern human thought and behavior. However, when we speak of professional ethics, it is the second of the above definitions to which we refer. To the philosopher, this is the layman's definition of ethics; a set of standards by which a group or community decides to regulate its behavior, to distinguish what is legitimate or acceptable in pursuit of their aims from what is not. Ethics as a philosophical concept thus differs from specific ethics, or the layman's concept, in that it is the analysis and exposition of theoretical doctrine rather than the creation of a practical guide to living.

In this chapter we will examine specific ethics in relationship to what the archival profession has done to create and to implement an ethical code for its members; and consider the question of whether the profession also needs to address the philosophy of ethics.

The governing principle in creating a code of ethics is that the rules must not be arbitrary. They must be necessary for, or an aid to, the purposes of the field in which they apply. Once these purposes have been clearly established, then a code of ethics can be drawn up, and any rule of conduct or moral principle can be assessed in terms of the contribution which it makes toward these ends.

The purpose of an ethical code is to delineate, for the members of the profession and for the public at large, the issues of greatest concern and the areas of potential conflict between individual action and the purposes of the group, and to guarantee that the special expertise of the group will be used for the good of society. A code of ethics sets standards of behavior for the members of a profession to follow, and establishes bounds within which they should operate to achieve its goals.

Ethical concerns also involve adherence to legal responsibilities. A code of ethics is not a code of law. It does not, and need not, enumerate the laws which govern the operations of the group, but it presumes that the membership will be familiar with the pertinent laws, and that they will strive for full compliance with the law while maintaining the highest standards of personal and professional conduct and excellence of performance.

A history of the code of ethics for archivists

American archivists have developed, reviewed, and revised their ethical code over the years. The first published discussion of the issue of ethics and the need for a code appeared in 1939, in an article by Robert C. Binkley, an historian at Western Reserve University. Binkley believed that archivists needed a clear-cut ethic to deal with problems that arose while protecting privacy at the same time as they were providing information that ought to be publicly available. He called for those precepts to be defined in a code, so that a "duly certified archivist'' could claim the confidence of a client in the same way that doctors, lawyers, or journalists do in the course of their professional activities.

There was no immediate response by archivists to this call for an ethical code. Ultimately, though, two published codes of ethics appeared; the first in 1955, and the second in 1980. The first code was written by Wayne C. Grover, Archivist of the United States (1948–1965). It was originally intended as an internal document for use in the National Archives' Inservice Training Program, so naturally its focus was upon governmental archives. It was subsequently published, without revision, in the 1955 volume of the *American Archivist* for dissemination to the entire profession, but was never formally adopted by the profession. The second code was the product of the Society of American Archivists' ethics committee, which was created in 1976 and completed its task in 1980. The need for a new, revised code stemmed from a feeling that the archival profession had evolved in the twenty years since publication of the first code. Many archivists believed that since that code had been written specifically for the National Archives, it was neither applicable nor adequate to cover all the issues affecting the wide variety of institutions in the profession.

The Archivist's Code of 1955 was more an exposition of major responsibilities of the archivist than a guide to professional ethics, although it did address some matters of appropriate behavior in certain situations. It delineated the archivist's moral obligation to preserve and physically protect the valuable records of an institution; the duty to protect the integrity and evidential value of records; the moral constraint against profiting from the commercial exploitation of information; the obligation not to withhold information combined with the responsibility to observe legal restrictions on access; the duty to encourage research by others and to personally participate in scholarship. It was laced with practical reminders to maintain control of the budget while fulfilling these obligations.

The code was organized around seven points reflecting archival functions such as appraisal, security, reference, and access. The first point concerned the appraisal of records, and expressed the archivist's moral obligation to society to preserve the records of government which contain "evidence of how things actually happened and to take every measure for the physical preservation of valuable record". It linked this concept with the pragmatic view that the cost of records preservation must be taken into account in the appraisal process because the archivist "has an obligation not to commit funds to the housing and care of records that have no significance or lasting value". The second point also dealt with appraisal, calling for the realization that in the appraisal process the archivist "acts as the agent of the future in determining its heritage from the past". Archivists were exhorted to make impartial judgments, free from ideological, political, or personal biases.

The code next attended to the archivist's responsibility for the physical and intellectual protection of records, including the obligation to provide a properly controlled environment for their maintenance, to provide appropriate safeguards for their security, and to guarantee their integrity and provenance. Archivists should promote access to records, publish guides and finding aids to encourage their use, and be personally available to help researchers, at the same time observing "any established policies restricting the use of records". The code stipulated that archivists should behave courteously. They should not obstruct research, but need not waste time responding in detail to "frivolous or unreasonable inquiries". However, the code did not define what constituted a frivolous or unreasonable inquiry. It proposed that, while it is not appropriate to "idly discuss" the work of one researcher with another, it is proper to exchange such information when it is apparent to the archivist that there is a duplication of effort.

The code addressed the mutual ethical concern of all professions, that practitioners in a field should not profit from commercial exploitation of special information gained through their work, and also stated that archivists should not withhold information or records from others in order to engage in private research or publication projects. However, it held that archivists should take every legitimate advantage of their favored situation to conduct historical or archival research projects.

The final portion of the code encouraged archivists to share the fruits of their research with their colleagues to enlarge and enrich the body of archival knowledge, and to leave successors a "true account of the records in [their] custody and of their proper organization and arrangement".

Discussions of additional areas of ethical conflict continued in the literature after publication of the code, but a review of the code was not formally begun until the mid-1970s. During the 1960s and 1970s, articles were published that dealt with the ethics of institutional collecting policies, appraisal, and theft. A 1961 *American Archivist* article by David Duniway, "Conflicts in collecting", posited that competition and conflict in collecting were the inevitable results of the nature of the records and manuscripts being created and the legal mandates of the various agencies and institutions charged with the responsibility to collect and preserve them. In this seminal article, Duniway proposed ten principles which would establish guidelines for defining collecting areas, replevin of estrayed material (that is, the return of records to their legal custodians), policies for determining acceptance of collections of organizational or family records, and procedures for microfilming.[1]

In a 1966 article in the *American Archivist* on theft and alienation of records, James B. Rhoads, Archivist of the United States (1968–1979), called for the creation of a joint committee of the Society of American Archivists and the Manuscript Society to draw up a code of ethics including a definition of the rights and obligations of dealers, collectors, archivists, and manuscripts curators to their institutions and to one another "explicit enough to be effective and so fair that no public-spirited archives or manuscripts depository and no honest manuscript collector would have valid grounds for refusing to subscribe to it". Rhoads believed that addressing ethical issues was a priority for the profession.

In 1968 an incident occurred which dramatically pointed up a number of ethical concerns. It also vividly demonstrated that archivists had no mechanism to investigate and resolve alleged breaches of conduct. Francis L. Lowenheim, professor of history at Rice University, charged that the Franklin D. Roosevelt Library had denied him access to a file of 1933–1934 letters to Roosevelt from W. E. Dodd, American Ambassador to Germany, because an archivist at the Library was editing a three-volume work on foreign affairs during the Roosevelt administration and wanted to monopolize publication of these letters.

Additional charges made by Professor Lowenheim included that although he could not prove that he had specifically requested the Dodd file, nonetheless, knowing his research topic, the archivists at the Roosevelt Library had an obligation to inform him of its existence and pertinence to his project; that the Library deliberately had not notified scholars of the publication project; that the archivist–editor was "not a competent or formally trained scholar or editor"; that the Roosevelt Library and Harvard University Press, the publisher, had conspired to give away public property by contracting to publish and copyright material in the public domain; and that he deserved compensation for his expenses and research time at the Library because the staff had wasted his time by their conduct.

These charges were taken seriously by the press and the historical profession. Since the archival profession did not have any process in place for dealing with complaints against institutions or individuals for unethical conduct, the American Historical Association and the Organization of American Historians quickly stepped in to form a committee to investigate the Lowenheim allegations. The committee issued a report in August 1970 which found that the Library had not behaved dishonestly in its dealings with Lowenheim, but underscored the areas of potential conflict between the interests of historians and other researchers, and archivists and manuscript curators. The incident also demonstrated the potential damage to the archival profession in not having the machinery in place to investigate and mediate disputes. Richard Polenberg, professor of history at Cornell University, and Herman Kahn, a past president of the Society of American Archivists and former director of the Franklin D. Roosevelt Library, discussed the case and its implications in two articles in the July 1971 issue of the *American Archivist*. Despite the unhappiness of the archival profession that resolution of the Lowenheim matter was taken out of its hands, no immediate steps were taken to review professional ethics nor to create a formal process to handle future complaints and disputes.

New freedom of information and privacy legislation led to additional ethical concerns, as did revisions in the copyright law. These and other critical issues continued to be raised in the literature. Finally, in December 1976, the Council of the Society of American Archivists created an *ad hoc* committee on ethics. The committee's responsibilities were to explore and define ethical behavior in archival and manuscripts work, concentrating on the issues of collecting policies, service to patrons, and "managing record material". The committee was to prepare a draft code of ethics and make recommendations to Council on the appropriateness and feasibility of the Society's adopting sanctions against unethical conduct.

The committee worked for three years to complete the final version of the new code. They opened the process to input from the entire profession. Forums were held at three successive annual meetings of the Society, 1977–1979. A draft of the code was published in the July 1979 *SAA Newsletter*, and all responses were considered in the final revision. This final version was approved at an SAA Council Meeting in January 1980, and was published in the summer 1980 issue of the *American Archivist*.

The current code of ethics

A code of ethics for archivists has two sections, the text and a commentary. It begins with a definition of archivists as individuals, who "select, preserve, and make available records and papers that have lasting value to the organization or public that the archives serves". The definition goes on to say that archivists perform these functions in accordance with statutory requirements or institutional policy while subscribing to a code of ethics "based on sound archival principles and promote institutional and professional observance of these ethical and archival standards".

Having defined archivists and their basic duties, the new code is similar to the old. It enumerates major areas of archival responsibility, defining the accepted practices or behavior in each of them. Rather than having a numbered set of rules, the text has eleven unnumbered paragraphs. The first two paragraphs are concerned with the acquisition of records and papers. Acquisition or transfer or records or papers is to be done in accordance with the institution's purposes and resources. Grover is echoed in the statement that institutions do not compete for materials when the competition would endanger the integrity or safety of the items. The new code goes a step further to say that there should be cooperation to ensure that materials will be preserved in "repositories where they will be adequately processed and effectively utilized".

The second paragraph incorporates all of the considerations which affect negotiations for transfer of records or papers to a repository. It stipulates that archivists should seek fair decisions based on legal authority over the materials, financial arrangements, copyright, processing arrangements, and access.

Wayne C. Grover dealt with access by advising archivists "to promote access to records to the fullest extent consistent with public interest" while "carefully observ[ing] any established policies restricting the use of records". Access to records and papers, today, more so than in 1955, involves the most ethically complex issues which archivists in the United States face because they must thread their way through freedom of information and privacy legislation which governs the individual's right to access to information and laws which equally protect the right to privacy. These obligations may conflict with the primary duty archivists have to preserve and protect the records of significance and lasting value to society—as Grover said, "the evidence of how things actually happened"—and to make that information available for research.

Moreover, the United States is a litigious society. Fears about the possible misuse or abuse of information can tip the balance, for an archives, in favor of either not preserving certain materials or placing restrictions on access to them. Such restrictions, however, may open the profession to charges of unfairness and inequity in their creation and application. These considerations must be weighed against the duty of the archival profession, as Grover expressed it, "to promote access to records to the fullest extent consistent with public interest".

The new code addresses this multi-faceted issue by saying that, "Archivists discourage unreasonable restrictions on access or use, but may accept as a condition of acquisition clearly stated restrictions of limited duration and may occasionally suggest such restrictions to protect privacy". It admonishes archivists to faithfully observe all such agreements.

The next matters dealt with are appraisal, arrangement of records and papers, and the intellectual and physical security of archives. Whereas Grover spoke in philosophical terms of the archivist acting "as the agent of the future in determining its heritage from the past", as well as needing to make "decisions impartially without taint of ideological, political, or personal bias", the new code says: "Archivists appraise records and papers with impartial judgment based on thorough knowledge of their institution's administrative requirements and or acquisitions policies". Impartiality and institutional interests are the two new guideposts for the appraisal process.

Arrangement of materials is to be "in conformity with sound archival principles and [proceeding] as rapidly as . . . resources permit". Regarding security, it is the responsibility of the archivist to protect the evidential integrity of the records and papers, and to secure them against theft, defacement, and damage from use or improper storage. Further, as a reflection of the state of present-day society, archivists are adjured to "cooperate with other archivists and law enforcement agencies in the apprehension and prosecution of thieves". It is interesting to note that a reminder of this responsibility was necessary. This may be because archives are sometimes reluctant to take action on thefts, perhaps because of embarrassment at the circumstances, the difficulty in proving ownership due to inadequate administrative record-keeping, or the difficulty and costs of prosecution.

Respect of privacy is raised again in regard to the case of "individuals who created or are the subjects of records and papers, especially those who had no voice in the disposition of the materials". This refers particularly to case files from mental hospitals, orphanages, and other such institutions. Here is the point where profit from information gained or the revelation of information from restricted holdings is prohibited.

The consideration of reference also echoes Grover's 1955 code. "Archivists answer courteously and with a spirit of helpfulness all reasonable inquiries about their holdings . . .'' There follows an elaboration upon the old code on the exigencies and professional concerns which may place limitations on use. ''[Archivists] encourage use of [holdings] to the greatest extent compatible with institutional policies, preservation of holdings, legal considerations, individual rights, donor agreements, and judicious use of archival resources. They explain pertinent restrictions to potential users, and apply them equitably.'' The new code endorses Grover's proposition that it is appropriate for archivists to inform researchers of parallel projects using the same materials, and expands it to include the exchange of names of the researchers, if both parties agree. It reaffirms the legitimacy of archivists using their institutional holdings for personal research, with the caveats that the research have institutional approval and that others users of the same materials be informed of the research. There is an expansion of the principle of appropriate personal research and interest in historical documents by archivists to include review and comment on the works of others in their fields, even works based on research in their own institutions. It also states that archivists who personally collect manuscripts should not compete for acquisitions with their own repositories, and should keep complete records of their purchases available for scrutiny by their employers.

Additionally, the revised code covers the matter of professional criticism and complaints about professional or ethical conduct. Irresponsible criticism of other archivists or institutions should be avoided; complaints should be addressed to the individual or institution involved, or to a professional archival organization for resolution. However, none of our professional organizations has put in place a body to investigate or adjudicate such disputes. One of the responsibilities of the ethics committee was to suggest ways to implement sanctions for violations of the code. Although this was done, the Society of American Archivists did not formally adopt the proposed procedures. A serious complaint will, no doubt, serve as the catalyst for action in this area.

The code endorses the idea that archivists should share their knowledge and experience through professional activities, and that they have a responsibility to assist in the professional growth of junior colleagues. It closes with the statement, ''Archivists work for the best interests of their institutions and their profession and endeavor to reconcile any conflicts by encouraging adherence to archival standards and ethics''.

The body of the code is followed by a ''Commentary'' which is intended to explain the reasoning of the committee, and to further clarify various points. The committee kept the text brief for easy reading and reference. This section gives members of the committee an opportunity to comment on the areas where there was no unanimity of opinion. It provides information about some points of law with which archivists should be familiar. Taken with the body of the code, it gives as full an explanation of the agreed current standards of behavior for the profession as could easily be read and consulted.[2]

Conclusion

The *Code of ethics for archivists* provides needed guidance for coping with problems which may arise during the daily performance of professional duties. Within the limitations which exist for any ethical code, this is a good and workable document. As stated earlier, a code is only a general guide to standards of behavior. It can outline major areas of conflict and concern for the profession, recommend ways to avoid encountering problems, and suggest generally appropriate responses and remedies. It is an essential and useful instrument for professions which deal with the public and which must protect the interests of the public and the members of the profession in their interactions. It is, however, only one component of professional ethics. The other two necessary elements are education in the philosophy of ethics, and the development of a system for the adjudication of complaints and the implementation of sanctions for breaches of ethical conduct.

Both of these elements were mentioned in the final report of the ethics committee to the Council of the Society of American Archivists. The report said that, "Consideration of ethics for archivists should be an important part of instructional courses and workshops for beginning and other archivists". Regarding the issue of policing infractions, the committee suggested that the SAA should have a new committee of eight to ten members on professional standards and ethics, "constituted so that its members are people specially interested in ethical considerations and well informed about them". It was suggested that past presidents of the SAA might desire to serve, along with three or four *ex officio* members from the SAA Council.

Neither of these suggestions was approved or implemented by Council. The issue of professional ethics seems to have reached temporary resolution through the adoption of the code. Perhaps it will require another "Lowenheim Case" or a major inter-institutional conflict to awake archivists to the realization that the adoption of a code of ethics does not resolve the need for creating a climate of ethical concern and arbitrating questions of ethical conduct.

In any event, the archival profession needs to include ethics as a fundamental part of its basic educational programs. An understanding of professional ethics and of how to apply them in a professional capacity is not in-born in would-be archivists: it requires study. The reward for this effort comes from the elevation in the level of interaction between archivists and the public. When exposed to public scrutiny, there will be less chance that the profession can be accused of arbitrary or inequitable behavior if it has incorporated ethics in all levels of policy and performance. Moreover, the profession needs to create its own committees or panels to investigate and adjudicate alleged breaches of conduct. The existence of such a mechanism to review the conduct of individuals and institutions and the vigor and dedication with which it chooses to police itself provide clear indication of how seriously a profession adheres to its ethical principles. Concerned archivists should take the initiative lest this responsibility be taken away and placed in the hands of other professional organizations again.

Notes and references

1. Discussion of the literature is based on an unpublished presentation by James H. Conrad to the 7th Annual Meeting of the Society of Southwest Archivists, May 10, 1979, entitled "Archival ethics: perspectives on the literature". Full citations to the articles mentioned are in the list of sources for further reading.
2. There was a session devoted to the issue of ethics at the 50th Annual Meeting of the Society of American Archivists in August 1986. There were three presentations at that session which are as yet unpublished. Larry E. Burgess, "The archivist's code: is it of use?"; Elena S. Danielson, "Ethical dilemmas of the present and future archivist"; David E. Horn, "The development of ethics in archival practice".

14

Implementing an Archival Preservation Program

Norvell M. M. Jones
and *Mary Lynn Ritzenthaler*

Preservation is one of the defining concepts of archives administration. Without recognition that certain records are worth saving indefinitely, archives as they are presently known would exist only by accident. At the same time, although records may be preserved forever, if they are not accessible to a specific audience, the preservation effort will have been a dismal failure. This chapter will address those activities that go beyond the physical repair of damaged documents to include basic approaches to many aspects of archival work that ensure the preservation of records in a usable form.

Because preservation concerns affect so many archival activities, most institutions will benefit from a program approach that influences the execution of almost all other archival functions. The goal of preservation is to assure that records in archival custody survive as long as possible or, in some cases, as long as is legally necessary. This can be most easily achieved when the goals and basic principles of preservation are understood by all staff involved with the records, including everyone from the head of the archives, to the search-room attendants, to the person responsible for the heating, ventilating, and air-conditioning system—and everyone else along the way. The size of the group will vary, just as the specifics of the preservation program will vary, depending on the size and needs of the institution.

In addition to a well-informed staff, someone should have responsibility for oversight and implementation of the preservation program. Increasingly this person is a professional conservator or archivist who has had post-baccalaureate training in preservation. Because such training is still far from common, it is important to recognize that preservation is a vital part of the total archives program and should, accordingly, be afforded professional respect and status. The entire archives suffers when preservation is confined to the narrow limits of a technical service and viewed as the simple-minded work of repair technicians.

Archival preservation is the joint responsibility of a number of professional staff, each of whom brings unique knowledge to bear on the complex problem of preserving archival records. Archival materials are as diverse as man's creativity and ingenuity. While there are traditional materials and formats generally considered to constitute the archival record—such as loose or bound paper documents and a wide array of photographic and other graphic materials —emerging technologies are continually expanding archival horizons, and thus the preservation challenge.

The diversity of the archival record is more than matched by the complexity of individual record items. Archival records are composite objects, generally composed of a variety of papers, inks, adhesives, pigments, emulsions, animal skins, textiles, plastic films, and magnetic images, among many other substances. A single archival document thus may be composed of diverse materials, each of which may respond somewhat differently to changing environmental conditions and which may also have varying keeping qualities. Sound archival preservation programs must be based on a knowledge of the chemical and physical requirements of various materials *and* a knowledge of the intrinsic value of specific records and how they relate to the overall holdings of the institution. Traditional archival concerns have focused on the intellectual content of archival documents. This concern must be meshed with concern for the physical object, not only because the physical and chemical attributes affect possibilities for long-term preservation, but because the physical nature of a document can convey much about the past and how the historical record was created and valued.

Preservation issues should be addressed through the joint efforts of knowledgeable professionals. These include archivists, who are aware of the relative values of records and their expected uses, and conservators, who can provide information on the physical and chemical nature of archival materials, treatment options, and unique attributes of various physical forms. Conservation scientists can provide essential data, based on research and testing, that can help in identifying media and related problems of stability as well as in making sound decisions regarding storage environments. In addition, in response to rapidly changing technology in the areas of information creation and capture and the increasing interface between the information industry and archival concerns, technologists or media specialists can provide critical information on the preservation of film-based materials, sound recordings, and other magnetic media, such as machine-readable records, and optical and digital disks. Most archival repositories will not have technical specialists in all of the areas listed above. However, informed archivists and preservation specialists can acquire a broad knowledge of the archival record, using archival insights about the intellectual content and the physical needs of records in developing preservation programs that address questions about the storage, handling, and use of archival materials. This mature archival perspective dictates a response that addresses both unique and collective requirements posed by the informational content and the physical form of records.

Archival and library preservation, which share many of the same concerns, are relatively new professional specialities in the field of conservation. Historically, however, creators of records have always sought to preserve documentary materials by providing secure and environmentally stable storage conditions. However, it was the Florence flood of 1966, with the devastation wrought to library, archival, and museum collections by the waters of the Arno River, which marked, in the opinion of many concerned professionals, the starting point in the development of archival and library conservation as a field of specialization within the conservation profession.

The tragedy brought together international teams of book and paper conservators with diverse backgrounds and approaches, in massive attempts to share knowledge and information on the best techniques to recover and restore damaged manuscripts, books, and documents. As restoration efforts progressed, it became apparent that certain materials and structures had withstood the ravages of time—and the devastating flood—much better than others. This resulted in conservators beginning to consider the utility of incorporating the best elements of historical structures into modern conservation treatments.

While many of the lessons learned from the Florence flood related to treatment innovations and systems, it also became obvious that conservation and preservation programs had to focus on whole objects and whole collections, both in terms of restorative treatment of damaged materials and preventive maintenance of entire holdings. For example, the importance of disaster planning and preparedness could not be better exemplified than by the tragedy in Florence. Of equal significance was the fact that many members of the salvage teams went on to take positions in the cultural institutions of their home countries that allowed them to develop broadly-based preservation programs for library and archival collections. The lessons learned in Florence have played a continuing role in the emerging field of archival preservation at an international level.

A fundamental issue in archival preservation relates to the massive volume of many archival holdings. While some individual records have great intrinsic and artefactual value, most archival documents are valued for the information they contain, gaining significance not as individual items but as part of a whole, in relation to other documents and groups of records. These issues of mass and scale align archival preservation with problems being addressed by libraries and many museums, and serve to define the preservation solutions sought by such institutions. Faced with large and diverse holdings, it is expedient to direct limited resources to solutions that will have the greatest benefit for the collection as a whole. A systems approach—addressing such needs as improved environmental conditions or better housing for archival records—will have much greater impact on saving collective holdings than will providing conservation treatment for only a limited number of single items. Emphasis on *preservation activities* rather than on *conservation treatment* of archival records is necessary, although treatment plays an important role in the overall preservation program of an archival institution.

The elements of a preservation program and the underlying problems they must address are covered in the following pages. Issues such as assessing needs, establishing priorities, and developing effective solutions to preservation problems are also covered, within the overall context of integrating archival and preservation management.

Causes of deterioration

Archival records deteriorate due to a number of interrelated factors, including the chemical and physical stability of specific materials, storage under adverse environmental conditions, and such external causes as excessive or careless handling, and loss or destruction brought about by human-induced or natural disasters. Being aware of, and as far as possible, gaining control over these factors can do much to enhance the useful life of archival records.

Temperature, relative humidity, light, and air quality are the environmental factors that must be controlled if archival records are to be preserved in a usable state. As temperatures rise, the rate of chemical reactions accelerates, including the rate of deterioration of record materials. High temperatures (above 75 degrees Fahrenheit, 24 degrees Celsius) can also have adverse effects on some materials, causing, for example, gelatin emulsions on photographs to soften and stick to other surfaces, or certain types of sound recordings (such as wax cylinders or vinyl disks) to soften and take on distorted shapes. Relative humidity, which is defined as the amount of water vapor in a volume of air, expressed as a percentage of the maximum amount that the air could hold at the same temperature, is important for the effect it has on both the chemical and physical well-being of record materials. Relative humidity is temperature-dependent, that is, the warmer the air, the more water vapor it is capable of holding. Many chemical reactions are both temperature- and water-dependent; the higher the temperature and relative humidity, the greater the rate of reaction of degradative processes. Conditions of high relative humidity (generally above 65 percent) and temperature also encourage the growth of mold and mildew and enhance the possibilities of insect and rodent infestation. Humidity is a curious factor in that it can pose problems if it is either too high or too low. Under conditions of high relative humidity, moisture-sensitive inks can offset, photographic emulsions can become tacky, and coated papers can stick together. Conversely, very low relative humidity can cause cellulosic materials to dry out, become brittle, and fracture or crumble during use and handling. Parchment and vellum are examples of hygroscopic materials that are very responsive to changes in moisture level in the surrounding air; under conditions of low relative humidity such animal skins can become inflexible, cockle, and shrink and, if used as a covering material on books, can cause boards to warp and buckle. The moisture level in the air affects such physical characteristics as dimension and flexibility. Therefore, humidity levels must remain relatively constant so that the equilibrium moisture content of record materials is also constant, and papers and books retain mechanical stability.

Light, specifically ultraviolet radiation, is also capable of damaging archival materials. The shorter the wavelength, the more active or energetic the radiation, and thus the potential to cause photochemical degradation of paper and other archival materials. Visible light in the blue and blue-violet end of the spectrum can damage organic materials, although short-wave ultraviolet and near-ultraviolet radiation (beneath 400 nanometers) are most damaging. Damage from light is cumulative and is dependent on the wavelength and the duration and intensity of exposure. Chemical reactions initiated during exposure to light continue after records are placed in dark storage; thus, limiting the total exposure of a document to light over its life cycle is a primary preservation concern. Light speeds up the chemical reactions causing degradation of paper. For some materials, exposure to light has a bleaching effect, causing paper to lighten and colored papers and inks to fade. On the other hand, poor-quality groundwood papers will discolor and darken upon exposure to light. Light can also greatly damage such sensitive media as watercolors, color photographs, and blueprints, resulting in color loss, diminished contrast, and loss of information.

Air quality is another important concern in archival preservation programs, especially for repositories in urban areas or industrial centers. Gaseous pollutants, including oxides of sulphur and nitrogen, hydrogen sulfide, and ozone, are products of combustion and other chemical reactions that have a deleterious effect on paper and other record materials. Sulphur dioxide and oxides of nitrogen combine with water in the air to form acids, and ozone causes oxidation reactions which embrittle paper. Particulate matter, including dirt, dust, and oily soot, can damage record materials by abrading sensitive surfaces (as on photographs and sound recordings), and can also be corrosive or cause disfiguring stains that obscure information. In humid environments, dirt and soot that become imbedded in paper fibers often cannot be removed and must be considered permanent damage.

Other enemies of archival records include mold, insects, rodents, and similar micro-organisms and biological pests. Such agents can be controlled or eliminated entirely by maintaining recommended environmental conditions and establishing good housekeeping practices. Mold spores, which are always present in the air, will grow and flourish under warm and humid conditions (temperature generally above 75 degrees Fahrenheit, 24 degrees Celsius, with a relative humidity above 60 percent); darkness and little or no air circulation will also encourage the growth of mold. The precise conditions conducive to the growth of micro-organisms vary, however, depending on the type of mold and whether or not the materials have been previously infested. Mold can permanently stain, disfigure, and weaken paper and other record materials, resulting in cosmetic and physical damage, as well as loss of information.

Insects and rodents are attracted to cellulose, paste and glue, gelatin sizing and emulsions, and other materials composing archival records, both as a food and as a nesting source. Insects, including cockroaches, silverfish, and carpet and other beetles, are as likely to nibble delicately at the edges or surface of paper documents as to eat their way through stacks of paper and books, causing structural damage as well as loss of information. Rodents, such as mice, rats, and squirrels, are also attracted to archival records and are fond of shredding paper to recycle it as a nesting material. The droppings of such pests are corrosive and can permanently stain and disfigure record materials. Insects prefer warm, humid environments; and both insects and rodents will be more active at night when they are less likely to be interrupted in their destructive activities. Constant vigilance and careful attention to the details of archival housekeeping are thus important aspects of a preservation program.

Further threats to archival materials are posed by careless handling, inappropriate storage systems, and well-intentioned but misguided repair attempts or conservation treatments. Virtually every time a record is handled, whether by archival staff or researchers, it is in greater jeopardy of being damaged than if it were passively sitting in its storage container. Staff awareness and researcher orientation, therefore, are mandatory aspects of a preservation program, because they ensure that the special handling needs of various record materials will be respected and enforced.

Elements of a preservation program

Almost all repositories must deal directly with the full range of archival enemies: environments that are uncontrolled and far from ideal; storage systems that fail to protect and in some cases actually damage records; access run amok, with indiscriminate use and handling of records; records so popular that they are virtually being used up; records so important that they are permanently and proudly (or even absentmindedly) displayed; records that are torn, brittle, moldy, or otherwise damaged; and, at one time or another, an event as mundane as a burst water pipe or as overwhelming as a major fire. Well-designed preservation programs provide a framework to meet these and similar needs within unique institutional settings. Programs must be flexible enough to respond to changing institutional priorities while balancing the preservation needs of archival records against other, sometimes conflicting, repository goals.

A basic priority that the preservation program should address is the environment in which records are stored. The ideal environment is one which maintains a cool temperature and an even relative humidity. Atmospheric pollutants, especially oxides of sulphur and nitrogen, ozone, and just plain grit and dirt should be eliminated. Recommendations on specific temperature and relative humidity ranges vary depending on the type of holdings in the repository, how often the materials are used, and the location of the archives. Recommended temperatures for records that are frequently used and stored in space shared with people are usually the lowest temperatures that the people will tolerate. This is usually between 68 to 70 degrees Fahrenheit (20 to 21 degrees Celsius) in North America. In some parts of the world this will seem too hot while in other parts it will seem too cold. A degree or two in one direction or the other does not make that much difference, although cooler temperatures will greatly enhance the preservation of infrequently used records. Relative humidity recommendations also vary. Cellulose, which composes the bulk of most archival holdings, will last longest at a relative humidity of around 20 to 30 percent, much lower than that normally recommended in the past. However, skin materials, including vellum and leather, become quite dry and tend to loose flexibility or distort in such dry conditions. Therefore, for holdings of mixed materials a higher relative humidity, around 45 percent, is recommended. For both temperature and relative humidity, tolerances of two to four units are usually permitted. Ideally, changes in temperature and relative humidity should take place gradually over several days or weeks, rather than hours, to allow record materials to equilibrate gradually.

In some buildings, even with all of the money in the world, it is impossible to maintain desirable environmental conditions. Some buildings when heated in the winter cannot tolerate relative humidity at the specified level. Excessive condensation results at the point in the building where the warm moist air meets the cold, which can damage the building structurally. Aside from these problems, a weakened building can be a harbinger of disaster for the records. The control of temperature and humidity is an expensive and complex undertaking and one that must be approached with judgment and common sense. The goal should be as even an environment as is economically feasible, with fluctuations that are as gradual as possible.

If a building is located in a polluted industrial area, some control of air quality is highly desirable, and technologies exist to filter air coming into the archives for dirt as well as gaseous pollutants. Particulate matter is easiest to remove as the process is essentially physical removal by filtration; however, removal of very fine particulates is expensive both in terms of energy efficiency and maintenance. Removal of gaseous pollutants is more complex, involving equipment that removes the pollutants by neutralizing them in a chemical wash or by precipitating them using special scavenger filters. Engineers specializing in controlling air quality in buildings can assist in identifying appropriate filtration equipment. In addition to the initial investment, financial resources must be committed to support the scrupulous maintenance of the equipment once it is installed. A system that is not properly maintained is worse than none at all, since it leads to a false sense of security.

Storage of records can be the single most important aspect of a preservation program. In most archives, individual records are used infrequently; therefore, the way that they are housed becomes a very significant preservation issue. In some national archives, legislation determines which records have permanent value, what type of paper they should be created on, and how they should be housed for permanent storage. By terms of the law, when records are retired to the archives they are housed in good-quality boxes, labeled, and made ready to be used by researchers as the need arises. Most archives are, however, less fortunate. Records may arrive in a systematic way, or may simply be bundled up and sent forward when they are no longer used and are in the way of the creating agency. They may be housed in containers which are of poor quality, or housing may be non-existent. Access and preservation are both served by storing records in boxes and folders that are chemically and physically stable. Ideally, at the point of accession, records should be housed in folders and boxes made from high-quality paper stock that is resistant to abrasion and tearing, and which is buffered throughout with magnesium or calcium carbonate, or both, to assure that the stock itself will be long lasting and non-damaging to the records within. A number of excellent commercially-available box and enclosure designs meet the requirements of providing safe, sturdy protection for archival records.

Handling and use are a third area of concern in a preservation program. Although the seeds of much damage are sown as records degrade chemically, the actual break, tear, or dirty smudge does not occur until the record is handled; and even then damage can occur to relatively stable, sound records through thoughtless or excessive handling. It is important that repositories have a vigorous education program for staff and researchers in proper techniques for handling records, and that handling aids are readily available. For example, book supports and easels should be available in research rooms, as should tables that are large enough to accommodate the records being used. Rigid supports (such as large folders constructed of archival corrugated board) and flat carts should be provided for supporting oversize materials as they are moved between storage areas and research rooms; and trucks and trolleys used to transport records should be sturdy and easily maneuvered without vibration. Besides staff training seminars, there should be regular review sessions to assure that the information is fresh and not eroded by time. Strictly-enforced research-room rules help to prevent damage to records. Researchers should be given limited amounts of material, allowed to take notes only in pencil, monitored by staff at all times, and encouraged to bring preservation problems to staff attention.

Microreproduction and other transfer formats are an obvious adjunct to concerns about use and handling. Because reproduction introduces the possibility of making multiple copies of a record, and machine-readable copies such as optical digital disk introduce the possibility of quick search and access, transfer formats often serve two roles in an archives. As a preservation technique they allow archivists to retire the most valuable, vulnerable, or most used records from regular use and substitute a copy. The benefits are significant, although there is a continuing debate about the permanence of some transfer formats. Silver halide microfilm processed to archival standards and stored under appropriate conditions has excellent permanence. When the reproduction becomes the record copy and the original is discarded, which is suggested only for extremely vulnerable, unstable media or for records of no intrinsic value, verification of film and assurance of its stability are extremely important. New machine-readable technologies, such as optical digital disk, are unproven as a permanent media, yet offer very attractive features. Records can be searched rapidly and easily, eliminating much extra handling of original materials. Many institutions are now exploring these technologies, and in the future this way of restricting handling may become the method of choice. In the meantime, silver halide microfilm continues to be the recommended method for most preservation copying.

Exhibited records are often exposed to environmental conditions that are at variance with conditions in the rest of the institution. Lighting is often too bright, which can be damaging to most types of record materials. When, in addition, the light source generates heat, it can alter the established balance between temperature and relative humidity. The handling that records receive in preparation for display is often more stressful and vigorous than they would receive otherwise. Yet exhibition is a useful and quite valid form of access for many archival programs; when implemented properly, damage to records can be avoided and exhibition can actually enhance a preservation program. By carefully selecting the records to be exhibited and by evaluating the risks in each case; by controlling environmental conditions during exhibit; by assuring that exhibition handling and mounting techniques are non-damaging; and by including preservation information in captions where appropriate and planning an occasional preservation exhibit, archivists can incorporate exhibition as part of a preservation program.

Light damage is a product of the combined result of the intensity of the light, its radiant energy, and the duration of exposure. Just as a person's life expectancy cannot be predicted with absolute accuracy, it is not possible to tell exactly how exposure to a particular light for a specific amount of time will affect a record. A great deal is known about relative vulnerabilities, however, and some general recommendations can be made regarding exhibition lighting for archival records. First, all ultraviolet radiation should be eliminated by filtering all light sources, and, second, the intensity and duration of visible light exposure should be controlled. A limited lifetime exposure is recommended for vulnerable paper artefacts, and a record of the duration and intensity of exposure for all exhibited pieces should be maintained. Total exposure is calculated by multiplying the intensity of the exposure by its duration. A document exhibited at five footcandles for ten hours would thus receive the same total exposure—fifty footcandles—as it would if it were exhibited at twenty-five footcandles for two hours.

In addition to providing safe conditions for exhibit, which reduces the risk of chemical damage from light and uncontrolled temperature and relative humidity, it is important to assure that records are protected from physical damage before, during, and after being displayed. Only safe mounting materials and techniques should be used, and documents should be placed in contact only with archival-quality paper, boards, and plastics. Documents should always be framed under glass or acrylic sheeting such as Plexiglas® or Perspex®, or exhibited in closed cases. Staff who will be responsible for handling records in preparation for exhibits should be trained in the proper techniques, and policy governing the length of exhibits should be established and followed. If material is changed too frequently, staff may feel pressured to meet deadlines and adopt shortcuts and a casual approach to putting material on display; on the other hand, the damaging effects of long exhibition are all too well documented. Again, judgment is required to strike a compromise that meets the legitimate needs of access without excessive stress on the records being exhibited. Recommended exhibition times for paper records range from three months to one year. The important thing to remember is that lighting levels are just as important as duration, and that not all records are equally vulnerable. For example, a twentieth-century letter written on mechanical wood pulp paper with a watercolor illustration is usually much more vulnerable to damage by light than an eighteenth-century account book. The exhibit history and future exhibit potential of a document should also be considered when determining whether an item should be displayed and for how long. An obscure document that will probably never be exhibited again could be safely on view for a year, while a popular document that is requested repeatedly may need curtailed exhibit time.

Disasters happen to the unprepared. Planning for the occurrence of a major fire or even a burst pipe can minimize loss to an archives, and is an essential part of any preservation program. In the planning process, archivists should assess both the risks of the geographic area where their institution is located and those within the institution itself, and identify essential holdings as well as finding aids that can be very expensive or impossible to replace. It is also important to make contact with the local fire department, freezer plant, and other local immediate sources of essential recovery supplies. Throughout the planning exercise, it is useful to imagine what the very worst situation could be, as well as the much more probable burst pipe with its limited but still potentially devastating damage.

Without a well-thought-out plan, essential time is lost when disaster strikes. Effort is expended which not only does not help the situation, but which may actually damage records more than the disaster itself. The wrong people are notified, the wrong records are saved, and the wrong salvage techniques are used. Planning for the unexpected should involve consultation with staff representing all parts of the institution. For a small institution this may be only one or two people, but in a large one it should include representatives from facilities maintenance to upper management and every area in between. The staff member responsible for preservation may be in charge of instituting the planning process but should not, indeed cannot, do it alone.

The final element in a preservation program is the treatment of damaged or vulnerable records. It is not accidental that this comes at the end because, balancing effort and cost against results, it is the most expensive aspect of preservation. Conservation treatment, repair, restoration, or any of the other names that have been applied to the physical reparation of documents is, indeed, an important part of a preservation program. The work of skilled, sensitive practitioners, using only the highest quality, time-tested materials and techniques, will always stand up to the scrutiny of their successors. However, because treatment has often been viewed as the first line of defense, many institutions confronting massive quantities of ageing records have adopted a single treatment solution. As a result, records in sound condition have been laminated or reinforced with silk gauze, while others of relatively low importance have been treated and then returned to inadequate storage containers. The treatment plan for all archival holdings should consider the relative importance, condition, and anticipated use of the documents. The options available for treating records also must be considered, and whether it makes more sense to have a conservation laboratory or repair station within the institution, or whether work should be done on contract by outside conservation facilities.

Steps in implementing a preservation program

The most successful preservation programs share several important characteristics. First of all, they have archives-wide support. An institutional commitment of both human and monetary resources to preservation is a matter of policy. Secondly, there is a written statement of goals based on serious study of the preservation problems that the institution confronts, an assessment of available and needed resources, and decisions about which actions provide the greatest benefit and are most cost-effective. And finally, in practice, the program meets the stated goals and the preservation needs of the institution. This is a tall order; but with careful planning, commitment, and flexibility, it can be accomplished.

Before the planning can be started in a systematic way, someone, perhaps the head of the archives or another staff member with specialized training or a strong interest, must target preservation for attention. Then, in almost all cases, both subordinates and their superiors must be convinced that the time is right for action. Because preservation activities affect so many functional aspects of an archives, the initiative must come from high enough in the institution to command the broad support and participation required. With an institutional mandate and fixed responsibility for the program, the planning can begin.

The next steps will depend primarily on institutional size and style. An archives with three staff members will organize the process differently from one with fourteen departments, each with ten or twelve staff members; but the areas of concern, the milestones, and the goals are similar. In a small institution, one person may carry out the entire planning process with regular informal consultation with other staff members. In a medium-sized institution, the person responsible may head a committee where individual members take responsibility for small parts of the process and work both individually and as a group. In a large institution, the committee format may be expanded to include subcommittees or task forces to study different problems. The format is not critical as long as staff members at all levels are involved. The planning process serves several useful functions in addition to its primary one of developing a plan. It educates the staff about the preservation requirements of the archives' holdings and generates support for preservation activities to be included in the plan.

Acquiring a basic background knowledge is the next step of the preservation planning process. In addition to the information in this chapter, the list of sources for further reading will provide a good starting place. Conversations with preservation administrators in other institutions and with local conservators also can be helpful, as can participation in the preservation activities of professional organizations. Throughout the planning process, deadlines must be set for the completion of each phase.

Gathering and assessing preservation data

Once the planners have acquired some basic preservation background, they should be able to identify the areas of study, outline the questions that must be answered, and establish a timetable. The seven elements of a preservation program—environment, storage, handling and use, microreproduction and reformatting, exhibition, disaster planning, and treatment—outlined earlier, should each be considered. In addition, other elements not included here that may be specific to an individual institution should be incorporated as appropriate. A list of questions should be developed for each element that will, to some degree, be institution-specific. The list should be designed to obtain general information, such as: What is current preservation practice within the institution? What areas of the institution are involved? How is current practice most effective? What aspects need to be improved, and what stands in the way of improvement? Obviously, consideration of each element will require specific information as well. For example, in examining the environment within the institution, it will be necessary to consider the local climate, prevailing environmental conditions in the repository, and what means exist currently for controlling it, as well as any plans, such as renovation, which might have an impact on the environment.

There are several useful techniques for gathering both general and specific information, including interviews, reading, inspection, and surveys. Not all of them will be useful for every element, but most of them will be. Common sense will suggest which technique to emphasize in each instance. For example, in considering the environment, the investigation should include interviews with staff responsible for the operation and maintenance of heating, air-conditioning, and ventilating equipment, as well as with staff familiar with conditions in stack and other areas of the repository, to obtain information about the age and health of the equipment and whether there is flexibility in its operation. Assessment by both technical and non-technical staff can help to determine the efficiency of the system and to identify its weak and strong points. Monitoring of actual environmental conditions, which is a form of survey, will also be important, as will an inspection of the equipment and design and construction features of the building affecting environmental control. At some point in the process, it will probably be necessary to do some additional reading, including administrative files, equipment literature and specifications, or perhaps some slightly more technical materials.

On the other hand, in considering storage, the investigation might begin with a series of brief interviews with staff who have direct custody of and oversight over the storage of records, to determine current practice and areas of concern, and then concentrate on an inspection of actual storage conditions. If the institution's holdings are extensive, a survey to pinpoint problem areas might be in order. If a survey of storage is required, it might well be coordinated with a survey of the condition of the records themselves, which would be an important part of planning for the treatment needs of the holdings. Again, additional reading might be required.

Assessment of handling and use will rely heavily on both interviews and inspection. It will be essential to understand how all staff actually handling records perceive problems. In a large institution, it is almost always the case that records are thought to be damaged in the next department or, barring that, by researchers. Inspection in this case will involve observation, as unobtrusive as possible, of what actually happens in each type of situation where records are handled. The combination of talking and watching should identify problems caused by people and those caused by the wrong furniture or inadequate storage containers, as well as damage resulting to fragile records because of insufficient protection or safeguards. As the information-gathering process concludes, a clear picture of what the problems are should emerge. At this point, it should be possible to summarize those areas where change or improvement will benefit preservation of the institution's holdings and to suggest ways to accomplish this goal. The planners should resist ruling out any ideas for the time being, even the most outlandish. Sometimes ideas which at first seem to be impractical, too expensive, or a waste of time, ultimately prove useful or spark a solution which is perfect.

When the results from each element of the planning process are reviewed together, there will almost always be areas of overlap. A single solution may answer several different problems. For example, use of stronger alkaline buffered boxes for storage of records may (a) protect records from an environment which for the time being can be only imperfectly controlled, (b) improve storage conditions for and protect records that are currently housed in a wide array of unsuitable acidic boxes and wrappers, and (c) help to prevent damage to records as researchers struggle to remove them from inadequate or damaging containers. As each element is reviewed and the lists are consolidated, there will be a mix of major and minor projects.

Setting priorities and balancing resources

The next phase of the planning process involves assigning a cost to the solutions and assessing the impact of each, and determining whether they can or must be accomplished in a short period of time or spread over a longer time span. Monetary costs for particular preservation solutions can be determined by consulting catalogs, talking with suppliers, engaging potential consultants or contractors in preliminary conversations, calculating the cost of staff hours involved, contacting other preservation administrators—in short, using any and all means available. Assessing the impact of a particular solution relies on the background work and judgment of the planners. For example, filtering fluorescent tubes in stack areas to remove ultraviolet radiation may at first seem like a very useful project, but if all of the records are stored in closed boxes and if records are not used or exhibited for significant amounts of time in the stacks, the project would actually contribute little to the preservation of the records, and have low impact. On the other hand, in a region characterized by high relative humidities and widely fluctuating temperatures, an environmental control system would contribute substantially to the long-term preservation of the holdings and have a high impact. The third factor, scheduling, can obviously influence and interact with both cost and impact. It may be possible to spread a reboxing project over several years, permitting the use of existing staff with no change in program and requiring a smaller annual allocation of preservation money for the purchase of new boxes. If the project is completed in a more condensed period of time and all the boxes are purchased at once, the savings on the quantity purchase of the boxes could help pay the wages of someone to rebox the records.

Because cost, impact, and scheduling are so interrelated in preservation planning, it is important to keep some flexibility and perspective in the next stage, assigning priorities. The first priorities should be those items which have high impact and are relatively inexpensive. There may also, however, be some high-cost items which are so important that they must be included. It is not possible to be specific at this point since high cost is relative. What seems prohibitive for a small institution may be not only essential for a large one, but actually represent only a small portion of its preservation budget. What is important is that the priorities fit the institution. The middle and lower priorities generally include high-impact, high-cost items as well as low-impact, low-cost ones. If, for example, installing a dimmer switch on lights in the exhibit space will lower light levels a few footcandles it is beneficial, and since it does not cost much it is well worth doing. The items which usually drop off the list entirely are the low-impact, high-cost ones. They serve a purpose, however, by stimulating thought to produce other ideas.

The work up to this point is essential, but if it stops before the last stages its usefulness will be greatly diminished. Many hours in many institutions have been spent carrying out preservation surveys, with negligible results, because no one translated the findings into a plan of action with goals and a timetable. The last step in the planning process before implementation is to state clearly what needs to be accomplished, what the accomplishments will mean for the preservation of the archives' holdings and what resources will be required, and to establish specific target dates for the accomplishment. It is prudent before submitting the preservation plan to the director of the archives to have the document reviewed by key colleagues to assure that no obvious points have been overlooked and to generate support for implementation. The director may decide to use the plan as a tool to generate additional funds for preservation and may suggest some changes before it is accepted and implemented.

When the plan has been accepted and implementation starts, provision should be made to review progress against goals on a regular basis, perhaps quarterly. Such a review and a commitment to flexibility assures success. If something is not working, it is reasonable to revise the timetable, the goals, or the method of operation to be more realistic. The written goals in the plan are a target, but the ultimate objective is preservation of the archives' holdings. It is important to keep a sense of perspective. The plan is only a tool, though it can be an extremely useful one.

Integrating archival and preservation management

Administrative aspects of implementing an archival preservation program should be integrated at an early stage with ongoing archival functions such as appraisal, accessioning, arrangement and description, storage and housing, reference use, and exhibition. Preservation must be seen as an inherent part of all archival work rather than as a series of specialized activities relegated to alternate Thursdays. Everyone on the staff must be made to feel that the preservation of archival records is a specific part of their job. Explicit mention of appropriate preservation duties associated with various tasks should be written into position descriptions. This responsibility for preservation should be accepted by staff at all levels, from the director of the institution down to and including any student and volunteer workers. A preservation plan that focuses on archival functions has the potential for great impact in that many of the goals or identified areas of concern can be carried out with little expenditure of financial or staff resources. Simply articulating preservation as a major institutional goal, reordering priorities as necessary, and taking steps to orient all staff regarding the preservation implications of their actions can do much to move a preservation program forward.

Every time a record is handled there is potential for damage or loss. Therefore, it is important that all archival functions be carefully scrutinized to determine whether or not they are being carried out in a manner that may put records in jeopardy. There are a number of basic preservation procedures that should be incorporated into archival tasks. For example, during records appraisal, basic information on the physical form and condition of the records can be gathered. Archivists should consider not only the intellectual content of potential accessions and how they might fit into an overall collecting policy, but also assess them from a physical perspective. This ensures that decisions to acquire unstable or damaged records or records in unusual formats are made in the full knowledge of the responsibility to devote preservation resources to any necessary conservation treatment, copying, or specialized storage of such materials.

Preservation record-keeping should be incorporated into accessioning or arrangement processes. Such things as the need for better-quality storage enclosures or the presence of unstable media (such as cellulose nitrate film or thermographic copies) that require reproduction should be noted. Recording the location and quantity of unstable materials requiring preservation expedites planning and the execution of the appropriate responses. A preservation checklist (manually compiled or computerized) with such categories as media, format (bound, rolled, folded, oversize, etc.), housing, and condition simplifies the recording of preservation data. Also, because a basic goal of preservation is to minimize the handling of archival records, it makes good sense to carry out as many functions and gather as much information as possible in a single review and evaluation of records. Such an approach unifies archival and preservation goals and is also an economic way of expending staff resources.

Storage and housing can be improved at various stages during the life cycle of records but are often incorporated into accessioning or arrangement projects. Good-quality storage containers meeting archival specifications should be used, and sizes of enclosures and storage containers should fit and adequately support the records. Oversize and bound materials obviously require specialized housing, as do records that are fragile or in poor condition as well as those bearing such sensitive media as charcoal, pastel, or watercolor pigments. The presence of fasteners used to unite groups of records should also be evaluated to determine whether they are causing damage. Many metals are capable of rusting or corroding, thereby weakening and staining the surrounding paper. Many fasteners, such as tightly-clamping clips, exert too much pressure on weak, brittle pages; they should be removed from records, as should fasteners that function as a hard line or cutting edge against which paper will break as it is flexed. Rubber bands should never be used on archival records; nor should colored textile tapes or string, which may contain unstable, soluble dyes. Both rubber bands and cloth tapes can cause mechanical damage if wrapped around loose documents, causing the edges of the paper to break and tear. Also, rubber bands contain sulfur, which causes yellow–brown stains on paper; as rubber bands age they become soft and tacky, causing objects to stick together, and they eventually harden into accretions that can be difficult to remove without causing damage.

If preservation were the only concern, fasteners would be eliminated entirely from the archival repertoire of supplies. But in this as in other areas, sound preservation practice must be meshed with other valid archival concerns regarding security, handling, and the need to maintain records in their original order. When fasteners must be used, devices made of stable materials should be selected, such as stainless steel paperclips or rustproof, non-corroding staples. Both types of fasteners may be used to advantage in conjunction with small strips of archival bond paper that are folded in half and placed over the top edges of the documents to serve as a barrier and support for the fastener. In some instances, fasteners are always inappropriate, such as with records of high intrinsic value, documents that have artistic merit, or materials such as photographs where the image-bearing layer could be permanently damaged by the pressure or impress of a fastener.

Other preservation concerns should be considered during archival arrangement activities, such as the removal of foreign objects. Foreign objects include items which, because of their chemical make-up or dimensions, could damage adjacent records by staining them or causing physical distortion of flat paper. Materials that should be segregated from files of documents include campaign buttons, such mementos as pressed flowers or locks of hair, cased photographs, mineral samples, bullets, or any strange and wonderful items found in the midst of more traditional record materials. Depending upon the archival significance of such items, on institutional policies, or on agreements with donors, foreign objects may either be discarded or filed in separate, appropriate storage with necessary cross-references employed to maintain links between associated materials.

All institutional policies regarding identification or other markings placed directly on records should also be evaluated to ensure that only non-damaging techniques are employed. Such historical practices as embossing or perforating ownership markings are now considered inappropriate by many institutions because they permanently alter and damage paper. Any inks (whether manuscript, ballpoint pen, or stamp pad ink) used to mark documents should be non-acidic, non-bleeding, and colorfast. Identification or ownership markings can be useful as theft deterrents. Their use, however, must be balanced against other factors, such as the nature of the records in archival custody, whether aesthetic values would be altered, monetary or market value of the documents, and institutional security procedures. Because identification markings are generally considered in the context of theft deterrence, the use of invisible ink must be widely publicized to meet this goal. Institutions holding security-classified documents may also have to deal with the issue of marking records for the purpose of declassifying them; the same issues apply regarding the stability and non-damaging characteristics of the marking media.

Inks used to permanently mark file folders or other enclosures containing records should also be evaluated. Requiring that pencils rather than ink be used for such purposes will diminish the possibility of records inadvertently being damaged by staff rehousing records, and will also negate the possibility of descriptive information being lost in the event of a water-related disaster in which soluble inks will feather or bleed, sometimes to the point of staining archival materials.

Many of the preservation concerns described above may be broadly considered to be a part of what is termed holdings maintenance. Preservation actions grouped under this heading are basic procedures designed to prolong the useful life of archival records while deferring and, in many cases, eliminating the need for conservation laboratory treatment. Goals of holdings maintenance include the provision of a suitable, safe storage environment for record materials that takes into account their value, use, size, format, condition, and any special preservation concerns. Holdings maintenance actions include sleeving fragile documents in stable plastic, removing damaging fasteners, preservation photocopying, dusting the exteriors of boxes and bound volumes, and replacing poor-quality storage enclosures with those that meet archival specifications for long-term preservation. Given the specialized requirements of many archival records and related problems of identifying some media that either have special storage needs or that are unstable and therefore must be segregated from other records, holdings maintenance programs are often best jointly developed by archivists and conservators working together to achieve appropriate preservation solutions for institutional holdings. Holdings maintenance procedures, however, are intended to be carried out by archival staff in a non-laboratory setting.

Another important series of preservation activities that falls short of laboratory treatment involves evaluating the condition of records at the time they are requested for use by researchers. Staff trained in basic preservation procedures and trained to make sound judgments regarding the condition of records and their ability to withstand use should examine records before they are delivered to researchers. Such evaluation ensures that records that are heavily used will be looked at from a preservation perspective and that necessary protective measures will be taken, including dusting boxes and the exteriors of bound volumes, sleeving or copying fragile documents, aligning records neatly within boxes, and replacing damaged folders and boxes as necessary. Provision should also be made for withholding from use any document that cannot be safely handled without prior conservation treatment. This evaluation program should be carried out with the knowledge of the research community, and efforts should be made to gain their support in the archives' preservation mission. Notices describing the program can be posted or given to researchers as they sign into the reading room. Perhaps even more effective is to make the program an integral part of the procedure by which researchers request and receive records. Such a program can help to impress upon researchers the fact that the archives is serious about its preservation mandate, and that it expects researchers to take seriously their role in the process. An active evaluation program can be of assistance in ensuring that reading room regulations regarding the handling and use of records are followed; it can also assist in generating broad public support for the preservation mission of the institution.

The preservation actions described above should be fully incorporated into ongoing archival functions. Written guidelines and periodic training and refresher courses for staff, taught by persons with overall responsibility for the preservation program, help to ensure consistent approaches to preservation across the institution; they will likewise help instill a sense of the importance and serious nature of the mandate. Preservation work is obviously never complete, but the more it is fully integrated into archival functions the greater the likelihood of the records surviving. It is also efficient to take advantage of every opportunity to perform basic preservation functions and record preservation data in the course of accomplishing other archival work. False distinctions between preservation and archival activities are thus diminished, and more is gained each time a record is handled if multiple tasks are performed. This alone is a great preservation advantage, since the less records are handled the better off they are.

Conservation treatment

Preservation checklists and forms compiled while performing such tasks as rehousing, arrangement and description, or evaluation prior to research use, can be used as aids in identifying records requiring conservation treatment and in setting treatment priorities. The goals of archival conservation include chemical stabilization, physical support and protection, and improved appearance. For example, a document on early nineteenth-century paper with information written in iron gall ink might benefit from washing and deacidification, which would improve its chemical stability. This treatment, however, would not regenerate the paper or make it less brittle to the touch. Additional treatment, perhaps a lining with strong Japanese paper or simply encapsulating the document, would be required to provide physical support and make it possible to handle the document safely. Improved appearance as a result of such treatment procedures is often an added benefit. Although cosmetic improvement is generally not a primary goal in archival conservation, it may be required or desirable for objects intended for exhibition or for items of the highest intrinsic value.

Archival conservation is closely allied with other conservation specialities and shares with them common philosophical and ethical concerns. These relate to treatment considerations as well as the attitudes and practices of professional conservators. The American Institute for Conservation (AIC), for example, adopted a Code of Ethics and Standards of Practice which guide the professional behavior of its members. This code should be required reading for archivists working with conservators. The AIC Code of Ethics provides insights into the responsibilities accepted by United States conservators toward the historical, artistic, or other cultural objects with which they work, the need for documentation, and the mutual responsibilities and expectations of conservators and custodians of culture property. The International Institute for Conservation (IIC) is another important source of information on issues pertaining to conservation ethics and philosophy.

Ethical considerations in archival conservation begin with sensitivity to and understanding of the values and inherent qualities of historical records, knowledge of the materials employed in their creation, methods of fabrication, and uniqueness of physical form. This knowledge is then brought to bear on problems relating to condition and stability, and selecting appropriate treatment options. Conservation treatments must be safe and appropriate to the problem at hand, must not subject documents to trauma nor result in any loss or damage, either of information or the media or support. All materials used during the course of treatment must be stable and of known good quality.

The issue of reversibility of conservation treatments is very complex and is currently under discussion in the conservation profession. In general, the philosophy of using only reversible materials and techniques is sound and should be adhered to and advocated. The issue is really one of degree, however, since virtually every conservation treatment permanently alters a document. For example, there is no way to return a document that has been washed and deacidified to its pretreatment state; it has been permanently changed. While the decision to carry out a conservation treatment is usually reasoned and appropriate, it does not truly fit the requirement of being reversible. It is perhaps easier to consider this issue in a more familiar area, such as reversibility problems associated with cellulose acetate lamination. Theoretically, this treatment is often reversible, if inks and pigments are not soluble in the solvent used to delaminate the document. In practical terms, however, reversibility of collections of laminated documents is not feasible or realistic, given the large numbers of such materials, the time required to carry out the procedure, and the fact that the process cannot be completely reversed since it is impossible to remove entirely all of the cellulose acetate impregnated in the paper. Further complicating this issue is the fact that often in archival contexts there are records that have little intrinsic value but are in such poor condition that a treatment of last resort is sometimes the appropriate solution, given preservation responsibilities to whole collections, the need to preserve information rather than the artefact in many instances, and limited resources. In such situations, the question of reversibility is perhaps of less importance than the simple necessity to do *something* to preserve information.

Although archival conservation shares many approaches and concerns with the broader conservation community—and is debating the same issues—there are several important differences. The most obvious of these relates to the facts of mass and scale. Archival holdings are generally so massive that the possibility of providing conservation treatment for all items within an institution is out of the question. A further and somewhat intriguing difference between the goals of archival conservation and fine art conservation, for example, is the fact that archival records are intended to be used and handled in ways to which works of art will never be subjected. Archival records, in all of their amazing diversity, are generally mobile objects that must be in fit condition to be accessed and handled by staff and researchers. Paper must flex, and bindings must open. Thus, conservation treatment solutions for archival records must be applied in ways that somehow bridge the gap between the inherently conflicting goals of use and preservation.

Given the special character and needs of archival holdings, approaches to conservation treatment have evolved to incorporate the concepts of mass (or batch) and single-item treatment. The nature of the records will determine which approach is carried out, but in either case the quality of the treatment should meet the same high standard. Mass treatment is appropriate for groups of records that are similar in composition and which require straightforward and similar treatment. Such an approach is also appropriate when treatment has to be carried out relatively quickly (which is often the case with large masses of records requiring stabilization), and when individual treatment documentation is not required. Documents of the same age, the same paper and ink type, and exhibiting relatively the same condition are candidates for mass treatment. Mass-treatment approaches do involve a somewhat higher risk of damage and thus are generally not appropriate for records having high intrinsic value. Other factors to consider when establishing treatment approaches and systems include the facts that archival records are inherently non-standard and that documents similar in appearance may in fact carry quite different inks and media of varying solubilities. Documents of high intrinsic value may also be interfiled with documents of less significance. To avoid carrying out inappropriate treatments and resultant damage to records, it is as important with mass as with single-item treatment to carefully evaluate the records before treatment in order to assign correct treatment solutions and isolate unique or highly-valuable documents requiring special handling. It is equally necessary to be aware of the primary danger of mass conservation treatment, that is, letting a system or approach become so automatic or mechanized that individual treatment decisions are not made.

Single-item conservation treatment is necessary for documents having high intrinsic value or exhibit potential, as well as records that present complex conservation problems. Single-item approaches are also mandatory when additional time and experimentation may be necessary to develop appropriate treatment solutions and when individual treatment documentation is necessary because of the significance of the records. Examples of archival materials that require single-item approaches include original works of art, manuscript maps, treaties, and individual documents of great historical significance. The treatment steps in mass and single-item approaches are the same; however, in the latter instance, documents would be handled individually rather than in a group, and extensive examination and testing would be carried out both before and during treatment. Treatment documentation, including written treatment proposals and detailed reports, would specify materials and techniques employed, and would be supplemented by photographs of the items before, during, and after treatment.

Conclusion

Sound archival preservation programs can be developed when preservation is viewed as an institutional priority, and when the archival staff is informed about the specialized storage and handling requirements posed by archival records. Progress in implementing a preservation program will be made most quickly if emphasis is placed on improving conditions for entire holdings. Concerns that should be addressed first when implementing a preservation program include monitoring and improving environmental conditions, improving the storage and housing of archival records, and instituting inspection programs so that potential problems with unstable or deteriorating materials are caught early. In addition, it is important to evaluate institutional policies and procedures to ensure that records are not being inadvertently damaged or endangered. Since preservation and conservation are rapidly changing fields, it is important that staff keep current with the technical literature and attend professional conferences. A successful preservation program achieves a proper balance between sometimes conflicting archival requirements for access and preservation; and solutions to problems must be sought that do not compromise the records. In the final analysis, archival records need advocates, and preservation programs can serve this function by ensuring the long-term protection and availability of record materials.

15

Archival Security

Frederick J. Stielow

Despite a long legacy of curses, chained volumes, and locked *armaria*, the contemporary history of security is quite short. Library consciousness first stirred in the 1940s with the publication of Lawrence Thompson's landmark *Bibliokleptomania* and then awakened with the social unrest of the 1960s. Archival awareness was even more belated. Despite some earlier work, security interest in archival literature was only codified with the publication of Timothy Walch's *Archives and manuscripts: security* manual by the Society of American Archivists (SAA) in 1977. Such concerns were further legitimized by the rapid evolution of the *Library Security Newsletter*, first published in 1975, into the *Library and Archival Security* journal, the dominate source for current articles. Although awareness is still far from complete, archivists had begun to embrace security as part of the general professionalization of the 1970s and, lest it be overlooked, in particular response to the St Louis Records Center fire of 1973.

As Walch pointed out, the awakening of interest in archival security had been delayed because of misperceptions over its supposed high costs and great complexity. Some archivists may have sought to avoid unnecessary unpleasantness, while others ignored the issue or hesitated to announce thefts in the misguided belief that publicity would exacerbate the situation. Yet, according to Philip Mason in his perceptively titled "Library and archival security: new solutions to an old problem" (1975), the needs had long been around. Moreover, they were expanding. Library and archival thefts in the United States increased from a total value of five million dollars in 1963 to more than fifty million dollars a year in the 1980s. The problem of library and archival thefts can no longer be expected to vanish. Cultural repositories are being faced with almost unthinkable threats from bombings to increased incidents of arson, that now account for over 80 percent of all their fires.

If archivists accept the reality of the dangers and the imperative to preserve the documentary heritage, then security emerges as a necessary professional responsiblity. One way to approach this obligation is to treat security as a subset of preservation management. Archival security is "preservative". It is charged with deterring unwarranted access to and the mutilation or theft of archival materials and, because of the impossibility of immediately differentiating between human and natural causes, its purview must also overlap with disaster preparedness.

The addition of such elements to the archival portfolio is not without its problems. Since preservation and security are best served by denying entry to or even a knowledge of holdings, they are in seeming conflict with the rest of archival theory—which is designed to make materials available for use. This inherent contradiction between the mandate to guarantee the continuation of a documentary heritage and the one to facilitate access demands resolution, but has yet to be debated on a theoretical level. Even a full synthesis will probably fail to achieve perfection, and the rest of this chapter will focus on establishing the frame for a workable set of compromises.

There are no final answers or perfect security systems—just a series of trade-offs to provide the most feasible and affordable protection. Each situation is unique and calls for variable responses. Archivists and administrators will be called upon to make distinct policy decisions at each institution. They must first be aware that effective archival security does not stem from crisis responses or even reliance on superior locks and alarm systems. Proper responses will only come from professional awareness and a systematic management perspective.

In keeping with modern management theory, all aspects of security should be evaluated against the ideal of an "open systems" framework which will support the fulfillment of the institution's mission and the attainment of its goals. This concept offers much to a security program. Its effectiveness is rooted in the idea of considering security as an integral part of all aspects of archival practice. Instead of dramatically altering other archival functions, the key is to enhance their inherent security elements. In practice, such an approach increases overall efficiency and even helps to demonstrate that the simple awareness and publication of a concern for security are key deterrents.

As with any strategic effort, a security program starts with formal authorization and proceeds to an essential data-gathering phase before analysis, planning, and implementation. This particular overview stresses the utility of an integrated perspective, which begins with a complex assessment of facilities, other archival functions, and of staff, as well as an understanding of legal implications and outside liaisons.

Facilities assessment

Perhaps the easiest way to initiate an investigation of security needs is through physical surveys of the general building and its services and the specifics for the archives. Such a study must be broadly cast: for example, taking into account time or use cycles to differentiate among the periods when the archive is active, when it is inactive with adjacent areas still open, and when the institution is fully closed.

Outside opening hours, one can conceive of physical layers of defense. Leaving aside any external fencing and assuming that the building is not situated on a flood plain or other unfortunate location, the outer perimeter of defense consists of clean, well-lighted and easily-observed grounds. The next layer of defense is the exterior of the building itself. Its condition is crucial, not only to defeat human miscreants, but also as the essential element for protection against natural disasters—such as storms, floods, fires and earthquakes.

Although a high-level security program would call for expert structural assessments of the building itself, archivists should be capable of an adequate initial effort. Using a published check list, or the questions indicated in this chapter and their own common sense, archivists should survey the layout for danger areas and note the presence or absence of physical barriers to unwanted entry, as well as of devices to scare off intruders and alert staff if such penetrations should occur. Surveyors should pay particular regard to the roof and to doors and locks, as well as alternative forms of ingress like windows, skylights, or coal chutes. For more specific advice, the reader may wish to turn to guidelines established by the National Archives for records centers. In keeping with these standards, outside walls should be "type A", or four-hour fire-resistant, with two-hour fire-resistant columns, a non-combustible roof and two sources of water supply. The recommendations also suggest alarm systems to alert against both human and natural agents. The examination of building systems will also need to take into account accumulations of flammable supplies, as well as the plumbing and electrical systems, plus such details as automatic fire doors, a fire-resistant inclosure for the furnace, and a closable vent system to prevent smoke transfer.

Since most archives occupy only part of a building, archival security will tend to concentrate on the next layer, or the internal defenses of the repository itself. Fortunately, the lack of facilities for browsing and the norm of closed stack operations mean that archives, manuscript repositories, and records centers are natural security areas. Researcher exit and entry should normally be restricted to one doorway. Ideally too, for general preservation purposes, an archives should be located on an intermediate level and not in a basement, which may be vulnerable to water damage, or an exposed top floor.

Whatever the reality, the research room serves as the main arena for potential thefts and mutilations during working hours. Any equipment belonging to the archives should be firmly fastened and permanently marked or etched to deter pilfering. Closed-circuit television cameras or less expensive dummy cameras may also be employed, but a control desk is the defensive focus, since it is the location for both the initial screening and the later monitoring of users.

Although a degree of propriety and politeness is necessary, the room and its control section should be designed with a mind to implementing the institution's circulation control policies and an eye to clear sight lines without hidden nooks. It should also be noted, however, that current library electronic book detection devices are of little use, too expensive, and physically too dangerous, because of the adhesives they use, for unbound archival materials. A more effective solution is the designation of a "clean" research room, where researchers are required to leave all extraneous parcels and materials outside, and where, at its "cleanest", the archives even provides all paper and pencils. This step also typically entails the installation of a security gate and secure storage for researchers' belongings.

Although most breaches of security by humans occur during working hours, the configuration of the building at others times must not be ignored. Windows in public areas should be locked, and any such openings protected by gratings or screens in high-security areas or where within easy reach of the ground. Interior walls, doors, and locks come under special scrutiny during periods when the archives is closed but the building itself is open. Attention must also be paid to ensuring good sight lines for security guards and to the dangers from less obvious points of possible entry—such as through the panels in modern suspended ceilings.

The physical division between the research and storage areas in a closed stack operation is a major line of defense against human intrusion when the archive is in operation. The storage area itself is the main bastion of protection at all hours. It should be windowless and regarded as off limits to unauthorized personnel, unless they are strictly observed. Such safeguards should provide basic protection against theft, vandalism or arson, but the facilities assessment should also be concerned with further guaranteeing the safety of the materials from these and from natural dangers by checking whether or not proper warning devices are present, in particular for fire, smoke and water, and whether the shelving is strong enough and properly braced so that it will not collapse or tilt, whether from a weak earthquake or through vandalism.

Attention also needs to be given to individual storage containers. The placement of documents in rather nondescript and uniform boxes is actually a further security feature, and the standard archival box-type container has proved itself quite an effective barrier against water, smoke, and even fire damage. But such boxes need to be at least four to six inches above the floor and preferably below the top level of shelving. The documents themselves should be filed perpendicular to the shelf line, so that they cannot spill out directly on to the floor and thus inadvertently feed a conflagration.

A facilities survey will also take special account of fire-prevention equipment, such as lightning deflectors and especially sprinkler units. What type of sprinklers, are they functioning, and are they in any way impeded (for example, by boxes piled too closely to their outlets)? Earlier emphasis on the consequences of water damage to archives have now receded before the realization of the more devastating effects of total incineration. Fire-suppressant systems have proved remarkably successful in localizing damage by catching the fire at an early stage. Moreover, the cost of such systems can often be amortized by savings in insurance costs. There are several types of these automatic systems. In ascending order of cost, they include: pipe systems, the most ubiquitous, where individual sensors in the sprinkler heads release water in a continuous stream; dry pipe, where water is only drawn into the pipe after a sensor has been set off; pre-action, a dry pipe system with an early alarm to allow for human intervention first; recycle or automatic range to act individually over a fire; and high-expansion foam or inert gas, most notably the Halon 1301 flooding system used to protect the most valuable holdings.

There is a wide variety of alarm and detection systems to warn of the presence of smoke or flame, or of sudden increases in temperature, plus devices that attempt to scare off or inform of the presence of a possible arsonist. It is most important that such devices are either constantly monitored or that they are certain to alert the responsible personnel. Other precautions include a cache of disaster equipment, which could include emergency backup generators, wet/ dry shop vacuum cleaners, fans, mops, flashlights, marking labels, and plastic sheets and containers.

The ultimate layer of physical defense is a vault for the most sensitive and valuable pieces. The vault area will offer the highest degree of protection against fire, flood, and theft. Since its very presence calls attention to the material within, one may want to insure a concomitant enhancement in warning devices and circulation procedures.

A vault is also increasingly associated with storage for machine-readable records. The rapid onset of computer technologies makes it imperative that discussion of data security and integrity be firmly introduced into the literature of archival security. Since these media are routinely backed up by duplicates, some of the dangers from theft or vandalism by localized fires or direct magnetic attacks can be alleviated. Magnets should obviously be banned, but magnetic media and newer optical devices are surprisingly tough and more easily insulated from natural disasters than are paper records. Equipment too should be safeguarded and registered, yet alarms and disaster equipment, with the possible addition of specialized tape winders and cleaners, can actually be much the same for all media. The presence of electrical equipment obviously should alert one to potential dangers from electrocution in a water-related disaster.

The chief defense in an archival setting is simply physical access. Tapes, optical disks, "floppies" and the like are best safeguarded as off-line storage, so that they can only be mounted and used with the archivist's knowledge.

Security control is much more difficult when the use of on-line systems is involved. Typical problems are those of guaranteeing that the site at the other end of the line is the intended one and of preventing outsiders from intercepting or manipulating the message. Typical responses are the exchange of unique identification protocols between sites, careful shielding of transmission lines and the encryption of data. The advent of "untappable" fiber-optic cables is projected as an ultimate solution to this transmission problem in the immediate future.

The identification of individual users before allowing them access is a more usual area of archival concern. While the existence of esoteric mechanisms designed to match voice inflection or eye retina patterns may be noted, passwords will probably continue to provide the normal defense in most cases. Passwords need to be subject to their own security procedures. The best are randomly-generated groups of symbols. Whether this type, or the more normal pattern of understandable phrases or mnemonics is used, one should always try to insure that passwords are frequently changed and that neither they nor any of their written locations are easily guessed. In addition, one should seek software that limits the number of attempts at entry to the system, plus reporting on and perhaps attempting to trace unsuccessful attempts. Tracing itself will be greatly facilitated by the use of digitized telephone systems, enabling telecommunications authorities to keep track of every call made to or from any telephone in the system. In addition, the security of passwords can be enhanced by linking them to specific machines ("home site only" access in which each machine has its own unique password).

Archivists can also expect increasing involvement with authorization rules to determine the actions that different classes of users can take with collections of data bases and their own automated finding systems. On the latter, one needs to insure that only a select group, preferably at a particular site, are capable of changing or making entries, while limiting general users to queries only: for example, ensuring that only a cataloger can change a record, while allowing anyone to use it. Similarly, care must be taken that data in master archival files is not altered by unauthorized persons during later data manipulations or juxtapositions with other records. This would normally mean that the master files should never be mounted except to provide duplicate user copies; only the latter would be given to users.

An integrated function

The previous discussions have already indicated the difficulty of separating an analysis of structures from their related functions. Indeed, the heart of a successful security program and a prime daily concern is its integration with other ongoing activities.

Archival security proper begins from the moment ownership or control is passed to the archival institution. This activity may entail the external transfer controls and procedures of a records management program or be isolated to direct entry in an in-house acquisitions register. The key is to record ownership as soon as possible and to safeguard that documentation. Without such proof, legal attempts to regain ownership (replevin) of lost (estray) property are effectively worthless. Collections should also be brought under inventory control as quickly as possible; for they are most susceptible to undetectable pilfering while awaiting processing. Similar cautions and a change of policy are in order for libraries that demand the temporary transfer of valuable or restricted manuscripts from the controlled environment of the archives to the uncontrolled shelves of the catalog department for library cataloging.

With acquisition policies in place, appraisal emerges as central to the security effort. Here appraisal is used to determine artefactual values, confidentiality levels, and vital records status for the establishment of security priorities (machine-readable appraisal excludes artefactual values). If possible, the procedure will also establish cash values for reporting in case of later theft. Assuming the institution cannot afford full protection for each document, the appraisal process may single out those materials that require special treatment: for example, which documents should be placed in vault storage; which should be duplicated, so that only the facsimile is given to users; or, which should be marked to display ownership.

Such steps, especially duplication, imply additional costs. The inclusion of an indelible ownership mark heightens one's chances of recovering stolen materials in court and is a useful deterrent, but also demands a policy decision in regard to the possible loss of artefactual values. If marking is acceptable, it is well to turn to the guidelines put forth by the security committee of the Rare Books and Manuscripts Section (RBMS) of the American Library Association. These recommend stenciling in permanent ink in small size. (about 5-point) the initials of the owning institution—especially those based on National Union Catalog symbols. The initials should not disfigure and be easily located, specifically on the lower inner margin and near the last line of text on the verso of single-leaf documents or the verso of the first page of the principal text on bound papers.

Arrangement and description should also be adapted for security purposes, but with a consciousness of trade-offs among the ideal level of control and the realities of budgets and staffing. Thus, even though security and preservation are both enhanced by the processing of individual items, such desirable detail must be balanced with the economic and personnel realities that have led archival institutions to concentrate on broader series-level descriptions. An obvious compromise rests with the appraisal process and the designation of different levels of treatment based on the projected value of the holdings. The caution here is to avoid unnecessarily calling attention to the monetary value of a collection, for example, by listing cash amounts or purchase costs in public catalogs.

Research-room practices provide the main active defenses against theft and mutilation by outsiders, but may also be overly burdensome on researchers. The ironies here are that, whereas irresponsible users are likely to object to these controls, responsible researchers will respect the need for them and such efforts may actually elevate the archives and archivists in their eyes. A number of procedures are already well accepted, but may require enhancement. Typical research-room etiquette, for example, prohibits the use of foodstuffs and smoking, as well as ink pens. Thus, prohibitions on the introduction of outside belongings an the escalation to a "clean" research room could be viewed as part of an established continuum; moreover, this step avoids the prospect of greater embarrassment arising from the inspection of researchers' personal belongings when they leave the room. Yet thoughtful consideration must be given to this step, for even responsible researchers are likely to object to being totally denied access to their outside notes and forms. Other practices—such as ownership marks, user copies, posted security policies, daily sign-in logs and researcher registration forms—are normally more accepted. Taken together, however, such measures may create the sense of a rather élitist milieu which has the psychological effect of discouraging casual visitors.

Researcher registration may be a routine procedure, but it is also an essential element in any security program. Registration forms are best promulgated as contracts, which acknowledge the mutual exchange of value and point out the institution's restrictions. Beyond its potential for recording user interests and even evaluations, the contract requires a signature block and should have space for addresses (local and permanent), plus the form of identification presented. In high-security or suspect situations, procedures might dictate a double check on this identification and formal passes or letters of introduction.

Circulation documentation is equally important. When married to registration forms and logs, it provides the major resources for tracing back discrepancies to the last known users. More significantly, check-in protocols may provide a major deterrent against thefts and mutilation. A detailed verification of the return of all requests against an item-level description serves as the ultimate defense during operating hours. Although such a practice may be prohibitively expensive for all collections, some inspection is in order. Collections with special significance or those used in suspect circumstances would require more intensive scrutiny. In general, one should at least publicize the fact that collections are inspected on return and ask users to report any absences or destruction. In addition, the dangers from razoring or small thefts can be partly eliminated by reprographic policies that facilitate the copying of non-classified documents.

Especially in highly sensitive or secretive atmospheres, security extends to the final disposal or de-accessioning process. Typical procedures require a written authentication of destruction. Disposal methods themselves are varied and should be based on the degree of confidentiality of the documents involved. Techniques range from dumping in the trash, shredding, burning, and pulping for paper products to degaussing for magnetic materials.

What should be evident is the necessity of integrating security considerations into the management of records throughout the life cycle, rather than letting them stand on their own. Without this integration, a security program will probably fail. Such a program demands that a series of formal, conscious decisions be taken and properly recorded in supporting documentation, and calls for a written policy manual with a clear articulation of purpose. These guidelines must be seen as living volumes, which require constant updating and staff awareness. A manual is a basic sign of professionalism, which can be used both for training and to establish the propriety of the required actions. It would also include policy considerations, such as the degree the institution is interested in casual visitors and willing to sacrifice artefactual integrity to the deterrent value of marking.

Similar implications exist for written disaster plans, which are even more susceptible to being overlooked because of their lack of continuity with other procedures. The disaster plan is only functional if it is kept in the active consciousness of the staff and retrievable in an emergency. This requires that copies be kept in several known locations, and that alternative light sources be available to enable staff to read the plan in case of power failure. A typical plan should have a list of those designated to lead the recovery effort, key expert contacts, and specific responses for each type of emergency. A final warning is to include in the plan cautions against the possibility of thefts occurring during disasters.

The staff

Employees and administrators encompass the essential strengths and inherent weaknesses of security management. Any effort ultimately relies on their diligence and honesty—thus, the conundrum, for who watches the watchers? One procedural innovation would be a random inventory of the collections, which could also be used to collect information on their physical condition for preservation purposes. Random inspections offer one of the few remedies against internal thievery. They should be introduced as an automatic procedure without bias, which operates with the full knowledge of the staff as part of an integrated preservation program.

Other usual safeguards include the careful screening of job applicants. In some cases, screening can be facilitated by the requirement of a fidelity bond and the bond company's credit check. Another measure may be to augment or replace the research room clerk with a uniformed guard. Training sessions, which stress the seriousness of the mission and instruct in proper security techniques, are even more important. Rather than relying solely on negative deterrents, an educational program is a positive step that can help build a sense of *esprit de corps* among the staff. Security needs to be a staff effort, but it can also be used to motivate that same staff. For example, one can recognize the talents of individuals by giving them authority in guiding the various disaster recovery teams, or by including them in a security oversight planning group.

Since they often have keys and free, unobserved run of the institution, cleaning, custodial, and even non-archives security staff represent a particular—but more controllable—danger. Although precautions must be taken for ready access in emergencies, the best resort is to deny direct access after hours. Whenever possible, the activities of non-essential personnel should be observed and confined to working hours. Certainly, special care should be given to guarantee the integrity of the vault area in this regard.

Another major move is selecting a security officer from the senior staff. Such persons have primary responsibility for the coordination and continuity of the program. The security officer will work closely with the institution's legal council and any security force, as well as its public relations officer. Or, in smaller institutions, security officers may combine a number of those functions under their own purview. Security officers are also on the front line in the aftermath of a theft. They will insure that the matter is properly reported and initiate the collection of supporting evidence.

Legal factors and liaisons

Zeal for security must be tempered by proper decorum and a knowledge of the legal factors involved. Security programs walk a tightrope between the desire to protect the documents and the rights of individuals, including researchers and staff. Self-protection and the interests of the institution again call for careful planning, a publicly stated determination to stop theft, and a written security plan, all of which should be reviewed by legal authorities.

A knowledge of the law and where to go for help are both essential to the security effort. Unfortunately, laws are still so varied and occasionally so underdeveloped that one finds it hard to generalize. RBM's sample draft legislation on theft and mutilation, for example, calls for three classes of offenses: minor offenses, or misdemeanors, in respect of damage or theft to the value of 500 dollars or less; more serious offenses, described as "Class I felonies" for damage or theft between 500 and 5,000 dollars in value; and the most serious category, "Class II felonies", for damage or theft valued at more than 5,000 dollars. The draft legislation generally follows the State of Virginia's 1975 extension of its shoplifting statute to cultural property and allows archivists to hold and inspect suspects. Yet most archivists in the United States are still not free to detain a supposed thief without the danger of a false arrest suit and may not even be permitted to inspect parcels and purses. Even in protected areas, archivists should always be tactful, call for assistance, and avoid holding the suspect up to public ridicule. Another rule of thumb for archivists in potentially hazardous situations is to be certain to minimize any risk of physical danger to themselves and others in the event of thefts, mutilations, or natural disasters.

Legal knowledge apart, the recovery of stolen or damaged materials still depends heavily on prior work and contacts. Archivists must be able to identify and establish the monetary value of their holdings. They can benefit from a cultivated relationship with police and prosecutors. In addition, post-theft responses also call for ties with manuscript dealers and an awareness of their own security structures.[1] Similar liaisons are even more advantageous and necessary for disaster preparedness. These include a working relationship with local experts, emergency suppliers, and cold-storage locations. The spring 1987 "Emergency Management" issue of *Special Libraries* brings out an interesting relationship in this regard, with the possibility of the archival institution serving as a resource center for others in certain emergencies.

Other key ties are with the fire department, which should also be alerted to the peculiar requirements of archival repositories and the value of their holdings before turning on the high-pressure hoses. But the fire department and police can be a great source of information and training, as can insurance agents, whose business is risk management. The latter are often particularly adept at helping to plan all aspects of a security program and are a good source of technical expertise and guidelines. The final and most overlooked liaisons are with the users. The archivist's work is actually facilitated by communicating the reasons for a security inconvenience to researchers and attempting to enlist them in the effort. Informed researchers are a valued ally. They can, on occasion, report suspect activities and, more normally, tell of missing or misfiled documents they encounter.

Conclusions

If truth be told, most archivists would prefer not to have to deal with security. Security seems somewhat seedy and fascistic. The reality, however, is that archives are cursed—that unprotected cultural property is an invitation to thieves and vandals. From the basic proposition that documentary material of enduring value merits preservation, it simply follows that repositories must take steps to insure the integrity of their holdings. This imperative must be balanced by the reality of countervailing requirements for access—but cannot be ignored. Efficiency and professionalism suggest a management perspective and the integration of security as a factor within the full range of archival activities. Thus, security management and expertise emerge as basic elements within the modern archivist's portfolio.

Notes and references

1. For example, Bookline Alert/Missing Books and Manuscripts (BAMBAM), P O Box 1236, Washington, D.C., USA (tel (212) 737–2715) lists missing or stolen documents internationally.

16

Public Programs

Kathleen D. Roe

Excitment radiates as students pore over a letter from the Depression era, reliving the pain, stress and tension of "hard times'. Memories flow as community residents meet in a historic local bar, passing around old advertisements and newspaper clippings that elicit stories of by-gone social customs and notable neighborhood characters. A novelist weaves a tale of pioneer life based on the diaries and letters of a woman settler. A lawyer retrieves a cache of old property maps from the office basement and donates them after an archivist speaks to a professional luncheon meeting. These activities and many more result from innovative public programs.

Public programs serve a crucial function for archives by acting as the interpreter between a repository and the public. While the purpose of archives is to preserve and make available historical resources, that goal lacks substance if the resources remain unused. Public programs can promote archival goals to acquire and preserve valuable resources, encourage and expand the use of historical records, and raise public awareness of archives and their purpose.

A variety of terms are used for public programs: outreach; educational programs; external programs; developmental services; and public service. In addition, public programs are less clearly defined than other parts of the total archival process. Some archives have entire sections or individuals assigned to the development and maintenance of public programs; others conduct such activities, but do not clearly identify them as a distinct program element; still other archives dismiss the concept entirely. Public programs often receive less administrative and financial support than other archival functions; nonetheless their impact is beginning to demand increased attention.

Public programs do not share the longer history of other archival processes. Although occasional efforts at what may be called public programs can be identified from the early years of this century, the predominant methods for raising awareness and encouraging use were reference service, exhibits, and documentary transcription, editing and publishing. Archivists initially defined their public as the serious scholar, and the programs they provided were essentially in reaction to that scholar's needs. Archives were largely the sphere of an élite, educated class, and the needs of the general public were ignored. Not until the 1960s and 1970s did archivists begin to clearly and consistently articulate a theoretical framework for public programs.

Effective public programs consist of several basic elements. First, the purpose of developing such a program should be carefully defined. The institution needs to know what productive results will come from the program, and how it will support basic archival functions and further the needs of archival administration. The audience for whom a public program is designed must also be clearly defined to maximize impact. Finally, each archives needs to find program ideas that are both interesting and useful to its audiences while producing viable results for the archives. A detailed discussion of these three basic elements follows.

The purpose of public programs

As a comparatively new branch of archival practice, public programs have had to establish their legitimacy as a purposeful function. Some of the early complaints lodged against such programs have, in fact, been that they are not essential and do not contribute to the overall process. Public programs have been accused of treating archival materials and research lightly, or worse, smacking of public relations or marketing, drawing resources and attention away from substantive archival functions. When the goals of public programs are not well defined, such criticism is likely, just as it is when any endeavor is neither explained nor justified. There are several essential reasons for developing public programs. First, the basic archival functions of acquiring and preserving records with archival value can be expanded through the use of public programs. Secondly, public programs can increase and encourage the use of archival materials. Finally, they can raise awareness of archives and their holdings, as well as identifying the role and uses of records in society. Public programs can be used by archival institutions to encourage and improve communication with their parent institutions and with groups who allocate funds.

Public programs can be an important factor in assuring more complete documentation in a number of crucial areas. A substantial number of valuable resources have been lost in the past, and may continue to be lost in the future if people are not exposed to information about what is, and what should be retained permanently. Public programs can provide the vehicle for identifying and preserving records that might not have been retained otherwise. Public programs are a major means both for increasing the types and numbers of archival users, and for encouraging new and better usage. Many users already come to archives, but need to improve their skills in how to locate and use resources. Besides improving current reference services, public programs can be used to assist in identifying and encouraging new users for archival resources. Depending on its holdings and collection scope, an archive may develop programs to encourage use by professionals ranging from city planners, land surveyors, and engineers to novelists and playwrights.

Related to the issue of identifying new users is the potential of public programs for raising awareness of what archives are and what they contain. The general lack of understanding of archives is painfully evident to the archival profession. Concern has been expressed over the lack of a clear identity, as evidenced when archivists find themselves being called anarchists, and activists. Raising public awareness of archives will help in bringing archival information into the mainstream of the larger information community. For most people, books, magazines, newspapers, and sometimes government publications are the parameters of the information world. Using public programs to draw attention to archival resources and encourage their use will help archives to become another standard source of information, rather than a curiosity.

For sheer survival purposes, public programs can be used to encourage communication between archivists and the officials who allocate the resources needed to maintain an archival program. Few archives are so well-endowed or financed that they do not need to campaign actively in their own behalf. Resource allocators, like the rest of the public, often have only a cursory sense of what archives are and do. When these key persons are not sufficiently supportive of the archival program, the archives is an easy target for budget cuts, especially where budgetary competition is substantial, as in business, university, and governmental settings. Well-designed public programs can draw the attention of resource allocators to the role of the archives. Further, they can be used to gain the support of constituencies which, while not necessarily regular users, nonetheless recognize the importance and benefits of archival programs. Having a source of support and advocacy can be essential, not only to the survival of an archival program, but to its further growth.

The public program audience

Successful programs require a careful consideration of audience characteristics and needs. A thorough investigation is needed of the interests, experience levels, and learning styles of potential audiences. Too often archivists have relied on their own knowledge and general assumptions about certain potential user groups when planning public programs. Specific information can be gathered by various methods: reading the literature of a particular professional group; surveying a potential audience; holding individual discussions with users; or conducting in-depth user studies. By carefully studying a potential group, the archivist can tailor programs to meet identified characteristics, make planning time more efficient, and enhance program effectiveness and impact.

The results are well worth the initial time investment.

In practice to date, archivists have identified a number of audiences. The most obvious group to address has been that of scholarly and historical researchers. Their concern with archival resources has been the mainstay of many repositories' reference service. While their commitment might suggest that this group needs no further attention, study may suggest areas for improvement. Most archivists are armed with tales of historians who have no conception of how primary sources are organized, what they might contain, or how to access them. And if historians are not fully prepared in their graduate training, it is unlikely that scholarly researchers in such fields as criminal justice, social welfare, mental health, geography, and environmental conservation, among others, are any more prepared. Archives having, or desiring, a substantial research population must determine not only what specific information scholars need, but what information they need about how to identify, access, and use the repository's holdings. Programs designed to meet those needs will benefit the scholar and improve use.

Students are another user group that comes readily to mind when designing public programs. History, social studies, or government classes are the logical target subject-areas; nonetheless, other areas of student curricula should be considered. Students in literature, science, mathematics, theater, art, communications, and writing classes are involved in study that could be enhanced by the use of archival records. In addition to being aware of the potential subject-areas, archivists need to be familiar with educational goals and curricular requirements. Archival resources can be used for considerably more than teaching students to "appreciate" history and historical facts. Educators may use documents in the field of the social studies, for example, to teach students critical thinking skills, the ability to read, discern viewpoints, and develop interpersonal skills. Programs designed for students should take into account these educational needs.

When designing public programs for students, archivists also need to be aware of teachers as part of the user public. Considerable mythology exists in society about the interest, knowledge, and competence of teachers; those assumptions cannot be relied on in program development. It is imperative that archivists make direct contact with teachers, hopefully those who will be involved in a particular public program. Teachers are an important resource for information on the issues of educational skill development and curriculum. Further, their interest in carrying out a public program is crucial to its success. Some teachers prefer maximum amounts of information to be provided by the repository; others are very willing to take on a major role in developing and using materials. Programs being conducted in local areas can be tailored to the specific needs of a few individuals or school districts. For those aimed at larger, regional areas, an approach must be designed that will address the largest number of needs.

To become familiar with the teacher/student community, archivists can review the educational literature for trends and for information on the skills which are being emphasized by educators. Familiarity with mandated curricula is also essential. Many local, regional, and national teaching organizations sponsor conferences where considerable information may be gained and where contacts with teachers may be established. Finally, archivists can visit local classrooms to learn at first hand what the learning styles, interests, and capacities of students are.

Other user groups for whom archives are beginning to design programs are those of professionals in various fields. These users provide an important opportunity for archives to expand beyond the traditional historical research community. Archivists can begin by assessing the subject strengths of their holdings, then identifying professions related to that area. For business, government, or university archives, such professionals may be the individuals employed in their parent institution. Policy research, statistics, celebrations of institutional milestones, exhibits, publicity, or providing data for reports, speeches, and articles may all be areas where institutions can draw on archival resources.

Again, useful programs for these audiences require the archivist to do background research to identify areas of potential development. Archivists must become familiar with the basic activities involved in various professions in order to determine when and how archival materials might prove useful. This may require research into professional literature, attendance at corporate or governing body meetings, familiarization with basic institutional mission statements and reports, and active discussions with professionals on possibilities for providing them with enhanced service. Since these groups may have less understanding of and less commitment to the use of archival resources, archivists must assume more responsibility for identifying connections between a given profession and archival materials. An advisory committee of professionals may serve as a useful vehicle for confirming the archivist's conclusions about a profession's needs and the usefulness of certain programs.

Another group which is often taken for granted as a user public is that of researchers who are following their personal interests. Archives have, however, recently begun to pay more attention to public programming for local historians, genealogists and collectors, and for those pursuing research as a hobby rather than a profession, in a variety of areas such as postal history, military history, and historic home restoration. Often archives are not quite sure how many such researchers they have, what areas they are interested in, or how they use collections.

Several tools might be used to gather information on this user public. Research-room registration forms may be adapted to include the identification of research topics being pursued and records being used. Periodic summaries of the information contained on these forms could indicate interest areas. Archivists might conduct more in-depth reference interviews with such researchers to identify their needs. If time is a limiting factor, local library school students might be willing to undertake a survey as a class project, or interviews might be conducted on a sampling basis.

A final group being targeted is the general public. In its broadest sense, this group includes people who have a casual interest in documentary evidence or historical issues. That such a group exists is obvious from the lines of visitors who come to see exhibits of the Magna Carta, the Declaration of Independence, and other basic documents of national interest. The fascination, however, is not just with these major works. Archivists are often asked for assistance in preserving family letters, military commissions or ancestral birth certificates, or asked about autographs, broadsides, photographs, and maps destined to be displayed in homes. There is a large common interest in the unique and archaic nature of documents. While this interest may not be so compelling that individuals actually begin to pursue research of their own, it nonetheless identifies a group who are sympathetic to archives and their holdings.

To develop programs for this type of public, archivists must match the general interest areas within their own particular holdings with groups who would find them of interest. Those groups may be as diverse as the holdings of the archives. Doctors may be curious about old medical bills or remedies applied; engineers may enjoy decoding structural drawings; political groups may be interested in campaign posters and ephemera; and senior citizens may enjoy reviewing documents from eras they remember. Such groups can become active supporters and "friends" of an archival institution.

Kinds of public programs

Although archival public programs are relatively new, the range and variety of programs has developed rapidly. It is impossible to enumerate all the possibilities in this chapter. Instead, general approaches will be summarized, with basic and successful directions in current practice being highlighted. An impressive array of creative, innovate programs are under way. Currently the network for information on public programs is very informal; professional conferences, newsletters, and journals may provide exposure to people and institutions involved, and new developments in programs. Programs fall into three basic categories: documentation programs; programs to expand and encourage use; and public awareness programs.

Public programming can be used to support basic archival acquisition policies. They add a dimension to regular strategies for collecting and ensuring the permanent retention of historically valuable information. In certain subject-areas or social groups, documentation has been irregularly kept or has failed to survive. For example, the recent trend in social history has shown the deficiencies of documentation of blacks, women and ethnic groups, and in subject-areas such as working life, small business development, and social customs. Archivists sensitive to the lack of adequate records in these areas have attempted to find alternative methods for acquiring and ensuring the survival of this information.

Oral history can be used to fill in or add to paper records in a subject area. Extensive programs have been developed for methodical, comprehensive interviewing of individuals on a range of topics from the automotive industry to ethnic community life. It is a particularly useful way to capture the human experience. Chapter Eleven in this book may be referred to for more extended discussion of this technique.

Public programs may also be used to fill in documentary gaps. Many records are destroyed or neglected because many people simply do not recognize the value of family or business records, or realize that they may be of interest to a repository. The general public sustains a pervading myth that archives and manuscript repositories only preserve records of community leaders, or on subjects of national interest. A number of repositories have begun sponsoring events in which residents of an area are invited to bring their photographs and documentary resources on a subject theme or geographical region. Frequently a central site such as a senior citizens' center, local library, community center or even a shopping center is chosen. Archivists, curators, conservators, and photographers assess the resources and make copies of those items with significant informational value. In return, they provide the individuals with information on how to store and care for the objects. Basic acid-free materials are made available for sale at a minimal cost. Such efforts provide at least for the survival of information in a copied form. In a number of cases, the owners are made aware of the value of their records, and decide to donate their resources at that time, or provide for their eventual donation to a repository.

Basic information programs such as brochures, slide shows, tours, and speeches can also be used in the effort to collect and preserve documentation. Many records creators and keepers often simply fail to think about the permanent value of their records. Clear illustrations raise their consciousness so they may either contact the archives or respond to requests for information on the existence of records.

A wide range of public programs have been developed to promote the use of archival resources. Educational programs are designed to bring historical records to students at primary, secondary, and university level. Other programs are directed at increasing the number of adult users of archives, and at helping them develop better skills in accessing and using archival resources. Finally, publications continue to be an important method to inform potential users of the research possibilities of archival holdings.

Educational programs are basically characterized by their relationship to the formal institutional setting. They are one of the most popular forms of public programming. Such programs expand the use of archival materials substantially, since one teacher will have anywhere from 30 to 150 students. In addition, teachers are a receptive audience, because they readily recognize the usefulness of documents for achieving educational goals, as well as their high level of interest for students. Finally, the enthusiasm generated by students when exposed to historical resources provides a very rewarding experience for archivists.

Archival teaching packets are a particularly popular method for reaching student populations. These generally consist of facsimile documents, along with other supporting materials such as teachers' guides, questions and activities for the students. Archivists must be aware that the construction of useful, usable teaching packets requires considerable familiarization with curriculum, teaching methods, and attention to the needs of teachers and students.

In a related approach, some archival institutions offer workshops for teachers to assist them in developing their own materials for classroom use. The development of teaching packets requires time, staff, and educational expertise that may not be available in every repository. Teachers are skilled at educating; few, however, are familiar with historical resources and primary research. The skills of archivists are usually the reverse. By teaching educators how to use historical resources and helping them to identify relevant materials for their classroom, archivists can encourage the development of educational materials without having to do the actual work.

Other archival repositories have developed educational programs in which students are brought to the archives to do research directly with original records. This provides students with the opportunity to see records in their "natural" surroundings, rather than as single documents. It provides students with a realistic experience in historical research, evaluation of evidence, and drawing conclusions. With careful advance training in the handling and interpretation of records, this can be a highly successful method. Experiences of archivists conducting such programs indicate that students are extremely careful with documents, perhaps more so at times than their elders.

Some archivists have begun expanding their researcher public by sharing their expertise in documentary access and use with students in university courses. Many university archivists, in fact, assist professors in planning projects to familiarize students with the use of primary resources. Specific collections may be identified for students to use with coursework, or special assistance in research projects may be provided.

Archives also use publications to provide information and impetus for increasing the use of their resources. Brochures serve as a basic method for identifying collecting areas and the research potential of resources. To be effective, a clearly-defined plan for the distribution of such brochures needs to be developed. Mailings to target audiences may be conducted, or brochures may be made available at conferences and meetings. In addition to general brochures on their holdings, special brochures may be developed to address specific potential user groups. Particular care needs to be taken to ensure that such publications are both visually and informationally interesting to potential users. Careful study of the audience and planning of content and distribution greatly increases effectiveness.

Finding aids are a traditional tool of archivists that can be a powerful resource if coordinated with public programming. Whether dealing with a special subject, organization, or area of interest, finding aids can be prepared with the specific goal of increasing use, in addition to those developed for in-house access. Such finding aids need good-quality illustrations, special sections identifying potential research uses of records, and user-oriented features such as indexes, historical background, and information on how to use both the finding aid and particular types of historical records. A careful plan for distributing such finding aids to interested professional and research groups can plant information with potential users that may germinate into substantial use.

Gaining support and understanding of archives is one of the most amorphous, but much-needed goals of public programs. To maintain programs, much less expand them, archival administrators must have sources of support and advocacy. The general trend of the archival profession is to shy away from "public relations" efforts, yet they are essential if archives are to survive in an age of limited resources.

A wide range of techniques may be used to bring the holdings, goals, and accomplishments of archives to public attention, and win support. Tours may be conducted for professional organizations and groups who recognize the importance of historical documentation. Slide shows or videotapes are a useful mechanism for disseminating basic information to educate the public to the existence and uses of archives. They can also be developed to address special ongoing issues, such as the need for records management, or attention to local government records.

Archivists concerned with the public's lack of awareness of archives, or even their avoidance of "research" facilities have begun sponsoring a range of events to encourage people to become familiar with the repositories. Conferences on popular topics such as military history, family history, or historic preservation can often be used as a vehicle to introduce the purposes and role of archives. Some institutions have sponsored theatrical and musical events based on their holdings. Such techniques help to expand the image of archives as having a role beyond service to historians. These efforts help bring archives and their mission to the attention of the general public.

Conclusion

Because of their "public" nature, particular care must be given to the development of public programs to ensure their impact and success. Public programs should be designed to help the institution meet specific goals. Few archives can afford the luxury of conducting programs for sheer interest or entertainment. Defining a clear purpose for a public program is essential to its success. A careful consideration of potential users is similarly important. The number and variety of possible users is enormous, but to reach them requires assessing and clearly addressing their information needs. Once program audiences and purposes are defined, public program options are limited only by imagination and the ever-present budget constraints.

Public programs are an essential element of a healthy archival program. The enormous effort expended to acquire, describe, and make resources available merits an equally strong commitment to facilitating use. Archival resources have tremendous potential to inform, protect, justify, and educate; yet these resources have been seriously under-utilized. Active public programs have the capability to bring archives forward into the position of strength and impact they deserve in the information community.

17

Archival Exhibits

James Gregory Bradsher
and *Mary Lynn Ritzenthaler*

Archival exhibits are mounted to interest, inform, stimulate, entertain, and educate viewers. Well-planned exhibits designed to meet these goals can be an important tool in encouraging public appreciation and use of archives and archival institutions, and an understanding of historical events. Exhibits, which are a major component in public outreach programs, are useful in drawing attention to the resources available in archival institutions and serve as an invitation to further research. Perhaps no other aspect of public programs reaches so many people or touches them in such a manner that graphically illustrates the goals and contributions of archival institutions in preserving historical records. Exhibits can encourage people to study the past; donate records, money, or services to the institution; and even stimulate civic pride. For these reasons, most archives find that some type of exhibit program is worthwhile.

Despite the diversity of the mission statements, policies, and resources of archival institutions, there are a number of general principles and considerations that are applicable when establishing and conducting exhibit programs. The creation of effective exhibits requires a knowledge of the conceptual and technical methods associated with their preparation, coupled with the realization that they require a commitment of staff time and money and an awareness of conservation and security requirements.

Archival institutions vary widely in numbers and types of staff, size of holdings, financial resources, and physical plant. These factors will have a direct bearing on the extent of the exhibit program that is developed. Some institutions will have a dedicated staff of exhibit curators, designers, and conservators, while others may contract for such services as necessary. It is just as likely that small institutions will rely on a single archivist to mount exhibits. In a similar vein, the space available for exhibits within an archives may range from a separate gallery with built-in exhibit cases and a security staff, to exhibits mounted in foyers or research rooms. The scale of the exhibit program must be tailored to the needs, capabilities, and resources of the institution, and a proper balance must be achieved between exhibits and other archival functions. All exhibits, no matter their size, should contribute to the stated mission of the archives. This chapter will briefly address policy issues, conceptual approaches, and technical areas to be considered when developing exhibit programs. This information can be adapted to fit the specific needs of individual archival institutions.

Establishing a program and defining an audience

Because exhibits, regardless of size, require often scarce institutional resources and can also pose conservation and security problems, implementation of an exhibit program requires careful consideration. Exhibits, like other institutional activities, should be adopted to fulfill a need. All exhibits, whether consisting of several dozen items displayed in a gallery or ten documents placed in an exhibit case in the reading room, can and should meet conservation standards; however, they must be scaled to fit the resources and expertise available to carry them out.

Once it is determined to have an exhibit program, a written policy statement defining the objectives of the program and its place in the overall priorities of the institution should be adopted. This statement should include regulations and guidelines that govern the type, size, complexity, and frequency of exhibits; security and environmental requirements; and loan policies for incoming and outgoing loans.

In developing the policy statement, the archives will need to identify who will be viewing its exhibits, or the audience it wishes to attract. In defining a target audience, archival institutions should initially consider all of their potential publics, including the parent institution, the local community, scholars, tourists, genealogists, and students. Based upon this analysis and a review of institutional goals and user profiles, a primary audience should then be defined. A national or state archives may be required to develop exhibits with broad general appeal, whereas a university archives may identify a much narrower audience of scholars and students. The time devoted to determining the profile of the target audience is well spent, for this information can be used to develop exhibit goals and parameters. Such guidelines help to provide a sense of what exhibits can accomplish and the types of presentations that are most suitable. Once these elements of the exhibit policy are articulated, they help serve as a gauge for evaluating the success or failure of future exhibits.

Institutions may find it necessary or expedient to have semi-permanent as well as changing exhibits. However, to give vitality to their exhibit programs, institutions should annually install new exhibits or revise existing ones. Changes need not be elaborate or complex. For some exhibits, items can be replaced or rotated at intervals without altering the subject. Such an approach is necessary to meet conservation requirements, but also has the added benefit of maintaining audience interest.

An overly ambitious exhibit program can collapse of its own weight and possibly jeopardize other archival functions and responsibilities, as well as lose staff support. Therefore, it is wise to start with a manageable effort, and to create only a limited number of well-done exhibits. The general rules are to think big, but start small. Remember that subject-matter, placement, and quality of materials and exhibit items take priority over size or complexity.

Types of exhibits

Once the audience is identified, the next task is to determine how to attract and hold its interest. There are two basic types of archival exhibits. First, there are those that are organized around a subject or a type of object, or that commemorate or celebrate an event. Secondly, there are those that present archival institutions and their holdings in a favorable light by focusing on various archival activities, functions, and services.

Thematic or subject exhibits can explain and interpret historical events, activities, and topics, as well as simply introduce visitors to the raw materials of history. They can emphasize the activities and contributions of a specific institution, organization, family, or individual that is important to a local community, region, or nation. They can also commemorate anniversaries, celebrate holidays, or focus on a certain year or era that is significant to the target audience. Thematic exhibits generally exploit the subject strengths of the archives, thereby publicizing its holdings and possibly attracting new accessions.

Exhibits that focus on the institution can explain the nature and value of archives, describe the mission of the archival institution, and depict specific archival operations. While such institutional exhibits are not, as a rule, of great interest to the general public, they do serve a purpose and should be considered on a modest basis. These exhibits can provide an overview of the institution's holdings or highlight an important document or artefact acquired during the previous year. Such exhibits can also reflect the diversity of the archival record by presenting an historical survey of materials and techniques used to generate records and maintain information. Institutional exhibits can explain such archival activities as preservation and reference services. For example, an exhibit on preservation could explain reasons why archival records deteriorate, and then present such institutional responses to this problem as microfilming, conservation treatment, and access and handling regulations. An exhibit on reference could assist researchers in exploiting information contained in archival records, focus on copyright and privacy issues, or explain how research is best accomplished in an archival setting. Such exhibits can be useful to the institution, for they may save staff time that would otherwise be spent in instructing researchers or reminding them of their expected conduct.

Finally, institutional exhibits can be mounted to show the contributions the archival institution has made to the community or the world of scholarship, by showing how records have been used to advantage by its various constituencies. For example, photographs used by historical preservationists to restore a neighborhood or a sampling of published articles and books based on the holdings of the archives might be displayed. Exhibits can be used to generate support or acknowledge contributions of a friends group. Anniversaries of the institution can also provide an opportunity for a celebratory exhibit.

Choosing a subject

After defining the audience and the type of exhibit to be mounted, a subject must be selected to meet the interests of both the viewer and the institution. Since archival institutions are often competing with other organizations offering cultural programs, they must produce exhibits that focus on the unique and appealing characteristics of archival records, using them to depict fresh, innovative, and insightful subjects.

Good judgment and taste must be exercised in selecting an exhibit topic. While it might be appropriate to exhibit a given subject in a particular locality, the same subject might be considered offensive in another. Additionally, in selecting a subject, the archival staff should carefully consider exhibit themes that ask "why" questions, such as "why did the American Civil War happen?", or metaphysical questions, such as "was the Civil War inevitable?" Just as historians have trouble answering the former and find it next to impossible to resolve the latter by empirical means, exhibit curators will find the same difficulties and impossibilities. The exhibit staff should try to pose questions that evoke concrete rather than theoretical responses, such as "who", "when", "where", "what", and "how", in developing exhibits. By doing so they can empirically answer and interpret these questions with their documents and captions, and thereby produce exhibits with greater relevance, accuracy, and utility.

Frequently exhibits are mounted in connection with a specific event, such as a speech, a conference, or an anniversary. Thus, the event itself dictates the subject of the exhibit. The exhibit staff will find it useful to keep a calendar of forthcoming events and anniversaries, and archivists, who come across many interesting records during the course of their work, should keep a file of potential exhibit subjects as well as of records that have visual appeal or other exhibit potential.

It is important for archivists, public affairs specialists, educators, exhibit curators, and designers to work together in developing exhibit themes, and subsequently in reviewing materials selected for exhibition. Not only will better exhibits be mounted but the closer interaction can improve morale and foster enthusiasm within the institution.

Planning

Once an idea for an exhibit is proposed, the first step is research to determine if resources exist within the archives to develop the topic. If they do, then planning for the exhibit begins with the preparation of a proposal outlining its purpose, scope, and major themes, as well as the tentative dates, production schedule, budgetary requirements, and related activities. Once this proposal has been approved, an action plan should be developed, specifying the sequence of tasks that must be carried out and by whom. Sufficient time must be alloted for researching the subject, selecting material, and designing and installing the exhibit. Ample lead time must be allowed for carrying out necessary conservation work as well as evaluating environmental conditions in the exhibit space and implementing required improvements. Time must also be devoted to publicizing the exhibit, planning related special events and, as appropriate, producing a catalog or checklist and related sales items, such as posters and postcards.

The site chosen for the exhibit depends on the size and nature of the institution; it may be a separate exhibit gallery, research room, or hallway. Whichever site is selected, it should provide an appropriate setting for the materials to be displayed and accommodate the expected audience. It should be secure, well-maintained, and capable of meeting conservation standards, as well as attractive, tasteful, inviting, and centrally located.

Off-site and traveling exhibits of original material, because of the cost and risks involved, should be undertaken with great care. Most institutions cannot afford the insurance, shipping costs, and related expenses, nor adequately provide for the physical security and environmental requirements while the items are in transit or on exhibit in the off-site location. The risks can be eliminated by substituting facsimiles for original documents. The costs can be reduced by obtaining funding from the organizations that will host the exhibit. Traveling exhibits of facsimiles, if they are well done, can greatly benefit the institution by making it better known to a wider audience. Slide shows or videotapes prepared to accompany an exhibit can also be a useful tool in introducing the institution and the manifold uses of archival records.

Selecting exhibit materials

Items selected for exhibition must be integral to the subject being presented and must help advance the theme or idea behind the exhibit. They should have strong documentary value and visual impact, and also be in stable enough condition to withstand exhibition. A compelling subject will be a failure as an exhibit if it cannot be presented visually.

While it is natural to want to show off all items related to the exhibit theme, restraint should be exercised, for quality is more important than quantity. A case crowded with objects, even if all are relevant to the subject, will overwhelm and distract viewers. Usually a few items, attractively displayed and carefully documented, will interpret a subject more clearly than a display case full of similar items that differ in details only of interest to specialists or *aficionados*.

Although textual (that is, written) documents are commonly perceived as dull and uninteresting, many have extraordinary visual appeal. Some documents are so significant as symbols, or their content is so moving, that they can be the sole subject of an exhibit. Most exhibits, however, consist of more than one item. Too many textual documents, however, with their interpretative labels, will overwhelm viewers with text. As a general rule, the fewer textual documents, the more chance of their being read. It is also better to have a mix of material for both visual appeal and liveliness. Textual documents can be integrated to advantage with appropriate graphic or pictorial items, such as photographs, maps, broadsides, cartoons, prints, posters, architectural drawings, advertisements, and three-dimensional artefacts.

In selecting material, just as in choosing a subject, good judgment and taste are essential. Archivists and curators must be sensitive to privacy issues and always weigh the right to privacy against the right to know. For example, contemporary photographs depicting recognizable individuals in awkward or embarrassing circumstances are best not displayed, despite their interest or historical significance.

Because visitors assume that what they see and learn in an archival exhibit is authentic, accurate, and true, the exhibits must be objective and truthful. Therefore, careful attention must be paid to the selection of exhibit items and the writing of accompanying captions. Failure to do so could not only embarrass an institution but ruin its reputation. Just as "history" is a personal opinion about the past, so too are exhibits a form of opinion about the past. To provide balance, exhibits should present different versions of an event or indicate differences of opinion about its significance, when appropriate, via eyewitness accounts or other contemporary records. To ensure historical accuracy and objectivity, the exhibit content should be reviewed by knowledgeable staff or other subject specialists prior to the production of captions and installation.

Designing an exhibit

A well-organized exhibit enables viewers to quickly grasp the subject, to view the exhibit in a logical manner, and to understand and enjoy each display case or panel. Good planning and design expertise are critical elements in achieving these goals.

A primary concern is to coordinate the number, size, thematic placement, and format of the items to be exhibited, as well as space available for the presentation of each theme. Each object should be displayed in a manner that encourages viewing and study. A logical intellectual and physical progression of display units, each containing a well-arranged group of related items, is essential to a successful exhibit. The layout in each case or panel should be sufficiently attractive and interesting to gain and hold the attention of the viewer, and yet should also clearly indicate its relationship to the other components of the exhibit. Planning the exhibit on paper in detail, long before starting installation, is vital. The creation of schematic plans and diagrams is an important aspect of planning the design and layout, which ensures at an early stage not only that the number, format, and size of documents selected for exhibition are appropriate, but also that the mounting requirements of individual documents will be met. During this process it is necessary to accurately measure the dimensions of the exhibit items, both to assure that adequate space is available for each object and to minimize costly errors in estimating required exhibit supplies or the construction of wall mounts and panels.

The visitor traffic patterns need to be studied and planned in relation to the distribution of display cases, free-standing panels, and overall room size in order to eliminate traffic hazards. Audio-visual components of the exhibit or such participatory displays as push-button question-and-answer panels must be located so as to minimize traffic bottlenecks.

Colors and textures are important design elements in an exhibit. They create mood and can be used to indicate a change in subject or emphasis. The background colors in individual display cases should harmonize with the exhibited items and show them to advantage. Color schemes and design motifs can be used effectively to unite an exhibit visually with its catalog, associated publications, publicity materials, such as posters and press releases, and the invitations to the exhibit opening.

Proper lighting is an important factor, not only from a conservation point of view, but also in producing an attractive exhibit. The illumination in exhibit rooms should be subdued and the cases should be arranged to eliminate reflections caused by windows, overhead lights, or other light sources. Sources of illumination should be shielded from the observer and placed to avoid distracting shadows.

Facsimiles can be used effectively in an exhibit to maximize the visual impact of documents. For example, enlargements of photographs can be used as backdrop panels, and textual documents or selected passages can be enlarged to assist viewers in reading them. However, facsimiles and enlargements not only change the viewer's perception of an historical artefact, but possibly also the original intent of the creator by altering the emphasis or manner in which information is conveyed. Therefore, the use of such visual tools should be clearly indicated in exhibit labels and catalog notes, along with information on actual sizes, and in the case of excerpted passages, a note that only a portion of a document is presented.

Labels are of critical importance in an exhibit. They should place the subject within its historical context and explain the significance of the materials displayed. They should also answer specific questions aroused by the exhibit and furnish sufficient information to stimulate interest or perhaps further study in it. Headline labels consisting of single words or short phrases should be used to identify the subject of an exhibit as well as its major thematic subdivisions. Subject labels, which are extended statements of short sentences describing essential facts about topics covered within a display unit, must be as brief as possible because visitors generally will not read labels containing more than one hundred words. Object labels identify individual items, and convey such information as date, place, author or maker, source, and medium, as appropriate. Instead of paraphrasing documents, labels should explain their origins and significance. If several related documents are exhibited together, a single label can be used to describe their subject matter and relation to one another, along with small individual labels noting specific information about each document or item. In writing the labels, just as at all other stages of developing an exhibit, it is wise to allow time for review and establish a mechanism for evaluation by colleagues and subject specialists. Once in final draft, labels should be edited to ensure stylistic uniformity and proper use of the language. After production, all labels must be carefully proof-read to avoid embarrassing errors or omissions.

The physical appearance and placement of the labels is as important as their content. All labels should be clear and concise. Regardless of how they are produced, the letters should be legible. Labels should also be produced with sufficient contrast between the background and the type to make for easy reading in the low light level of the exhibit gallery. Labels, just as with textual documents, should be placed within easy reading distance at eye level. Items of special interest to children should be placed lower than the other items.

Preservation

At the most basic level, there is an inherent conflict between the exhibition and the preservation of archival records. Records on exhibit are more vulnerable to damage or theft than those in passive storage, and some documents are more susceptible than others to exposure to light or fluctuating temperature and relative humidity. Documents on display are subject to an environment that is generally more difficult to control than that of a records storage area. Exhibitors must therefore always weigh the potential educational and publicity values of a planned exhibit against the disastrous consequences that could result from careless handling and inappropriate exhibition of archival records. Ensuring that exhibits meet preservation requirements, including proper handling and storage of materials while they are being prepared and installed, is critically important.

It is virtually certain that some damage will occur as documents are exhibited. The degree of damage may be almost imperceptible, but it is important to acknowledge that damage *will* occur and to determine whether this is acceptable and to what degree. The types of damage most likely to occur include the darkening of poor-quality (groundwood) paper, fading of dyes used to color paper and inks, or physical distortion such as pages curling as a result of fluctuating or high relative humidity.

The first step in dealing with potential exhibit materials is to determine if they are in stable enough condition to be displayed. No documents should be scheduled for exhibition until their condition and suitability for exhibition are evaluated by a conservator or knowledgeable archivist. During the evaluation the exhibition history of the materials should be reviewed to determine whether the items have been previously displayed, for how long, and under what conditions. The intrinsic value of the documents should also be considered in this context, to provide a framework for considering the need for special security or conservation measures, or whether the items are simply too valuable or vulnerable to exhibit. The condition of the records should be evaluated to determine the stability of the materials, vulnerability to light damage, structural features that are weak or vulnerable, and the need for conservation treatment prior to exhibition. Depending on the number of items in an exhibit, their condition, and the availability of conservation treatment resources, the conservation aspects of exhibit planning and preparation can be quite time-intensive. Under the exhibit policy guidelines, a procedure should exist for prohibiting the exhibition of archival records because of their physical condition, the institution's inability to carry out necessary conservation treatment in the time available, or the likelihood of deterioration due to uncontrolled exhibit conditions or the vulnerability of the records.

During the conservation evaluation, mounting and installation requirements and limitations should be noted for each item. Mounting considerations for flat, loose documents include whether the edges of objects may be overlapped by a mat or whether they must "float" (that is, have all edges visible) within the window mat, type of mounting (hinges, polyester encapsulation, or corners), and whether a need exists for a special structure, such as a sink mat to protect vulnerable surfaces. For bound volumes, the type of book cradle must be specified, as well as the permissible angle of opening and degree of incline, and the need for polyethylene straps to secure the volume in its cradle.

Temperature, relative humidity, air quality, and light levels in the exhibit area should be comparable to environmental conditions in storage areas. Thus, depending on the materials exhibited, temperature should be maintained between 68 to 70 degrees Fahrenheit (20 to 21 degrees Celsius), with a relative humidity of about 45 percent. Fluctuations should be minimal. All sources of ultraviolet radiation should be filtered, using filtering sleeves over fluorescent tubes and filtering film or glazing on windows, exhibit cases, and in frames; window shades and curtains should also be drawn to eliminate direct sunlight and excess illumination and to avoid problems with interior heat build-up. Light levels should be kept low; normally, a maximum of five footcandles is recommended for light-sensitive materials, while less vulnerable documents can be exhibited at ten footcandles, although overall duration of exposure to light must be considered as well (see Chapter Fourteen). Light-related problems will be easiest to control if light sources are kept separate from exhibit case interiors, relying instead upon the illumination in the room. Given the normal high light levels (approximately 100 footcandles) in reading rooms and other areas where archival exhibits have typically been located, it is advisable to limit displays in such spaces to facsimiles or other non-record materials.

The duration of exhibits of archival documents should be limited from a few months to a year, depending upon the condition, light-sensitivity, and value of the documents. It is generally not appropriate or feasible to consider permanent exhibition, except in such unique situations as the permanent display of the Constitution of the United States. Not many documents warrant permanent exhibition, nor do many institutions have the requisite security and conservation resources to make it possible. Facsimiles should be used in place of documents that are unstable or particularly vulnerable to exhibit conditions. They can also be used to replace items in an exhibit that have reached their exhibition limit.

Exhibit cases should be sturdy and fitted with pick-resistant locks and screw closures. Cases should not be air-tight, but rather equipped with unobtrusive ventilation holes to allow environmental conditions within the case to equilibrate with conditions within the exhibit room. If dirt is a problem, filters should be placed over ventilation holes to keep the interiors of the cases clean. Exhibit cases and wall panels must be evaluated in terms of their construction materials, paints, adhesives, sealants, and finishes, to ensure that unstable, volatile substances that will emit gases that can damage archival records have not been used. The materials currently considered most acceptable for exhibit cases are softwoods coated with a latex paint. Oak, which emits acetic acid, should be avoided, as should any polyurethane varnish containing formaldehyde. Newly-constructed exhibit cases should be allowed to "cure" in a well-ventilated space for several months before enclosing archival documents within them.

Framed documents hanging on walls or exhibit panels must be mechanically secured with screws and brackets. Metal frames (such as aluminum) are the preferred choice from a conservation perspective, although wooden frames may be more aesthetically pleasing from the point of view of design. If wooden frames are used, the rabbets, or inner edges, must be sealed. Documents should not be placed in direct contact with the cover glass, to avoid problems caused by condensation or flaking of loosely-adhered media. If possible, several standard sizes for mats and frames should be selected so that they can be re used for subsequent exhibits.

During the course of an exhibition, routine security and maintenance inspections should be undertaken. Documents should be examined to ensure that no movement has occurred and that there is no evidence of damage or alteration. The exteriors of exhibit cases must be cleaned on a regular basis to remove dirt and fingerprints. The case interiors should be lightly dusted as required. Environmental conditions, including temperature, relative humidity, and light levels, must also be monitored regularly.

Program coordination

Mounting an exhibit is a complex undertaking. To help ensure the success and visibility of the exhibit, and thereby warrant the resources expended in its creation, a variety of public programs should be considered.

Exhibits must be publicized if the target audience is going to be aware of their existence. The type and extent of publicity should reflect the magnitude and importance of the exhibit. There are many ways of informing the public about exhibits, including press releases for the media; notices in specialized publications; distribution of posters, brochures, and banners; direct mailings; and listings in tour guides. Press conferences to convey the significance of the exhibit and to explain the importance of the archival program can be held before major exhibits open.

Special events associated with an exhibit, such as lectures, seminars, workshops, film showings, anniversary celebrations, preview parties, and receptions, can be used to publicize the exhibit and the institution. Receptions at which refreshments are served should have a designated area for food and drink to keep them well away from exhibited documents. Receptions and other public programs are expensive both in money and staff time, and thus the costs and benefits of such activities must be weighed.

Since exhibits are ephemeral, archivists should consider producing a catalog or checklist. These publications serve to document the exhibit and provide an inventory of the items exhibited, and can be of great value to the viewer, both during and after the exhibit. They can be very elaborate hardbound editions or simply a handout. Exhibit publications should contain an introduction which explains the subject of the exhibit, as well as a list of all the items displayed, including detailed descriptions and annotations, when appropriate.

Because it is important to make visitors feel welcome and at ease, a friendly atmosphere in a hospitable and relaxing environment must be established and maintained. Volunteers, guards, and staff should be informed about the exhibit, so that when asked about it they can give answers or at least direct the questioner to knowledgeable staff members.

Volunteers can serve a very important function as the link between the exhibition and the visitor. They can provide assistance to visitors and, perhaps better than anyone, can help to create a welcoming environment. They can also provide feedback to the staff regarding the effectiveness of the exhibit. However, volunteer programs require an investment of staff time in supervising their activities, and therefore their adoption must be carefully considered.

Administrative considerations

Exhibits are expensive. When considering the establishment of an exhibit program, archivists must assess all costs, including staff dedicated to exhibit support (research, curatorial, design and installation, conservation, editorial, security, maintenance, etc.), equipment, supplies, and construction (exhibit cases, panels, frames, matting and mounting materials), as well as insurance, printing, mailing, and associated publicity expenditures. The extent of such costs will, of course, depend on the size and complexity of the exhibit program. However, even small exhibits represent substantial costs in staff time as well as some financial outlay. Given the many benefits of professionally-executed exhibits, the allocation of institutional funds to support the effort is normally warranted. As with any other area of the archives program, if a function is considered to be important and is integral to the mission of the institution, it is worthy of institutional support. While outside funding from public grant-funding agencies or private benefactors may be used to underwrite all or part of the costs of a special exhibit, it is not realistic to expect that outside funding can be used indefinitely to support a major program area. The sale of exhibit-related products, such as catalogs, slide sets, posters, and postcards, can offset some, but normally not a significant part, of the costs of putting on an exhibit.

In some cases it is possible that an exhibit theme cannot be fully advanced solely through an institution's holdings, and would be enhanced by the use of carefully selected loan items. At archives that have systematically avoided acquiring or keeping three-dimensional objects, for example, the problem of integrating such artefacts with textual documents for visual appeal and interest in an exhibit is most easily solved by borrowing needed objects. However, because of the costs and risks involved, both borrowing items from and lending items to other institutions must be carefully considered.

Before agreeing to the loan of any materials, their condition and value must be evaluated—just as with in-house exhibits—to determine whether exhibition, plus the added dangers of travel, are feasible. It is also necessary to solicit information from the borrowing institution, by way of a facilities report, regarding the following concerns: staff who will be handling and installing borrowed items, security provisions, fire protection, temperature and relative humidity in storage and exhibit spaces, and types of light sources and capabilities for controlling them. Loan agreements must be executed in writing and should specify the terms of the loan, including the duration, required security provisions, permissible light levels, and any special mounting or display requirements. Borrowing institutions must be prepared to underwrite shipping and insurance costs, and many archives require that loaned items be hand-carried to the exhibit site at the borrowing institution's expense.

Because many types of exhibit materials, whether published or unpublished, are copyrighted, permission must be acquired from the copyright owner before they are published or reproduced. Even though a work may be in the public domain or the copyright has lapsed—and permission is therefore not required—it is appropriate to use a credit line. Additionally, any borrowed items must be properly credited as specified in the loan agreement.

For record-keeping purposes, a permanent file on each exhibit should be created. This should contain a complete list of all items exhibited along with appropriate citations. This file can document the exhibit history of individual archival records and thereby help eliminate the over-exhibition of specific treasures in the future. The exhibit file should also contain copies of the script, labels, checklist, and any associated catalogs or publicity materials. Installation photographs of the entire exhibit, design and layout diagrams, and information on supplies and contractors should also be retained. For security and conservation purposes, photographs of each item should be taken before exhibition to help assess any damage that may occur during the course of the exhibit as well as to provide reference access to materials on display. These photographs should form part of the exhibit file. Such documentation provides institutional memory of past exhibits, can help to avoid repetition of past mistakes, and can be of great assistance in developing long-range exhibit plans.

Despite the difficulty of assessing the effects that exhibits have on people, some effort should be made to evaluate them and determine if they met their goals. Simply counting the number of viewers is a gross measure of impact and effectiveness, but it is also important to develop, use, and refine other performance measures. Brief questionnaires may work in some instances or, depending on the nature of the exhibit, it may be possible to incorporate a participatory element at the exit point that elicits viewers' responses to specific ideas or themes developed in the exhibit. Reviews of exhibits in the media can serve as another gauge of their effectiveness.

Archivists can increase their exhibit knowledge and skills, including technical abilities, by various means. These include: viewing many exhibits; developing contacts with exhibits staffs at other institutions; taking courses on exhibit design and preparation; and attending sessions on exhibits at meetings of archival, library, and museum associations. They should also become acquainted with appropriate literature, beginning with the works cited in the list of sources for further reading for this chapter and Chapter Fourteen.

Conclusion

Through an exhibit program an institution has an opportunity to develop and project its identity. It is important, therefore, to present attractive, interesting, and stimulating exhibits that are viewed, understood, and enjoyed by the audience for whom they were constructed. Viewers should leave an exhibit with a better understanding of the subject treated and with a greater appreciation of archives and the archival institution. Good exhibit programs require institutional commitment, initiative, ingenuity, imagination, planning, and aesthetic discrimination. With these general guidelines in mind, the results will always be worth the effort.

18

Archival Management

Michael J. Kurtz

The preceding chapters in this volume explore the management of archives and information resources from a variety of functional perspectives. This chapter will explore the basic principles and practices involved in the daily "nuts and bolts" management of archival organizations. Because archives exist in such diverse settings, this discussion of management theories and practices will be in a broad, profession-wide context. The ideas and suggestions are intended for use in small and large institutions, whether public or private in nature. Based on information collected by the Society of American Archivists for its Census of Archival Repositories, any archival program employing thirty or more staff members is considered large. That census also clearly demonstrated that the vast majority of archival programs are located within larger, parent bodies such as corporations, religious institutions, universities, historical societies, public libraries, and government entities.

The goal of this chapter is to assist new or existing archival programs in improving management practices. Because of their involvement in areas of complex professional concern such as preservation and access, archivists tend to forget that effective management is one of the cornerstones for a successful archival program. This cornerstone rests on the archival manager's mastery of the areas of administrative expertise, especially organization, planning and reporting, budget planning and execution, work standards, personnel management, public information, and facilities design and maintenance.

The critical role of the archival manager requires the development of a variety of skills that at first glance seem disparate. The manager must be a skilled archivist *and* an effective administrator. Senior-level archivists functioning as administrators normally have extensive experience with archival records and a solid understanding and appreciation of archival theory. As administrators, though, archivists often lack an equal foundation in organizational and management theory. Though there is extensive professional literature for the various aspects of modern management, as well as numerous seminars and academic offerings in relevant disciplines such as business administration, industrial engineering, and personnel management, the archival manager too often develops administrative expertise through trial and error. Effective archival administration requires successful integration of the principles and practices of archives administration with the management techniques of business or public administration.

Development of management skills is basically similar to the development of archival expertise. Both require a methodical and well-conceptualized program of academic coursework, on-the-job training and experience, keeping abreast of professional literature, and active participation in professional organizations. Those who aspire to be successful archival administrators must be competent archivists *and* managers. Depending on the size and complexity of the archival organization, this is a demanding task. For those who successfully integrate archival and managerial skills, the rewards in terms of program achievements and professional development are substantial.

In addition to archival and administrative competence, managers must develop the interpersonal skills necessary to balance and meet the needs of researchers, the general public, oversight officials, donors, colleagues, and last but not least, subordinates. This is quite as demanding and essential as developing archival and administrative expertise. Effective managers must understand the personal and political dynamics within the archival program, as well as the dynamics of a parent body or oversight group, and external constituencies. Managers must build an influence base, understand the limitations and opportunities that exist and, upon occasion, take acknowledged risks.

Specifically, managers must develop an understanding and appreciation for the basic needs and drives that motivate people in the workplace. They must challenge their own assumptions about why people work and what motivates them. Culturally-based differences relating to the work ethic, money, and authority, among other issues, are often subtly played out in the workplace, and thus difficult to manage.

While managers need not become amateur psychologists or sociologists, they do need to develop skills in the areas of individual and group dynamics. Colleges, consulting firms, and government-sponsored programs are potential sources for necessary training in human relations. Seminars or workshops focusing on topics such as group dynamics, leadership styles, effective listening, and performance counseling are particularly useful. Also, training courses usually provide references to relevant literature that managers can read and study long after the course has ended. Managers who can successfully navigate the potential minefield that is interpersonal relations are far along the path to success.

While archival and administrative competence and interpersonal skills are essential for effective archival administration, one other factor must be noted. Many archivists who spend years developing their subject-matter and technical expertise fail to appreciate the contribution of a well-executed administrative operation to the overall success of the archival program. Planning, preparing reports and budgets, and measuring productivity certainly are not glamorous activities. But these tasks are critical to the successful accomplishment of all archival functions. The discussion that follows should foster an appreciation for the role of administrative excellence in archival management.

Placement and organization

Because archival programs are located within larger institutions, the issues of placement and organization are critical to their success. The following seven guidelines encompass principles applicable to small or large archives located in a variety of institutional frameworks:

1. The archives must have a distinct identity within the larger, organizational framework.
2. For reasons of political viability and access to resources, the director of the archives program should report directly to the head of the parent organization or the governing body of the institution.
3. The archives must develop and issue a mission statement that identifies the purpose of the program and the archives' relationship to the larger organization. The mission statement can be based on statutory requirements, charters of incorporation, or a charge from the parent organization. Mission statements educate the public that the archives serves, and are used as the basis for internal planning and budgeting. (This latter point will be developed later.)
4. Policy statements that define the specific services and functions performed by the archives flow from the broad, general mission statement. Critical areas covered should include collections policies, processing materials, reference services, and access restrictions, if any.
5. Internally, archives should be organized on a subject-matter basis. This would, of course, reflect the provenance of the records of the organization or organizations for which the archives has custody. Ancillary administrative and support services are staffed and organized to facilitate the basic archival functions.
6. Brief functional statements of responsibility for each organizational component of the archives should supplement the mission and policy statements. Also included are any delegations of authority from the parent organization to the archives program and any delegations within the archival program itself.
7. The final step in the organizational process is the creation of detailed operational procedures for use by the archives staff. These "how to do it" instructions cover the critical areas defined in the policy statements.

Implementing these proposed guidelines may seem complicated but, as always, common sense should prevail. The organizational documentation required for small or medium-sized archival programs probably will not be as detailed as that needed for larger more complex programs. The goal is a rational organizational structure, with clear written policies and procedures adequate to guide both the archives staff and the public served by the archives.

Planning and reporting

Planning and reporting are key activities in the management of a successful archival program. While extensive professional literature discussing planning in modern management exists, until recently there was little archival literature on planning. In the last fifteen years the archival profession has increasingly realized the need for systematic continuous planning. Efforts such as the Society of American Archivists' Goals and Priorities Task Force have resulted in more sophisticated archival planning. The list of sources for further reading contains several basic works on management planning theories, particulary management by objectives, as well as literature specifically devoted to archival planning.

Many archival managers and their staffs remain reluctant to engage in detailed planning efforts. They seem to feel that the time "wasted" on planning could be better spent on doing actual work. There is some truth in this if planning becomes an end in itself, and results in "tending" an overly complicated and rigid plan by means of an elaborate reporting system. Despite these concerns, though, a modern archival program cannot survive without a creative planning process that results in well-defined written goals and objectives.

Effective planning allows managers to control their program and make the best use of scarce budgetary and staff resources. Staff involvement in planning can lead to a better understanding of and commitment to the program's goals and objectives. A flexible plan that addresses the core responsibilities of the program's mission will aid the archives in moving forward, and not just reacting to everyday crises and problems. All kinds of institutions require each of their programs to justify its existence continually. An archival program is no exception. Planning is the best tool for explaining the mission of the archives and its importance to the parent organization, to researchers, and to the general public. Lastly, planning provides a framework for evaluating the performance of archival managers and staff. Whether the plan under development is long-term or short-term, certain basic principles and procedures are essential for a successful planning effort:

1. Planners must analyze the environment in which the archives operates and determine, realistically, what resources are available. While a management plan can be used to request and justify additional resources, the manager must understand what is politically realistic.
2. As part of the process of defining how the archives can serve the needs of its parent organization and other constituencies, planners must set priorities that concentrate resources on the most critical program areas.
3. To the greatest extent possible, managers and staff should work together in creating the plan that implements these priorities. The sense of participation stimulates staff commitment. Also, the plan can serve as the basis for performance evaluations that are perceived as equitable and effective.

4. Before the actual process begins, managers must determine what type of plan will be produced (strategic or operational), how the staff will participate, and the plan's format. At this point it should be understood clearly how the plan will be used both for internal management purposes and for furthering the archives program with its public.

5. Based on the mission statement of the archives and the overall priorities set by archival managers, planners develop program goals, objectives, and tasks or activities. While the definitions of these terms may vary somewhat, goals are generally regarded as broad statements of overall program direction designed to further the basic mission of the archives. Objectives are set for each goal. These are measurable and realistic steps necessary to achieve the goal. Objectives are then broken down into specific activities that reflect the most elemental work activities of the archives. The activities and objectives must have concrete outputs and deadlines in order to complete the program goals within the timeframe of the overall plan.

6. When the plan is drafted, support from within the archives and the parent organization is essential to its effective implementation. The plan should be used for monitoring progress in achieving program goals, and for evaluating staff performance. The plan always should be viewed as a flexible document subject to revision as circumstances change or new requirements arise.

An important part of implementing the archival management plan is the development of an effective reporting system. Ideally, the reporting system should capture only the statistical and narrative information needed to evaluate progress in achieving the goals set in the management plan. Depending on the size of the archives and the complexity of the programs, reports can be on a monthly or quarterly basis. It is important that the plan and the reporting system be kept as simple as possible. This is an antidote to a situation where the plan becomes an end in itself.

Another effective way to implement the plan includes structuring staff meetings around the progress and problems involved with achieving the goals, objectives, and activities identified in the plan. Also, wherever possible, work assignments should be based on specific activities in the management plan. Achieving the plan should always be kept in the forefront of staff consciousness.

Likewise, the attention of the archives' public should be refocused continually on its efforts to successfully achieve its goals. This can be done through well-prepared annual reports, periodic briefings for senior managers of the parent organization, and presentations to outside constituencies. Presentations should not only focus on the holdings and services of the archives, but also on any obstacles impeding the archives in fulfilling its basic mission.

Management and measurement

Success in implementing the management plan is, of course, dependent on effectively managing work. The issues involved with the management and measurement of work are probably the most controversial in the field of archival management. Work that is not assigned and measured effectively will thwart even the best-conceived organizational structure and detailed management plan.

Many archivists believe that the unique nature of their holdings and of archival work itself makes it impossible to manage work through the setting of productivity goals and standards. In the last few years a growing body of archival literature has argued that measurement *is* possible. For example, those advocating work measurement state that while each archival collection has its unique characteristics such as size, complexity, and physical condition, there are certain similarities among collections that permit measurement and comparison.

Apart from the issue of theoretical feasibility, practical considerations force managers to adopt additional resource management techniques. Many archival programs are faced with static or declining resources (budgetary and personnel) and increasing holdings. Within larger institutions, archival managers must engage in fierce competition for resources. Requests must be justified in terms of output and the numbers and type of personnel needed to perform major activities. It is essential that managers accurately estimate what level of resources are needed for processing collections, providing reference services, or completing preservation actions.

The tools needed to measure productivity basically come from the field of industrial engineering. While they may seem intimidating to many archivists, the concepts are essentially common-sense approaches to organizing, managing, and measuring work. Archival managers interested in work measurement should consult relevant professional literature (see the list of sources for further reading) and, where the size of the archival program merits, obtain the services of a consultant experienced in the various techniques of work measurement. Basic ideas involved with analyzing and measuring work can be employed in archives of any size and relate closely to archival planning and budgeting. Work analysis ensures that tasks are carried out efficiently *and* effectively. Work-flow patterns must be identified to evaluate methods of work assignment, utilization of staff, and the adequacy of space and equipment. Work measurement and establishing productivity standards should occur after the most effective work methods are identified and put into place.

There are various methodologies available to determine the time and costs associated with performing archival functions. Identifying the most appropriate methodology depends on the size of the archival institution, the volume of holdings, and the variety of services performed by the archives.

Work measurement methodologies can be grouped into two broad categories: historical data analysis and direct measurement. The use of historical data presupposes that reliable statistics are available for a given period of time, such as a fiscal or annual year, and that they show total volume of work produced (records processed, letters answered, etc.) by category of activity, and the total number of hours spent by all archival personnel. In addition, fairly accurate estimates must be made for the percentage of staff time (by number and type of personnel) for each archival function. From this type of analysis, statistical summaries are possible that show estimated time and costs for each category of activity.

The difficulty with this method is that archival institutions often do not have even fairly accurate historical data. Even when such data are available, historical data analysis provides information on categories of activity, and does not account for time differences in processing, referencing, or preserving individual collections. Nonetheless, for smaller archival programs this may be the most cost-effective method for projecting work times and costs. Institutions without such statistics must begin collecting this summary-level data so that future work and budget planning can be conducted in as rational a manner as possible.

Larger archival programs, which by nature are labor-intensive, must consider using the tools of direct measurement. This is a difficult issue. Archival managers and professional staff often believe that such measurement is both demeaning and wasteful of scarce resources. In fact, institutions with large and complex holdings requiring extensive projects, reference, and preservation activities need to determine accurately how much work is accomplished and the costs involved for individual projects and functions.

There are two basic techniques in direct measurement. Usually a combination of the two is appropriate to capture both the repetitive and cognitive aspects of archival work. Briefly described these techniques are:

1. *Pre-determined time systems.* These are times established over the years in various industrial and governmental environments for performing routine clerical and manual tasks. Pre-determined times are appropriate for such activities as pushing carts, shelving boxes, paper-to-paper copying, and microform filming and duplication. Information on pre-determined time standards is readily available from professional industrial engineering societies, and government organizations such as the United States Department of Defense.
2. *Direct observation.* This is required to measure work involving decision-making and a variety of non-routine tasks. Most commonly, direct observation involves the use of time and motion studies. Other examples of direct observation include work sampling and self-observation and reporting by the staff.

Through the use of these techniques, exact costs can be developed for specific activities in the various archival areas. Staff hours spent on each function can be idenfitied, as well as the amount of work produced. Though work measurement is often viewed by archival staff as wasteful of resources, it is vital for planning staff assignments, developing budget data and projections, and managing and evaluating work.

In dealing with staff resistance, certain common-sense precepts should be kept in mind. As often as possible, managers should structure work so that employees can begin and complete entire tasks or projects and thus experience the greatest satisfaction possible (the "closure concept"). In addition, archival staff should receive tangible rewards for quality work performed in a timely manner. Such rewards can range from "employee of the month" certificates to cash incentives. It is very important that staff be involved in evaluating work and developing standards. Their sense of involvement and commitment will ultimately determine the success of productivity standards. Of course, only activities or collections that are heavily used and significant should be measured and monitored.

Budget planning and execution

With the tools of the management plan and the statistical data of the work measurement system, archival managers can prepare a budget that supports and justifies the resource needs of the archives. Accurate, realistic budget projections provide an aura of legitimacy for the archival program in the competition for resources within a larger organization or from an appropriating body. In addition, the budget is a key element in effective internal management.

There are several budgeting techniques that can be used, such as management by objectives, zero-based budgeting (justifying program components and then ranking in priority order) and a system often used by libraries known as the Planning-Programming-Budgeting System. In general, these systems require: (a) identifying each major activity such as processing, reference services, preservation; (b) establishing the appropriate workload measurement for each activity, such as cubic feet per staff hour for processing; and (c) calculating the expected levels or standards of production. From these workload indicators, the total hours and dollars for staff (broken down by categories) are calculated. Also calculated in budget planning are the estimated costs of supplies, equipment, and space, if appropriate.

Budget execution is as important as budget planning. At the least, quarterly and semi-annual reviews should be held to ensure that the goals of the management plan as well as the budget targets are on track. Careful monitoring can identify poorly-conceived goals and objectives, inadequate work measurement statistics, or faulty budget projections.

Personnel management

The finest organizational structure and planning process will be to no avail without a quality archival staff. Personnel management is a major element in the success of an archival program. The essential elements of personnel management include personnel selection, performance evaluation, and professional development.

The first, and most important, step in personnel selection is identifying the requirements for the position being filled. Tools to be used include the archival unit's functional statement of responsibility; the program's goals and objectives; and the knowledge, skills, and abilities needed to perform the duties involved. Based on this thorough analysis, the manager prepares the position description. The archival manager must also provide evaluation factors that will identify the most highly-qualified applicants.

Depending on the organizational structure and rules of the parent institution, the archival manager may or may not be involved with job advertising and the initial screening of applicants. At the least, he should ensure that the position is advertised in all appropriate registers, lists, and scholarly journals. Regardless of involvement with initial screening, the archival manager will have the final say in determining which highly-qualified applicant is selected.

In selecting from the list of finalists, the manager would be well advised to follow common personnel practices. All references and previous employers should be checked carefully. In addition, interviewing each highly-qualified applicant is essential. Only in the interview can the archival manager form an opinion on intangible but real factors such as judgment, adaptability, and general interpersonal skills. Ask all interviewees the same questions. For purposes of further evaluation, the interviewer should take notes on the answers that the applicants give to each question.

The selection process may seem tedious, often it is. But the successful identification of job requirements and the selection of the best applicants available are the foundation of a competent and progressive archival program. Given the fact that approximately 75 percent of an archival program's budget is devoted to personnel costs, the time and effort put into selection and supervision is quite worthwhile.

Effective supervision is another critical aspect of personnel management. The key element in supervision is a sound written performance plan that spells out the critical tasks or elements of the job, and identifies the standards for judging performance. The critical elements are tasks drawn from the job description and, where appropriate, from the goals and objectives of the archival program's management plan. The performance standards list specific tasks and end products designed to fulfil the critical elements. The standards must, to the greatest extent possible, contain both time-frames for task completion and quality benchmarks for evaluation purposes. Where possible, standards should be based on productivity standards developed through the work measurement process.

Employee participation in preparing the performance plan is recommended highly. Staff investment in both the management plan and the performance plan will improve morale and productivity. While managers are in daily contact with their staff concerning work progress, formal counseling sessions reviewing employee performance should be held at least semi-annually. Managers and staff members should re-evaluate performance plans each year in the light of changes in job descriptions or the management plan.

Continuing professional development is the third pillar on which successful personnel management rests. Professional archival training, depending on the locality, is offered in a variety of settings. Most archival training is provided "in-house" or through courses taught in colleges and universities. While most academic archival courses are offered through history departments, many library science schools are expanding their curricula to include courses on archives and manuscripts.

A good professional development program should include most, if not all, of the following elements:

1. "On-the-job" training in basic archival theory and practices. This should be supplemented by available academic course offerings, and by seminars or workshops sponsored by professional organizations.
2. Wherever appropriate, staff hired to work in one particular aspect of the archives program should be temporarily assigned, on a rotational basis, to other parts of the program. This will enhance their understanding of the archives' total holdings.
3. Archivists with managerial duties must receive systematic professional training for their areas of responsibility. Courses in statistical analysis, planning, budgeting, and personnel management, for example, are offered by government agencies, professional societies, and academic institutions.
4. A coordinator is needed to identify training opportunities and organize in-house classes and rotational assignments.
5. Archival institutions should consider actively supporting staff members interested in conducting research for publication in the areas of archival theory and practice, archival management, and topics of historical interest. Support could be expressed through underwriting publications costs, providing research time during duty hours, or other such options.
6. Archival managers should also encourage staff members to participate in local, regional, national, and international professional archival societies. Giving papers at conferences or serving as officers of these societies aid new archivists in maturing professionally and also sustain the motivation of archival veterans.

Public information

One area of responsibility for the archivist as manager that receives relatively little attention is public information. In this context, the term does not mean activities such as exhibits and educational programs. Rather it means identifying constituencies, actual or potential, that can support the archival program, and explaining how the archives can serve the needs of these groups. Archival institutions should have a planned system for disseminating information about the archives. The methods used could include speeches or lectures to local organizations, press releases, and articles for publication in newspapers, newsletters, or journals. Other information tools include annual reports, guides to the archival holdings, and pamphlets describing services. All such communication should address current societal needs through the information contained in the archives. Continually reinforcing this message is one way to gain a broader base of support in the community for the archives.

Facilities planning and maintenance

Space precludes an extended discussion on the role of the archivist in facilities planning and maintenance. Though some may see this topic as more appropriate for architects and engineers, quality facilities are essential for a truly successful archival program. All too often archives exist in cramped quarters with inadequate environmental conditions. Upon occasion, archivists have the opportunity to plan a new facility or, more likely, assist in renovating or refurbishing archival space.

Whichever may be the case, the archival manager has certain key responsibilities. Only the archivist can determine program needs through identifying the kind of storage space required for the particular holdings of the archives, projecting the growth of holdings, and documenting the most effective workflow patterns. The last point is important in providing direction to architects on which functions need to be performed near one another. Archivists must also be familiar with the literature and with issues relating to matters such as environmental standards and archival storage media. When archival program requirements are clearly defined, then the archivist can begin working with other professionals in constructing, renovating, or maintaining facilities.

Automation

A final component for consideration in the area of archival management is the use of ADP for administrative applications. This may be most appropriate for larger archival programs. Administrative applications could include tracking workload statistics, developing budget projections and monitoring spending, and tracking the status of personnel actions. Automation could speed the processing of administrative actions, monitor work, and improve the use of statistics. Of course, for small programs, manual systems will continue to be most cost-effective.

Professional literature

Unfortunately, there is still little professional literature for many areas of archival management. The best sources for identifying what has been published are *Modern archives and manuscripts: a select bibliography*, compiled by Frank B. Evans and published in 1975; and *Writings on archives, historical manuscripts, and current records*, compiled by the staff of the National Archives since 1942, and published in the *American Archivist* from 1943 to 1980. The compilation for the years 1979–1982 was published by the National Archives (1985), and the yearly compilations for 1983 and 1984 appeared in the *American Archivist* (Summer, Fall 1986 issues).

Included in the list of sources for further reading for this chapter are several major works in archival and library science literature that have chapters or sections focusing to some extent on management issues. These include T. R. Schellenberg's *Modern archives: principles and techniques*, Kenneth Duckett's *Modern manuscripts: a practical manual for their management, care and use*, and *The modern manuscript library* by Ruth B. Bordin and Robert M. Warner. Also included are books and periodical literature relevant to the major topics of this chapter.

Conclusion

Archival programs will never achieve their full potential without the effective application of sound management techniques. Whether the archival program is large or small, the aspiring manager must develop expertise in two fields—archival administration and institutional management. Professional achievement and personal satisfaction await those who can successfully bridge the two worlds.

19

Archival Effectiveness

James Gregory Bradsher

Archivists experience many rewards. But like all professionals, they also encounter many frustrations. This concluding chapter looks at the causes of some of these frustrations and some of the means of overcoming them. Its purpose is to suggest how archivists may become more effective managers and administrators of their institutions and archives.

The frustrations

Much of the frustration which archivists and other professionals experience comes from change. Change is unfamiliar; its uncertainties distress and unsettle us. Many professions respond to change by attempting to ignore, avoid, or even resist it. Archivists, in some respects, are the enemies of change. They spend much time protecting and preserving their archives and institutions from the fiscal and physical elements of change. Much time is spent simply keeping archives and the sources of financial support from deteriorating and all types of backlogs from appearing or increasing.

All professions must face change, for mutability and transitoriness are traits of nature and of all life in it. Change has been especially rapid in all facets of life during the last forty years. However, archivists have a special relationship to these changes, for perhaps there has been no greater change than in the shift from a society based on manufacturing and industry to one based on information. Today, more than ever before, societies are dependent upon information to function effectively and to cope with change. We are experiencing an information revolution, where information is the principal resource, the vital commodity.

An integral and crucial aspect of this information revolution is technology.

New technologies have increased our ability to gather, store, manipulate, analyze, retrieve, and communicate information. But they have also added to the archivist's problems. Information in data base management systems constantly changes; hardware and software quickly become obsolete; and copiers and computers produce staggering amounts of paper records almost instantly. Once it was thought that the 1980s would witness the birth of the paperless office. This has not happened. Instead, the computer has created more—not less—paper and information.

Thus, archivists increasingly are faced with the problem of bulk as records accumulate rapidly in staggering quantities. The fault does not lie completely with technology. More records are being created as a result of the growing multiplicity of record-creating programs that document more activities and more people. This results in more archives and more problems for archivists, including the burdens of storage, preservation, and administration. Records are also becoming more complex, reflecting the inherent complexity of the entities and individuals they document. This complexity causes numerous problems for archivists in deciding what records should be retained as archives and how they should be administered.

Because information is the principal resource of the new revolution, archivists are being called upon increasingly to make the information in their archives available to more and varied researchers. Researchers are also demanding more. They want more information, more recent information, and they want it faster and in a form and manner such that it can be easily used and cheaply reproduced.

Archivists, faced with change, the ever-increasing volume and complexity of records, and reference demands, are encountering difficulties in managing their institutions and administering their archives. To some degree these difficulties arise because archival institutions lack the financial resources to cope adequately with the problems facing them. However, many of them also arise from the way in which archival institutions are managed and led. Most such institutions are designed for stability and predictability, places where routine and repetition are organized efficiently through standard operating procedures. Under current conditions of rapid change and increased complexity, uncertainty often leads to ambiguity, confusion, and disarray as archivists experience the frustrations of dealing with conditions for which their institutions were never designed. This is often the case when archival institutions are part of larger bureaucratic organizations or are themselves large bureaucracies.

By their nature, bureaucracies, designed for stability and routine operations, resist change. In many archives, institutional thinking is frequently rigid and inflexible. Archival managers too often come to new ways of thinking and acting only with great difficulty. In many archival institutions, managers have either lost or never acquired the desire and skill for making tough decisions, taking significant risks, or coping with change. In some institutions the managers and staff are so afraid of the risk of any decisive action that they adopt a style of avoiding problems and opportunities, and employ various techniques for delaying decisions.

Archival administrators often do not have an articulated, understood, and accepted vision that provides meaning and direction to their institution and inspires the staff and creates a sense of purpose, focus, and commitment. In large institutions, managers often unconsciously slip into authoritarian roles. They become commanders who command their staffs, rather than leaders who lead them. They often forget that their staffs are not really working for them, but *with* them, for themselves and for the institution.

It is not surprising, therefore, to find that many archival institutions are overmanaged and underled. Managers are often concerned too much with the short-term and too little with their staffs' motivation, job satisfaction, and ideas. They tend to over-emphasize numbers, management information systems, and quantitative analysis. In doing so they become too remote from the heart of the operation or institution and the concerns of their staff. Many managers have become so scientific-minded in terms of management that they have forgotten that good management involves more than just planning, organizing, and controlling. It also involves leadership, motivation, creativity, and a concern for organizational environment and staff feelings.

These overmanaged and underled institutions all too often promote uniformity and dullness. They inhibit innovation by over-emphasizing group or committee thinking at the expense of individual effort. All too often, staff appraisal and reward systems may not give sufficient credit for creative thinking, either for new ideas or for suggestions for improvements. In many institutions, archivists often feel hampered by strict controls and limitations on their participation in management activities that affect their work. In such institutions, not only problems, but good, innovative ideas are often overlooked in a bureaucratic channeling of information, thereby preventing the staff from adopting better ways of working.

Because archivists are increasingly being called upon to play an important role in the information age in managing and making their archives available, they need to contend effectively with these difficulties. In previous chapters, the contributors have provided many specific answers and approaches to how archivists can contend effectively with the problems, changes, challenges, and frustrations facing them. The remaining pages offer some general thoughts in the context of the management functions of planning, organizing, leading, and controlling.

Planning

Planning, that is, determining what, when, how, and by whom work is to be carried out, is fundamental to an archival institution because it gives the institution its goals and sets up a procedure for reaching them. Planning takes precedence over the performance of the other management functions of organizing, leading, and controlling, and it is more important than those functions, because it gives them purpose and direction. Planning helps archivists focus their attention on institutional goals and makes it easier to apply and coordinate institutional resources more efficiently. It provides benchmarks against which accomplishments can be measured and allows managers and institutions to minimize risk and uncertainty, helping them prepare for and deal with change. Despite the time involved, a commitment to planning throughout an institution is vital if it is to increase its chances for success in reaching its goals and, to some measure, ensuring its survival.

The first and most important aspect of planning is to establish appropriate goals, objectives, and strategies. Goals provide the basic sense of direction for an institution's activities. For archival institutions, there are two ultimate goals: preserving records of archival value, and making them available for research. Hierarchically below the ultimate goals are major goals such as "making records available to researchers as efficiently as possible". Objectives are the ends an archival institution must achieve to reach its goals. For example, in order to accomplish the major goal stated above, an archives may adopt the objective of "ensuring all series of records are adequately described". Strategies are broad programs for achieving the institution's objectives. To achieve the above objective, for example, an archive may adopt the strategy of "reviewing all series in the institution to ensure that they are adequately described".

Many institutions, in the midst of changing environments, lose their effectiveness by not focusing clearly on their goals. They end up tinkering with their structures, priorities, and practices, in response to change, often doing more harm than good. Archivists, therefore, must remember that their ultimate goal is preserving archives and making them available. By focusing on their central mission and maintaining a clear perspective about the functions and purposes of their institutions, they will help focus energy on what needs to be done and provide an environment where decisions can be made logically and efficiently.

To make themselves more effective planners, archivists must not accept with complacency the *status quo* or become so preoccupied with meeting established goals and objectives that they cease to question them. Deciding to change or abandon goals and objectives when necessary is as important as setting them up in the first place. If archivists are satisfied with the *status quo* they will see no reason to innovate, and will not be able to see needs, problems, and opportunities. Refusing to give up unproductive or obsolete goals and objectives is a common cause of organizational failure. An important part of moving into the future is letting go of an unusable past. This means that archivists must develop a healthy dissatisfaction with the *status quo* and continually question the value of their goals and objectives.

After reviewing and firmly establishing their goals and objectives, archivists need to look for better ways of reaching them. They must regularly re-examine everything they do and how they do it to see whether improvements can be made. Theories, principles, programs, policies, procedures, methods, practices, and even definitions must be examined in the light of the major technological changes that are occurring in our ability to create, store, process, access, and use information. Those things which no longer make sense or do not contribute anything to reaching the goals and objectives should be abandoned.

In an age of scarce resources, anything that leads to more efficient and effective operations increases an institution's chances to survive and succeed in fulfilling its goals. Therefore, archivists must be willing to look at whole new approaches to solving a problem or seizing an opportunity. They will inevitably find that the most effective archival practices, like the rules of life, are learned from experience and not necessarily from logic. Archivists must experiment and exercise creativity and innovation to generate new ideas and translate them into improved programs or methods of operation.

To successfully solve current problems and meet the challenges of change, archivists must constantly enlarge the pool of techniques and ideas from which they can draw to create or improve processes and services. Therefore, they must build on the ideas and experiences of others, and share information, resources, and research and development costs, not only with other archivists but also with other professions. They must work especially with preservation and information specialists to solve storage and preservation problems and to make more efficient and effective the intellectual control of and access to information.

If archivists are to identify, arrange, describe, and preserve archival records efficiently, they must also cooperate closely with those who produce records in order to establish and maintain control over their quality at the source. This is particularly true with respect to automated systems. Archivists need to intervene constantly to exert a positive influence on technological development to ensure that valuable information is not lost and that information in electronic environments can be administered effectively.

Automated information systems are needed to contend with the bulk and complexity of modern records. But, in the rush to automate, archivists must not become too enraptured with automation. Automation is a useful tool only to the degree that it is handled with skill, knowledge, and a keen sense of its limits. Archivists must be careful to adopt systems only when they will improve service without unduly disrupting program activities. Careful planning is needed to determine which systems are best suited to an archival institution in both the short and long term, especially when technologies are changing so fast.

The most important thing to remember about the future is that there is nothing permanent except change, accompanied by increasing complexity. As an archival institution's internal and external environments (including technologies) change, archivists must either change with them or become increasingly frustrated as the changes overwhelm them. Archivists must make change work for them, not against them. Because changes are occurring so rapidly that there is often little time to react, archivists must anticipate and plan for the future. They must anticipate change, institutional needs, and potential problems, and plan the steps to be taken to avoid the problems or respond to them as they arise.

Many changes cannot be imagined. However, many others and the resultant problems, can be anticipated. Despite the accelerating rate of change, the early warning signals are almost always evident to those who choose to see them. This is the case with technological innovation which takes years to reach fruition. Therefore, archival institutions should continuously monitor technological developments that affect the creation and preservation of records, as well as their own external and internal environments, to anticipate emerging issues, challenges, and opportunities.

All innovation, including establishing new goals and objectives, involves risks because change is involved. However, by knowing what is important to the success of an archives, risk-taking can be encouraged and the right risks taken. The best and most effective change is orderly change. The best way to achieve orderliness and to minimize risks is to plan change as carefully and thoroughly as possible. Also, the approach taken to effect change greatly affects its acceptance. Archival staffs will resist change if they see no reason for it or if they have had little or no opportunity to be involved in planning for it. Archivists, who are closest to archival problems and thus most aware of opportunities for, and difficulties in making change, must participate fully in planning for change. High levels of staff participation will yield greater acceptance of the change and greater support for its maintenance because people understand and believe in what they help to create.

In finding ways to improve their work, archivists should not rely too much upon prepackaged programs and rigid methods to provide an easy, structured approach to decisions. The information revolution is too fluid to be wholly contained by any method. Therefore, archivists should not become slavishly devoted to any one method. No method can substitute for creativity. Many professions have been hindered by the mistaken idea that the most serious difficulties are "methodological" and that if only the right methodology is found, progress is sure to follow. This attitude is not merely unproductive, but potentially destructive. By pressing methodological norms too far, bold and imaginative ideas may be inhibited. Archivists must always remember that there are a variety of good answers to good questions.

In the process of re-examination and subsequent redirection, archivists must also remember that much of what they do results from hard-won experience. Therefore, they should not be too quick to change for the sake of change. Inertia can play a constructive role. It warns us against facile conceptions of "progress" and disabuses us of the notion that change is easy. Simplistic ideas of progress see only the near face of events when they look to the future. Typically, they underrate its complexities and often do not consider that the solution of one problem is only the formulation of another.

Thus, studies should be undertaken to determine whether a potential change will be necessary or effective, or both, and to better understand its consequences and uncertainties as well as the consequences of not changing at all. Alternatives must be analyzed and evaluated with a concern for probable and possible consequences, both positive and negative, as well as for how decisions relate to the major goals and objectives. The effects of potential change on people and on organizational structures must also be considered, as well as their interrelationship with other decisions.

An important aspect of effective decision-making is knowing when to leave things alone. Progress is often made by freeing ourselves from past practices, but without them, orderly archival institutions would hardly have been possible in the first place. The art of progress is to preserve order amid change and to promote change amid order. The real challenge is to accept, adopt, and adapt the positive aspects of the past for use in the present and the future.

To deal effectively with present and future problems and opportunities, archival institutions must develop a sense of commitment to decisive decision-making. Decisions deserve careful study, but archivists must avoid "paralysis caused by analysis", that is, so much planning or searching so long for more information, alternatives, and assessments of risks that decisions are never made, or by the time they are, events and even opportunities have passed by. The desire of some archivists to find the "best" has kept them from the "good". Archivists must be willing to make intelligent compromises with perfection lest they wait forever before taking action. Few things can be more wasteful of time, energy, and spirit than the necessity of trying to live up to a completely irrelevant and useless standard of perfection. Archivists should remember the Puritan dilemma of the seventeenth century—the attempt to create a perfect world using imperfect material, that is, humans. Much archival material is imperfect, reflecting mankind's untidy nature in the way that records are created, filed, maintained, used, and retired. Therefore, archivists will often find that the most effective means of dealing with their archives is to adjust their methods to fit the records, rather than the other way round.

Because there is much work to be done and often not enough resources to tackle all problems and opportunities, archivists must set priorities, identifying tasks as "must do", "should do", and "nice to do". Attention should be given first to those opportunities and problems that truly affect the entire institution. Archivists will be more successful in achieving goals if they moderate their aspirations to reasonable levels and tackle only those issues that are commensurate in scale with the tools available for grappling with them.

Organizing

Once goals and objectives are established and plans and strategies developed to reach them, an effective organizational structure must be designed to carry out the plans successfully. Designing this structure requires careful analysis to organize activities for their most effective and efficient performance. Because fulfilling different objectives may require different kinds of organizational structures, there is no one ideal way for all archival institutions to be organized. The most desirable structure will vary from one archives to another and for the same archives over time. Archival leaders must constantly review their institution's structure because the staff, technologies, and internal and external environments inevitably change with the passage of time. They should also build in flexibility to permit the archives to adapt to changing conditions.

Organizing an institution for orderly and efficient operations is often an extremely complicated task. Archival leaders must exercise conceptual skills. They must be able to see their institution as a whole, understanding how changes in any one part affect all the others. They must coordinate and integrate the activities of the separate units or programs in order to achieve their goals and institutional objectives efficiently. Without this coordination and integration, the staff and the various units will lose sight of their roles within the institution. As part of this process, the staff must be informed of the methods by which objectives are to be reached and how their efforts can contribute to reaching them.

Additionally, the organization must be balanced with the psychological and social needs of the staff who want to enjoy their work and not consider it a boring routine. Archival work must be specialized to promote efficiency, but not so specialized that tasks become meaningless to those who peform them. Furthermore, the needs of individual staff members should be considered in assigning work. While many archivists prefer to specialize in one or more tasks, many find that they are more effective, energetic, and productive if they alternate almost simultaneously or periodically among various, if not most, tasks. Therefore, managers need, whenever possible, to allow their archivists to work in a manner best suited to their individual needs.

Leading

Effective archival leadership involves getting the staff to perform in ways that will help to achieve goals and objectives with the least amount of time, effort, discomfort, and resources. This leadership is important because the well-being and resilience of an archives are direct reflections of the vigor, enthusiasm, and imagination of its leaders. This is particularly true of administrators, for they frequently establish the personality of the archives. What they do and how they do it is often copied throughout the institution.

The archival profession has many effective leaders who operate with vision and foresight, inspire trust, and encourage others to realize their full potential. Unfortunately, there are not enough of them. Thus, there is a need for a commitment to archival leadership, as distinct from archival management. There is a clear difference between the two. To manage is to direct the daily operations, to oversee the effectiveness of the routine, and to ensure the efficiency of the existing system. But leadership involves much more than management. To lead is to grasp the wider picture, to understand relationships, to clarify choices, to recognize both needs and opportunities, to encourage agreement, to inspire cooperation, and to instill confidence.

Change, complexity, and uncertainty increasingly make the leadership job ever more critical. To be effective, archival leaders must anticipate and deal with the uncertainties, frustrations, and ambiguities that changes produce in their institutions. They must implant predictability, stability, consistency, and harmony, making the archives stand for something in which the staff can believe. They must clear away ambiguity by clarifying purpose and setting direction so that the staff knows what has to be done and why.

To accomplish this, administrators must have a vision: a realistic, credible, desirable, and achievable future for their institutions. But merely to have a vision without sharing it comprehensively with the staff constitutes a major shortcoming in many large institutions. It deprives the staff of the opportunity to use their talents fully, and deprives the institution of the total potential contributions of its staff. Therefore administrators must espouse their vision and persuade their staffs to accept it as worthwhile and meaningful. To be accepted, it must grow out of a participatory process, where the staff shares, and is willing to work to achieve, the vision, because they understand their relationship to it. An articulated and accepted vision can become a strong, integrating, motivating force within the institution, and create a momentum which enriches the staff with such a feeling of pride and energy that production increases.

Many managers believe that people have to be directed according to certain motivations—fear, greed, praise—to perform their functions. But increasingly managers are finding that, to achieve the best results, their task is not to motivate workers, but to enable or encourage them to motivate themselves. By doing so, managers encourage their staffs to do the work that needs to be done. In this sense, leadership is the creation of power in others by inspiring them, energizing them, and aligning their motivation with that of the institution as a whole. This works because it supports the deepest psychological needs of people in an organizational context. People want to make a difference, to feel that they are doing something important. They want their creativity to have a purpose and direction. Leaders who thus enable their staffs to share some authority with management will have little difficulty in stimulating them and capturing their commitment to a common purpose.

Because archival institutions will benefit when the staff is allowed to exercise creativity, initiative, and individual discretion, institutions must be structured and a climate created that fosters creativity and innovation. These are best nurtured in a climate which encourages the exploration of new ideas and new ways of doing things. Such a climate is fostered when leaders make it clear that they welcome new approaches as well as calculated risk-taking, and when they recognize that time and resources will be invested in the generation and development of new ideas, concepts, and approaches, many of which may not work out. Leaders must tolerate failure, as many ideas may prove impractical or useless. They must realize that mistakes are to be expected. The important thing is to examine them, learn from them, and go on. The only real mistake is being afraid to make one.

An important element in establishing a creative and productive atmosphere is an insistence upon open and honest communication within the institution. Leaders need to know the limits of their abilities and to be open to criticism and advice. Recognizing that something is wrong and then taking action to correct it is a great skill that must be exercised by archival leaders. Therefore, they should develop a climate that emphasizes asking questions about why things are done in a certain way and not in another way. Their staffs must feel free and be given the opportunity to influence decisions that affect their work. Employee participation generally breeds positive motivation. Additionally, the free flow of information is essential to an archives, for it is only by knowing the realities of internal and external environments that management can hope to manage effectively.

The organizational climate will determine, to a large extent, how the institution performs and how the staff interprets and responds to its experience within the institution. Leaders will be more successful when they create and maintain an environment that allows staff members to act professionally and competently, to develop confidence in themselves, and to exercise their talents and skills to the best advantage. This means that leaders must nurture and help their staffs to reach their true potential as workers, as colleagues, and as human beings. Archivists, like all people, have a need to belong, to be liked, appreciated, praised, respected, and rewarded. They will work harder and be more productive if they are challenged, feel pride and self-satisfaction in achieving goals, know they are needed and appreciated, and also meet their own personal needs by working toward institutional goals and objectives. Managers thus need to create an invigorating and challenging atmosphere, where the staff is continually challenged, amply rewarded, and allowed to develop. The latter is important in producing future leaders.

Controlling

Although they may allow their staffs a good deal of discretion, managers must nevertheless ensure that staff actions move the institution toward its goals. A combination of well-planned objectives, sound organization, capable direction, and motivation has little chance of success unless there exists an adequate system of control. This should monitor progress by establishing standards of performance, measuring current performance and comparing it against these standards; and taking any necessary corrective action.

To be effective, controls should be specific, objective, logical, and simple to understand; economically and organizationally realistic; coordinated with the institution's work flow; acceptable to staff; focused on key objectives at critical points in operations; and flexible and responsive enough to adapt to changing circumstances. The latter is important because institutions, people, environments, and technologies keep changing. Thus, any control system will require continuing modification for it to remain effective.

In developing controls, managers must achieve a balance between control and creativity. Too much control produces archives that are stifling, inhibiting, and unsatisfying places in which to work; too little leads to archives that are inefficient and ineffective in achieving their goals. A balance can be best achieved with vigilant oversight, where managers are interested, concerned, involved, and available.

By approaching the staff as people who are capable of self-discipline, managers create challenging work situations in which individuals attempt to meet objectives. Self-discipline cannot be taught. People must develop it on their own. One of the best ways to help the staff become aware of the importance of self-discipline is for managers to set a good example; many times a subordinate's work behavior merely reflects that of the superior.

No control system will work unless there is a reporting system that is objective, accurate, and timely, so that the information gathered is useful and necessary corrective action can be taken. Similarly, an archives needs a good information system, one that facilitates the decision-making process and enables the planning, controlling, and operational functions to be carried out effectively. To make this process more efficient, archivists must harness the computer. However, in developing automated management systems, archivists must ensure that they facilitate, not hinder, their work. Archivists must not become the captive and functional slaves of computers, computer personnel, and automation; they must avoid situations where they are constantly feeding information to a computer as though this was their primary function instead of the archival tasks for which they were hired.

Conclusion

Increased funding and better management practices will go a long way toward improving archival operations, but these alone will not end the frustrations, meet the challenges, nor solve the problems. These can only be ended, met, and solved by archivists making themselves more efficient—using their mental and financial resources more wisely—and by making themselves more effective.

While archivists look for ways to make themselves more efficient and effective and while they experiment, speculate, and anticipate and plan for the future, much basic archival work exists. To succeed takes constant effort. Persistence is an indispensable ingredient of the archival profession. Those institutions that abandon persistence in the search for some quick solution, or in the quest for perfection, will end up hindering their effectiveness and wasting precious resources—including the most precious resource—time.

If archivists are to appraise and manage records and preserve and administer their archives more effectively in the future, they must adapt to changes in the ways information is created, stored, used, and accessed. In adapting to change they must keep or modify theories, principles, and practices that are still useful, and discard those that are outdated. They must also create or find better ways of administering information and archives, and develop strategies to cope with both the opportunities and problems created by the information revolution. To survive and succeed in the decade ahead, archivists must make the most of their opportunities, their industry, their curiosity, and their intelligence. The 1990s will require the basics—planning, organizing, leading, and controlling—as well as commitment, efficiency, and imagination. Anything less will deprive those whom archivists serve of the full value of the information contained in archives.

Sources for Further Reading

Full citations for and affiliations of works cited in a short form, and affiliations of works cited in full, are as follows:

The American Archivist. Published by the Society of American Archivists.
Archivaria. The Journal of the Association of Canadian Archivists.
Archives. The Journal of the British Records Association.
Archives and Manuscripts: The Journal of the Australian Society of Archivists.
Archivum. Published by the International Council on Archives.
Georgia Archive. Journal of the Society of Georgia Archivists (1972–1982).
The Indian Archives. Published by the National Archives of India.
The Midwestern Archivist. Published by the Midwest Archives Conference, United States.
Prologue: Journal of the National Archives. Published by the National Archives and Records Administration, United States.
Provenance: Journal of the Society of Georgia Archivists (1983–)
The Public Historian: A Journal of Public History. Sponsored by the National Council on Public History, United States.

Introduction to archives

Basu, Purnendu. Records and archives: what are they? *The Indian Archives*, vol. 2, nos. 2–4, April, July and October 1948. 75–81.
Baumann, Roland M., ed. *A manual of archival techniques*. rev. ed. Harrisburg, Pennsylvania Historical and Museum Commission, 1982.
Bechor, Malvina B. Bibliographic access to archival literature. *American Archivist*, vol. 50, no. 2, Spring 1987. 243–247.
Berner, Richard C. *Archival theory and practice in the United States: a historical analysis*. Seattle and London, University of Washington Press, 1983.
———. Manuscript collections, archives, and special collections: their relationships. *Archivaria*, no. 18, Summer 1984. 248–254.
Bradsher, James Gregory. Federal records and archives. *Government Information Quarterly*, vol. 4, no. 2, 1987. 127–134.

265

———. When one percent means a lot: the percentage of permanent records in the National Archives. Organization of American Historians *Newsletter*, vol. 13, no. 2, May 1985. 20–21.

Brooks, Philip C. Archivists and their colleagues: common denominators. *American Archivist*, vol. 14, no. 1, January 1951. 33–44.

Buck, Solon J. Let's look at the record. *American Archivist*, vol. 8, no. 2, April 1945. 109–114.

Burke, Frank G. The future course of archival theory in the United States. *American Archivist*, vol. 44, no. 1, Winter 1981. 40–46.

Burke, J.L. and Shergold, C.M. What are archives? *Archives and Manuscripts*, vol. 6, no. 6, February 1976. 235–240.

Burnette, O. Lawrence, Jr. *Beneath the footnote: a guide to the use and preservation of American historical sources*. Madison, State Historical Society of Wisconsin, 1969.

Cappon, Lester J. What, then, is there to theorize about? *American Archivist*, vol. 45, no. 1, Winter 1982. 19–25.

Clark, Robert L., Jr., ed. *Archives–library relations*. New York, R.R. Bowker Co., 1976

Connor, R.D.W. Adventures of an amateur archivist. *American Archivist*, vol. 6, no. 1, January 1943. 1–18.

Cook, Michael. Professional training: international perspectives. *Archivaria*, no. 7, Winter 1978. 28–40.

———. *Guidelines for curriculum development in records management and the administration of modern archives: a RAMP study*. Paris, UNESCO, 1982.

———. *Archives administration: a manual for smaller and intermediate organisations and for local government*. Folkestone, Kent, England, Dawson. 1977.

Couture, Carol and Rousseau, Jean-Yves. *The life of a document: a global approach to archives and records management*. translated by David Homel. Montreal, Vehicule Press, 1987.

Cox, Richard J. Professionalism and archivists in the United States. *American Archivist*, vol. 49, no. 3, Summer 1986. 229–247.

Cronin, Blaise. *The transition years: new intiatives in the education of professional information workers*. London, Aslib, 1984.

Daniels, Maygene F. and Walch, Timothy, eds. *A modern archives reader: basic readings on archival theory and practice*. Washington, D.C., National Archives and Records Service, 1984.

Davies, J. Conway, ed. *Studies presented to Sir Hilary Jenkinson*. London, Oxford University Press, 1957.

Dearstyne, Bruce W., issue ed. Archives and public history: issues, problems, and prospects. *The Public Historian*, vol. 8, no. 3, Summer 1986. 6–98.

Dodds, Gordon. Canadian archival literature: a bird's-eye view. *Archivaria*, no. 17, Winter 1983–84. 18–40.

Durr, W. Theodore, Some thoughts and designs about archives and automation, 1984. *American Archivist*, vol. 47, no. 3, Summer 1984. 271–289.

Ellis, Roger H. The British archivist and his training. *Journal of the Society of Archivists*, vol. 3, no. 6, October 1967. 265–271.

———. The British archivist and his society. *Journal of the Society of Archivists*, vol. 3, no. 2, October 1965. 43–48.

Evans, Frank B. Indian archival training and the archival training needs of Asia: some observations. *The Indian Archives*, vol. 30, no. 2, July–December 1981. 1–14.

———. Postappointment archival training: a proposed solution for a basic problem. *American Archivist*, vol. 40, no. 1, January 1977. 57–74.

———. *Writings on archives published by and with the assistance of UNESCO: a RAMP study*. Paris, UNESCO, 1983.

————, comp. *Modern archives and manuscripts: a select bibliography.* Chicago, Society of American Archivists, 1975.

Evans, Frank B., Himly, Francois-J. and Walne, Peter, comps. *Dictionary of archival terminology/dictionnaire de terminologie archivistique.* edited by Peter Walne. International Council on Archives Handbook Series no. 3 Munich, K.G. Saur Verlag KG, 1984.

Fang, Josephine Riss and Songe, Alice H., comps. *International guide to library, archival, and information science associations.* 2nd ed. New York, R.R. Bowker Co., 1981.

Grolier, Eric de, comp. and ed. *Register of education and training activities in librarianship, information science and archives.* Paris, UNESCO, 1982.

Grover, Wayne C. Archives: society and profession. *American Archivist,* vol. 18, no. 1, January 1955. 3-10.

Gupta, R.C. Training of archivists in south and west Asia. *The Indian Archives,* vol. 31, no. 1, January–June 1982. 1-24.

Gurnsey, John. *The information professions in the electronic age.* London, Bingley, 1985.

Helmuth, Ruth W. Education for American archivists: a view from the trenches. *American Archivist,* vol. 44, no. 3, Fall 1981, 295-303.

Hesselager, Lise. Fringe or grey literature in the national library: on "papyrolatry" and the growing similarity between the materials in libraries and archives. *American Archivist,* vol. 47, no. 3, Summer 1984. 255-270.

Hollaender, Albert E.J., ed. *Essays in memory of Sir Hilary Jenkinson.* Chichester, Sussex, Moore and Tillyer, 1962.

Holmes, Oliver W. Public records: who knows what they are? *American Archivist,* vol. 23, no. 1, January 1960. 3-26.

Hull, Felix. "Modern records" then and now. *Journal of the Society of Archivists,* vol. 4, no. 5, April 1972. 395-399.

Jenkinson, Hilary. *A manual of archive administration.* a reissue of the revised second edition with an introduction and bibliography by Roger H. Ellis. London, Percy Lund, Humphries and Co., 1965.

————. Twenty-five years: some reminiscences of an English archivist 1923-1948. *The Indian Archives,* vol. 3, nos. 1-4, January–December 1949. 12-35.

————. The future of archives in England. *Journal of the Society of Archivists,* vol. 1, no. 3, April 1956, 57-61.

————. The problems of nomenclature in archives. *Journal of the Society of Archivists,* vol. 1, no. 9, April 1959. 233-239.

————. Roots. *Journal of the Society of Archivists,* vol. 2, no. 4, October 1961. 131-138.

Kahn, Herman. Some comments on the archival vocation. *American Archivist,* vol. 34, no. 1, January 1971. 3-12.

Lamb, W. Kaye. The changing role of the archivist. *American Archivist,* vol. 29, no. 1, January 1966. 3-10.

————. Keeping the past up to date. *Journal of the Society of Archivists,* vol. 2, no. 7, April 1963. 285-288.

Leavitt, Arthur H. What are archives? *American Archivist,* vol. 24, no. 2, April 1961. 175-178.

Lee, Charles E. Persons, places, and papers: the joys of being an archivist. *American Archivist,* vol. 36, no. 1, January 1973. 5-14.

Love, J.H. What are records? *Archives and Manuscripts,* vol. 14, no. 1, May 1986. 54-60.

Lytle, Richard, ed. *Management of archives and manuscript collections for librarians.* Chicago, Society of American Archivists, 1980.

McCrank, Lawrence J. Prospects for integrating historical and information studies in archival education. *American Archivist*, vol. 42, no. 4, October 1979. 443–455.

———, ed. *Archives and library administration: divergent traditions and common concerns*. New York and London, Haworth Press, 1986.

Mason, Philip P. Archives in the seventies: promises and fulfillment. *American Archivist*, vol. 44, no. 3, Summer 1981. 199–206.

Miller, Fredric. Archives and historical manuscripts. *In*: Howe, Barbara J. and Kemp, Emory L, eds. *Public History: an Introduction*. Malabar, Florida, Robert E. Krieger Publishing Co., 1986. 36–56.

Moltke-Hansen, David. Reflections on the problems of access to archival literature. *American Archivist*, vol. 47, no. 3, Summer 1984. 293–295.

[Norton, Margaret Cross]. *Norton on archives: The writings of Margaret Cross Norton on archival and records management*. edited with an introduction by Thornton W. Mitchell. Chicago, Society of American Archivists, 1979.

Orlovich, Peter. Some basic assumptions underlying the education and training of archivists. *Archives and Manuscripts*, vol. 6, no. 6, February 1976. 204–225.

Orr, William J. Archival training in Europe. *American Archivist*, vol. 44, no. 1, Winter 1981. 27–39.

Parker, J. Stephen, comp. *Library and information science and archive administration: a guide to building up a basic collection for library schools*. Paris, General Information Programme and UNISIST, UNESCO, 1984.

Peace, Nancy E. and Chudacoff, Nancy Fisher. Archivists and librarians: a common mission, a common education. *American Archivist*, vol. 42, no. 4, October 1979. 456–462.

Pederson, Ann, ed.-in-chief. *Keeping archives*. Sydney, Australian Society of Archivists Inc., 1987.

Peterson, Trudy Huskamp. The National Archives and the archival theorist revisited, 1954–1984. *American Archivist*, vol. 49, no. 2, Spring 1986. 125–133.

Pinkett, Harold T. Professional development of an archivist: some ways and means. *Georgia Archive*, vol. 3, no. 2, Summer 1975. 107–115.

———. American archival theory: the state of the art. *American Archivist*, vol. 44, no. 3, Summer 1981 . 217–222.

[Posner, Ernst]. *Archives and the public interest: selected essays by Ernst Posner*. edited by Ken Munden with an introduction by Paul Lewinson. Washington, D.C., Public Affairs Press, 1967.

Posner, Ernst. The National Archives and the archival theorist. *American Archivist*, vol. 18, no. 3, July 1955. 207–216.

Raymond, Andrew and O'Toole, James M. Up from the basement: archives, history, and public administration. *Georgia Archive*, vol. 6, no. 2, Fall 1978. 18–32.

Reingold, Nathan. Confessions of a reformed archivist. *American Archivist*, vol. 31, no. 4, October 1968. 371–377.

Rhoads, James B. *The role of archives and records management in national information systems: a RAMP Study*. Paris, UNESCO, 1983.

Roberts, John W. Archival theory: much ado about shelving. *American Archivist*, vol. 50, no. 1, Winter 1987. 66–74.

Russell, Mattie U. The influence of historians on the archival profession in the United States. *American Archivist*, vol. 46, no. 3, Summer 1983. 277–285.

Schellenberg, T.R. *Modern archives: principles and techiques*. Chicago, University of Chicago Press, 1956

———. *The management of modern archives*. New York, Columbia University Press, 1965.

———. The future of the archival profession. *American Archivist*, vol. 22, no. 1, January 1959. 49–58.

Smith, Wilfred I. Broad horizons: opportunities for archivists. *American Archivist*, vol. 37, no. 1, January 1974. 3–14.
Taylor, Hugh A. The discipline of history and the education of the archivist. *American Archivist*, vol. 40, no. 4, October 1977. 395–402.
———. The collective memory: archives and libraries as heritage. *Archivaria*, no. 15, Winter 1982–83. 118–130.
UNESCO. *List of documents and publications of the General Information Programme and UNISIST*: 1977–1983. Paris, UNESCO, 1985.
Walch, Victoria Irons. *Information resources for archivists and records administrators: a report and recommendations*. Albany, New York, National Association of Government Archives and Records Administrators, 1987.
Walne, Peter, comp. *Modern archives administration and records management: a RAMP reader*. Paris, UNESCO, 1985.
Welch, Edwin. Archival education. *Archivaria*, no. 4, Summer 1977. 49–59.
Weldon, Edward. Archives and the practice of public history. *The Public Historian*, vol. 4, no. 3, Summer 1982. 49–58.
Wosh, Peter J. Creating a semi-professional profession: archivists view themselves. *Georgia Archive*, vol. 10, no. 2, Fall 1982. 1–13.

History of archives administration

Allen, C.G. Central African archives: some aspects of their development. *The Indian Archives*, vol. 2, no. 1, January 1948. 82–89.
Andersson, C. Ingvar. Swedish archives, their history and organisation. *Journal of the Society of Archivists*, vol. 3, no. 1, April 1965. 7–14.
Basu, Purnendu. Why preserve records? *The Indian Archives*, vol. 3, nos. 1–4, January–December 1949. 88–95.
Bell, Harold Idris. The custody of records in Roman Egypt. *The Indian Archives*, vol. 4, no. 2, July–December 1950. 116–125.
Bond, Maurice F. The formation of the archives of Parliament, 1497–1691. *Journal of the Society of Archivists*, vol. 1, October 1957. 151–158.
Born, Lester K. Baldassare Bonifacio and his essay "De Archivis". *American Archivist*, vol. 4, no. 4, October 1941. 221–237.
———. The "de Archivis Commentarius" of Albertino Barisoni (1587–1667). *Archivalische Zeitschrift*, vols. 50–51, 1955. 13–22.
Bradsher, James Gregory. Ebla's royal archives. *Information Development: The International Journal for Archivists, Librarians, and Information Specialists*, vol. 1, no. 4, October 1985. 238–245.
———. A brief history of the growth of federal records, archives, and information, 1789–1985. *Government Publications Review*, vol. 13, no. 4, 1986. 491–505.
———. Federal field archives: past, present, and future. *Government Information Quarterly*, vol. 4, no. 2, 1987. 151–166.
———. An administrative history of the disposal of federal records,1789–1949. *Provenance*, vol. 3, no. 2, Fall 1985. 1–21.
———. An administrative history of the disposal of federal records, 1950–1985. *Provenance*, vol. 4, no. 2, Fall 1986. 49–73.
Brooks, Philip C. *Research in archives: the use of unpublished primary sources*. Chicago and London, University of Chicago Press, 1969.
Clanchy, M.T. *From memory to written records: England, 1066–1307*. Cambridge, Harvard University Press, 1977.
Cocks, Pamela S. The development of the National Archives of New Zealand. *Journal of the Society of Archivists*, vol. 3, no. 3, April 1966. 121–126.
Cox, Richard J. American archival history: its development, needs, and opportunities.

American Archivist, vol. 46, no. 1, Winter 1983. 31–41.

Culham, Phyllis. Tablets and temples: documents in republican Rome. *Provenance*, vol. 2, no. 2, Fall 1984. 15–31.

Duchein, Michael. Archives at the service of the administration, of the researcher, and of the private citizen. *The Indian Archives*, vol. 27, no. 2, July–December 1978. 1–13.

Evans, Frank B, com. *The history of archives administration: a select bibliography.* UNESCO Bibliographies and Reference Works no. 6, Paris, UNESCO, 1979.

——. Promoting archives and research: a study in international cooperation. *American Archivist*, vol. 50, no. 1, Winter 1987. 48–65.

Ghosh, Pradyot Kumar. Archives for everybody. *The Indian Archives*, vol. 28, nos. 1–2, January–December 1979. 32–36.

Giusti, Martino. The Vatican secret archives. *Archivaria*, no. 7, Winter 1978. 16–27.

Grimstead, Patricia Kennedy. Regional archival development in the USSR: soviet standards and national documentary legacies. *American Archivist*, vol. 36, no. 1, January 1973. 43–66.

——. Lenin's archival decree of 1918: the Bolshevik legacy for soviet archival theory and practice. *American Archivist*, vol. 45, no. 4, Fall 1982. 429–443.

Grover, Ray. The National Archives of New Zealand: its historical context. *Archivaria*, no. 18, Summer 1984. 232–240.

Hallam, Elizabeth M. The Tower of London as a record office. *Archives*, vol. 14, no. 61, Spring 1979. 3–10.

Helfenstein, Ulrich. Swiss archives. *American Archivist*, vol. 37, no. 4, October 1974. 565–571.

Holmes, Oliver W. History and theory of archival practices. *In:* Stevens, Rolland E. ed. *University archives: papers presented at an institute by the University of Illinois Graduate School of Library Science, November 8, 1964*, Champaign, The Illinois Union Bookstore, 1965. 1–21.

Hornabrook, Judith. Thoughts on New Zealand's National Archives. *Archives and Manuscripts*, vol. 6, no. 2, February 1975. 103–107.

Iredale, David. *Enjoying archives: what they are, where to find them, how to use them.* Newton Abbott, David & Charles, 1973.

Jorgensen, Harald. The present organization and working conditions of Scandinavian archives. *Journal of the Society of Archivists*, vol. 4, no. 1, April 1970. 23–30.

Lodolini, Elio. Archives organization in Italy. *The Indian Archives*, vol. 32, no. 1, January–June 1983. 27–30.

Lokke, Carl. Archives and the French Revolution. *American Archivist*, vol. 31, no. 1, January 1968. 23–31.

McCain, William D. The value oᶠ records. *American Archivist*, vol. 16, no. 1, January 1953. 3–11.

McCoy, Donald R. *The National Archives: America's ministry of documents, 1934–1968.* Chapel Hill, University of North Carolina Press, 1978.

Moss, William W. Archives in the People's Republic of China. *American Archivist*, vol. 45, no. 4, Fall 1982. 385–409.

Nauman, Ann K. The Archivo General De Indias. *Archives*, vol. 15, no. 68, October 1982. 216–223.

Ormsby, William G. The Public Archives of Canada, 1948–1968. *Archivaria*, no. 15, Winter 1982–83. 36–46.

Posner, Ernst. *Archives in the ancient world.* Cambridge, Harvard University Press, 1972.

——. *American state archives.* Chicago and London, University of Chicago Press, 1964.

——. Some aspects of archival development since the French Revolution. *American Archivist*, vol. 3, no. 3, July 1940. 159–172.

————. Archives in medieval Islam. *American Archivist*, vol. 35, nos. 3-4, July–October 1972. 291-316.

Prasad, S.N. Archives in India. *Archivaria*, no. 7, Winter 1978. 52-60.

Schwirthich, Anne-Marie. Archives in the Roman Republic. *Archives and Manuscripts*, vol. 9, no. 1, September 1981. 19-29.

Smith, Clive. The Australian archives. *Archives and Manuscripts*, vol. 8, no. 1, June 1980. 33-40.

Swift, Michael D. The Canadian archival scene in the 1970s: current developments and trends. *Archivaria*, no. 15, Winter 1982-83. 47-57.

Sykora, Vojtech. Czechoslovak archives—origin and growth. *The Indian Archives*, vol. 32, no. 2, July-December 1983. 45-54

Veit, Fritz, *Presidential libraries and collections*. New York, Greenwood Press, 1987.

Viola, Herman J. *The National Archives of the United States*. New York, Harry N. Abrams, 1984.

Walch, Timothy, ed. *Guardian of heritage: essays on the history of the National Archives*. Washington, D.C., National Archives and Records Administration, 1985.

Weilbrenner, Bernard. The Public Archives of Canada, 1871-1958. *Journal of the Society of Archivists*, vol. 2, no. 3, April 1961. 101-113.

Wilson, Ian E. "A noble dream": the origin of the Public Archives of Canada. *Archivaria*, no. 15, Winter 1982-83. 16-35.

Wilsted, Thomas. Kiwis, kangaroos and bald eagles: archival development in three countries. *The Midwestern Archivist*, vol. 4, no. 1, 1979. 35-51.

Records management

Angel, Herbert E. Archival janus: the records center. *American Archivist*, vol. 31, no. 1, January 1968. 5-12.

Aschner, Katherine, ed. *Taking control of your office records: a manager's guide*. Prairie Village, Kansas, Association of Records Managers and Administrators, 1983.

Austin, Robert B. and Skupsky, Donald S. How to determine cost-savings for a records/files management program. *Journal of Information and Image Management*, vol. 16, no. 11, November 1983. 30-36.

Bartkowski, Patricia. Records management and the walking archivist. *Georgia Archive*, vol. 3, no. 2, Summer 1975. 125-134.

Booth, Pat F. and South, M.L. *Information filing and finding*. Guildford, Surrey, England, ELM Publicaions, 1982.

Bradsher, James Gregory. The army historian and army records. *The Army Historian*, vol. 8, Summer 1985. 10-11.

Brown, Gerald F.The archivist and the records manager: a records manager's viewpoint. *Records Management Quarterly*, vol. 5, no. 1, January 1971. 21-22.

Charman, Derek. Archives and records management—an interface? *Journal of the Society of Archivists*, vol. 6, April 1981. 423-427.

————. *Records surveys and schedules: a RAMP study with guidelines*. Paris, UNESCO, 1984.

————. Standards and cost-benefit analysis for storage of records in records centres. *Records Management*, vol. 8, 1983. 10-17.

————. The expanding role of the archivist. *Records Management Quarterly*, vol. 14, no. 1, January 1980. 24-31.

Committee on the Records of Government. *Report*. Washington, D.C., Committee on the Records of Government, 1985.

Cook, Michael. *The management of information from archives*. Aldershot, Hants, England and Brookfield, Vermont, Gower Publishing Co., 1986.

Cronin, Blaise, ed. *Information management: from strategies to action*. Medford, New

Jersey, Learned Information, 1985.

Darling, Robert H. The relation between archivists and records managers. *American Archivist*, vol. 22, no. 2, April 1959. 211-215.

Daum, Patricia B. Coordinating records management and the special library for effectiveness. *Records Management Quarterly*, vol. 20, no. 1, April 1986. 36-38.

Dearstyne, Bruce W. Principles for local government records: a statement of the National Association of State Archives and Records Administrators. *American Archivist*, vol. 46, no. 4, Fall 1983. 452-457

———. *The management of local government records: a guide for local officials*. Nashville, American Association for State and Local History, 1988.

DePuy, LeRoy. Archivists and records managers—a partnership. *American Archivist*, vol. 23, no. 1, January 1960. 49-55.

Diamond, Susan Z. *Records management: a practical guide*. New York, American Management Associations, 1983.

Dodds, Gordon. Back to square one—records management revisited. *Archivaria*, vol. 1, no. 2, Summer 1976. 88-91.

Evans, Frank B. Archivists and records managers: variations on a theme. *American Archivist*, vol. 30, no. 1, January 1967. 45-58.

Evans, Frank B. and Ketelaar, Eric. *A guide for surveying archival and records management systems and services: a RAMP study*. Paris, UNESCO, 1983.

Fleckner, John A. *Archives and manuscripts: surveys*. Chicago, Society of American Archivists, 1977.

Gray, William J. Hiring an information and records management consultant. *Records Management Quarterly*, vol. 14, no. 4, October 1980. 15-18, 20, 26.

Haire, Douglas M. *An organizational concept for information management programs*. Prairie Village, Kansas, Association of Records Managers and Administrators, 1980.

Hammitt, J.J. Government archives and records management. *American Archivist*, vol. 28, no. 2, April 1965. 219-222.

Hernon, Peter. *Microforms and government information*. Westport, Connecticut and London, England, Microform Review, 1981.

Hives, Christopher L. Records, information, and archives management in business. *Records Management Quarterly*, vol. 20, no. 1, January 1986. 3-8, 17.

Hull, Felix. The transfer and documentation of records. *Records Management*, vol. 3, 1979. 33-43.

Hunter, Gregory S. Thinking small to think big: archives, micrographics, and the life cycle of records. *American Archivist*, vol. 49, no. 3, Summer 1986. 315-320.

Ingerwesen, Peter, ed. *Information technology and information use: towards a unified view of information and information technology*. London, Taylor Graham, 1986.

International Institute of Municipal Clerks. *Records management resources: an annotated bibliography for local governments*. Pasadena, California, International Institute of Municipal Clerks, 1987.

Jackson, B. A records management program. *Records Management*, vol. 5, 1981. 8-32.

Johnson, Mina M. and Kallaus, Norman F. *Records management*, Cincinnati, etc., Southwestern Publishing Co., 1982.

Jones, H.G. *Local government records: an introduction to their management, preservation, and use*. Nashville, American Association for State and Local History, 1980.

Katz, Richard N. and Davis, Victoria A. The impact of automation on our corporate memory. *Records Management Quarterly*, vol. 20, no. 1, January 1986. 10-14.

Kesner, Richard M. Automated information management: is there a role for the archivist in the office of the future? *Archivaria*, no. 19, Winter 1984-85. 162-172.

Ketelaar, Eric. *Archival and records management legislation and regulations: a RAMP study with guidelines*. Paris, UNESCO, 1985.

Lewellyn, Michael V. *The ARMA/ICRM bibliography on information management*.

Prairie Village, Kansas, Association of Records Managers and Administrators, 1980.

Lytle, Richard H. The relationship between archives and records management: an archivist's view. *Records Management Quarterly*, vol. 2, no. 2, April 1968. 5–8.

Majumdar, J.S. Neo-dynamics of records management: disposition of government records. *The Indian Archives*, vol. 31, no. 1, January–June 1983. 46–54.

Morgan, Dennis F. and Millican, Dennis D. A records manager's blueprint for the inventory and retention scheduling of information in electronic form. *Records Management Quarterly*, vol. 18, no. 3, July 1984. 43–47.

Motz, Arlene. Applying records management principles to electronic media. *Records Management Quarterly*, vol. 20, no. 2, April 1986. 22–24, 26.

Otten, Klaus W. Economics of image and document handling: the changing role of micrographics. *Journal of Information and Image Management*, vol. 17, no. 7, July 1984. 35–41.

———. Mass information storage systems and records management: competing technologies and systems concepts. *Journal of Information and Image Management*, vol 17, no. 10, October 1984. 33–39.

Paul, Karen Dawley. *Records management handbook for United States senators and their repositories*. Washington, D.C., US Senate Historical Office, 1985.

Penn, Ira A. Federal records management in the 1980's—just like it was in the 1780's. *Records Management Quarterly*, vol. 18, no. 3, July 1984. 5–15.

———. "The" records management problem: living records—dead management. *Records Management Quarterly*, vol. 13, no. 2, April 1979. 8–10.

———. Understanding the life cycle concept of records management. *Records Management Quarterly*, vol. 17, no. 3, July 1983. 5–8, 41.

———. Will the real records management stand up? *Records Management Quarterly*, vol. 15, no. 3, July 1981. 10–12.

Public Archives of Canada. *Records management guide for ministers' offices*. Ottawa, Minister of Supply and Services, 1977.

Public Record Office. *Manual of records administration*. London, Public Record Office, 1983.

Radoff, Morris L. What should bind us together? *American Archivist*, vol. 19, no. 1, January 1956. 3–9.

Records Management Quarterly. Cumulative index of articles (annotated)—January 1967–April 1984. *Records Management Quarterly*, vol. 18, no. 2, April 1984. 61–64, 66–74, 76–80, 82–93.

Rhoads, James B. Records management and the archivist. *Records Management Journal*, vol. 13, no. 1, Spring 1975. 4–8.

———. *The applicability of UNISIST guidelines and ISO international standards to archives administration and records management: a RAMP study*. Paris, UNESCO, 1981.

Rhoads, James B. and Smith, Wilfred I. Why records management is important? *Records Management Quarterly*, vol. 10, no. 1, January 1976. 5–8, 20.

Ricks, Artel. Records management as an archival function. *Records Management Quarterly*, vol. 11, no. 2, April 1977. 12–18, 20, 35.

Ridge, Allan D. Records management: the archival perspective. *Records Management Quarterly*, vol. 9, no. 1, January 1975. 11–15, 25.

Robek, Mary F. Brown, Gerald F. and Maedke, Wilmer O. *Information and records management*. Encino, California, Glencoe Publishing Co., 1987.

Roper, Michael. *Dictionary of national standards relating to archives administration and records management: a RAMP study*. Paris, UNESCO, 1986.

Saffady, William. *Micrographics*. 2nd ed. Littleton, Colorado, Libraries Unlimited, 1985.

Shiff, Robert A. Dynamic records management: opportunities and caveats. *Journal of Information and Image Management*, vol. 17, no. 2, February 1984. 29–32.

———. The archivist's role in records management. *American Archivist*, vol. 19, no. 2, April 1956. 111–120.

Skupsky, Donald S. Legal issues in records retention and disposition programs. *Records Management Quarterly*, vol. 18 no. 3, July 1984. 72, 74–76, 78.

Snyder, Barton E. A cost-benefit analysis method for various storage media. *Journal of Information and Image Management*, vol. 17, no. 5, May 1984. 41–47.

Special Libraries Association. *Government information: an endangered resource of the electronic age*. Washington, D.C., Special Libraries Association, 1987.

Taylor, Hugh A. Information ecology and the archives of the 1980s. *Archivaria*, no. 18, Summer 1984. 25–37.

Thomas, Violet S., Schubert, Dexter R. and Lee, Jo Ann. *Records management: systems and administration*. New York, John Wiley & Sons, 1983.

Waegemann, C. Peter. *Handbook of record storage and space management*. Westport, Connecticut, Greenwood Press, 1983.

Weise, Carl E. Records management: the management science too long ignored. *Records Management Quarterly*, vol. 20, no. 2, April 1986. 30–35.

Records appraisal and disposition

Bauer, G. Philip. *The appraisal of current and recent records*. National Archives Staff Information Circular no. 13. Washington, D.C., National Archives, June 1946.

Benedict, Karen. Invitation to a bonfire: reappraisal and deaccessioning of records as collection management tools in an archives—a reply to Leonard Rapport. *American Archivist*, vol . 47, no. 1, Winter 1984. 43–49.

Boles, Frank. Sampling in archives. *American Archivist*, vol. 44, no. 2, Spring 1981. 125–130.

Boles, Frank and Young, Julia Marks. Exploring the black box: the appraisal of university administrative records. *American Archivist*, vol. 48, no. 2, Spring 1985. 121–140.

Bradsher, James Gregory. The FBI records appraisal. *The Midwestern Archivist,* vol. 13, no. 2, 1988. 51–66.

Brichford, Maynard J. *Archives and manuscripts: appraisal and accessioning*. Chicago, Society of American Archivists, 1977.

Brooks, Philip C. The selection of records for preservation. *American Archivist*, vol. 3, no. 4, October 1940. 221–234.

Collingridge, J. H. The selection of archives for permanent preservation. *Archivum*, vol. 6, 1956. 25–35.

Evans, Max J. The visible hand: creating a practical mechanism for cooperative appraisal. *The Midwestern Archivist*, vol. 11, no. 1, 1986. 7–13.

Fishbein, Meyer H. A viewpoint on the appraisal of national records. *American Archivist*, vol. 33, no. 2, April 1970. 175–187.

Guptil, Marilla B. *Archival appraisal of records of international organizations: a RAMP study with guidelines*. Paris, UNESCO, 1985.

Haas, Joan K., Samuels, Helen Willa and Simmons, Barbara Trippel. *Appraising the records of modern science and technology: a guide*. Cambridge, Massachusetts Institute of Technology, 1985.

Ham, F. Gerald. Archival choices: managing the historical record in an age of abundance. *American Archivist*, vol. 47, no. 1, Winter 1984. 11–22.

Hull, Felix. *The use of sampling techniques in the retention of records: a RAMP study with guidelines*. Paris, UNESCO, 1981.

Kepley, David R. Sampling in archives: a review. *American Archivist*, vol. 47. no. 3, Summer 1984. 237–242.

Kromnow, Ake. The appraisal of contemporary records. *Archivum*, vol. 26, 1979. 45-54.

Lamb, W. Kaye. The fine art of destruction. *In*: Hollaender, Albert E. J., ed. *Essays in memory of Sir Hilary Jenkinson*. Chichester, Sussex, England, Moore & Tillyer, 1962. 50-56.

Lewinson, Paul. Archival sampling. *American Archivist*, vol. 20, no. 4, October 1957. 291-312.

National Archives and Records Service. Intrinsic value in archival material. *In*: Daniels, Maygene F. and Walch, Timothy, eds. *A modern archives reader: basic readings on archival theory and practice*. Washington, D.C., National Archives and Records Service, 1984. 91-99.

———. *Appraisal of the records of the Federal Bureau of Investigation: a report to Hon. Harold H. Greene, U.S. District Court for the District of Columbia*. 2 vols. Washington, D.C., National Archives and Records Service, 1981.

Peace, Nancy E., ed. *Archival choices: managing the historical record in an age of abundance*. Lexington, Massachusetts and Toronto, Canada, D.C. Heath & Co. 1984.

Rapport, Leonard. No grandfather clause: reappraising accessioned records. *American Archivist*, vol. 44, no. 2, Spring 1985. 143-150.

Rieger, Morris. Modern records retirement and appraisal practice. *The Indian Archives*, vol. 30, no. 1, January-June 1981. 1-14.

Schellenberg, T.R. The appraisal of modern public records. *In*: Daniels, Maygene F. and Walch, Timothy, eds. *A Modern archives reader: basic readings on archival theory and practice*. Washington, D.C., National Archives and Records Service, 1984, 57-70.

Sly, Margery N. Sampling in an archival framework: mathoms and manuscripts. *Provenance*, vol. 5, no. 2, Spring 1987. 55-75.

Smith, Wilfred I. Archival selection, a Canadian view. *Journal of the Society of Archivists*, vol. 3, October 1967. 275-280.

Wilson, Duncan. *Modern public records: selection and access. Report of a committee appointed by the Lord Chancellor* (Cmd. 8204). London, Her Majesty's Stationery Office, 1981.

Young, Julia Marks, comp. Annotated bibliography on appraisal. *American Archivist*, vol. 48, no. 2, Spring 1985. 190-216.

Archival arrangement and description

Bearman, David A. and Lytle, Richard H. The power of the principle of provenance. *Archivaria*, no. 21, Winter 1985-86. 14-27.

Berner, Richard C. Arrangement and description: some historical observations. *American Archivist*, vol. 41, no. 2, April 1978. 169-181.

Berner, Richard C. and Haller, Uli. Principles of archival inventory construction. *American Archivist*, vol. 47, no. 2, Spring 1984. 134-155.

Boles, Frank. Disrespecting original order. *American Archivist*, vol. 45, no. 1, Winter 1982. 26-32.

Bureau of Canadian Archivists. *Toward descriptive standards, report and recommendations of the Canadian Working Group on Archival Descriptive Standards*. Ottawa, Bureau of Canadian Archivists, 1985.

Cook, Michael. Standards of archival description. *Journal of the Society of Archivists*, vol. 8, no. 3, April 1987. 181-188.

Duchein, Michel. Theoretical principles and practical problems of *respect des fonds* in archival science. *Archivaria*, no. 16, summer 1983. 64-82.

Enwere, J.C. Arrangement of public records in Nigeria. *The Indian Archives*, vol. 32, no. 1, January–June 1983. 11–26.

Evans, Max. Authority control: an alternative to the record group concept. *American Archivist*, vol. 49, no. 3, Summer 1986. 249–261.

Gracy, David B., II. Finding aids are like streakers. *Georgia Archive*, vol. 4, no. 1, Winter 1976. 39–47.

——. *Archives and manuscripts: arrangement and description*. Chicago, Society of American Archivists, 1977.

Hildesheimer, Francoise. *Guidelines for the preparation of general guides to national archives: a RAMP study*. Paris, UNESCO, 1983.

Hill, Edward E. *The preparation of inventories*. National Archives and Records Service staff information paper no. 14. Washington, D.C., National Archives and Records Service, 1982.

Holmes, Oliver W. Archival arrangement—five different operations at five different levels. *American Archivist*, vol. 27, no. 1, January 1964. 21–41.

Jenkinson, H.A. *A manual of archive administration*. Oxford. Clarendon Press, 1922.

Lucas, Lydia. Efficient finding aids: developing a system for control of archives and manuscripts. *American Archivist*, vol. 44, no. 1, Winter 1981. 21–26.

Lytle, Richard H. Intellectual access to archives: i. provenance and content indexing methods for subject retrieval. *American Archivist*, vol. 43, no. 1, Winter 1980. 64–75.

——. Intellectual access to archives: ii. report of an experiment comparing provenance and content indexing methods of subject retrieval. *American Archivist*, vol. 43, no. 2, Spring 1980. 191–207.

Muller, S., Feith, J.A. and Fruin, R. *Manual for the arrangemnt and description of archives*. a translation by A. H. Leavitt of the Dutch edition of 1920. New York, H.W. Wilson, 1940.

Peterson, Trudy Huskamp. Archival principles and records of the new technology. *American Archivist*, vol. 47, no. 4, Fall 1984, 383–393.

Posner, Ernst. Max Lehman and the genesis of the principle of provenance. *In*: Munden, Ken, ed. *Archives and the public interest: selected essays by Ernst Posner*. Washington, D.C., Public Affairs Press, 1967. 36–44.

Rabins, Joan. Records redux: enhancing subject access through redescription. *The Midwestern Archivist*, vol. 8, no. 2, 1983. 17–27.

Roper, Michael. Modern departmental records and the record archives. *Journal of the Society of Archivists*, vol. 4, no. 5, April 1972. 400–412.

Sahli, Nancy. Finding aids: a multi-media systems perspective. *American Archivist*. vol. 44, no. 1, Winter 1981. 15–20.

Schellenberg, T.R. *Modern archives: principles and techniques*. Chicago, University of Chicago Press, 1956.

Scott, P.J. Archives and administrative change—some methods and approaches (part 5). *Archives and Manuscripts*, vol. 9, no. 1, September 1981. 3–18

Stapleton, R. Jenkinson and Schellenberg: a comparison. *Archivaria*. no. 17, Winter 1983–84. 75–85

Personal papers

Berner, Richard C. Arrangement and description of manuscripts. *Drexel Library Quarterly*, vol. 11, no. 1, January 1975. 34–54.

Bordin, Ruth B. and Warner, Robert M. *The modern manuscript library*. New York, Scarecrow Press, 1966.

Brichford, Maynard. *Archives and manuscripts: appraisal and accessioning*. Chicago, Society of American Archivists, 1977.

Desnoyers, Megan Floyd. When is a collection processed? *The Midwestern Archivist*, vol. 7, no. 1, 1982. 5–23.

Duckett, Kenneth W. *Modern manuscripts: a practical manual for their management, care and and use*. Nashville, American Association for State and Local History, 1975.

Garay, K.E. Access and copyright in literary collections. *Archivaria*, no. 18, Summer 1984. 220–227.

Gracy, David B., II. *Archives and manuscripts: arrangement and description*. Chicago, Society of American Archivists, 1977.

Gwiazda, Henry J., II. Preservation decision-making and archival photocopying: twentieth century collections at the Kennedy Library. *Restaurator*, vol. 8, May 1987. 55–62.

Hackman, Larry J. and Warnow-Blewett, Joan. The documentation strategy process: a model and a case study. *American Archivist*, vol. 50, no. 1, Winter 1987. 12–47.

Honhart, Frederick L. The solicitation, appraisal, and acquisition of faculty papers. *College and Research Libraries*, vol. 44, May 1983. 236–241.

Hurley, Christopher. Personal papers and the treatment of archival principles. *Archives and Manuscripts*, vol. 6, no. 8, February 1977. 351–365.

Kane, Lucille M. *A guide to the care and administration of manuscripts*. Nashville, American Association for State and Local History, 1966.

Kesner, Richard M. Archival collection development: building a successful acquisitions program. *The Midwestern Archivist*, vol. 5, no. 2, 1981. 101–112.

McCarthy, Paul H., Jr. Overview: essentials of an archives or manuscript program. *Drexel Library Quarterly*, vol. 11, no. 1, January 1975. 5–20.

McCree, Mary Lynn. Good sense and good judgment: defining collections and collecting. *Drexel Library Quarterly*, vol. 11, no. 1, January 1975. 21–33.

Peterson, Trudy Huskamp. The deed and the gift. *American Archivist*, vol. 42, no. 1, January 1979. 61–79.

Phillips, Faye. Developing collecting policies for manuscript collections. *American Archivist*, vol. 47, no. 1, Winter 1984. 30–42.

Powell, Graeme T. Archival principles and the treatment of personal papers. *Archives and Manuscripts*, vol. 6, no. 6 February 1976. 259–268.

Rendell, Kenneth W. Tax appraisals of manuscript collections. *American Archivist*, vol. 46, no. 3, Summer 1983. 58–69.

Seton, Rosemary E. *The preservation and administration of private archives: a RAMP study*. Paris, UNESCO, 1984.

Skelton, Robin. The acquisition of literary archives. *Archivaria*, no. 18, Summer 1984. 214–219.

Slotkin, Helen W. and Lynch, Karen T. An analysis of processing procedures: the adaptive approach. *American Archivist*, vol. 45, no. 2, Spring 1982. 155–163.

Society of American Archivists. *Archival forms manual*. Chicago, Society of American Archivists, 1982.

———. *Inventories and registers: a handbook of techniques and examples*. Chicago, Society of American Archivists, 1976.

Stewart, Virginia R. A primer on manuscript field work. *The Midwestern Archivist*, vol. 1, no. 2, 1976. 3–20.

Taylor, R.J. Field appraisal of manuscript collections. *Archivaria*, vol. 1, no. 2, Summer 1976. 44–48.

Walle, Dennis F. The deposit agreement in archival collection development. *The Midwestern Archivist*, vol. 10, no. 2, 1985. 117–127.

Whyte, Doug. The acquisition of lawyers' private papers. *Archivaria*, no. 18, Summer 1984. 142–153.

Yoxall, Helen. Privacy and personal papers. *Archives and Manuscripts*, vol. 12, no. 1, May 1984. 38–44.

Cartographic and architectural archives

Archivaria, no. 13, Winter 1981–82. This entire issue is devoted to managing cartographic archives.

Brown, Lloyd A. *Notes on the care and cataloguing of old maps*. rev. ed. Fort Washington , New York, Kennikat Press, 1970.

Bryan, M. Leonard. Remote sensing data in geography and map libraries. *Special Libraries*, vol. 66, November 1975. 520–527.

Cruise, Larry, ed. *Microcartography: applications for archives and libraries*. Santa Cruz, California, Western Association of Map Librarians, 1981.

Drazniowsky, Roman, comp. *Map librarianship: readings*. Metuchen, New Jersey, Scarecrow Press, 1975.

Drexel Library Quarterly, vol. 9, no. 4, October 1973. This entire issue is devoted to map librarianship.

Ehrenberg, Ralph E. *Archives and manuscripts: maps and architectural drawings*. Chicago, Society of American Archivists, 1982.

Galneder, Mary. Equipment for map libraries. *Special Libraries*, vol. 61, July–August 1970. 371–374.

Kidd, Betty and Cardinal, Louis. The map user in libraries and archives. Association of Canadian Map Librarians *Bulletin*, no. 23, January 1977. 12–20

Kidd, Betty. Preventive conservation for map collections. *Special Libraries*, vol. 71, December 1980. 529–538.

Knight, James. Architectural records in Canada: toward a national programme. *Archivaria*, no. 3, Winter 1976–77. 62–72.

Larsgaard, Mary. *Map librarianship: an introduction*. Littleton, Colorado, Libraries Unlimited, 1978.

Lathrop, Alan K. The archivist and architectural records. *Georgia Archive*, vol. 5, no. 2, summer 1977. 25–32.

———. The provenance and preservation of architectural records. *American Archivist*, vol. 43, no. 3, Summer 1980. 325–326.

———. Copyright of architectural records: a legal perspective. *American Archivist*, vol. 49, no. 4, Fall 1986. 409–423.

Madan, P.L. Record character of maps and related problems. *The Indian Archives*, vol. 31, no. 2 July–December 1982. 13–22.

Missen, John. Air photos and the map curator. Australian Map Curator's Circle *Proceedings*, 1975. 39–42.

Nason, Roger P. *Plans and drawings classification system*. Fredericton, Provincial Archives of New Brunswick, 1975.

Oppen, William A. The archivist and cartograpic collections. *The Canadian Archivist*, vol. 2, 1974. 65–72.

Perry, Joanne M. Map storage methods: a bibliography. Special Libraries Association Geography and Map Division *Bulletin*, no. 131, March 1983. 14–15.

Singh, Ranchandra and Scherz, James P. A catalog system for remote sensing data. *Photogrammetric Engineering*, vol. 40, June 1974. 709–772.

Audio-visual archives

Betz, Elisabeth, comp. *Grapic materials: rules for describing original items and historial collections*. Washington, D.C., Library of Congress, 1980.

Bowser, Eileen and Kupier, John. *A handbook for film archives* , Brussels, FIAF, 1980.

Collins, T. J. *Archival care of still photographs*. Information Leaflet no. 2, Sheffield, Society of Archivists, 1984.

Dooley, Jackie. *LC thesaurus for graphic materials: topical terms for subject access*. Washington, D.C., Library of Congress, 1987.

Eastman Kodak Company. *Preservation of photographs*. Rochester, New York, Eastman Kodak Co., 1979.

——. *The book of film care*. Rochester, New York, Eastman Kodak Co., 1982.

Gill, Arthur T. *Photographic processes: a glossary and a chart for recognition*. London, Museums Association, 1978.

Harrison, Helen P. *Film library techniques*. New York, Hastings House, 1973.

——, ed. *Selection in sound archives: collected papers from IASA conference sessions*. Vienna, IASA, 1984.

Hendricks, Klaus B. *The preservation and restoration of photograpic materials in archives and libraries: a RAMP study with guidelines*. Paris, UNESCO, 1985.

International Federation of Film Archives Cataloging Commission. *Film Cataloging*. New York, Burt Franklin, 1979.

Kula, Sam. *The archival appraisal of moving images: a RAMP study with guidelines*. Paris, UNESCO, 1983.

Lance, David, ed. *Sound archives: a guide to their establishment and development*. Vienna, IASA, 1983.

Leary, William H. *The archival appraisal of photographs: a RAMP study with guidelines*. Paris, UNESCO, 1985.

Malan, Nancy. *Administering historical photograph collections*. Nashville, American Association for State and Local History, 1981.

McWilliams, Jerry. *Preservation and restoration of sound recordings*. Nashville, American Association for State and Local History, 1979.

Noble, Richard. *Archival preservation of motion pictures: a summary of current findings*. Technical Leaflet no. 126. Nashville, American Association for State and Local History, 1980.

Reilly, James M. *The care and identification of 19th century photographic prints*. Rochester, New York, Eastman Kodak Co., 1986.

Ritzenthaler, Mary Lynn, Munoff, Gerald J. and Long, Margery S. *Archives and manuscripts: administration of photographic collections*. Chicago, Society of American Archivists, 1984.

Roberts, David. Archives and sound archives—what's the difference? *Archives and Manuscripts*, vol. 12, November 1984. 116-124.

Robol, Ernest H. *Organizing your photographs*. New York, Amphoto, 1986.

Sound Archives Section, National Film Archives. *Sound archives: guide to procedures*. Ottawa, Public Archives of Canada, 1979.

Stielow, Frederick J. Subject indexing a large photographic collection. *American Archivist*, vol. 46, no. 1, Winter 1983. 72-74.

Volkman, Herbert, ed. *The preservation and restoration of colour and sound in films*.Brussels, FIAF, 1977.

Weinstein, Robert A. and Booth, Larry. *Collection, use, and care of historical photographs*. Nashville, American Association for State and Local History, 1977.

White-Hensen, Wendy. *Archival moving image materials: a cataloging manual*. Washington, D.C., Library of Congress, 1985.

Machine-readable archives

Ambacher, Bruce I. and Dollar, Charles M. The National Archives and secondary analysis. *New Directions for Program Evaluation*, vol. 4, Fall 1978. 1-5.

———. National Archives: data transfer and storage. *In*: Baruch, Robert F. et al., eds. *Reanalyzing program evaluations*. San Francisco, Josey-Bass, 1981.

Arad, A. and Olsen, M. E. *An introduction to archival automation*. Koblenz, Committee on Automation, International Council on Archives, 1981.

Cameron, Ross J. Appraisal strategies for machine-readable case files. *Provenance*, vol. 1, no. 1, Spring 1983. 49–55.

Cook, Michael. *Archives and the computer*. 2nd ed. London, Butterworths, 1986.

Dodd, Sue A. *Cataloging machine-readable data files: an interpretative manual*. Chicago, American Library Association, 1982.

Dollar, Charles M. Appraising machine-readable records. *American Archivist*, vol. 41, no. 4, October 1978. 423–430.

———. *Electronic records management and archives in international organizations: a RAMP study with guidelines*. Paris, UNESCO, 1986.

Fishbein, Meyer H. *Guidelines for administering machine-readable archives*. Washington, D.C., Committee on Automation, International Council on Archives, 1980.

———. *A model curriculum for the education and training of archivists in automation: a RAMP study*. Paris, UNESCO, 1985.

Geller, Sidney B. *Care and handling of computer magnetic storage media*. Washington, D.C., National Bureau of Standards, 1983.

Hedstrom, Margaret L. Privacy, computers, and reseach access to confidential information. *The Midwestern Archivist*, vol.6, no. 1, 1981. 5–18.

———. *Archives and manuscripts: machine-readable records*. Chicago, Society of American Archivists , 1984.

Hickerson, H. Thomas. *Archives and manuscripts: an introduction to automated access*. Chicago, Society of American Archivists, 1984.

Kesner, Richard M. *Information management: machine-readable records and administration: an annotated bibliography*. Chicago, Society of American Archivists, 1983.

Knoppers, Jake V. Th. *Managing the electronic revolution, archiving the electronic heritage: a position paper on issues and problems in EDP records/data management*. Ottawa, Public Archives of Canada, 1981.

National Archives and Records Administration. *Electronic record keeping*. NARA Bulletin no. 87-5. Washington, D.C., National Archives and Records Administration, 1987.

Naugler, Harold. *The appraisal of machine-readable records: a RAMP study with guidelines*. Paris, UNESCO, 1984.

Peterson, Trudy Huskamp. Archival principles and records of the new technology. *American Archivist*, vol. 47, no. 4, Fall 1984. 383–393.

Roistacher, Richard C. *A style manual for machine-readable records and their documentation*. Washington, D.C., United States Government Printing Office, 1980.

Roper, Michael. The changing face of the file: machine-readable records and the archivist. *Archives*, vol. 1, no. 63, Spring 1980. 145–150.

State Historical Society of Wisconsin. *Archival preservation of machine-readable public records: the final report of the Wisconsin survey of machine-readable public records*. Madison, State Historical Society of Wisconsin, 1981.

Automation techniques

Allen, Marie. Optical character recognition: technology with new relevance for archival automation. *American Archivist*, vol. 50, no. 1, Winter 1987. 88–99.

American Management Systems, Inc. *Findings on strategy and proof of concepts for an expert system for information retrieval at the National Archives and Records Administration*. Arlington, Virginia, American Management Systems, Inc., 1986.

Bearman, David. *Optical media: their implications for archives and museums*. Pittsburg, Archival Informatics Technical Report, 1987.

———. *Towards national information systems for archives and manuscript repositories: the national information systems task force (NISTF) papers*. Chicago, Society of American Archivists, 1987.

Chalmers, Duncan. Computer indexing in the Public Record Office. *The Indian Archives*, vol. 30, no. 1, January–June 1983. 55–73.

Cloud, Patricia. RLIN, AMC, and retrospective conversion: a case study. *The Midwestern Archivist*, vol. 11, no. 1, 1986. 125–134.

Cook, Micheal. *An introduction to archival automation: a RAMP study with guidelines*. Paris, UNESCO, 1986.

Evans, Max J. and Weber, Lisa B. *MARC for archives and manuscripts: a compendium of practice*. Madison, State Historical Society of Wisconsin, 1985.

Gillenson, Mark L. *Database: step by step*. New York, John Wiley & Sons, 1985.

Hendley, A.M. *Optical disk systems: a guide to the technology and applications in the fields of publishing and library and information work*. IFLA Professional Report no. 12. The Hague, International Federation of Library Associations and Institutions, 1986.

Hendley, Tony. *A comparison of the archival storage potential of microfilm, magnetic media and optical data discs*. Bayfordbury, Herts, England, National Reprographic Centre for Documentation, 1982.

Hensen, Steven L. The use of standards in the application of the AMC format. *American Archivist*, vol. 49, no. 1, Spring 1987. 31–40.

Hirtle, Peter B. Artificial intelligence, expert systems, and archival automation. *Provenance*, vol. 4, no. 1, Spring 1987. 76–88.

Kesner, Richard M. *Automation for archivists and records managers: planning and implementing strategies*. Chicago, American Library Association, 1984.

Lambert, Steve and Ropiequet, Suzanne. *CD-Rom: the new papyrus, the current and future state of the art*. Richmond, Washington, Microsoft Press, 1986.

Library of Congress. *Library of Congress optical disk pilot project*. Washington, D.C., Library of Congress, 1986.

Morton, Katherine D. The MARC formats: an overview. *American Archivist*, vol. 49, no. 1, Winter 1986. 21–30.

National Archives and Records Administration. *The MARC format and life cycle tracking at the National Archives: a study*. National Archives Technical Information Publication no. 2. Washington, D.C., National Archives and Records Administration, 1986.

National Archives and Records Service. *Technology assessment report: Speech pattern recognition, optical character recognition, digital raster scanning*. Washington, D.C., National Archives and Records Service, 1984.

Ostroff, Harriet. From clay tablets to MARC AMC: the past, present, and future of cataloging manuscripts and archival collections. *Provenance*, vol. 4, no. 2, Fall 1986. 1–11.

Sahli, Nancy. *MARC for archives and manuscripts: the AMC format*. Chicago, Society of American Archivists, 1985.

Smith, W. I. Archives and technology: some experiences of the Public Archives of Canada. *The Indian Archives*, vol. 33, no. 2, July–December 1984. 1–18.

Soergel, Dagobert. *Organizing information: principles of data base and retrieval systems*. New York, Academic Press, 1985.

Weinberg, David. Automation in the archives: RLIN and the archives and manuscript control format. *Provenance*, vol. 4, no. 2, Fall 1986. 12–31.

Winston, Patrick Henry. *Artificial intelligence*. 2nd ed. Reading, Massachusetts, Addison-Wesley, 1984.

Oral history

Allen, Barbara and Montell, Lynwood. *From memory to history: using oral sources in local historical research*. Nashville, American Association for State and Local History, 1981.

Baum, Willa K. *Oral history for the local historical society*. 2nd ed. rev. Nashville, American Association for State and Local History, 1974.

———. *Transcribing and editing oral history*. Nashville, American Association for State and Local History, 1977.

Charlton, Thomas L. Videotaped oral histories: problems and prospects. *American Archivist*, vol. 47, no. 3, Summer 1984. 228–236.

Clark, E. Culpeper, Hyde, M.T. and McMahan, E. Communication in the oral history interview: interviewing problems of interpreting oral data. *International Journal of Oral History*, vol. 1, no. 1, February 1980. 28–40.

Davis, Cullom, Buck, Kathryn and MacLean, Kay. *Oral history from tape to type*. Chicago, American Library Association, 1977.

Douglass, Enid, ed. Oral history. *In*: Trask, David, ed. *The craft of public history: an annotated select bibliography*. Westport, Connecticut, Greenwood Press, 1983.

Dunaway, David K. and Baum, Willa K., ed. *Oral history: an interdisciplinary anthology*, Nashville, American Association for State and Local History, 1984.

Filipelli, R.L. Oral history and the archives. *American Archivist*, vol. 39, no. 4, October 1976. 479–483.

Finnegan, Ruth. A note on oral tradition and historical evidence. *History and Theory*, vol. 9, no. 2, 1970. 195–201.

Frisch, Michael. Oral history and hard times: a review essay. *The Oral History Review*, vol. 7, 1979. 70–79.

Grele, Roland J. *Envelopes of sound*. Chicago, Precedent, 1985.

Henige, David. Where seldom is heard a discouraging word: method in oral history. *The Oral History Review*, vol. 14, 1986. 35–42.

Ives, Edward D. *The tape recorded interview: a manual for fieldworkers in folklore and oral history*. Knoxville, University of Tennessee Press, 1980.

Lance, David. *An archives approach to oral history*. London, Imperial War Museum and the International Association of Sound Archives, 1978.

Lummis, Trevor. Structure and validity in oral evidence. *International Journal of Oral History*, vol. 2, no. 2, June 1981. 109–120.

McWilliam, Jerry. *The preservation and restoration of sound recordings*. Nashville, American Association for State and Local History, 1979.

Moss, William W. *Oral history program manual*. New York, Praeger, 1974.

———, ed. *Oral history evaluation guidelines*. n.p., Oral History Association, 1980.

Moss, William W. and Mazikana, P. *Archives, oral history and oral tradition: a RAMP study*. Paris, UNESCO, 1985.

Neuenschwander, John. *Oral history and the law* . Denton, Texas, Oral History Association, 1985.

Stephenson, Shirley E. Protect your collection: oral history and copyright. *The Public Historian*, vol. 9, no. 4, Fall 1987. 21–33.

Stielow, Frederick J. *The management of oral history sound archives*. Westport, Connecticut, Greenwood Press, 1986.

Thomas, Norman Myers. Oral history: a selected bibliography. *Provenance*, vol. 2, no. 2, Fall 1974. 73–80.

Thompson, Paul. *The voice of the past: oral history*. Oxford, Oxford University Press, 1978.

Vansina, Jan. *Oral tradition: a study in historical methodology*. London, Routledge and Kegan Paul, 1965.

Reference service and access

Bradsher, James Gregory. Researchers, archivists, and the access challenge of the FBI records in the National Archives. *The Midwestern Archivist*, vol.11, no. 2, 1986. 95-110.

Brauer, Carl M. Researcher evaluation of reference service. *American Archivist*, vol. 43, no. 1, Winter 1980. 77-79.

Chalou, George. Reference. *In*: Baumann, Roland, ed. *A manual of archival techniques*. rev. ed. Harrisburg, Pennsylvania Historical and Museum Commission, 1982.

Conway, Paul. Research in presidential libraries. *The Midwestern Archivist*, vol. 11, no. 1, 1986. 35-56.

———. Facts and frameworks: an approach to studying the users of archives. *American Archivist*, vol. 49, no. 3, Fall 1986. 393-407.

Cox, Richard J. Bibliography and reference for the archivist, *American Archivist*, vol. 46, no. 2, Spring 1983. 185-187.

Crawford, Michael J. Copyright, unpublished manuscripts, and the archivist. *American Archivist*, vol. 46, no. 2, Spring 1983. 135-147.

Dearstyne, Bruce W. What is the "use" of archives? a challenge for the profession. *American Archivist*, vol. 50, no. 1, Winter 1987. 76-87.

Duchein, Michel. *Obstacles to the access, use and transfer of information from archives: a RAMP study*. Paris. UNESCO, 1983.

Freeman, Elsie T. In the eye of the beholder: archives administration from the user's point of view. *American Archivist*, vol. 47, no. 2, Spring 1984. 111-123.

Goggin, Jacqueline. The indirect approach: a study of scholarly uses of black and women's organizational records in the Library of Congress manuscript division. *The Midwestern Archivist*, vol. 11, no. 1, 1986. 57-68.

Hamby, Alonzo L. and Weldon, Edward, eds. *Access to the papers of recent public figures: the New Harmony conference*. Bloomington, Indiana, Organization of American Historians, 1977.

Hayward, Robert J. Federal acccess and privacy legislation and the Public Archives of Canada. *Archivaria*, no. 18, Summer 1984. 154-165.

Holbert, Sue E. *Archives and manuscripts: reference and access*. Chicago, Society of American Archivists, 1977.

Joyce, William L. Archivists and research use. *American Archivist*, vol. 47, no. 2, Spring 1984. 124-133.

Keon, Jim. The Canadian archivist and copyright legislation. *Archivaria*, no. 18, Summer 1984. 91-98.

Kepley, Brenda Beasley. Archives: accessibility for the disabled. *American Archivist*, vol. 46, no. 1, Winter 1983. 42-51.

Maher, William J. The use of user studies. *The Midwestern Archivist*, vol. 11, no. 1, 1986. 15-26.

Mayer, Dale C. The new social history: implications for archivists. *American Archivist*, vol. 48, no. 4, Fall 1985. 388-399.

Peterson, Gary M. and Peterson, Trudy Huskamp. *Archives and manuscripts: law*. Chicago, Society of American Archivists, 1985.

Pugh, Mary Jo. The illusion of omniscience: subject access and the reference archivist. *American Archivist*, vol. 45, no. 1, Winter 1982. 33-44.

Purdy, Virginia C. Archivaphobia: its causes and cure. *Prologue*, vol. 15, no. 2, Summer 1983. 115-119.

Riley, Tom. Freedom of information acts: a comparative perspective. *Government Publications Review*, vol. 10, no. 1, January-February 1983. 81-87.

Sahli, Nancy. National information systems and strategies for research use. *The*

Midwestern Archivist, vol. 9, no. 4, 1984. 5–14.

Smart, John. The professional archivist's responsibility as an advocate of public research. *Archivaria*, no. 16, Summer 1983. 139–149.

Smith, Clive. *An introduction to archives and copyright*. Canberra, Australian Society of Archivists, Inc., 1986.

Speakman, Mary N. The user talks back. *American Archivist*, vol. 47, no. 2, Spring 1984. 164–171.

Stevens, Michael. The historian and archival finding aids. *Georgia Archive*, vol. 5, no. 2, Winter 1977. 69–74.

Taylor, Hugh A. *Archival services and the concept of the user: a RAMP study*. Paris, UNESCO, 1984.

Tener, Jean. Accessibility and archives. *Archivaria*, no. 6, Summer 1978. 16–31.

Timings, E. Kenneth. The archivist and the public. *Journal of the Society of Archivists*, vol. 2, no. 5, April 1962. 179–183.

Tissing, Robert W., Jr. The orientation interview in archival research. *American Archivist*, vol. 47, no. 2, Spring 1984. 173–178.

Turnbaugh, Roy C. Archival mission and user studies. *The Midwestern Archivist*, vol. 11, no. 1, 1986. 27–33.

Whalen, Lucille, ed. *Reference service in archives*. New York, Haworth Press, 1986.

Archival ethics

American Library Association. *Report of the commission on freedom and equality of access to information*. Chicago, American Library Association, 1986.

Barritt, Marjorie Rabe. The appraisal of personally identifiable student records. *American Archivist*, vol. 49, no. 3, Summer 1986. 263–275.

Baumann, Roland M. The administration of access to confidential records in state archives: common practices and the need for a model law. *American Archivist*, vol. 49, no. 4, Fall 1986. 349–369.

Binkley, Robert C. Strategic objectives in archival policy. *American Archivist*, vol. 2, no. 3, July 1939. 162–168.

Bok, Sissela. *Secrets: on the ethics of concealment and revelation*. New York, Pantheon Books, 1982.

Bradsher, James Gregory. Privacy act expungements: a reconsideration. *Provenance*, vol. 6, no. 1, Spring 1988. 1–25.

Cooke, Anne. A code of ethics for archivists: some points for discussion. *Archives and Manuscripts*, vol. 15, no. 2, November 1987. 95–104.

Duniway, David C. Conflicts in collecting. *American Archivist*, vol. 24, no. 1, January 1961. 55–63.

Elston, Charles B. University student records: research use, private rights and the Buckley law. *The Midwestern Archivist*, vol. 1, no. 1, 1976. 16–32.

Geselbracht, Raymond H. The origins of restrictions on access to personal papers at the Library of Congress and the National Archives. *American Archivist*, vol. 49, no. 2, Spring 1986. 142–162.

Grover, Wayne C. Archives: society and profession. *American Archivist*, vol. 18, no. 1, January 1955. 3–10.

[Grover, Wayne C.] The archivist's code. *American Archivist*, vol. 18, no. 4, October 1955. 307–308.

Hoff-Wilson, Joan. Access to restricted collections: the responsibility of professional historical organizations. *American Archivist*, vol. 46, no. 4, Fall 1983. 441–447.

Kahn, Herman. The long-range implications for historians and archivists of the charges against the Franklin D. Roosevelt Library. *American Archivist*, vol. 34, no. 3, July 1971. 265–275.

Lamb, W.K. Acquisition policy: competition or cooperation? *The Canadian Archivist*, vol. 2, 1970. 21–25.

Lankford, Nancy. Ethics and the reference archivist. *The Midwestern Archivist*, vol. 8, no. 1, 1983. 7–13.

Mason, Philip P. Ethics of collecting. *Georgia Archive*, vol. 5, no. 1, Winter 1977. 36–50.

Peterson, Gary M. and Peterson, Trudy Huskamp. *Archives and manuscripts: law*. Chicago, Society of American Archivists, 1985.

Polenberg, Richard. The Roosevelt Library case: a review article. *American Archivist*, vol. 34, no. 3, July 1971. 277–284.

Reitman, Alan. Freedom of information and privacy: the civil libertarian's dilemma. *American Archivist*, vol. 38, no. 4, October 1975. 501–508

Robbin, Alice. State archives and issues of personal privacy: policies and practices. *American Archivist*, vol. 9, no. 3, Spring 1986. 163–175.

Russel, E.W. Archival ethics. *Archives and Manuscripts*, vol. 6, no. 6, February 1976. 226–234.

Society of American Archivists. A code of ethics for archivists, Draft "B". *SAA Newsletter*, July 1979. 11–14.

――――. A code of ethics for archivists. *American Archivist*, vol. 43, no. 3, Summer 1980. 415–418.

Standards for ethical conduct for rare book, manuscript, and special collections librarians. *College and Research Libraries News*, vol. 45, July–August 1984. 357–358.

Stewart, Virginia R. Problems of confidentiality in the administration of personal case records. *American Archivist*, vol. 37, no. 3, July 1974, 387–398.

Preservation

AIC code of ethics and standards of practice. *In: American Institute for Conservation of Historic and Artistic Works Directory, 1986–87*. Washington, D.C., American Institute for Conservation, 1986. 10–19.

American National Standards Institute. *Methylene blue method for measuring thiosulfate and silver densitometric method for measuring residual chemicals in films, plates, and papers* (PH 4.8-1978). New York, American National Standards Institute, 1978.

――――. *Specifications for photographic films for archival records, silver-gelatin type, on polyester base* (PH 1.41-1976). New York, American National Standards Institute, 1976.

Banks, Paul N. *A selective bibliography on the conservation of research library materials*. Chicago, Newberry Library, 1981.

Barton, John P. and Wellheiser, Johanna G., eds. *An ounce of prevention: a handbook on disaster contingency planning for archives, libraries and records centers*. Toronto, Toronto Area Archivists Group Education Foundation, 1985.

Bohem, Hilda. *Disaster prevention and disaster preparedness*. Berkeley, University of California Press, 1978.

Brown, Margaret R., comp. and illustrator. *Boxes for the protection of rare books: their design and construction*. Washington, D.C., Library of Congress, 1982.

Calmes, Alan, Schofer, Ralph and Eberhardt, Keith R. *National Archives and Records Service (NARS) twenty year preservation plan*. Gaithersburg, Maryland, National Bureau of Standards, 1985.

Clapp, Anne F. *Curatorial care of works of art on paper: basic procedures for paper preservation*. New York, Nick Lyons Books, 1987.

Crespo, Carmen and Vinas, Vicente. *The preservation and restoration of paper records and books: a RAMP study with guidelines*. Paris, UNESCO, 1984.

Darling, Pamela W. *Preservation planning program resource notebook*. Washington, D.C., Association of Research Libraries, 1982.

Darling, Pamela W. and Webster, Duane E. *Preservation planning program: an assisted self-study manual for libraries*. Washington, D.C., Association of Research Libraries, 1982.

Deken, Jean Marie. Recovering from a major disaster. *The Midwestern Archivist*, vol. 9, no. 1, 1984. 27-34.

Eastman Kodak Company. *Storage and preservation of microfilms*. Rochester, New York, Eastman Kodak Co., 1981.

Edwards, Stephen R., Bell, Bruce M. and King, Mary Elizabeth, comps. *Pest control in museums: a status report (1980)*. Lawrence, Kansas, Association of Systematics Collections, 1981.

Gwinn, Nancy E., ed. *Preservation microfilming: a guide for librarians and archivists*. Chicago, American Library Association, 1987.

Harrison, Alice W., Collister, Edward A. and Willis, Ellen R. *The conservation of archival and library materials: a resource guide to audiovisual aids*. Metuchen, New Jersey, Scarecrow Press, 1982.

Hunter, John. *Emergency preparedness for museums, historic sites and archives: an annotated bibliography*. Lincoln, Nebraska, National Park Service, 1981.

Keck, Caroline K. *Safeguarding your collection in travel*. Nashville, American Association for State and Local History, 1970.

Keene, James A. and Roper, Michael. *Planning, equipping and staffing a document reprographic service: a RAMP study with guidelines*. Paris, UNESCO, 1984.

Kemp, Toby. Disaster assistance bibliography: selected references for cultural/historic facilities. *Technology & Conservation*, vol. 8, no. 2, Summer 1983. 25-27.

Kyle, Hedi. *Library materials preservation manual: practical methods for preserving books, pamphlets and other printed materials*. Bronxville, New York, Nicholas T. Smith, 1983.

Library of Congress. *Polyester film encapsulation*. Washington, D.C., Library of Congress, 1980.

McCrady, Ellen, ed. and pub. *The Abbey Newsletter: Bookbinding and conservation*. Preservation Department, Brigham Young University Library, 6216 HBLL, Provo, Utah 84602.

Morrow, Carolyn Clark and Schoenly, Steven B. *A conservation bibliography for librarians, archivists, and administrators*. Troy, New York, Whitson Publishing Co., 1979.

National Research Council. *Preservation of historical records*. Washington, D.C., National Academy Press, 1986.

Ontario Museum Association and the Toronto Area Archivists Group. *Museum and archival supplies handbook*. rev. 3rd ed. Toronto, Ontario Museum Association and the Toronto Area Archivists Group, 1987.

Petherbridge, Guy, ed. *Conservation of library and archive materials and the graphic arts*. London, etc., Butterworths, 1987.

Plenderleith, H. J. and Werner, A. E. A. *The conservation of antiquities and works of art: treatment, repair, and restoration*. 2nd ed. London, etc., Oxford University Press, 1979.

Price, Robin. Preparing for disaster. *Journal of the Society of Archivists*, vol. 7, April 1983, 167-172.

Ritzenthaler, Mary Lynn. *Archives and manuscripts: conservation. A manual on physical care and management*. Chicago, Society of American Archivists, 1983.

Roberts, Matt T. and Etherington, Don. *Bookbinding and the conservation of books: a dictionary of descriptive terminology*. Washington, D.C., Library of Congress, 1982.

Smith, Merrily A., comp. *Matting and hinging works of art on paper*. Washington, D.C., Library of Congress, 1981.
Sung, Carolyn Hoover. *Archives and manuscripts: reprography*. Chicago, Society of American Archivists, 1982.
Thompson, Garry. *The museum environment*. 2nd ed. London, etc., Butterworths, 1986.
Waters, Pe.er. *Procedures for salvage of water-damaged library materials*. 2nd ed. Washington, D.C., Library of Congress, 1979.
Williams, John C., ed. *Preservation of paper and textiles of historic and artistic value II*. Washington, D.C., American Chemical Society, 1981.
Winger, Howard W. and Smith, Richard Daniel, eds. *Deterioration and preservation of library materials*. Chicago, University of Chicago Press, 1970.

Archival security

Berkley, Edmund Jr. Archival security: a personal and circumstantial view. *Georgia Archive*, vol. 4, no. 1, Winter 1976. 3-19.
Best, Reba and Picquet, D. C., comps. *Computer crime, abuse, liability and security: a comprehensive bibliography, 1970-1984*. Jefferson, North Carolina, McFarland & Co., 1985.
Brand, Marvine, ed. *Security for libraries: people, buildings, collections*. Chicago, American Library Association, 1984.
Brown, Marion. *Problem patron manual*. Schenectady, New York, Schenectady Public Library, 1981.
Fennelly, Laurence J. *Museum, archival and library security*. London, etc., Butterworths, 1983.
Fernandez, E. D., Summers, R. C. and Wood, C. *Database security and integrity*. Reading, Massachusetts, Addison-Wesley, 1981.
Gandert, Slade Richard. *Protecting your collection: a handbook, survey, and guide for the security of rare books, manuscripts, archives, and works of art*. New York, Haworth Press, 1982.
Jenkins, John H. *Rare books and manuscripts thefts: a security system for librarians, booksellers, and collectors*. New York, Antiquarian Booksellers' Association of America, 1982.
Mason, Philip P. Library and archival security: new solutions to an old problem. *American Archivist*, vol. 38, no. 4, October 1975. 477-492.
O'Neill, James E. Replevin: a public archivist's perspective. *College and Research Libraries*, vol. 40, January 1979. 26-30.
Post, Richard. *Security manager's desk reference*. London, etc., Butterworths, 1986.
Rhoads, James B. Alienation and thievery. *American Archivist*, vol. 29, no. 2, April 1966. 197-208.
Sable, Marin H., ed. *The protection of the library and archives: an international bibliography*. New York, Haworth Press, 1983.
Strassberg, Richard. *Conservation, safety, security and disaster considerations in design*. Ithaca, New York, Cornell University Press, 1984.
Turn, Rein. *Advances in computer system security*. Deadham, Massachusetts, Artech, 1981.
Walch, Timothy. *Archives and manuscripts: security*. Chicago, Society of American Archivists, 1977.
Welch, Edwin. Security in an English archive. *Archivaria*, vol. 1, no. 2, Summer 1976. 49-54.
Zeidberg, David. *Collection security in ARL libraries*. Kit 100. Washington, D.C., Association of Research Libraries, 1984.

Public programs

Chepesiuk, Ron. Archives and the child: educational services in Great Britain and Ireland. *Provenance*, vol. 1, no. 2, Fall 1983. 45–58.

Duboscq, Guy. The educational role of the archives. *UNESCO Bulletin for Libraries*, vol. 24, July–August 1970. 205–210.

Franz, Eckhart G. *Archives and education: a RAMP study with guidelines*. Paris, UNESCO, 1986.

Freeman (Freivogel), Elsie T. Education programs: outreach as an administrative function. *American Archivist*, vol. 41, no. 2, April 1978. 147–153.

——. Buying quarter-inch holes: public support through results. *The Midwestern Archivist*, vol. 10, no. 2, 1985. 89–97.

Kyvig, David E. and Marty, Myron A. *Nearby history*. Nashville, American Association for State and Local History, 1982.

Metcalf, Fay D. and Downey, Matthew T. *Using local history in the classroom*. Nashville, American Association for State and Local History, 1982.

Myres, Sandra. Public programs for archives: reaching patrons, officials and the public. *Georgia Archive*, vol. 7, no. 1, Spring 1979. 10–15.

Palmer, M. Archive packs for schools: some practical suggestions. *Journal of the Society of Archivists*, vol. 6, no. 3, April 1979. 145–153.

Pederson, Ann E. Archival outreach: SAA's 1976 survey. *American Archivist*, vol 41, no. 2, April 1978. 155–162.

Pederson, Ann E. and Casterline, Gail Farr. *Archives and manuscripts: public programs*. Chicago, Society of American Archivists, 1982.

Roe, Kathleen. *Teaching with historical records*. Albany, New York, State Education Department, 1981.

Sheik, Atique Zafar. The academic and educational uses of archives. *The Indian Archives*, vol. 33, no. 2, July–December 1984. 41–46.

Taylor, Hugh A. Clio in the raw: archival materials and the teaching of history. *American Archivist*, vol. 23, no. 3–4, July–October 1972. 317–330.

Wurl, Joel. Methdology as outreach: a public mini-course on archival principles and techniques. *American Archivist*, vol. 49, no. 2, Spring 1986. 184–186.

Archival exhibits

Bradsher, James Gregory. Taking America's heritage to the people: the Freedom Train story. *Prologue*, vol. 17, no. 4, Winter 1985. 229–246.

Casterline, Gail Farr. *Archives and manuscripts: exhibits*. Chicago, Society of American Archivists, 1980.

Cushman, Judith. Creating and managing an exhibit program. *The Midwestern Archivist*, vol. 1, no. 2, 1976. 28–37.

Dunlap, Ellen S. and Reed, Kathleen. Borrowing of special collections materials for exhibition: a draft. *Rare Books and Manuscripts Librarianship*, vol. 2, no. 1, Spring 1987. 27–37.

Eutick, Mal. On the display of archives. *Archives and Manuscripts*, vol. 12, no. 1, May 1984. 17–23.

Gallery Association of New York State. *Insurance and risk management for museums and historical societies*. Hamilton, New York, Gallery Association of New York State, 1985.

Miles, Catherine E. Wood coatings for display and storage cases. *Studies in Conservation*, vol. 31, 1986. 114–124.

Neal, Arminta. *Exhibits for the small museum*. Nashville, American Association for State and Local History, 1976.

O'Connor, Joan L. Conservation of documents in an exhibit. *American Archivist*, vol. 47, no. 2, Spring 1984. 156–163.
Powers, Sandra. Why exhibit? the risks versus the benefits. *American Archivist*, vol. 41, no. 3, July 1978. 297–306.
Stolow, Nathan. *Conservation standards for works of art in transit and on exhibition.* New York, UNESCO, 1980.
Tyler, Barbara and Dickenson, Victoria. *A handbook for the travelling exhibitionist.* Ottawa, Canadian Museums Association, 1977.
Vernon, John and Wood, Richard E. Baseball, bubble gum, and business: the making of an archives exhibit. *Prologue*, vol. 14, no. 2, Summer 1982, 79–91.
Witteborg, Lothar P. *Good show! a practical guide for temporary exhibitions.* Washington D.C., Smithsonian Institution Traveling Exhibition Service, 1981.

Archival management

Abraham, Terry, Balzarini, Stephen E. and Frantilla, Anne. What is backlog is prologue; a measurement of archival processing. *American Archivist*, vol. 48, no. 1, Winter 1985. 31–44.
Albrecht, Karl. *Successful management by objectives.* Englewood Cliffs, New Jersey, Prentice-Hall, 1978.
Alegbeleye, Bumni. The application of the C.I.P.P. (context, input, process and product) model to archival planning. *Archives and Manuscripts*, vol. 12, November 1984. 136–146.
Andrews, Patricia A., comp. Writings on archives, historical manuscripts, and current records: 1983. *American Archivist*, vol. 49, no. 3, Summer 1986. 277–303.
Andrews, Patricia A. and Grier, Bettye J., comps. *Writings on archives, historical manuscripts, and current records: 1979–1982.* Washington, D.C., National Archives and Records Administration, 1985.
Bordin, Ruth and Warner, Robert M. *The modern manuscript library.* New York, Scarecrow Press, 1966.
Brown, William E., Jr. Group processing: planning and management strategies. *Provenance*, vol. 2, no. 2, Fall 1984. 1–14.
Christian, John F. and Finnegan, Shonnie. On planning an archives. *American Archivist*, vol. 37, no. 4, October 1974. 573–578.
Conway, Paul. Perspectives on archival resources: the 1985 census of archival institutions. *American Archivist*, vol. 50, no. 2, Spring 1987. 174–191.
Cox, Richard J. Strategies for archival action in the 1980's and beyond: implementing the SAA goals and priorities task force report. *Provenance*, vol. 3, no. 2, Fall 1985. 23–31.
Davis, W. N., Jr. Budgeting for archival processing. *American Archivist*, vol. 42, no. 2, Spring 1980. 209–211.
Duchein, Michel. *Archive buildings and equipment.* International Council on Archives Handbook no. 1. Munich, Verlag Documentation, 1977.
Duckett, Kenneth W. *Modern manuscripts: a practical manual for their management, care, and use.* Nashville, American Association for State and Local History, 1975.
Evans, Frank B., comp. *Modern archives and manuscripts: a select bibliography.* Chicago, Society of American Archivists, 1975.
Fagerlund, Lisa. Performance planning for the Portland program. *Georgia Archive*, vol. 10, no. 2, Fall 1982. 60–70.
Gildemeister, Glen A. Recruiting and hiring in archives: qualifications, procedures, and techniques. *The Midwestern Archivist*, vol. 5, no. 2, 1981. 113–121.
Gracy, David B., II. Starting an archives. *Georgia Archive*, vol. 1, no. 1, Fall 1972. 21–24.

Haller, Uli. Variations in the processing rates on the Magnuson and Jackson senatorial papers. *American Archivist*, vol. 50, no. 1, Winter 1987. 100–109.

Hecht, Maurice R. *What happens in management: principles and practices.* New York, American Management Associations, 1980.

Hunter, Gregory S. Filling the GAP: planning on the local and individual levels. *American Archivist*, vol. 50, no. 1, Winter 1987. 110–115.

Klaassen, David J. The provenance of archives under library administration: organizational structure and organic relationships. *In*: McCrank, Lawrence J., ed. *Archives and library administration: divergent traditions and common concerns.* New York and London, Haworth Press, 1986.

Ladeira, Caroline Durant and Trautman, Maryellen, comps. Writings on archives, historical manuscripts, and current records: 1984. *American Archivist*, vol. 49, no. 4, Fall 1986. 425–454.

Lanning, Kaye. "Starting an archives": a decade later. *Provenance*, vol. 1, no. 2, Fall 1983. 35–44.

Lynch, Karen Temple and Lynch, Thomas E. Rates of processing manuscripts and archives. *The Midwestern Archivist*, vol. 7, no. 1, 1982. 25–34.

McCarthy, Paul H. Archives under library administration: points of convergence and conflict. *In*: McCrank, Lawrence J., ed. *Archives and library administration: divergent traditions and common concerns.* New York and London, Haworth Press, 1986.

McLean, Hugh A. *There is a better way to manage.* New York, American Management Associations, 1982.

Maher, William J. Measurement and processing costs in academic archives. *College and Research Libraries*, vol. 43, no. 1, January 1982. 59–67.

National Association of Government Archives Records Administrators and the Council of State Governments. *Program reporting guidelines for government records programs.* Lexington, Kentucky, Council of State Governments, 1987.

Perlson, Michael R. *How to understand and influence people and organizations: practical psychology for goal achievement.* New York, American Management Associations, 1982.

Schellenberg, T.R. *Modern archives: principles and techniques.* Chicago, University of Chicago Press, 1956.

Society of American Archivists. *Evaluation of archival institutions: services, principles, and a guide to self-study.* Chicago, Society of American Archivists, 1982.

———. *Planning for the archival profession.* Chicago, Society of American Archivists, 1986.

Swift, Michael. Management techniques and technical resources in the archives of the 1980's. *Archivaria*, no. 20, Summer 1985. 94–104.

Worthy, James C. Management concepts in archival administration. *The Midwestern Archivist*, vol. 4, no. 2, 1979. 77–88.

Archival effectiveness

Adams, James L. *Conceptual blockbusting: a guide to better ideas.* 3rd ed. Reading, Massachusetts, etc., Addison-Wesley, 1986.

———. *The care and feeding of ideas.* Reading, Massachusetts, etc., Addison-Wesley, 1986.

Bennis, Warren. *Leaders: the strategies of taking charge.* New York, Harper & Row, 1985.

Brown, Arnold and Weiner, Edith. *Supermanaging: how to harness change for personal and organizational success.* New York and Scarborough, Ontario, New American Library, 1985.

Burke, Frank G. Archival cooperation. *American Archivist*, vol. 46, no. 3, Summer 1983. 293–305.

Buskirk, Richard H. *Modern management and Machiavelli*. New York, A Mentor Book, 1975.

Child, Margaret S. Reflections on cooperation among professions. *American Archivist*, vol. 46, no. 3, Summer 1983. 286–292.

Cleveland, Harlan. *The knowledge executive: leadership in an information society*. New York, Truman Talley Books, 1985.

Constance, Joseph W., Jr. and Dinwiddie, Robert C. Time management for archivists. *Provenance*, vol. 3, no. 2, Fall 1985. 94–99.

Fleckner, John A. Cooperation as a strategy for archival institutions. *American Archivist*, vol. 39, no. 4, October 1976. 447–459.

Geneen, Harold and Moscow, Alvin. *Managing*. New York, Avon Books, 1985.

Ginsburg, Sigmund G. *Ropes for management success: climb higher, faster*. Englewood Cliffs, New Jersey, Prentice-Hall, 1984.

Groves, Andrew S. *High output management*. New York, Vintage Books, 1985.

Ham, F. Gerald. Archival strategies for the post-custodial era. *American Archivist*, vol. 44, no. 3, Summer 1981. 207–216.

LeBoeuf, Michael. *Working smart: how to accomplish more in half the time*. New York, Warner Books, 1980.

Martel, Leon. *Mastering change*. New York and Scarborough, Ontario, New American Library, 1987.

Peters, Thomas J. and Waterman, Robert H., Jr. *In search of excellence*. New York, Harper & Row, 1982.

Posner, Mitchell J. *Executive essentials*. New York, Avon Books, 1982.

Warner, Robert M. The National Archives and Records Service: the path ahead. *Prologue*, vol. 12, no. 3, Fall 1980. 154–157.

Weldon, Edward. Archives and the challenges of change. *American Archivist*, vol. 46, no. 2, Spring 1983. 125–134.

Wilson, Don W. The National Archives: new challenges, new opportunities. *Prologue*, vol. 19, no. 4, Winter 1987. 220–221.

Index